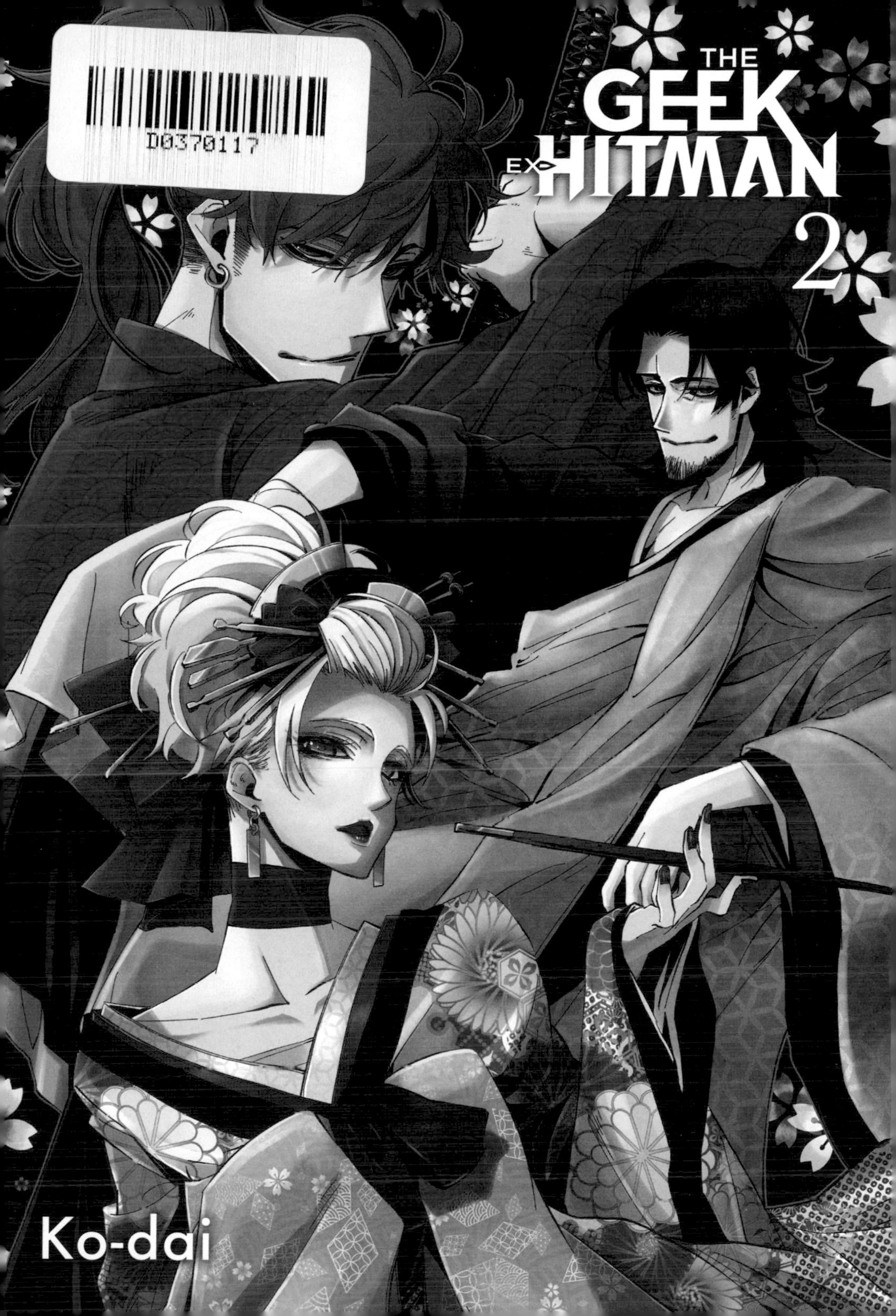
THE
GEEK
EX-HITMAN
2
Ko-dai

The Geek Ex-Hitman
CONTENTS

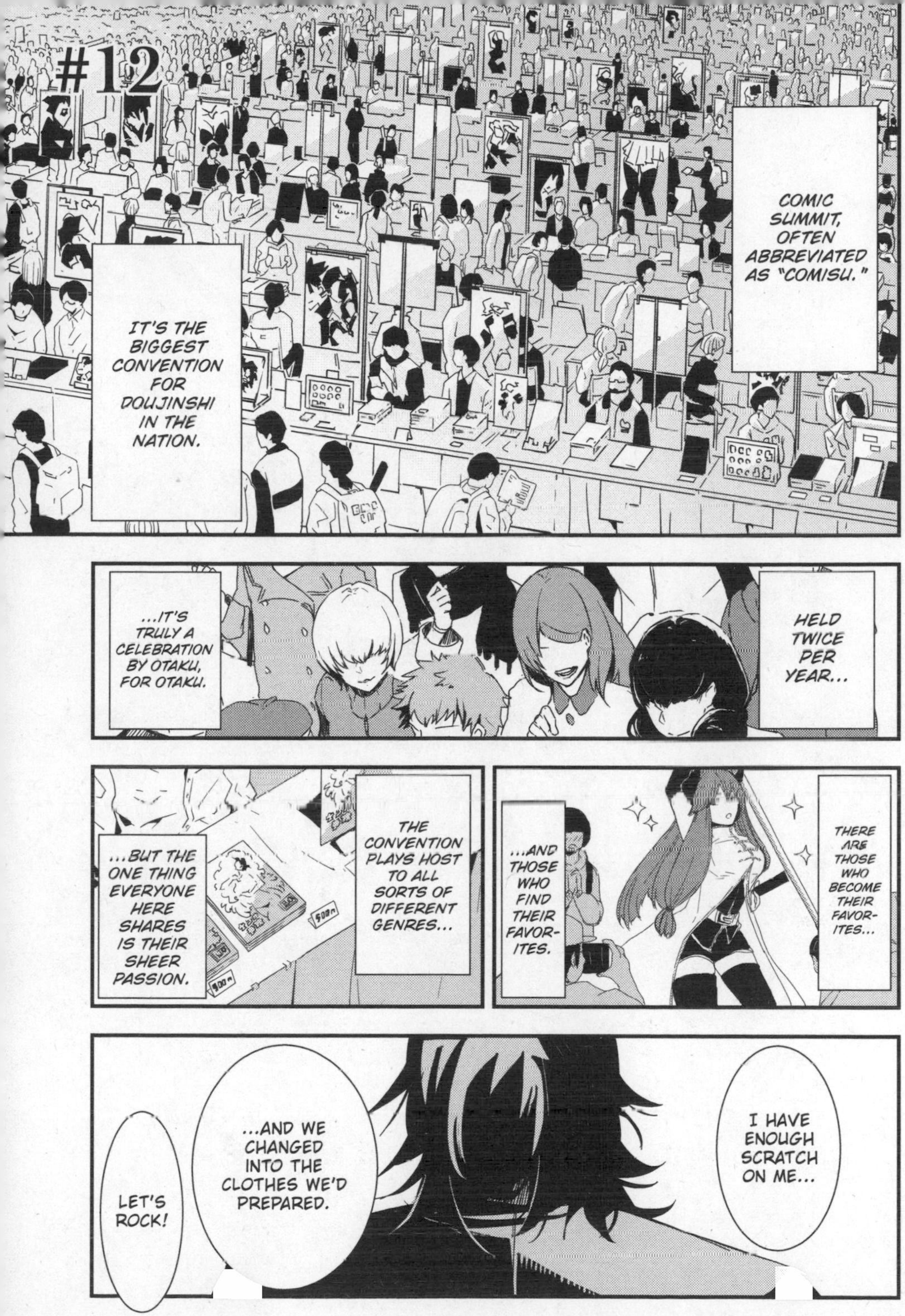
#12
COMIC SUMMIT, OFTEN ABBREVIATED AS "COMISU."
IT'S THE BIGGEST CONVENTION FOR DOUJINSHI IN THE NATION.
HELD TWICE PER YEAR...
...IT'S TRULY A CELEBRATION BY OTAKU, FOR OTAKU.
THERE ARE THOSE WHO BECOME THEIR FAVORITES...
...AND THOSE WHO FIND THEIR FAVORITES.
THE CONVENTION PLAYS HOST TO ALL SORTS OF DIFFERENT GENRES...
...BUT THE ONE THING EVERYONE HERE SHARES IS THEIR SHEER PASSION.
I HAVE ENOUGH SCRATCH ON ME...
...AND WE CHANGED INTO THE CLOTHES WE'D PREPARED.
LET'S ROCK!

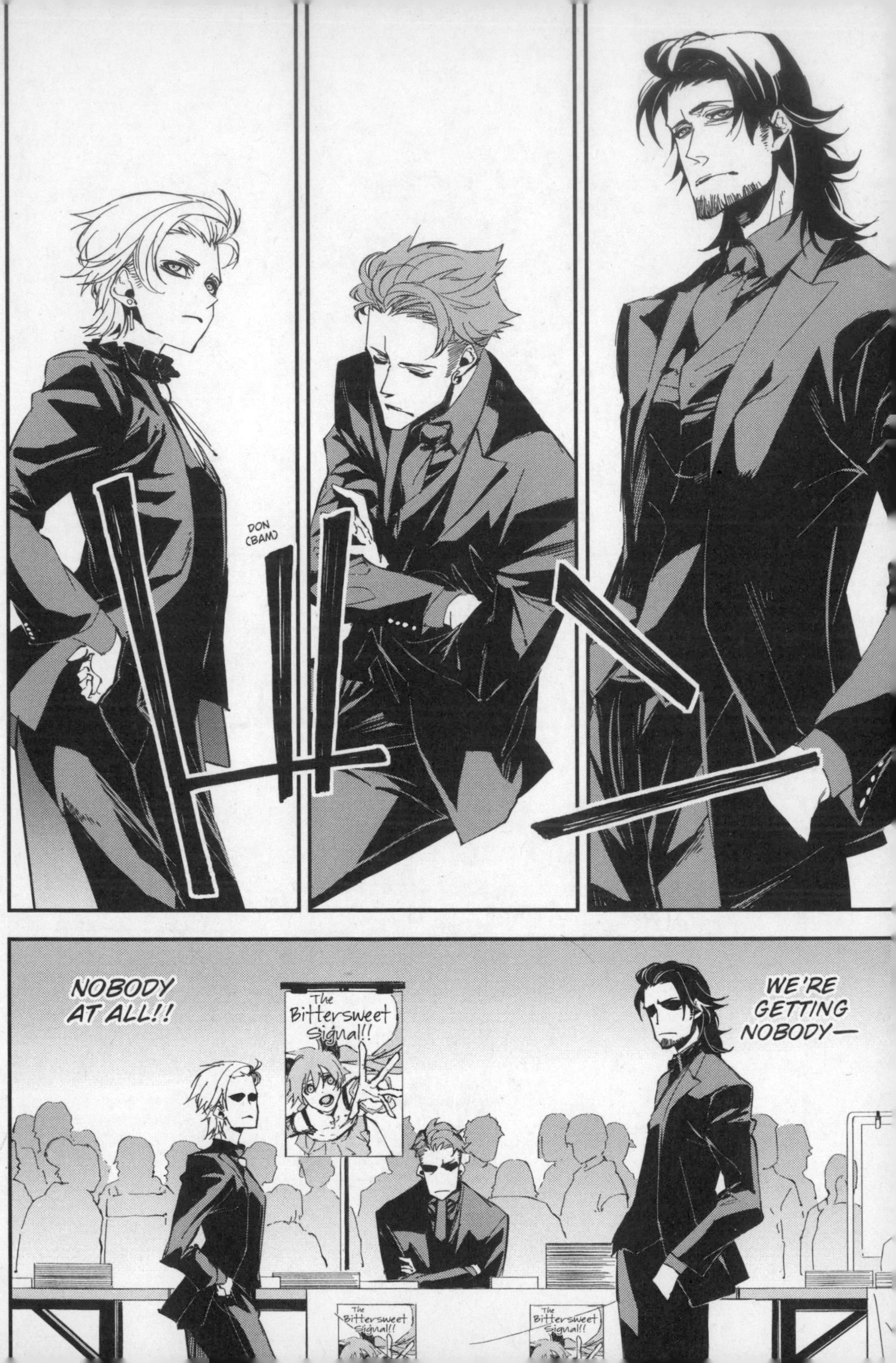
DON (BAM)
WE'RE GETTING NOBODY—
The Bittersweet Signal!!
NOBODY AT ALL!!
The Bittersweet Signal!!
The Bittersweet Signal!!

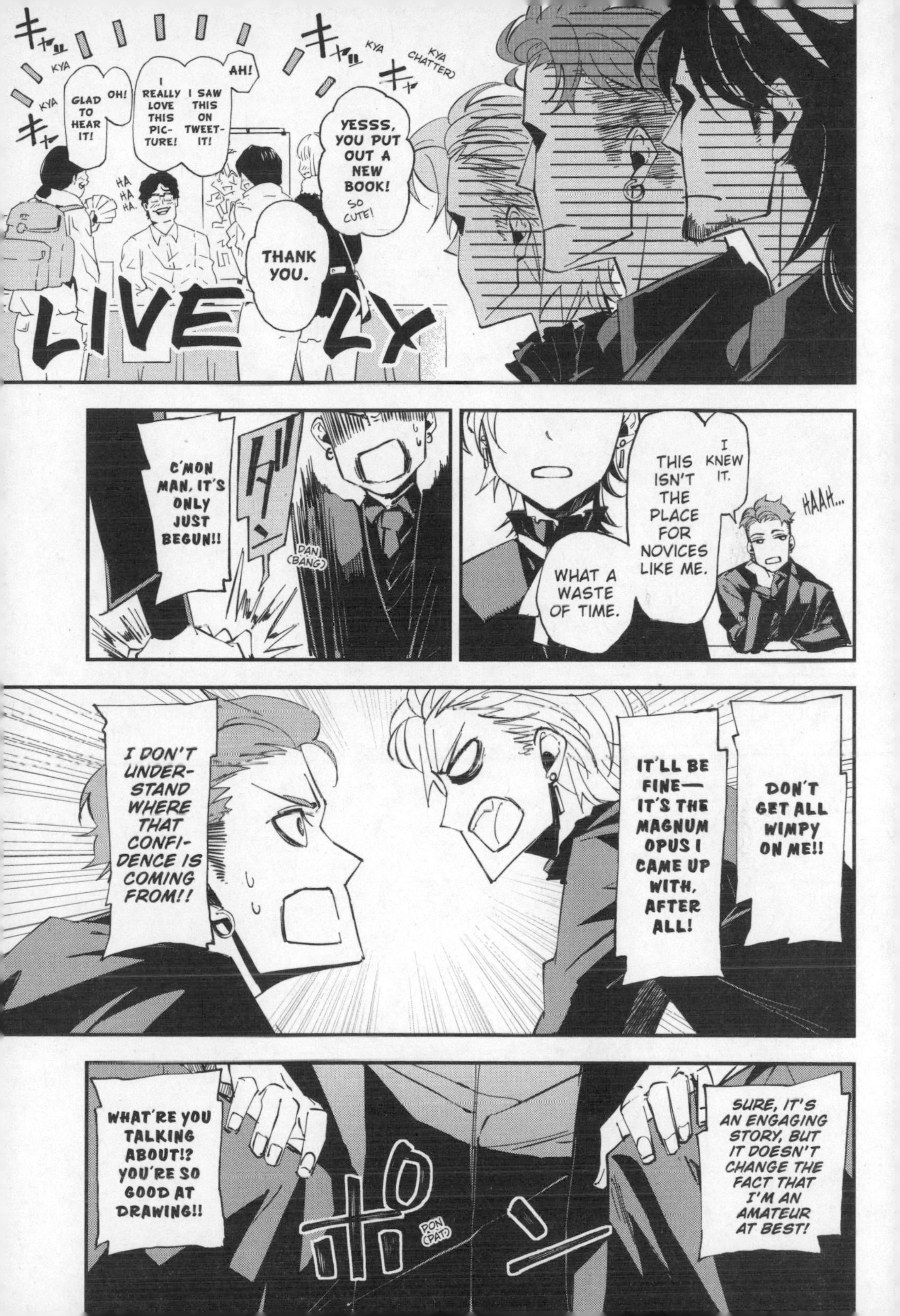
KYA CHATTER)
KYA
YESSS, YOU PUT OUT A NEW BOOK!
SO CUTE!
THANK YOU.
AH!
I SAW THIS ON TWEET-IT!
I REALLY LOVE THIS PIC-TURE!
OH!
GLAD TO HEAR IT!
KYA
KYA
HA HA HA.
LIVELY
I KNEW IT.
THIS ISN'T THE PLACE FOR NOVICES LIKE ME.
HAAH...
WHAT A WASTE OF TIME.
C'MON MAN, IT'S ONLY JUST BEGUN!!
DAN (BANG)
DON'T GET ALL WIMPY ON ME!!
IT'LL BE FINE—IT'S THE MAGNUM OPUS I CAME UP WITH, AFTER ALL!
I DON'T UNDERSTAND WHERE THAT CONFIDENCE IS COMING FROM!!
SURE, IT'S AN ENGAGING STORY, BUT IT DOESN'T CHANGE THE FACT THAT I'M AN AMATEUR AT BEST!
PON (PAT)
WHAT'RE YOU TALKING ABOUT!? YOU'RE SO GOOD AT DRAWING!!

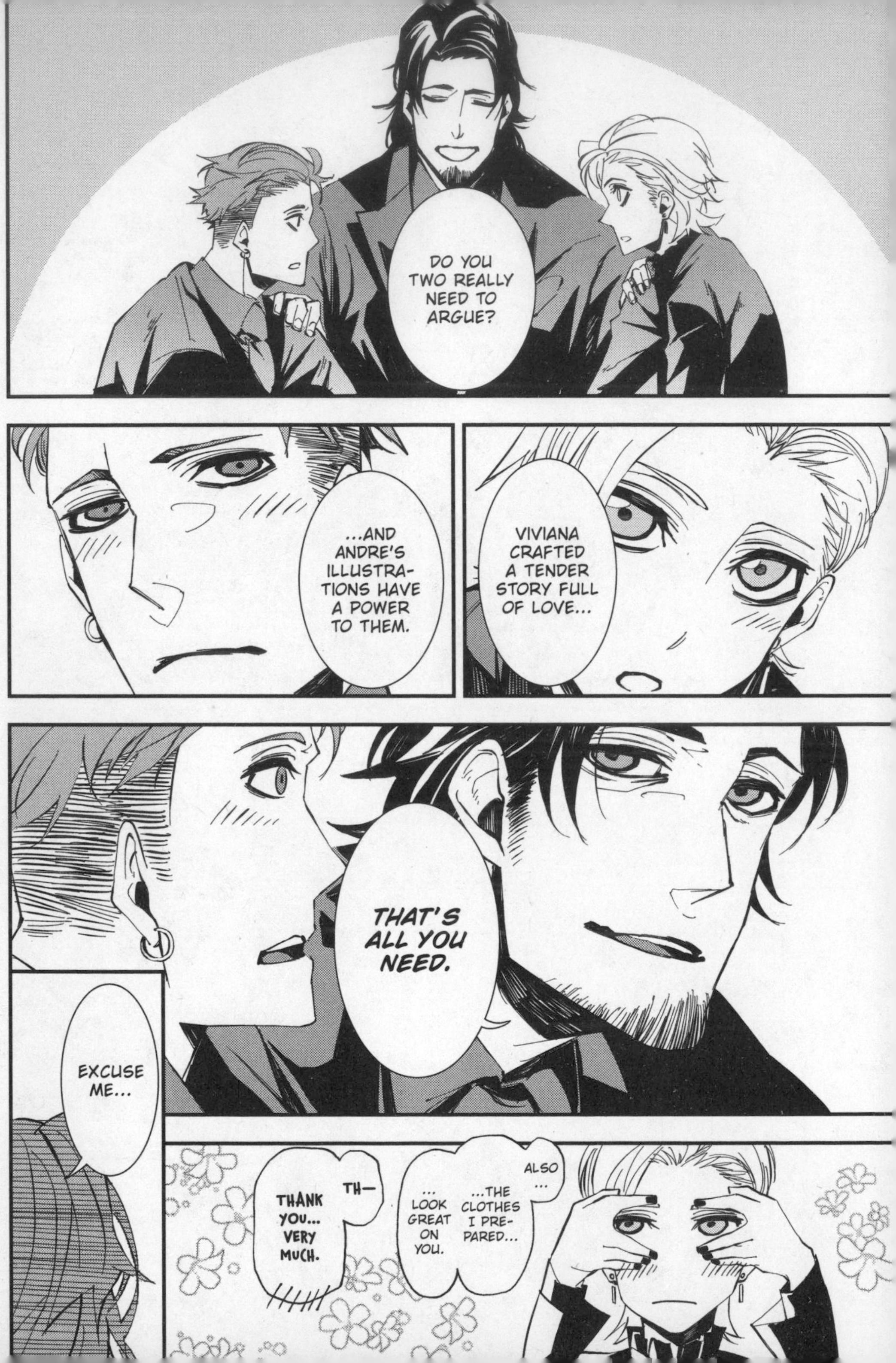
DO YOU TWO REALLY NEED TO ARGUE?
VIVIANA CRAFTED A TENDER STORY FULL OF LOVE...
...AND ANDRE'S ILLUSTRATIONS HAVE A POWER TO THEM.
THAT'S ALL YOU NEED.
ALSO...
...THE CLOTHES I PREPARED...
...LOOK GREAT ON YOU.
TH—
THANK YOU... VERY MUCH.
EXCUSE ME...

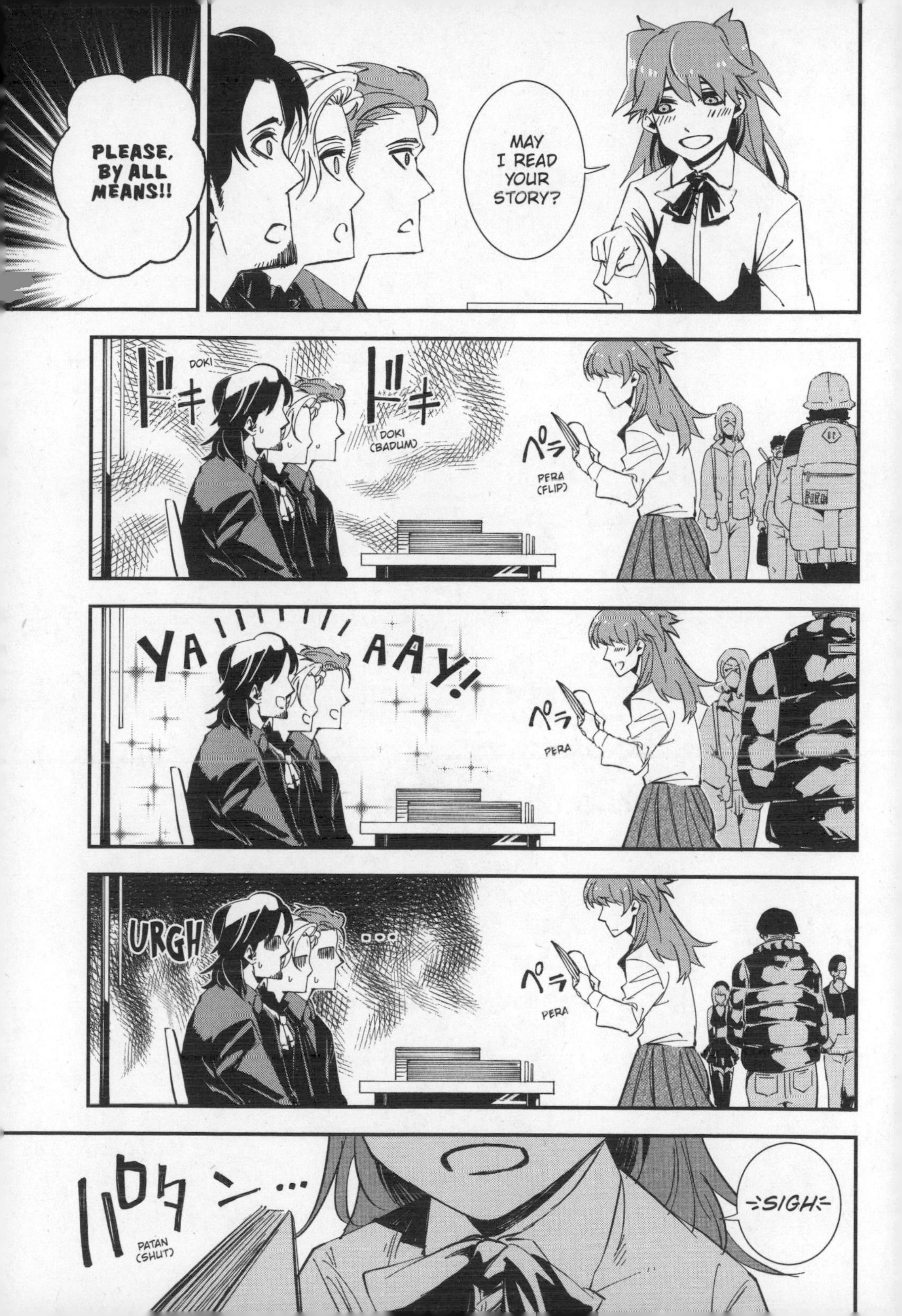
MAY I READ YOUR STORY?
PLEASE, BY ALL MEANS!!
ドキ
DOKI (BADUM)
ドキ
DOKI
ペラ
PERA (FLIP)
YA !!!!!!! AAY!!
ペラ
PERA
...
URGH
ペラ
PERA
SIGH
パタン…
PATAN (SHUT)

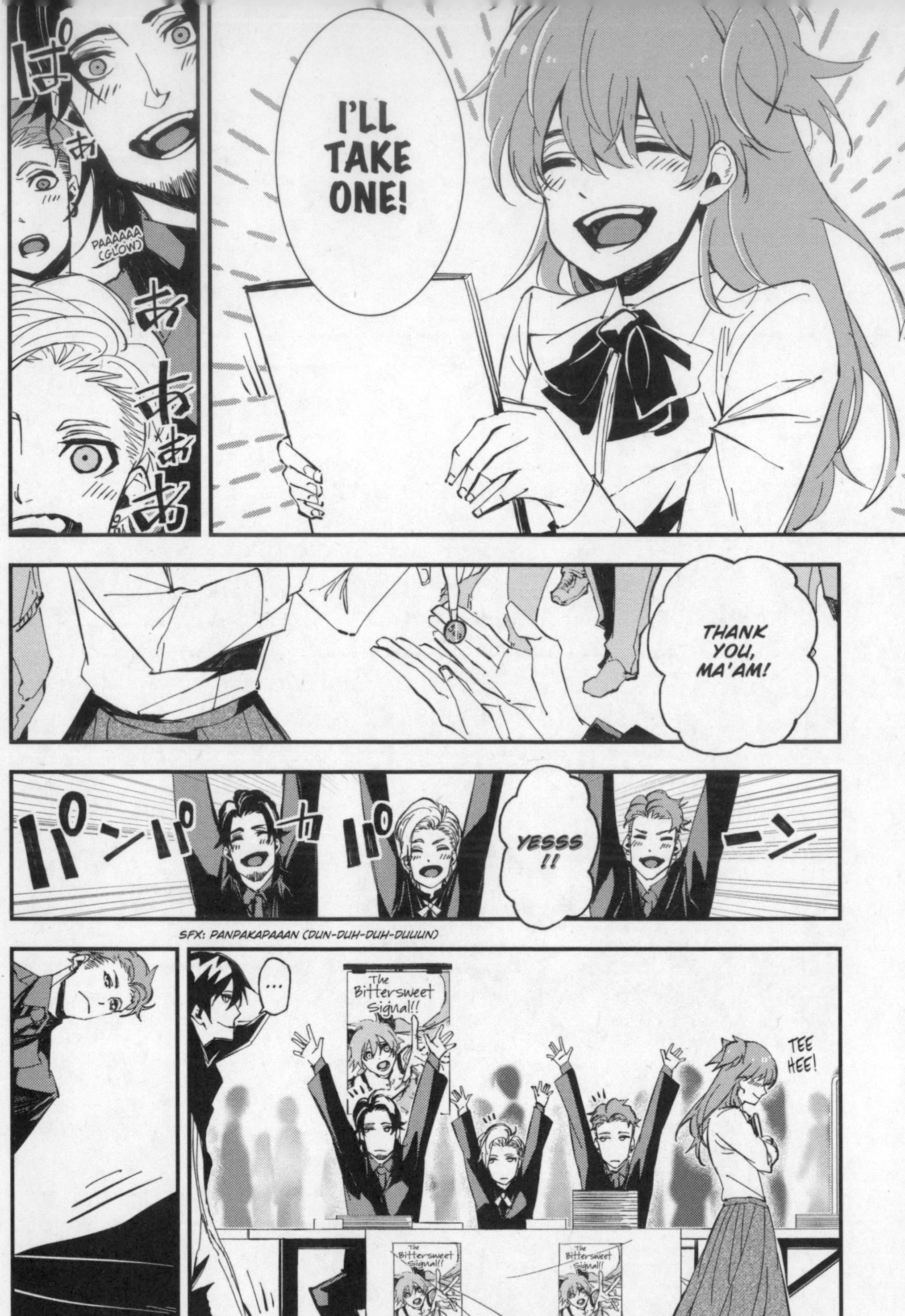
I'LL TAKE ONE!
ぱあ
ああああ
PAAAAAA (GLOW)
THANK YOU, MA'AM!
パンパカパーン
YESSS !!
SFX: PANPAKAPAAAN (DUN-DUH-DUH-DUUUN)
TEE HEE!
...
The Bittersweet Signal!!
The Bittersweet Signal!!
The Bittersweet Signal!!

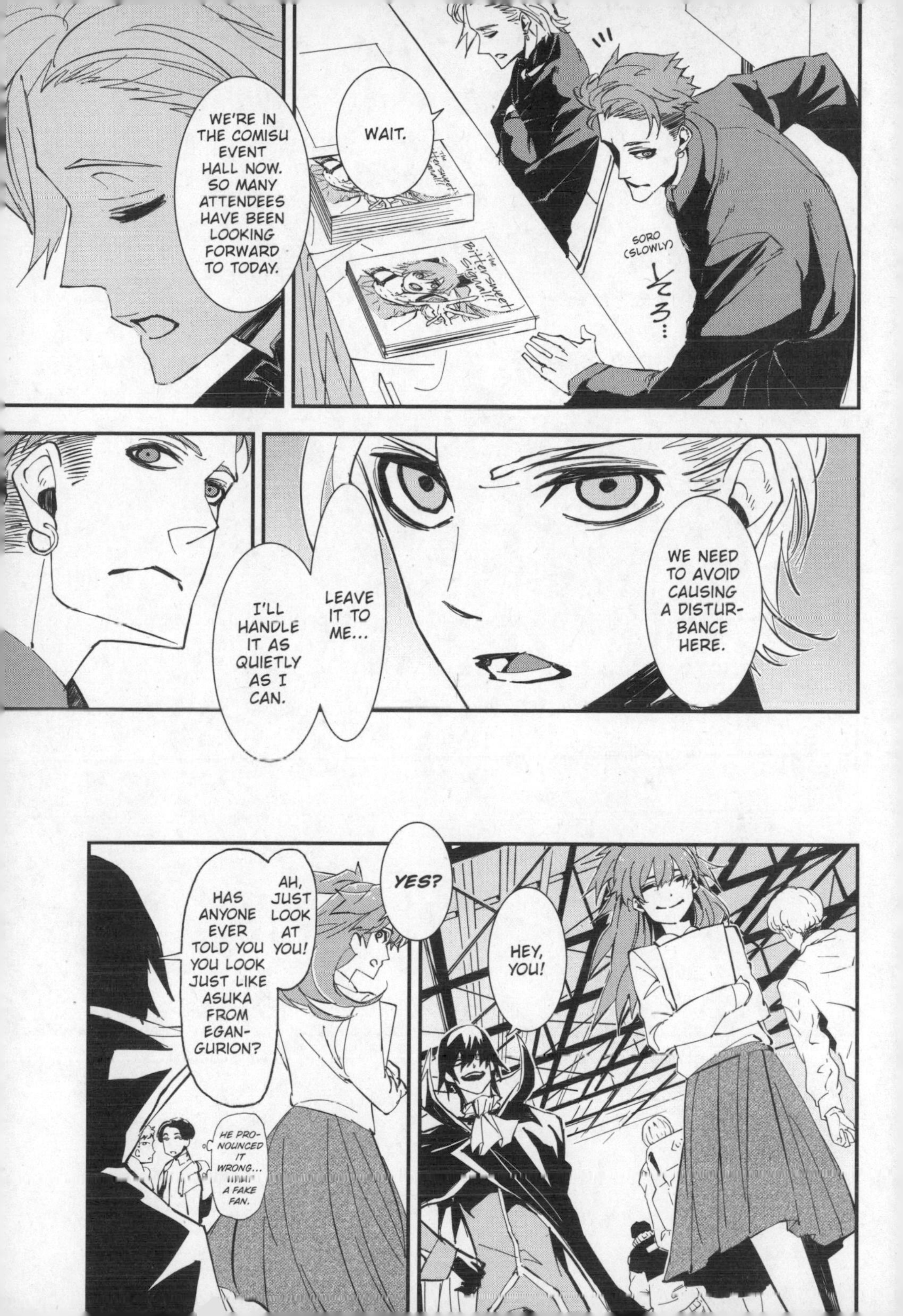
WAIT.
The Bittersweet Signal!!
SORO (SLOWLY)
そろ…
WE'RE IN THE COMISU EVENT HALL NOW. SO MANY ATTENDEES HAVE BEEN LOOKING FORWARD TO TODAY.
WE NEED TO AVOID CAUSING A DISTURBANCE HERE.
LEAVE IT TO ME...
I'LL HANDLE IT AS QUIETLY AS I CAN.
HEY, YOU!
YES?
AH, JUST LOOK AT YOU!
HAS ANYONE EVER TOLD YOU YOU LOOK JUST LIKE ASUKA FROM EGANGURION?
HE PRONOUNCED IT WRONG... A FAKE FAN.

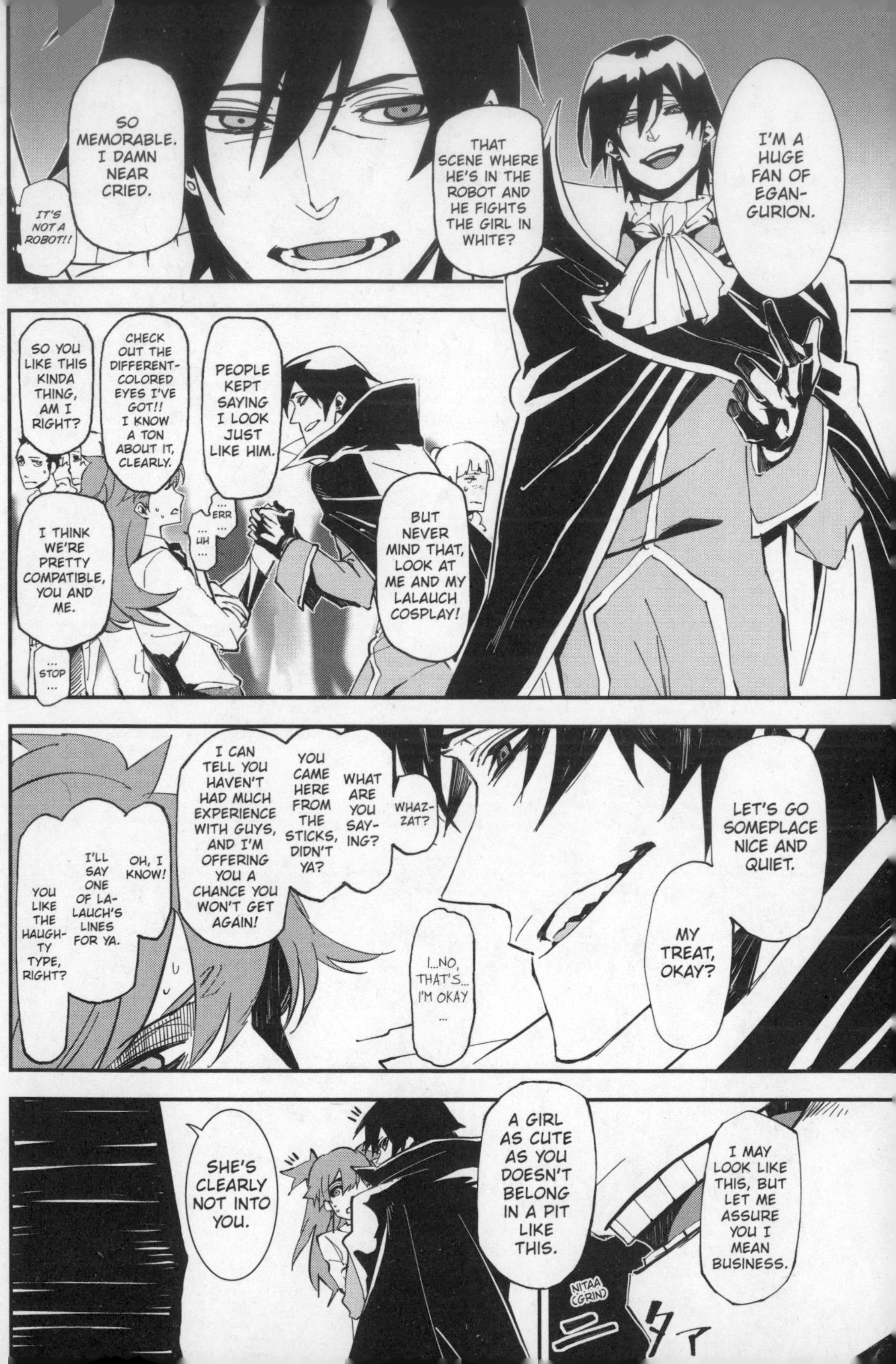
I'M A HUGE FAN OF EGAN-GURION.
THAT SCENE WHERE HE'S IN THE ROBOT AND HE FIGHTS THE GIRL IN WHITE?
SO MEMORABLE. I DAMN NEAR CRIED.
IT'S NOT A ROBOT!!
PEOPLE KEPT SAYING I LOOK JUST LIKE HIM.
BUT NEVER MIND THAT, LOOK AT ME AND MY LALAUCH COSPLAY!
CHECK OUT THE DIFFERENT-COLORED EYES I'VE GOT!! I KNOW A TON ABOUT IT, CLEARLY.
...ERR...
...UH...
SO YOU LIKE THIS KINDA THING, AM I RIGHT?
I THINK WE'RE PRETTY COMPATIBLE, YOU AND ME.
...STOP...
LET'S GO SOMEPLACE NICE AND QUIET.
MY TREAT, OKAY?
I...NO, THAT'S... I'M OKAY...
WHAZ-ZAT?
WHAT ARE YOU SAY-ING?
YOU CAME HERE FROM THE STICKS, DIDN'T YA?
I CAN TELL YOU HAVEN'T HAD MUCH EXPERIENCE WITH GUYS, AND I'M OFFERING YOU A CHANCE YOU WON'T GET AGAIN!
OH, I KNOW!
I'LL SAY ONE OF LA-LAUCH'S LINES FOR YA.
YOU LIKE THE HAUGHTY TYPE, RIGHT?
I MAY LOOK LIKE THIS, BUT LET ME ASSURE YOU I MEAN BUSINESS.
NITAA (GRIN)
A GIRL AS CUTE AS YOU DOESN'T BELONG IN A PIT LIKE THIS.
SHE'S CLEARLY NOT INTO YOU.

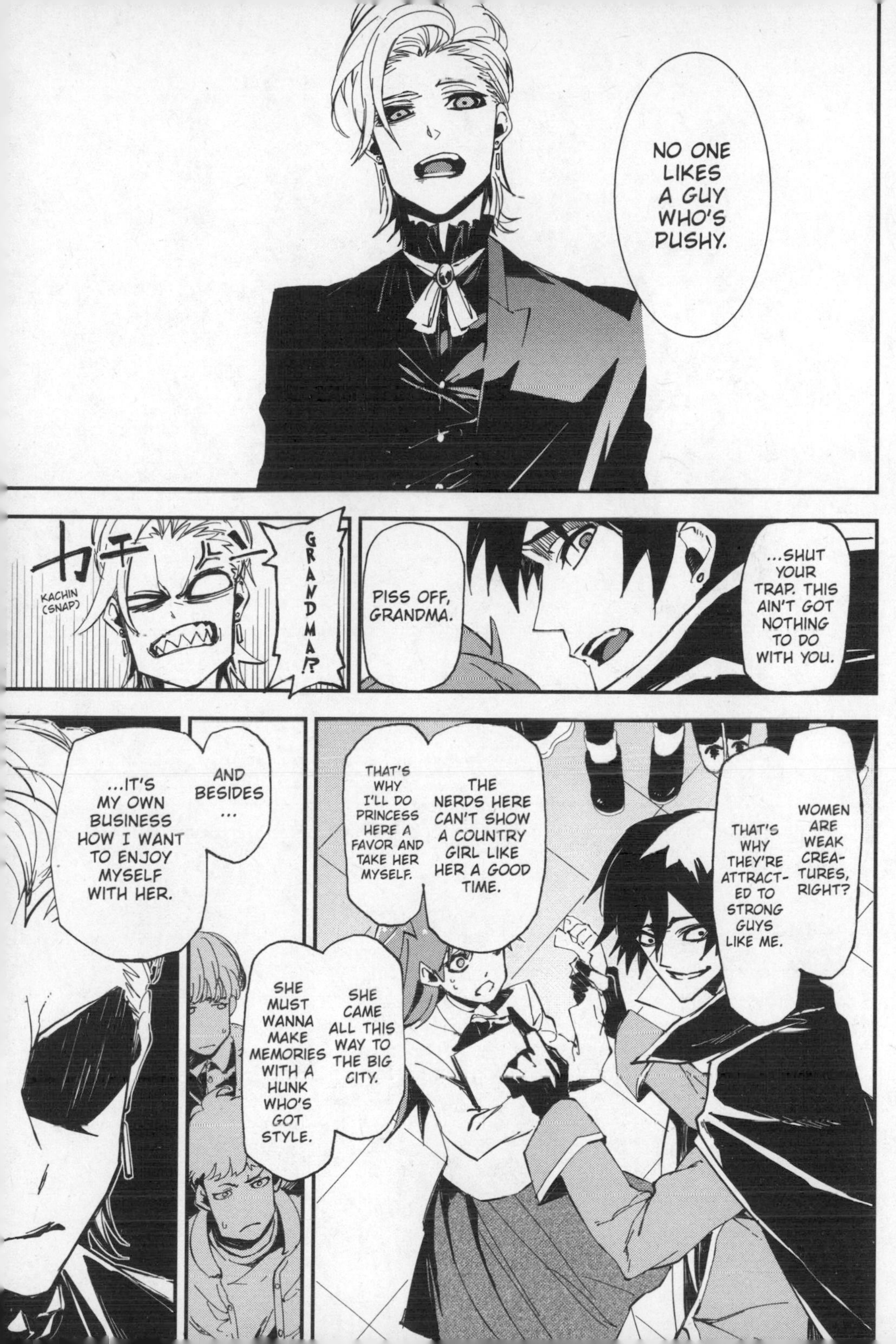
NO ONE LIKES A GUY WHO'S PUSHY.
...SHUT YOUR TRAP. THIS AIN'T GOT NOTHING TO DO WITH YOU.
PISS OFF, GRANDMA.
GRANDMA!?
KACHIN (SNAP)
WOMEN ARE WEAK CREATURES, RIGHT?
THAT'S WHY THEY'RE ATTRACTED TO STRONG GUYS LIKE ME.
THE NERDS HERE CAN'T SHOW A COUNTRY GIRL LIKE HER A GOOD TIME.
THAT'S WHY I'LL DO PRINCESS HERE A FAVOR AND TAKE HER MYSELF.
SHE CAME ALL THIS WAY TO THE BIG CITY.
SHE MUST WANNA MAKE MEMORIES WITH A HUNK WHO'S GOT STYLE.
AND BESIDES...
...IT'S MY OWN BUSINESS HOW I WANT TO ENJOY MYSELF WITH HER.

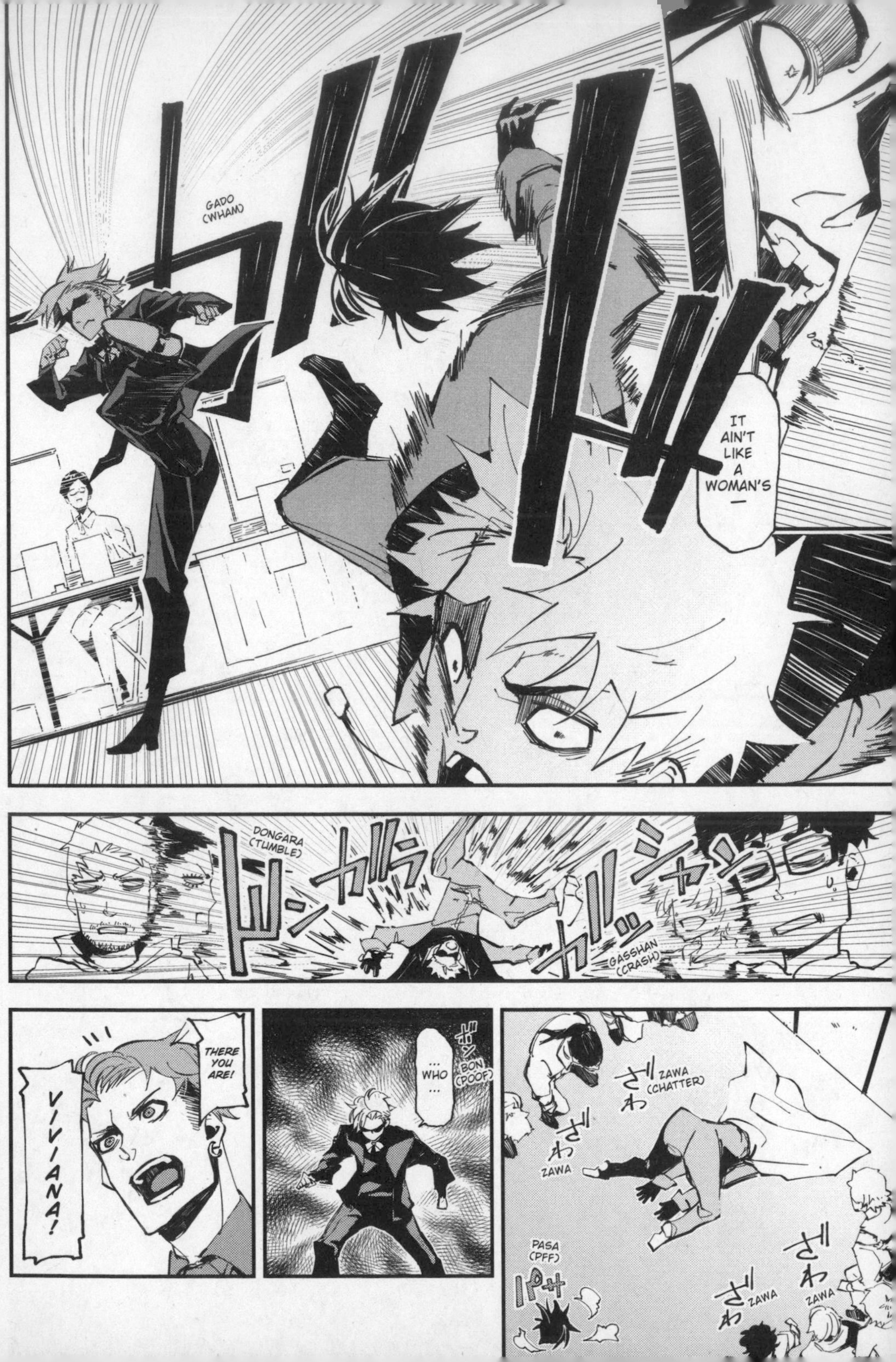
IT AIN'T LIKE A WOMAN'S—
GADO (WHAM)
GASSHAN (CRASH)
DONGARA (TUMBLE)
ZAWA (CHATTER)
ZAWA
ZAWA
ZAWA
PASA (PFF)
BON (POOF)
...WHO...
THERE YOU ARE!
VIVIANA!

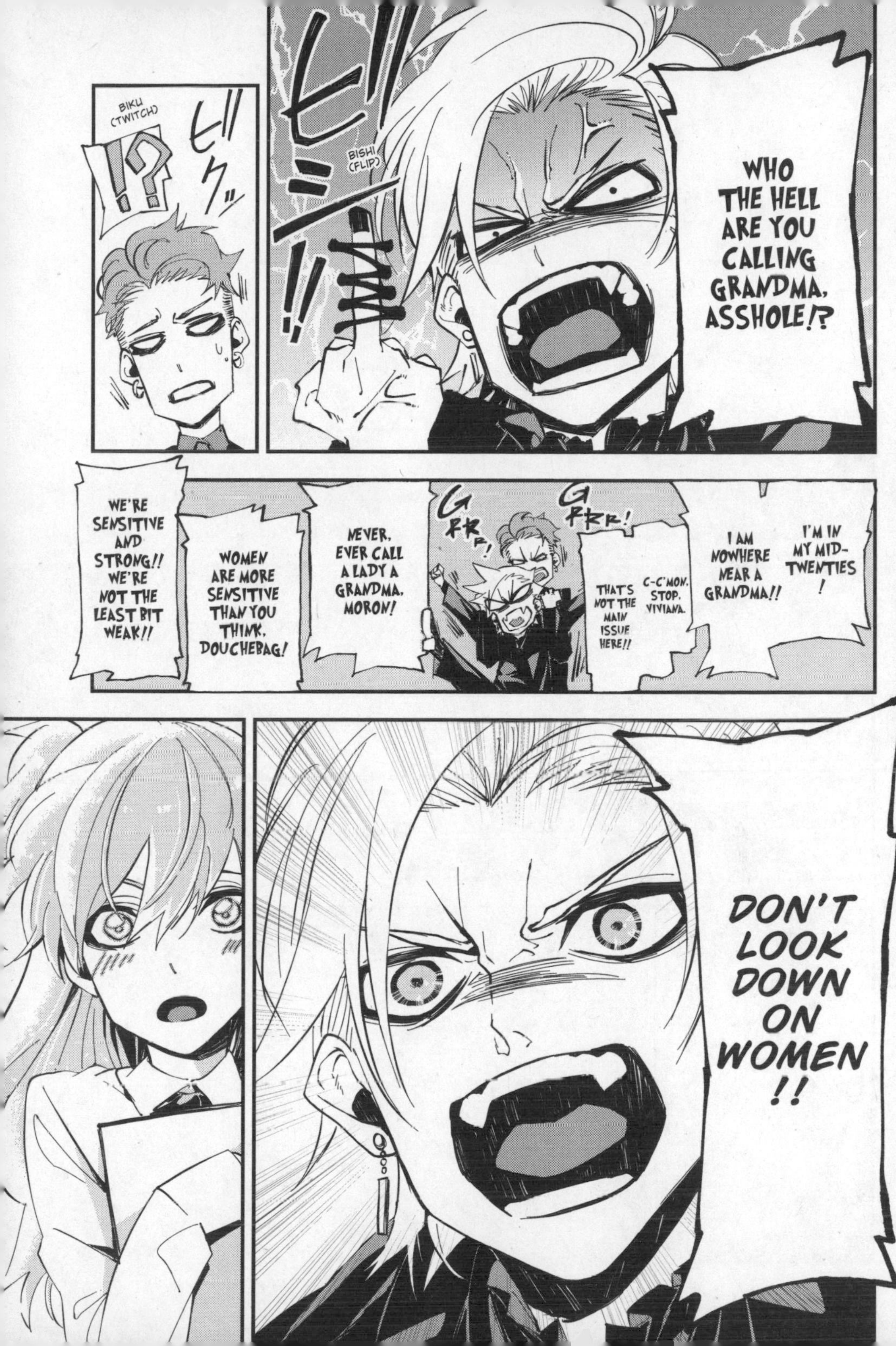
BISHI (FLIP)
WHO THE HELL ARE YOU CALLING GRANDMA, ASSHOLE!?
BIKU (TWITCH)
!?
I'M IN MY MID-TWENTIES!
I AM NOWHERE NEAR A GRANDMA!!
C-C'MON. STOP, VIVIANA.
THAT'S NOT THE MAIN ISSUE HERE!!
GRRR!
GRRR!
NEVER, EVER CALL A LADY A GRANDMA, MORON!
WOMEN ARE MORE SENSITIVE THAN YOU THINK, DOUCHEBAG!
WE'RE SENSITIVE AND STRONG!! WE'RE NOT THE LEAST BIT WEAK!!
DON'T LOOK DOWN ON WOMEN!!

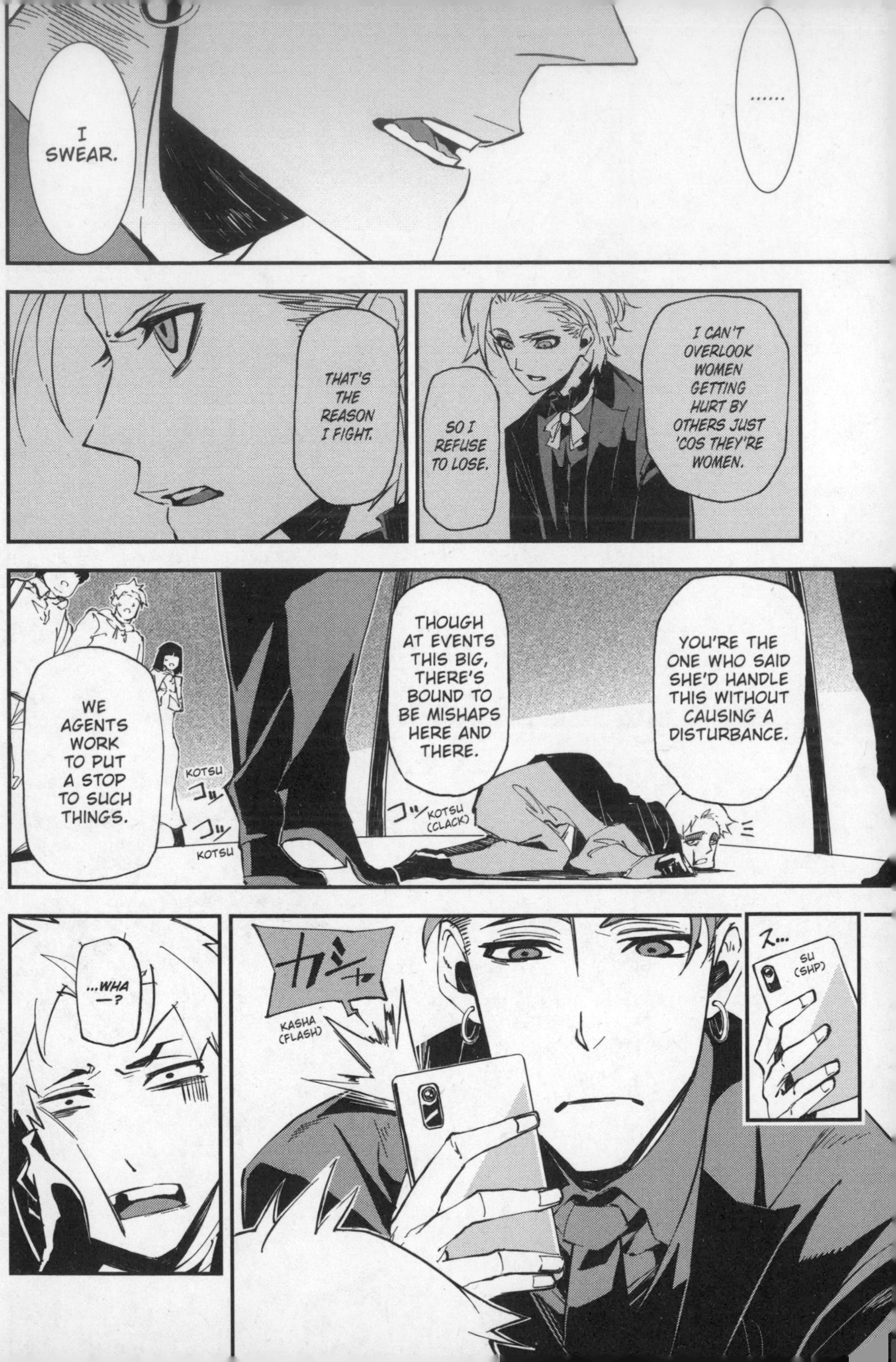
......
I SWEAR.
I CAN'T OVERLOOK WOMEN GETTING HURT BY OTHERS JUST 'COS THEY'RE WOMEN.
SO I REFUSE TO LOSE.
THAT'S THE REASON I FIGHT.
YOU'RE THE ONE WHO SAID SHE'D HANDLE THIS WITHOUT CAUSING A DISTURBANCE.
THOUGH AT EVENTS THIS BIG, THERE'S BOUND TO BE MISHAPS HERE AND THERE.
コッ
KOTSU (CLACK)
コッ
KOTSU
WE AGENTS WORK TO PUT A STOP TO SUCH THINGS.
コッ
KOTSU
ス…
SU (SHP)
カシャ
KASHA (FLASH)
...WHA—?

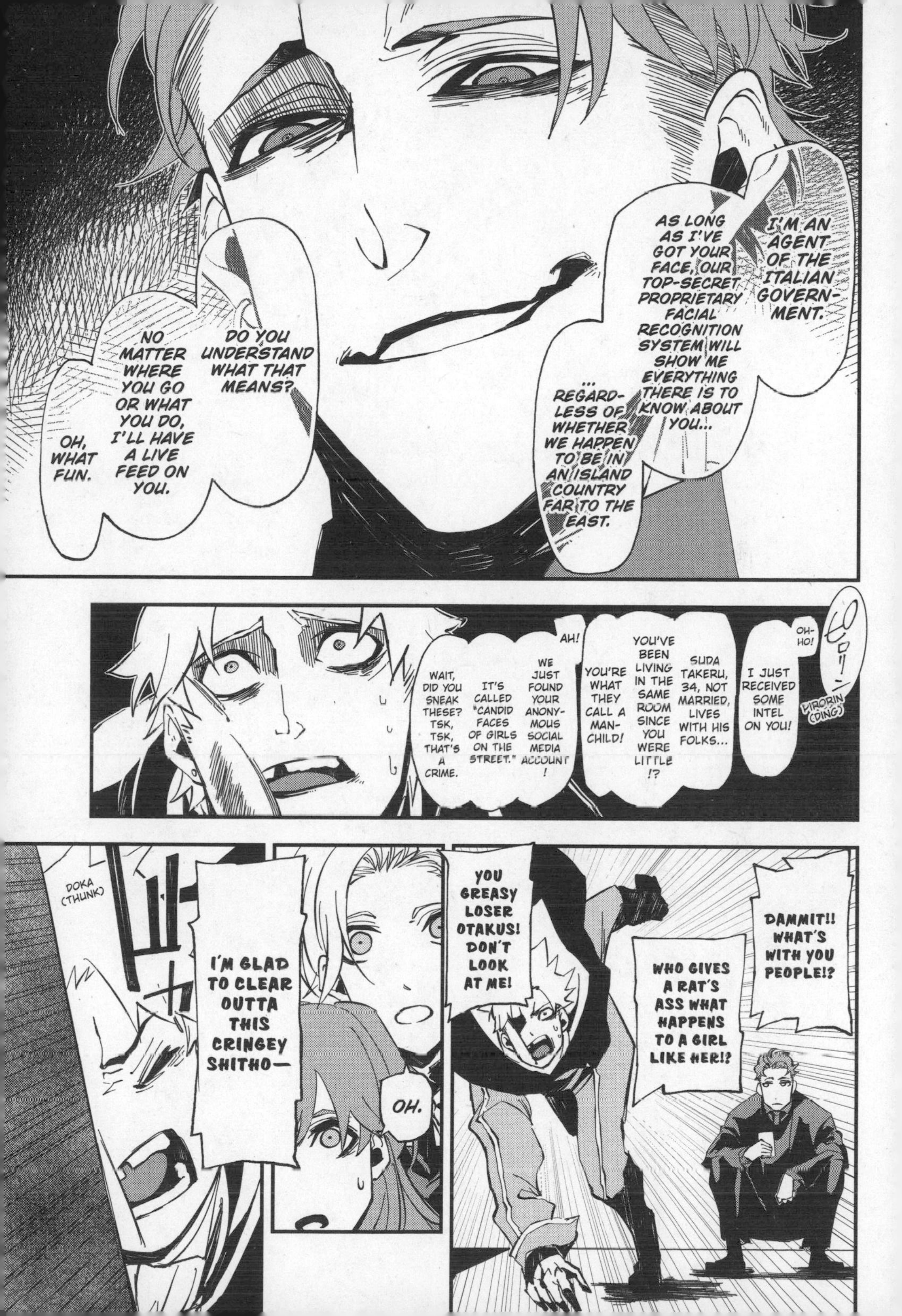
I'M AN AGENT OF THE ITALIAN GOVERNMENT.
AS LONG AS I'VE GOT YOUR FACE, OUR TOP-SECRET PROPRIETARY FACIAL RECOGNITION SYSTEM WILL SHOW ME EVERYTHING THERE IS TO KNOW ABOUT YOU...
...REGARDLESS OF WHETHER WE HAPPEN TO BE IN AN ISLAND COUNTRY FAR TO THE EAST.
DO YOU UNDERSTAND WHAT THAT MEANS?
NO MATTER WHERE YOU GO OR WHAT YOU DO, I'LL HAVE A LIVE FEED ON YOU.
OH, WHAT FUN.
PIRORIN (DING)
OH-HO! I JUST RECEIVED SOME INTEL ON YOU!
SUDA TAKERU, 34, NOT MARRIED, LIVES WITH HIS FOLKS...
AH! YOU'VE BEEN LIVING IN THE SAME ROOM SINCE YOU WERE LITTLE!?
YOU'RE WHAT THEY CALL A MAN-CHILD!
WE JUST FOUND YOUR ANONYMOUS SOCIAL MEDIA ACCOUNT!
IT'S CALLED "CANDID FACES OF GIRLS ON THE STREET."
WAIT, DID YOU SNEAK THESE? TSK, TSK, THAT'S A CRIME.
DAMMIT!! WHAT'S WITH YOU PEOPLE!?
WHO GIVES A RAT'S ASS WHAT HAPPENS TO A GIRL LIKE HER!?
YOU GREASY LOSER OTAKUS! DON'T LOOK AT ME!
I'M GLAD TO CLEAR OUTTA THIS CRINGEY SHITHO—
OH.
DOKA (THUNK)

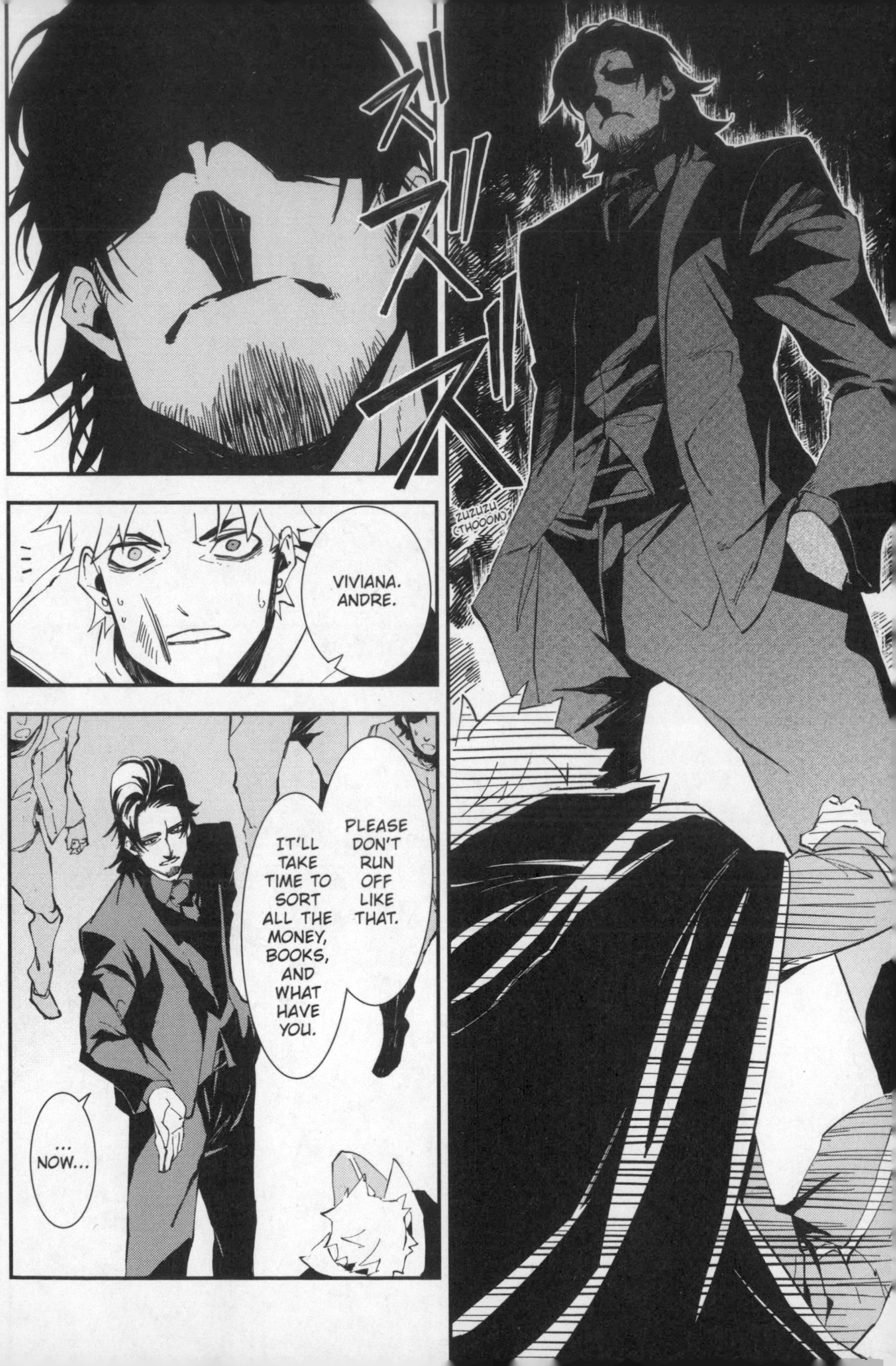
ZUZUZU (THOOOM)
VIVIANA. ANDRE.
PLEASE DON'T RUN OFF LIKE THAT.
IT'LL TAKE TIME TO SORT ALL THE MONEY, BOOKS, AND WHAT HAVE YOU.
...NOW...

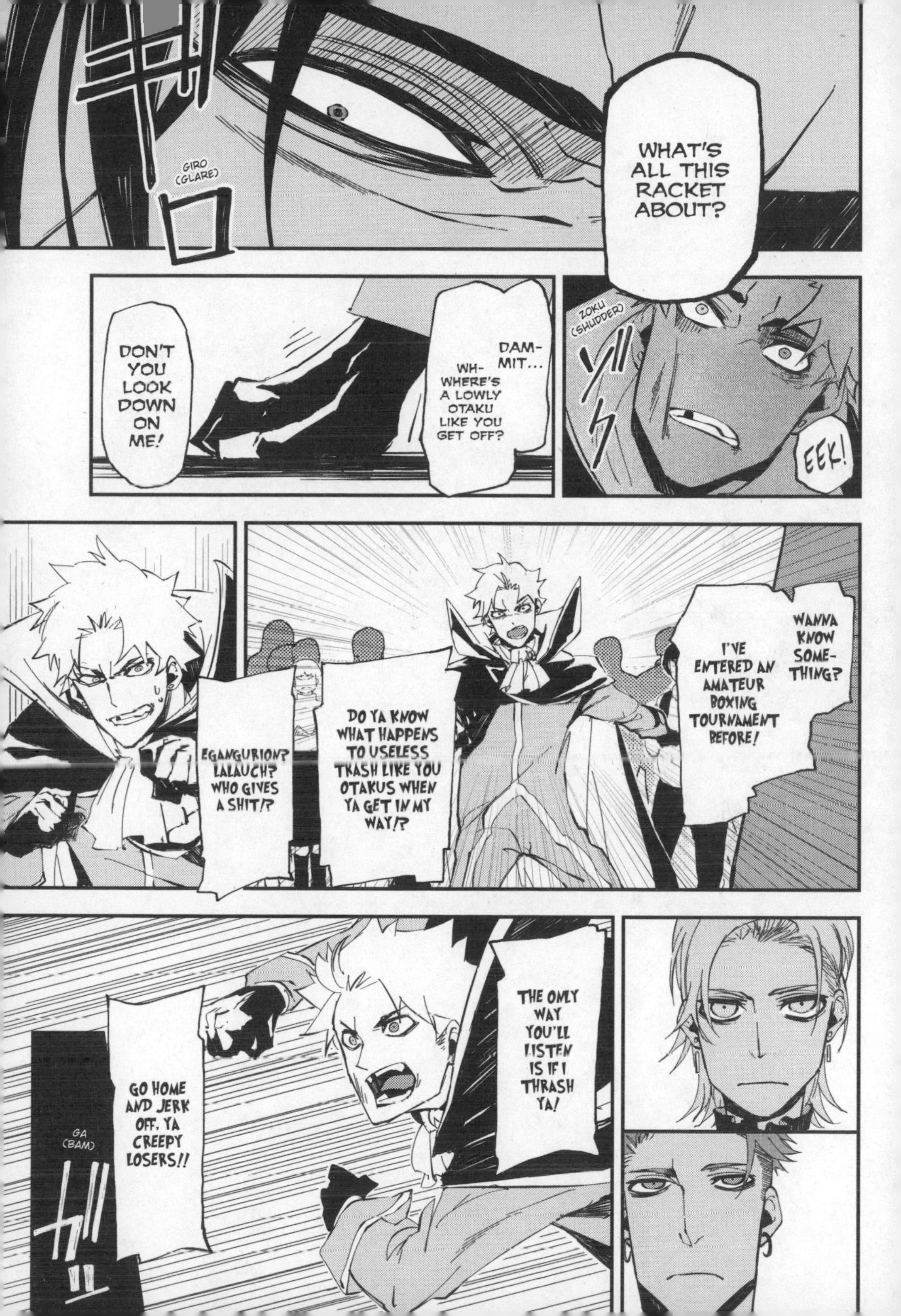
WHAT'S ALL THIS RACKET ABOUT?
GIRO (GLARE)
ZOKU (SHUDDER)
EEK!
DAM-MIT...
WH-WHERE'S A LOWLY OTAKU LIKE YOU GET OFF?
DON'T YOU LOOK DOWN ON ME!
WANNA KNOW SOME-THING?
I'VE ENTERED AN AMATEUR BOXING TOURNAMENT BEFORE!
DO YA KNOW WHAT HAPPENS TO USELESS TRASH LIKE YOU OTAKUS WHEN YA GET IN MY WAY!?
EGANGURION? LALAUCH? WHO GIVES A SHIT!?
THE ONLY WAY YOU'LL LISTEN IS IF I THRASH YA!
GO HOME AND JERK OFF, YA CREEPY LOSERS!!
GA (BAM)

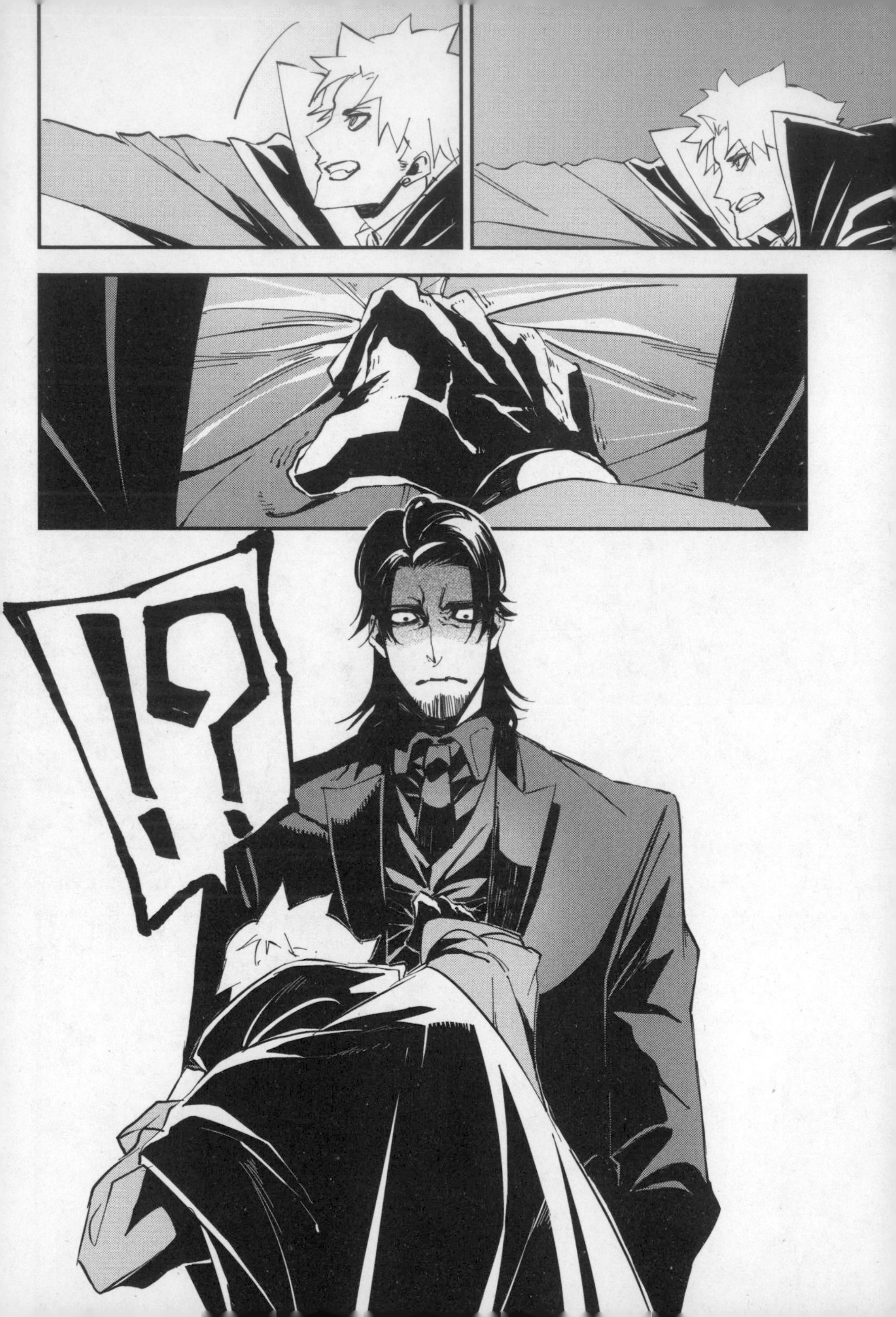
!?

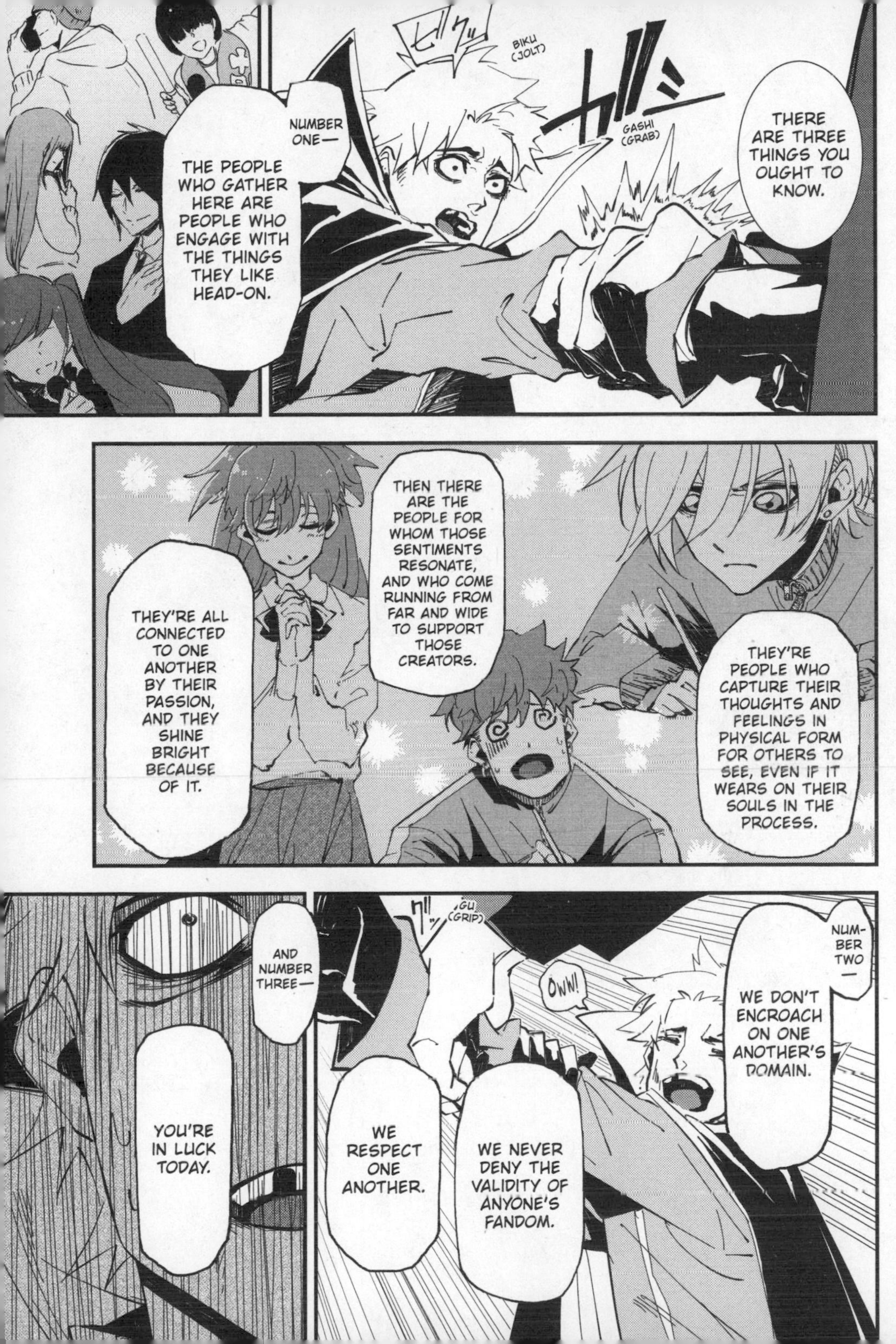
THERE ARE THREE THINGS YOU OUGHT TO KNOW.
GASHI (GRAB)
BIKU (JOLT)
NUMBER ONE—
THE PEOPLE WHO GATHER HERE ARE PEOPLE WHO ENGAGE WITH THE THINGS THEY LIKE HEAD-ON.
THEY'RE PEOPLE WHO CAPTURE THEIR THOUGHTS AND FEELINGS IN PHYSICAL FORM FOR OTHERS TO SEE, EVEN IF IT WEARS ON THEIR SOULS IN THE PROCESS.
THEN THERE ARE THE PEOPLE FOR WHOM THOSE SENTIMENTS RESONATE, AND WHO COME RUNNING FROM FAR AND WIDE TO SUPPORT THOSE CREATORS.
THEY'RE ALL CONNECTED TO ONE ANOTHER BY THEIR PASSION, AND THEY SHINE BRIGHT BECAUSE OF IT.
NUMBER TWO—
WE DON'T ENCROACH ON ONE ANOTHER'S DOMAIN.
OWW!
GU (GRIP)
WE NEVER DENY THE VALIDITY OF ANYONE'S FANDOM.
WE RESPECT ONE ANOTHER.
AND NUMBER THREE—
YOU'RE IN LUCK TODAY.

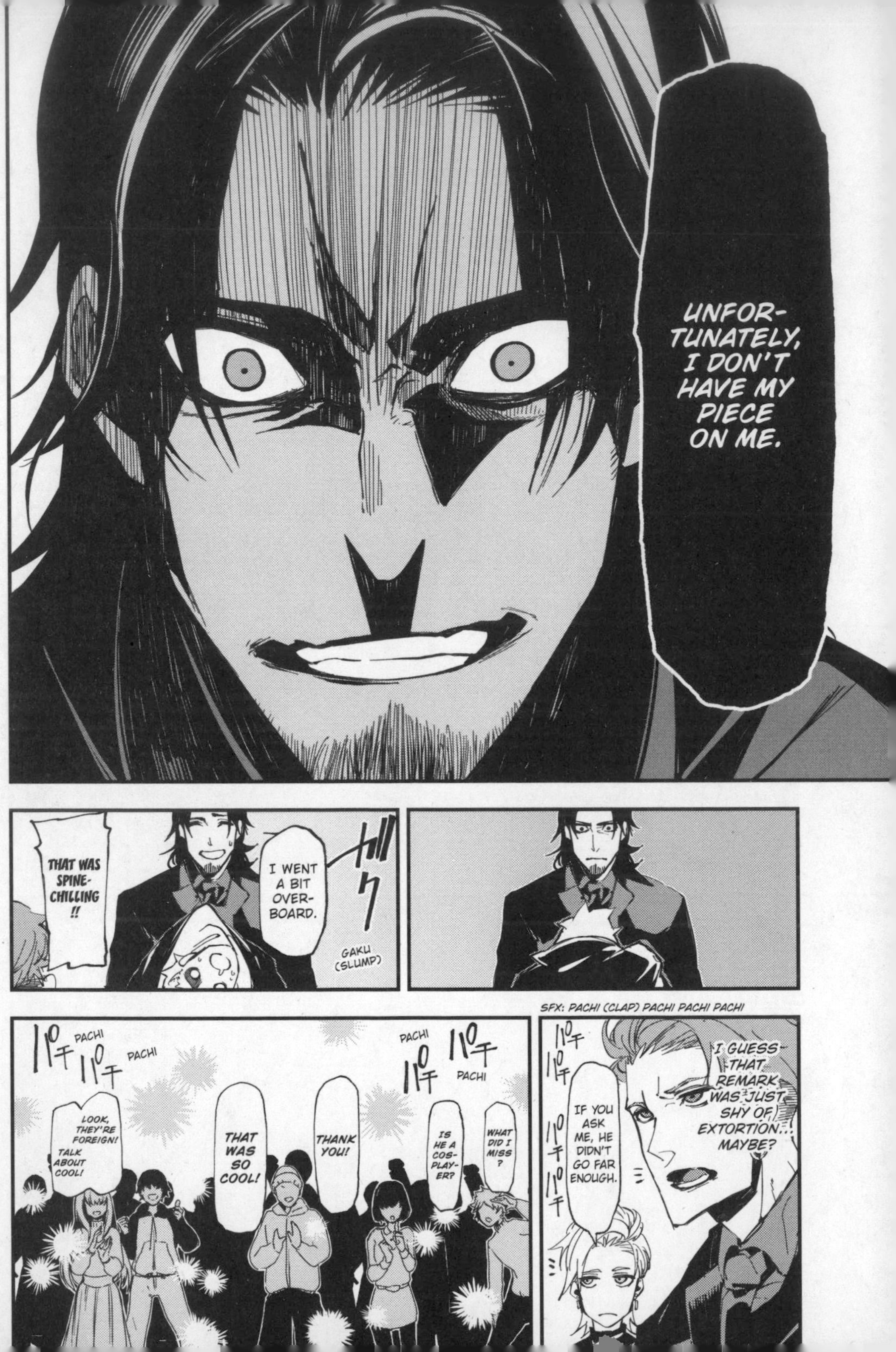
UNFOR-TUNATELY, I DON'T HAVE MY PIECE ON ME.
GAKU (SLUMP)
I WENT A BIT OVER-BOARD.
THAT WAS SPINE-CHILLING!!
SFX: PACHI (CLAP) PACHI PACHI PACHI
I GUESS THAT REMARK WAS JUST SHY OF EXTORTION... MAYBE?
IF YOU ASK ME, HE DIDN'T GO FAR ENOUGH.
PACHI
PACHI
WHAT DID I MISS?
IS HE A COS-PLAYER?
THANK YOU!
THAT WAS SO COOL!
LOOK, THEY'RE FOREIGN! TALK ABOUT COOL!
PACHI
PACHI

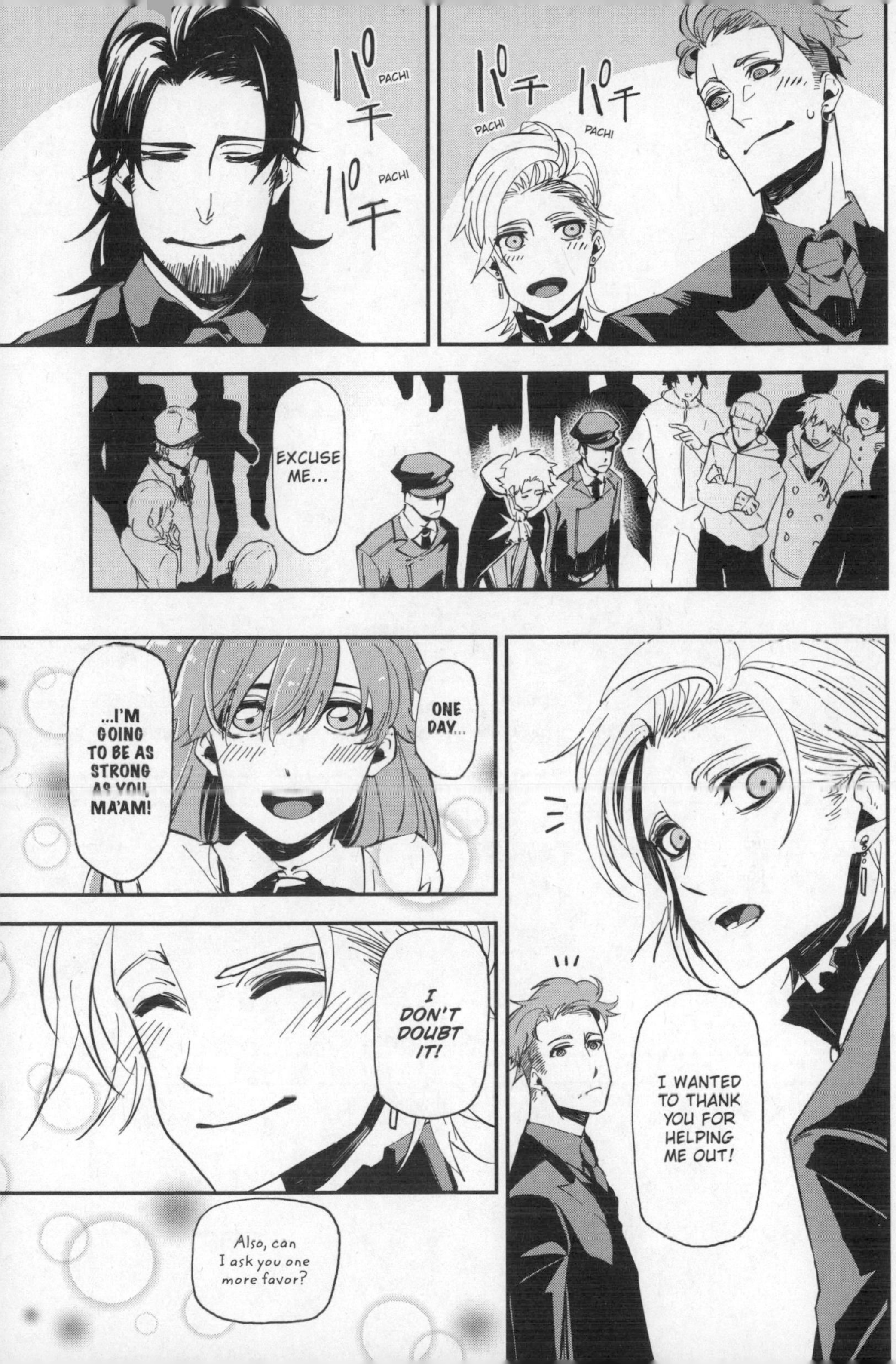
パチ
PACHI
パチ
PACHI
パチ
PACHI
パチ
PACHI
EXCUSE ME...
I WANTED TO THANK YOU FOR HELPING ME OUT!
ONE DAY...
...I'M GOING TO BE AS STRONG AS YOU, MA'AM!
I DON'T DOUBT IT!
Also, can I ask you one more favor?

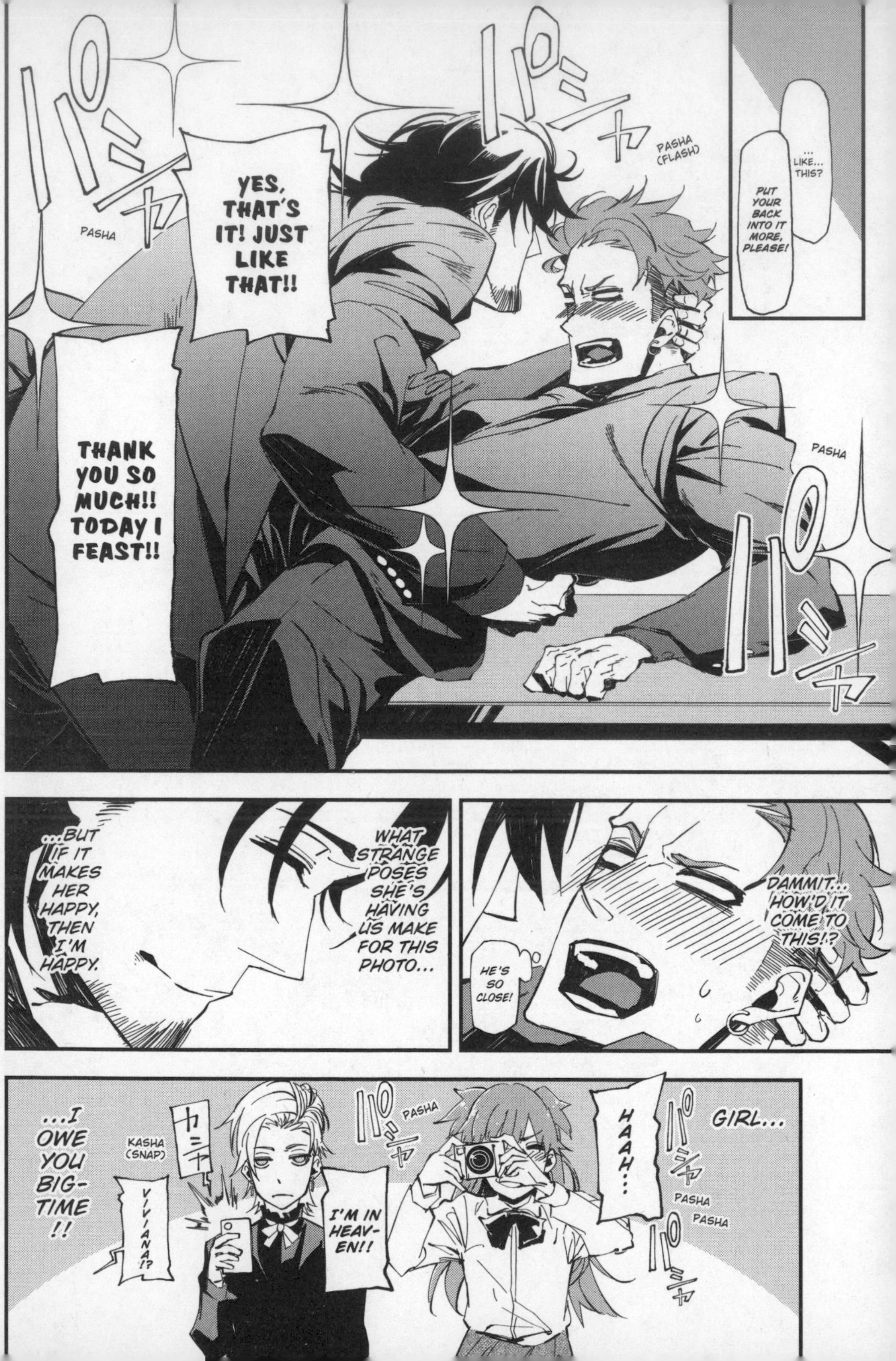
...
... LIKE... THIS?
PUT YOUR BACK INTO IT MORE, PLEASE!
PASHA (FLASH)
PASHA
YES, THAT'S IT! JUST LIKE THAT!!
PASHA
THANK YOU SO MUCH!! TODAY I FEAST!!
DAMMIT... HOW'D IT COME TO THIS!?
HE'S SO CLOSE!
WHAT STRANGE POSES SHE'S HAVING US MAKE FOR THIS PHOTO...
...BUT IF IT MAKES HER HAPPY, THEN I'M HAPPY.
GIRL...
HAAAH...
PASHA
PASHA
PASHA
I'M IN HEAVEN!!
VIVIANA!?
KASHA (SNAP)
...I OWE YOU BIG-TIME!!

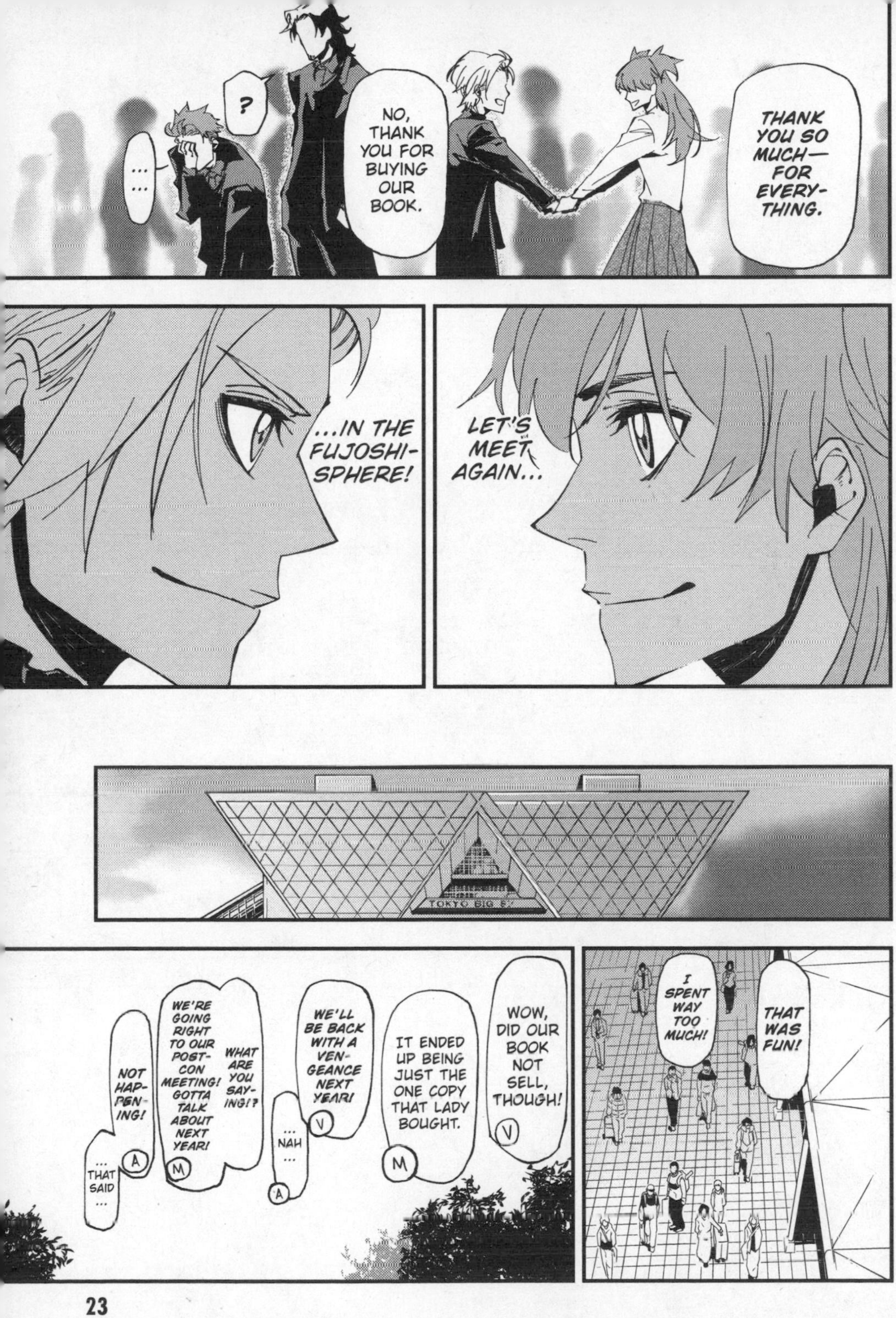
THANK YOU SO MUCH—FOR EVERYTHING.
NO, THANK YOU FOR BUYING OUR BOOK.
?
......
LET'S MEET AGAIN...
...IN THE FUJOSHI-SPHERE!
THAT WAS FUN!
I SPENT WAY TOO MUCH!
WOW, DID OUR BOOK NOT SELL, THOUGH!
IT ENDED UP BEING JUST THE ONE COPY THAT LADY BOUGHT.
WE'LL BE BACK WITH A VENGEANCE NEXT YEAR!
...NAH...
WHAT ARE YOU SAYING!?
WE'RE GOING RIGHT TO OUR POST-CON MEETING! GOTTA TALK ABOUT NEXT YEAR!
NOT HAPPENING!
...THAT SAID...

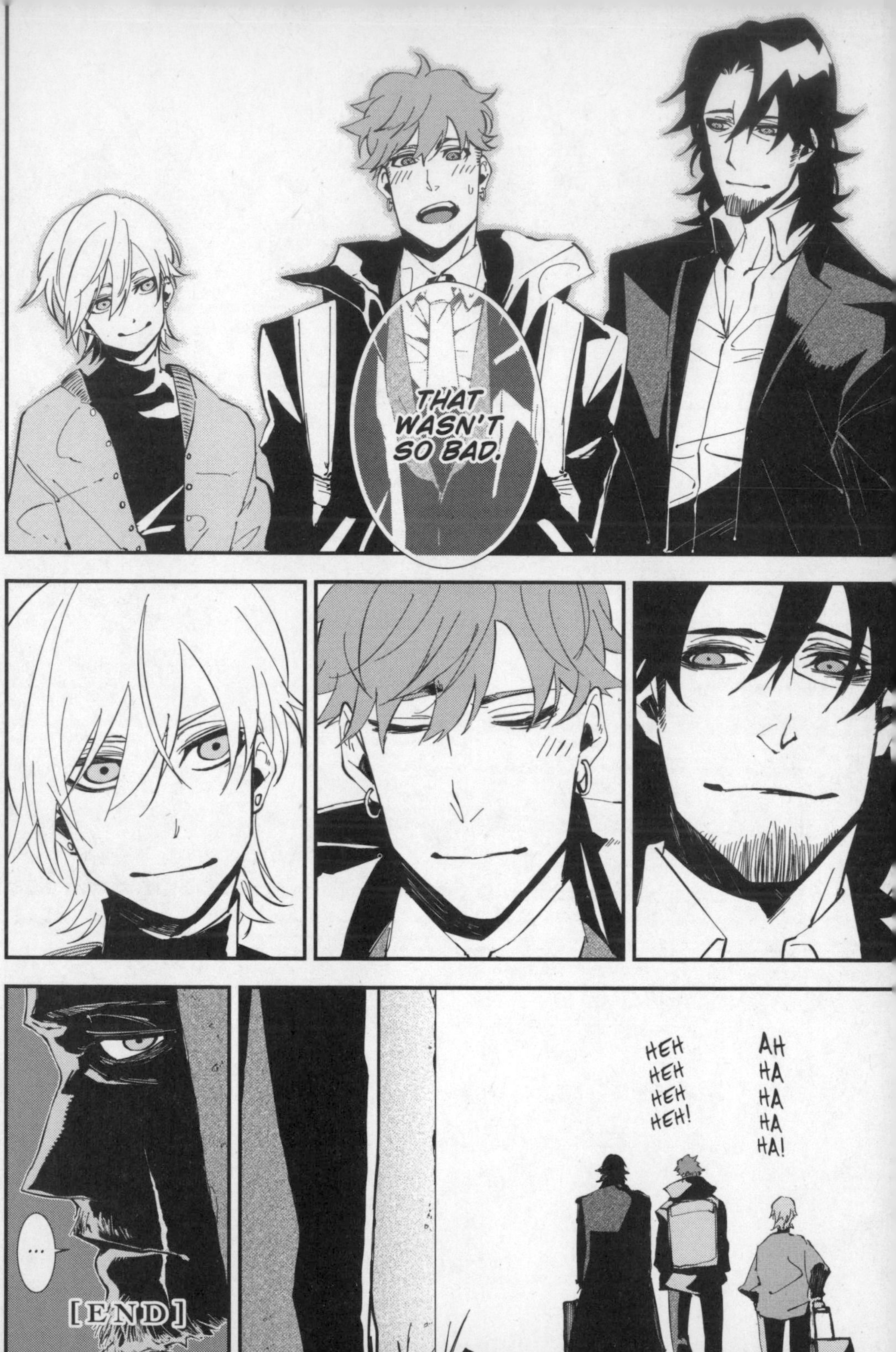
THAT WASN'T SO BAD.
AH HA HA HA HA!
HEH HEH HEH HEH!
...
[END]

#13

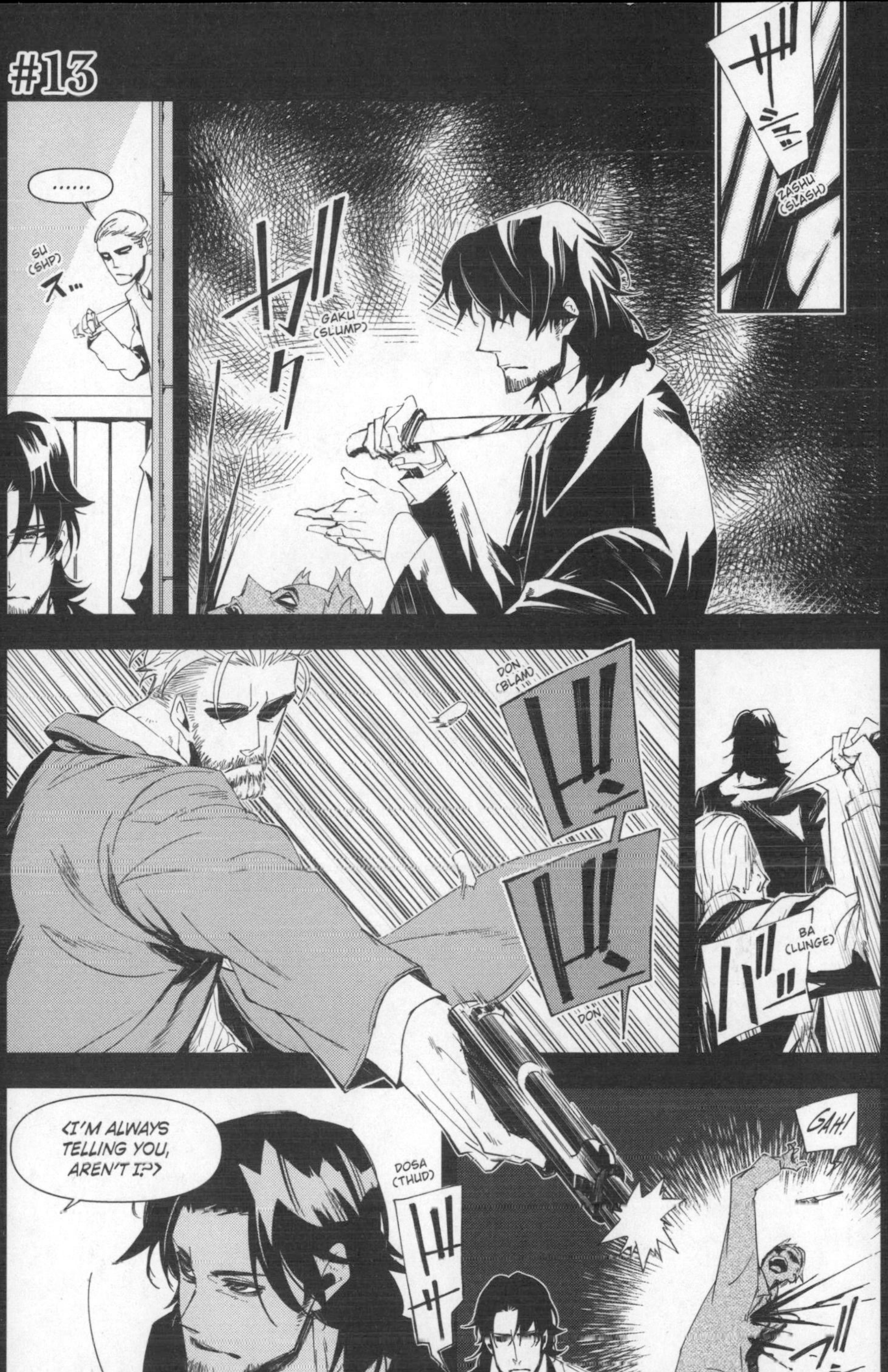
ZASHU (SLASH)
GAKU (SLUMP)
......
SU (SLIP)
BA (LUNGE)
DON (BLAM)
DON
GAH!
DOSA (THUD)
<I'M ALWAYS TELLING YOU, AREN'T I?>
BUSHU (SPURT)

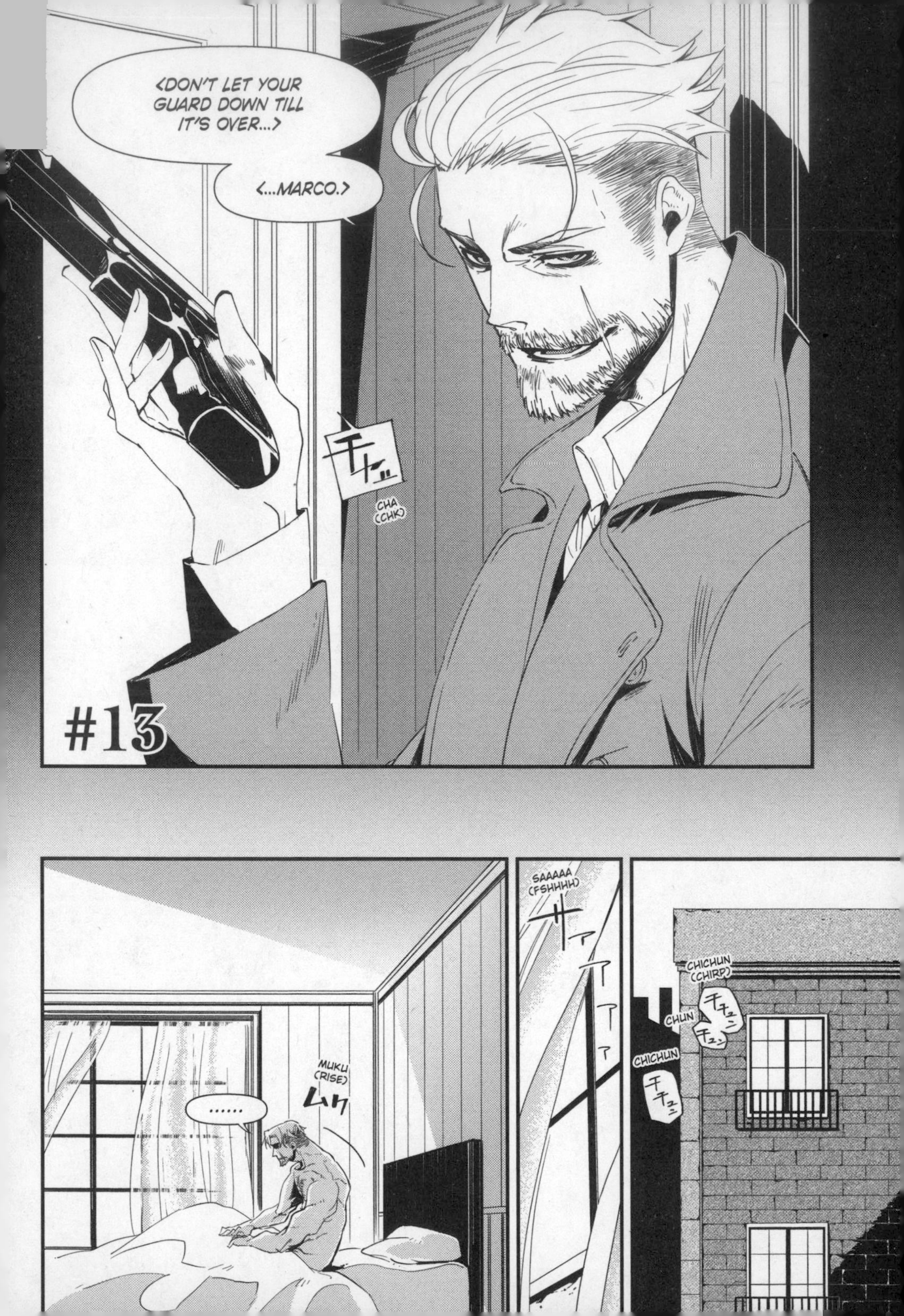
<DON'T LET YOUR GUARD DOWN TILL IT'S OVER...>
<...MARCO.>
CHA (CHK)
#13
CHICHUN (CHIRP)
CHUN
CHICHUN
SAAAAA (FSHHHH)
MUKU (RISE)
....

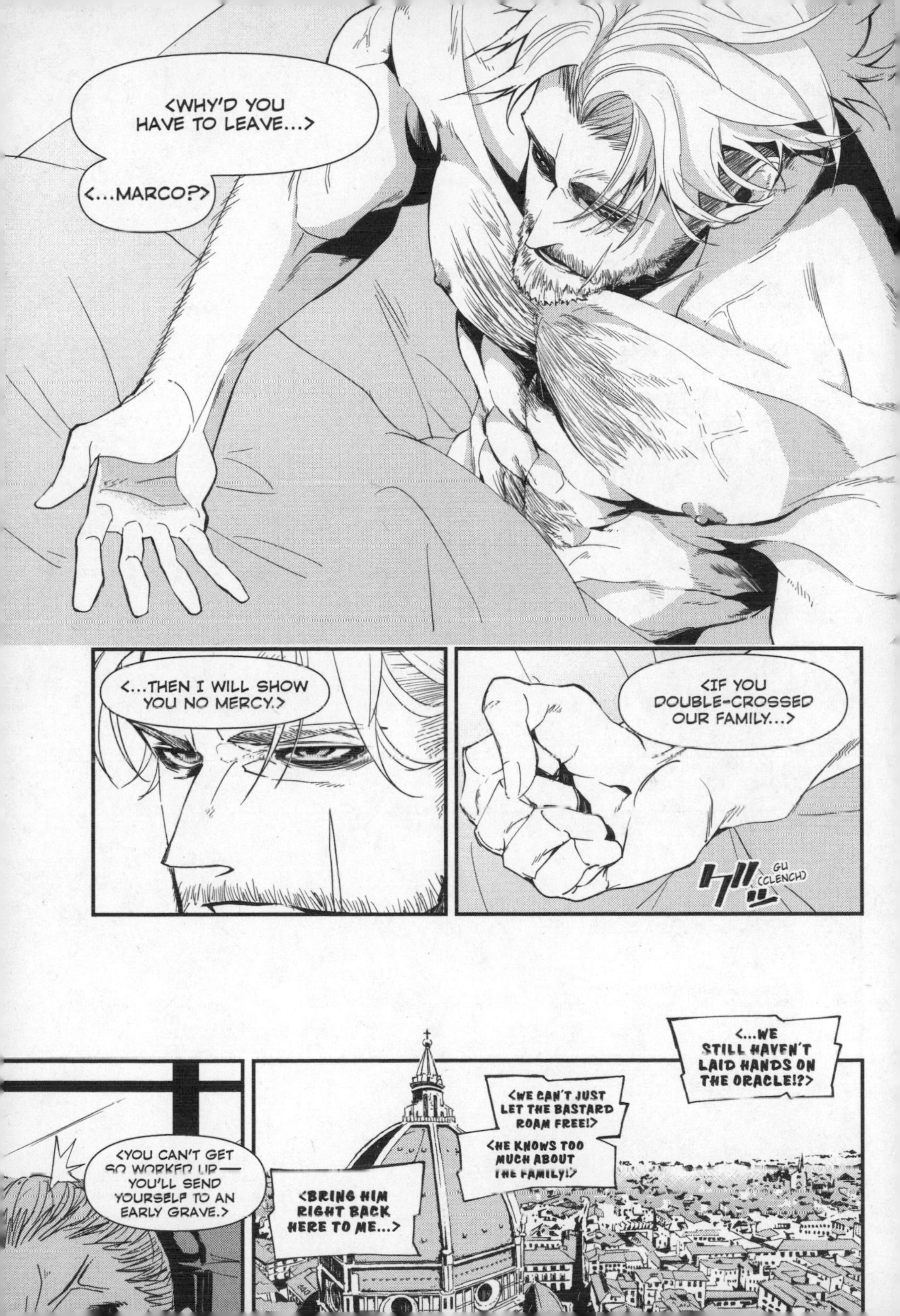
<WHY'D YOU HAVE TO LEAVE...>
<...MARCO?>
<IF YOU DOUBLE-CROSSED OUR FAMILY...>
GU (CLENCH)
<...THEN I WILL SHOW YOU NO MERCY.>
<...WE STILL HAVEN'T LAID HANDS ON THE ORACLE!?>
<WE CAN'T JUST LET THE BASTARD ROAM FREE!>
<HE KNOWS TOO MUCH ABOUT THE FAMILY!>
<BRING HIM RIGHT BACK HERE TO ME...>
<YOU CAN'T GET SO WORKED UP— YOU'LL SEND YOURSELF TO AN EARLY GRAVE.>

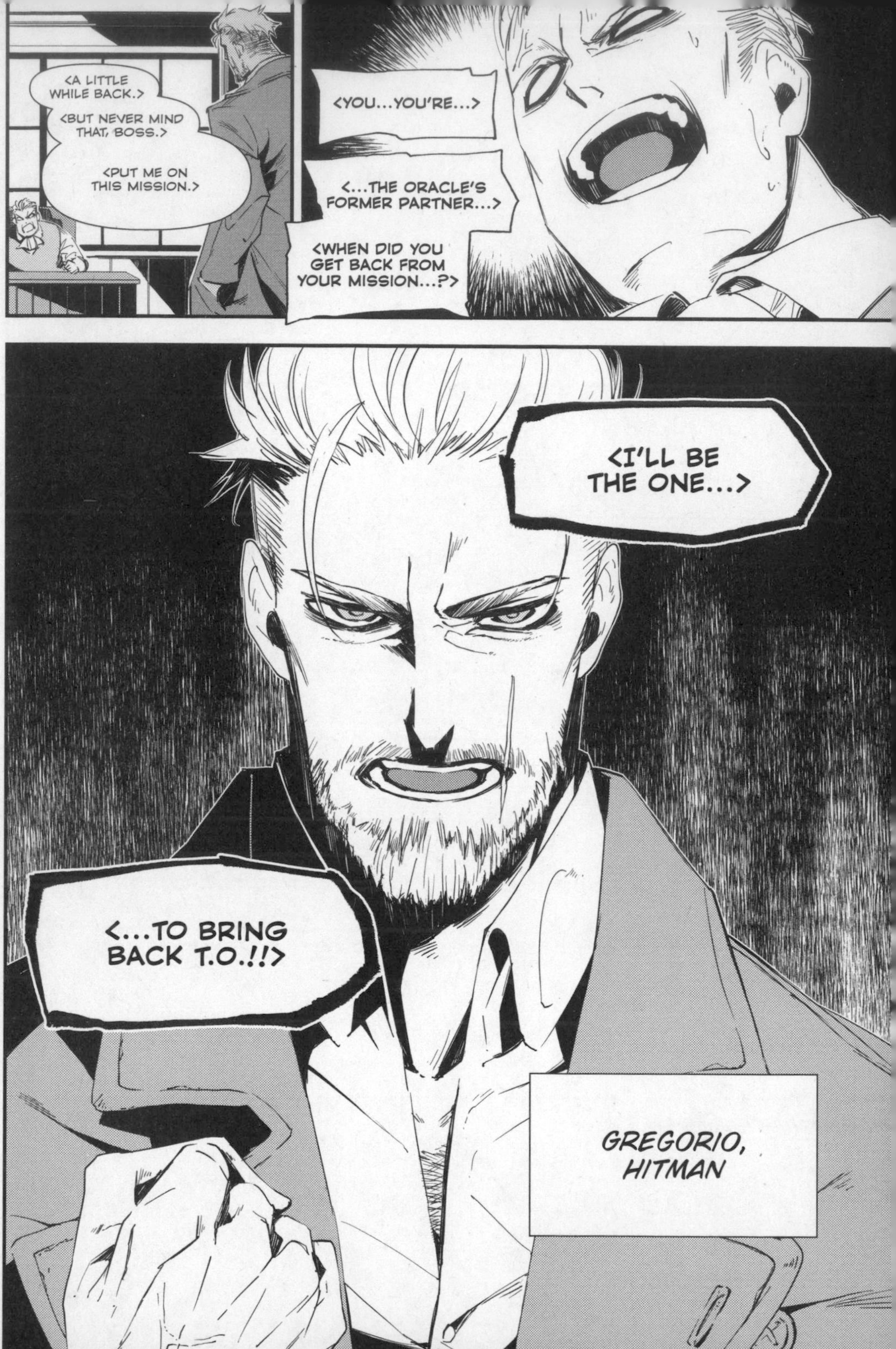
<YOU...YOU'RE...>
<...THE ORACLE'S FORMER PARTNER...>
<WHEN DID YOU GET BACK FROM YOUR MISSION...?>
<A LITTLE WHILE BACK.>
<BUT NEVER MIND THAT, BOSS.>
<PUT ME ON THIS MISSION.>
<I'LL BE THE ONE...>
<...TO BRING BACK T.O.!!>
GREGORIO, HITMAN

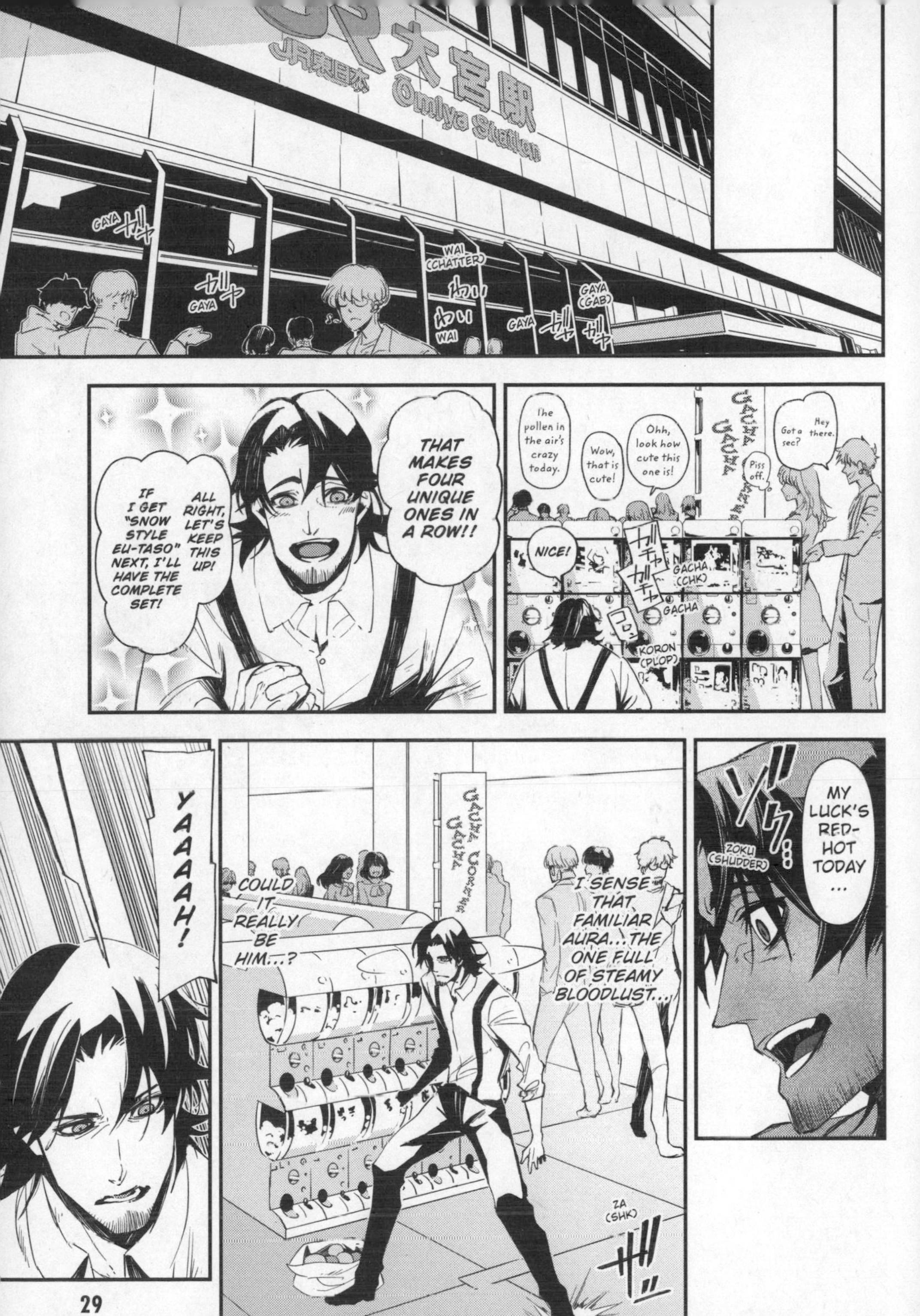
JR東日本
大宮駅
Ōmiya Station
GAYA (GAB)
WAI (CHATTER)
WAI
GAYA
GAYA
GAYA
Hey there. Got a sec?
Piss off.
Ohh, look how cute this one is!
Wow, that is cute!
The pollen in the air's crazy today.
NICE!
GACHA (CHK)
GACHA
KORON (PLOP)
THAT MAKES FOUR UNIQUE ONES IN A ROW!!
ALL RIGHT, LET'S KEEP THIS UP!
IF I GET "SNOW STYLE EU-TASO" NEXT, I'LL HAVE THE COMPLETE SET!
MY LUCK'S RED-HOT TODAY...
ZOKU (SHUDDER)
I SENSE THAT FAMILIAR AURA... THE ONE FULL OF STEAMY BLOODLUST...
COULD IT REALLY BE HIM...?
ZA (SHK)
YAAAAAH!

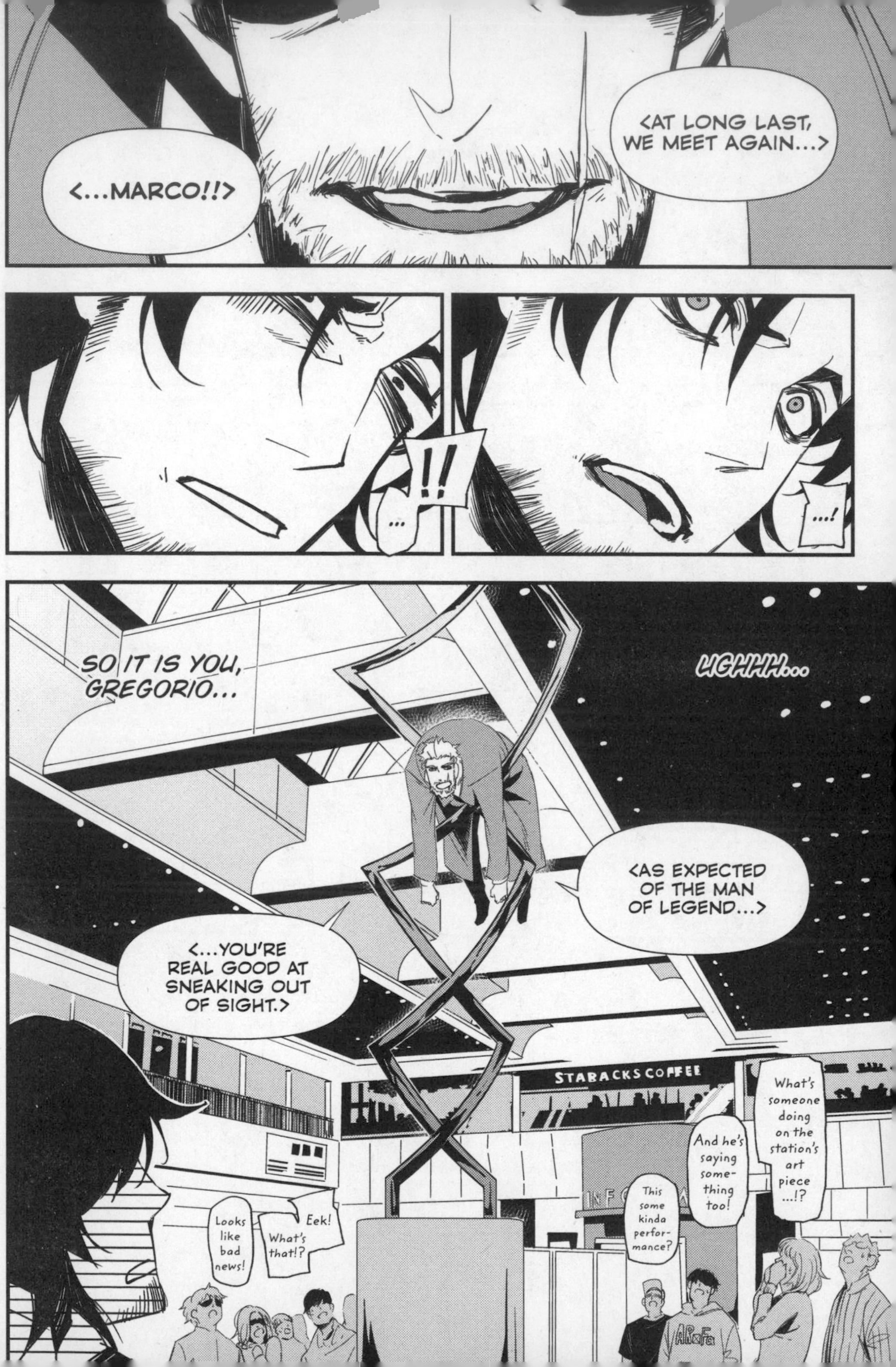
<AT LONG LAST, WE MEET AGAIN...>
<...MARCO!!>
...!
!!
...
UGHHH...
SO IT IS YOU, GREGORIO...
<AS EXPECTED OF THE MAN OF LEGEND...>
<...YOU'RE REAL GOOD AT SNEAKING OUT OF SIGHT.>
STABACKS COFFEE
What's someone doing on the station's art piece...!?
And he's saying something too!
This some kinda performance?
Eek!
What's that!?
Looks like bad news!

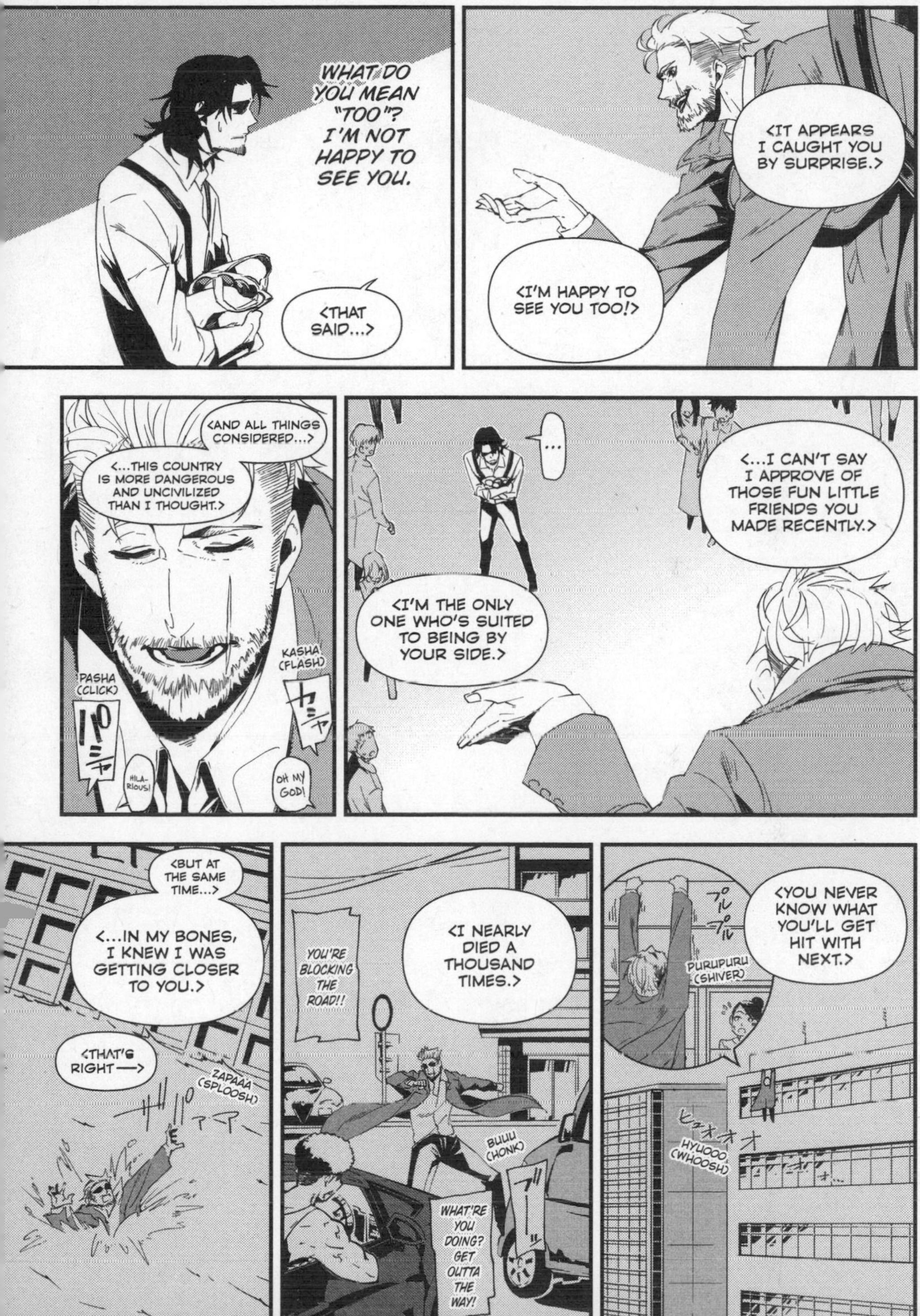
<IT APPEARS I CAUGHT YOU BY SURPRISE.>
<I'M HAPPY TO SEE YOU TOO!>
WHAT DO YOU MEAN "TOO"? I'M NOT HAPPY TO SEE YOU.
<THAT SAID...>
...
<...I CAN'T SAY I APPROVE OF THOSE FUN LITTLE FRIENDS YOU MADE RECENTLY.>
<I'M THE ONLY ONE WHO'S SUITED TO BEING BY YOUR SIDE.>
<AND ALL THINGS CONSIDERED...>
<...THIS COUNTRY IS MORE DANGEROUS AND UNCIVILIZED THAN I THOUGHT.>
KASHA (FLASH)
カシャ
PASHA (CLICK)
パシャ
OH MY GOD!
HILARIOUS!
<YOU NEVER KNOW WHAT YOU'LL GET HIT WITH NEXT.>
プルプル
PURUPURU (SHIVER)
HYUOOO (WHOOSH)
<I NEARLY DIED A THOUSAND TIMES.>
YOU'RE BLOCKING THE ROAD!!
BUUU (HONK)
ブー
WHAT'RE YOU DOING? GET OUTTA THE WAY!
<BUT AT THE SAME TIME...>
<...IN MY BONES, I KNEW I WAS GETTING CLOSER TO YOU.>
<THAT'S RIGHT—>
ZAPAAA (SPLOOSH)

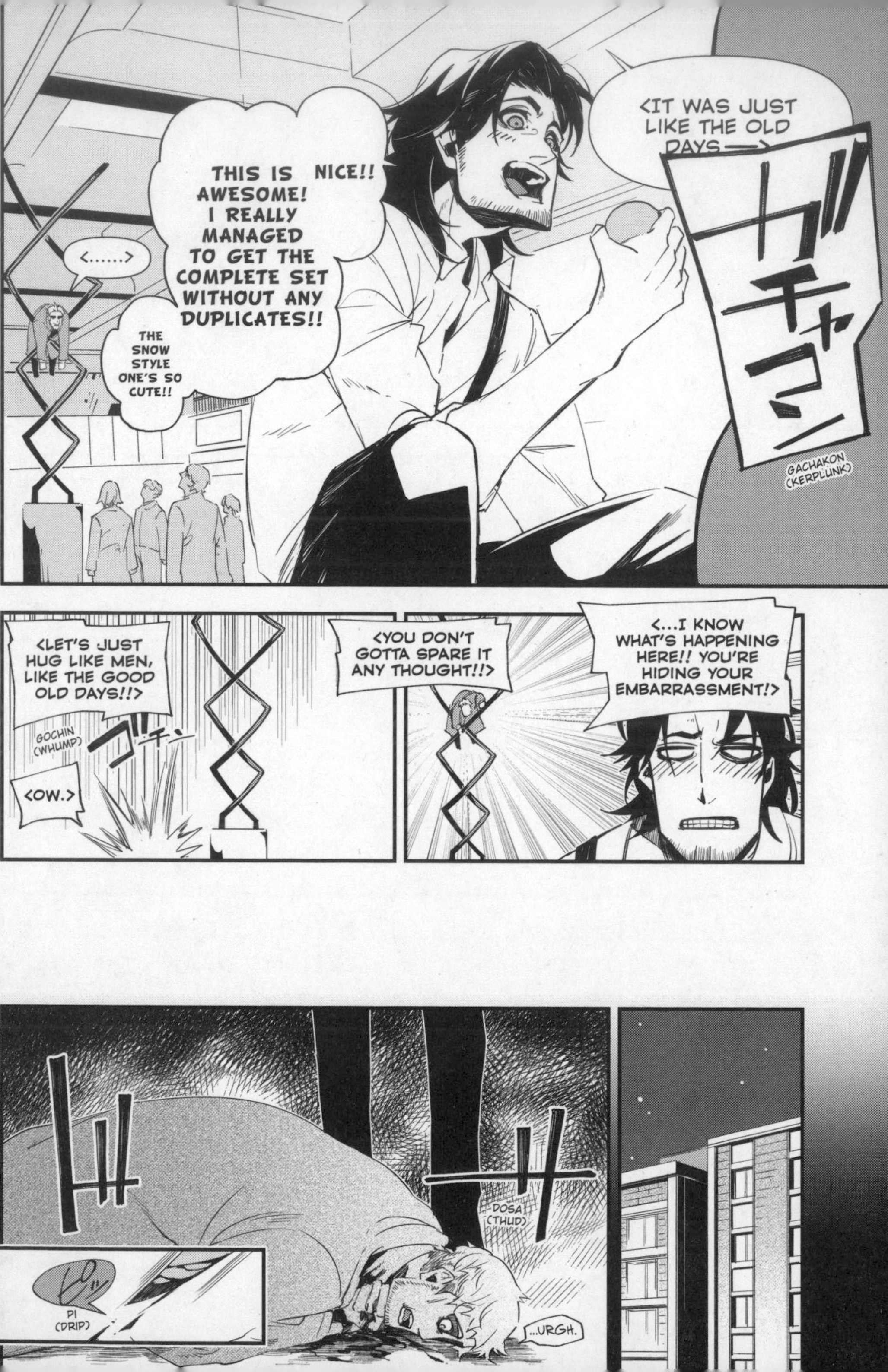
<IT WAS JUST LIKE THE OLD DAYS—>
ガチャコン
GACHAKON (KERPLUNK)
THIS IS NICE!! AWESOME! I REALLY MANAGED TO GET THE COMPLETE SET WITHOUT ANY DUPLICATES!!
THE SNOW STYLE ONE'S SO CUTE!!
<......>
<...I KNOW WHAT'S HAPPENING HERE!! YOU'RE HIDING YOUR EMBARRASSMENT!>
<YOU DON'T GOTTA SPARE IT ANY THOUGHT!!>
<LET'S JUST HUG LIKE MEN, LIKE THE GOOD OLD DAYS!!>
GOCHIN (WHUMP)
<OW.>
DOSA (THUD)
...URGH.
PI (DRIP)

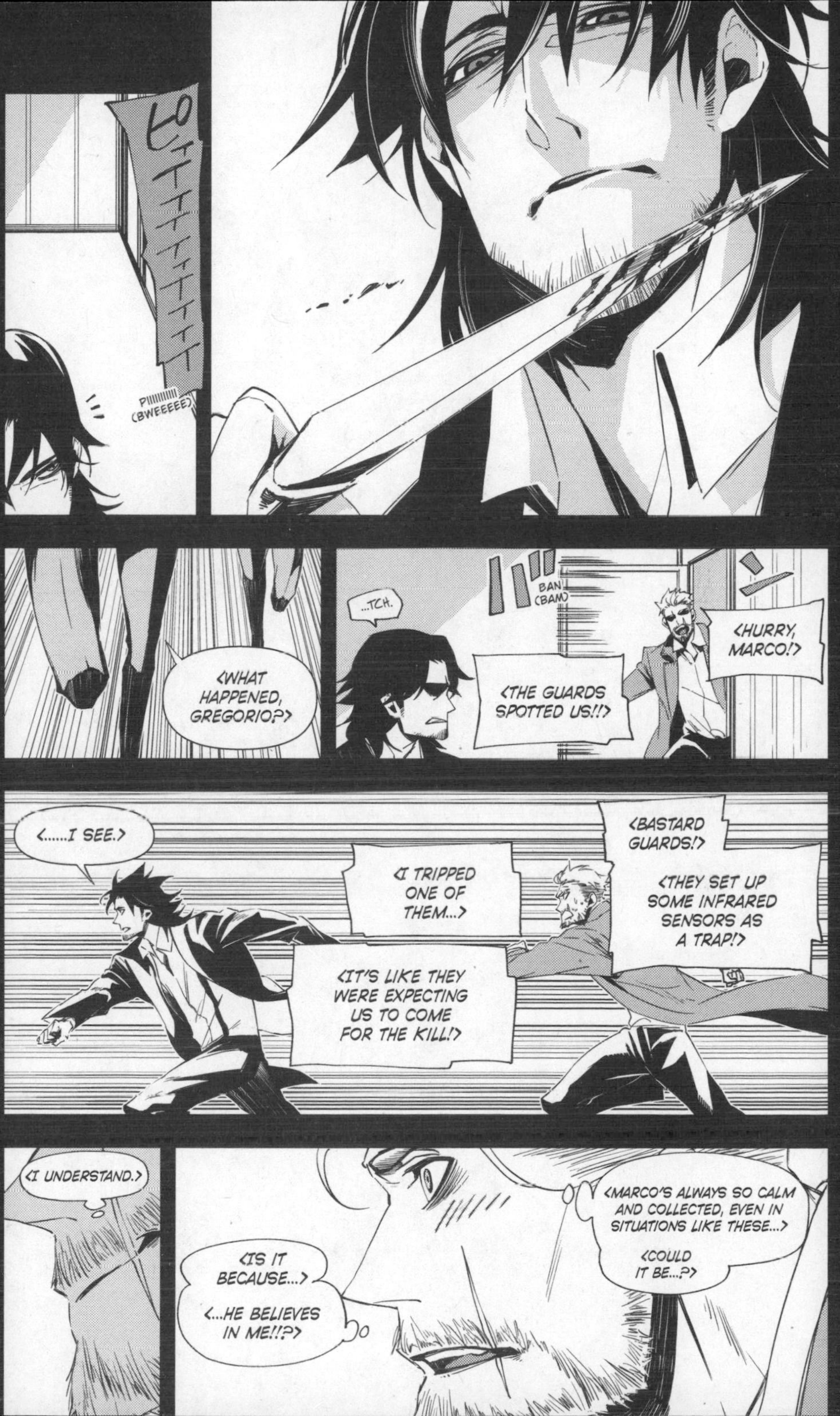
ピイイイイイイイイイイイ
PIIIIIIIII (BWEEEEEE)
BAN (BAM)
<HURRY, MARCO!>
...TCH.
<THE GUARDS SPOTTED US!!>
<WHAT HAPPENED, GREGORIO?>
<BASTARD GUARDS!>
<THEY SET UP SOME INFRARED SENSORS AS A TRAP!>
<I TRIPPED ONE OF THEM...>
<IT'S LIKE THEY WERE EXPECTING US TO COME FOR THE KILL!>
<......I SEE.>
<MARCO'S ALWAYS SO CALM AND COLLECTED, EVEN IN SITUATIONS LIKE THESE...>
<COULD IT BE...?>
<IS IT BECAUSE...>
<...HE BELIEVES IN ME!!?>
<I UNDERSTAND.>

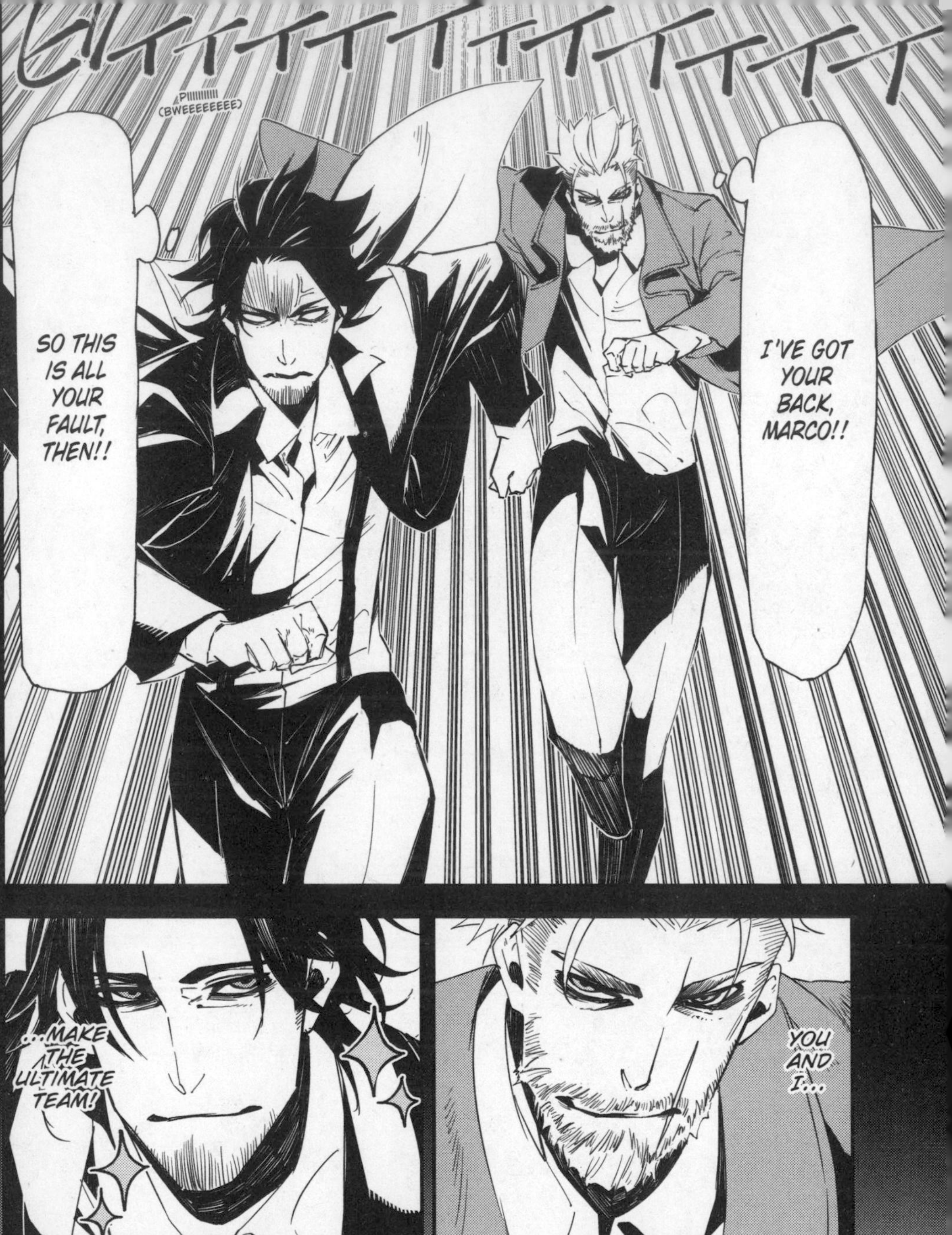
PIIIIIIIIII
(BWEEEEEEEEE)
I'VE GOT YOUR BACK, MARCO!!
SO THIS IS ALL YOUR FAULT, THEN!!
YOU AND I...
...MAKE THE ULTIMATE TEAM!
NOTE: GREGORIO'S FILTER

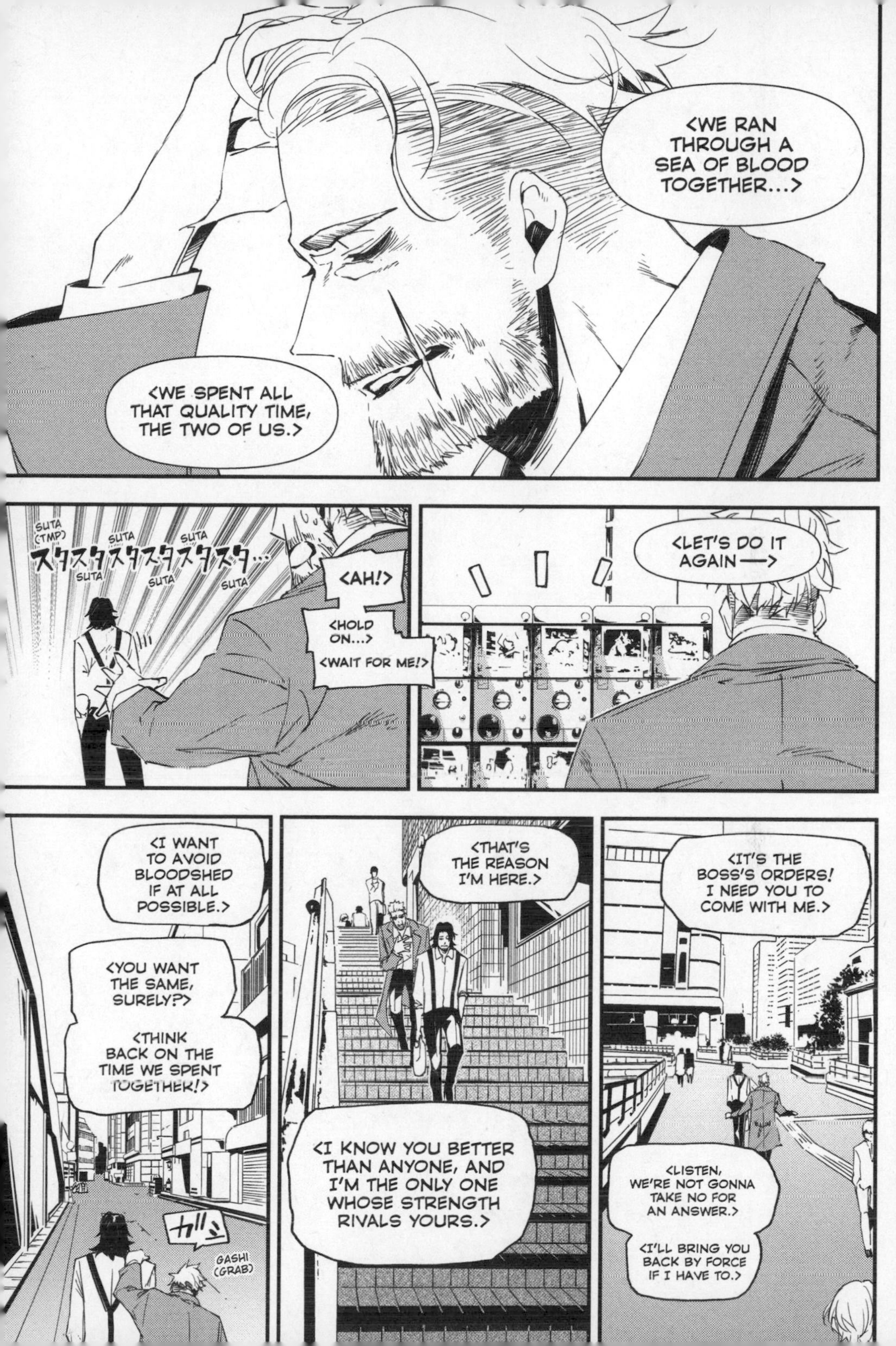
<WE RAN THROUGH A SEA OF BLOOD TOGETHER...>
<WE SPENT ALL THAT QUALITY TIME, THE TWO OF US.>
<LET'S DO IT AGAIN—>
SUTA (TMP) SUTA SUTA SUTA SUTA SUTA
スタスタスタスタスタ...
<AH!>
<HOLD ON...>
<WAIT FOR ME!>
<IT'S THE BOSS'S ORDERS! I NEED YOU TO COME WITH ME.>
<LISTEN, WE'RE NOT GONNA TAKE NO FOR AN ANSWER.>
<I'LL BRING YOU BACK BY FORCE IF I HAVE TO.>
<THAT'S THE REASON I'M HERE.>
<I KNOW YOU BETTER THAN ANYONE, AND I'M THE ONLY ONE WHOSE STRENGTH RIVALS YOURS.>
<I WANT TO AVOID BLOODSHED IF AT ALL POSSIBLE.>
<YOU WANT THE SAME, SURELY?>
<THINK BACK ON THE TIME WE SPENT TOGETHER!>
ガシ
GASHI (GRAB)

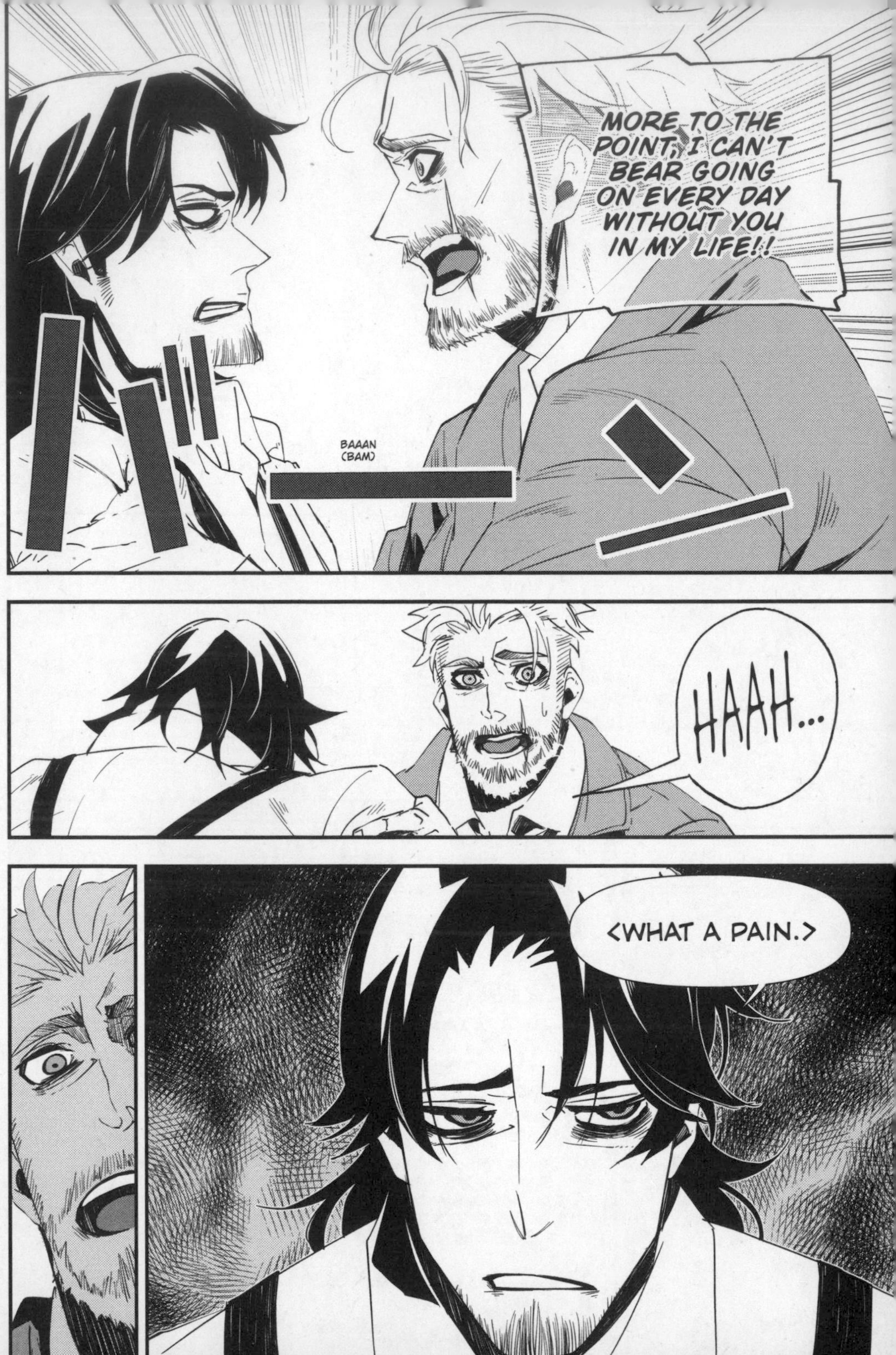
MORE TO THE POINT, I CAN'T BEAR GOING ON EVERY DAY WITHOUT YOU IN MY LIFE!!
BAAAN (BAM)
HAAH...
<WHAT A PAIN.>

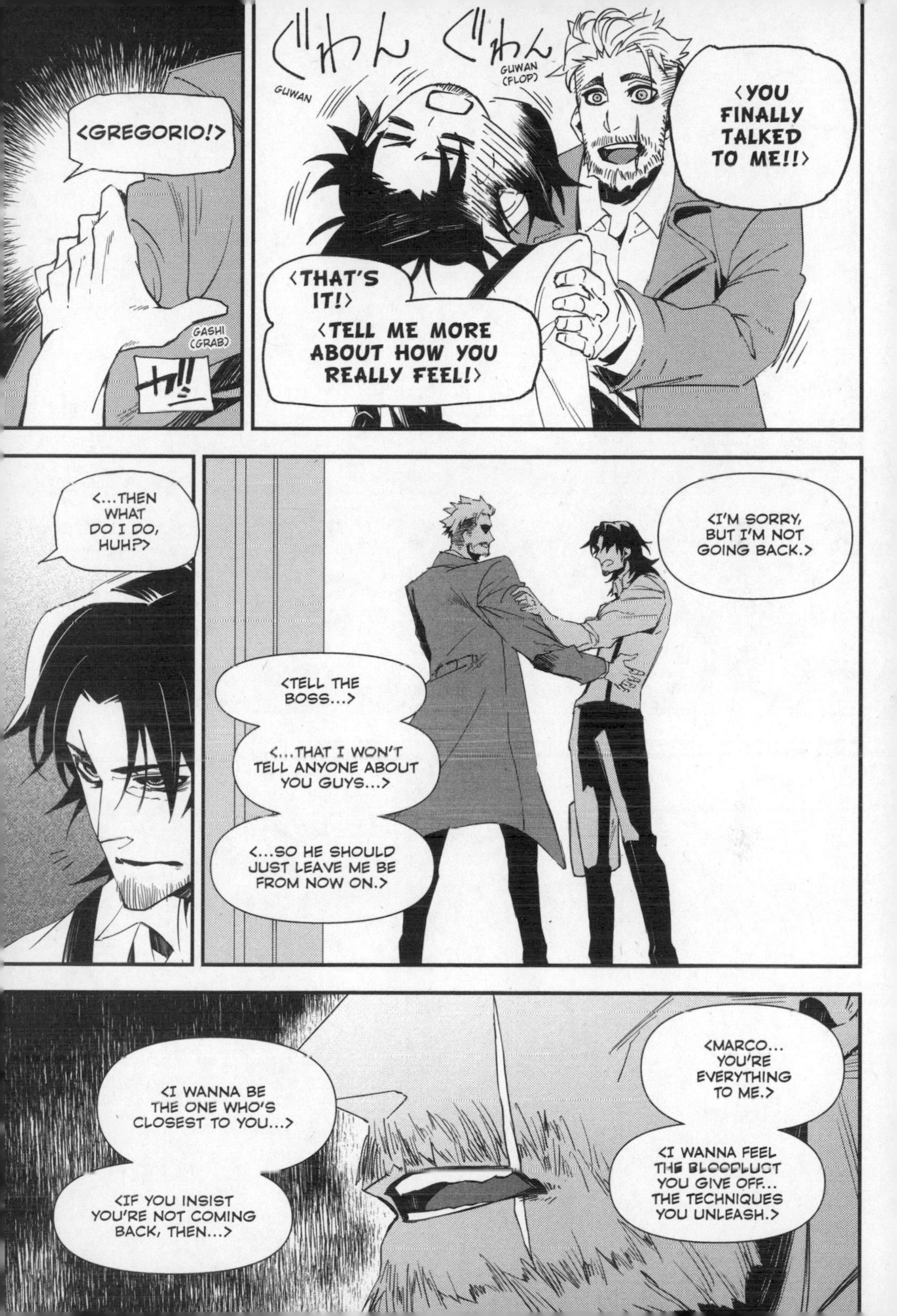
ぐわん ぐわん
GUWAN (FLOP)
GUWAN
<YOU FINALLY TALKED TO ME!!>
<THAT'S IT!>
<TELL ME MORE ABOUT HOW YOU REALLY FEEL!>
<GREGORIO!>
GASHI (GRAB)
ガッ!!
<I'M SORRY, BUT I'M NOT GOING BACK.>
<TELL THE BOSS...>
<...THAT I WON'T TELL ANYONE ABOUT YOU GUYS...>
<...SO HE SHOULD JUST LEAVE ME BE FROM NOW ON.>
<...THEN WHAT DO I DO, HUH?>
<MARCO... YOU'RE EVERYTHING TO ME.>
<I WANNA BE THE ONE WHO'S CLOSEST TO YOU...>
<I WANNA FEEL THE BLOODLUST YOU GIVE OFF... THE TECHNIQUES YOU UNLEASH.>
<IF YOU INSIST YOU'RE NOT COMING BACK, THEN...>

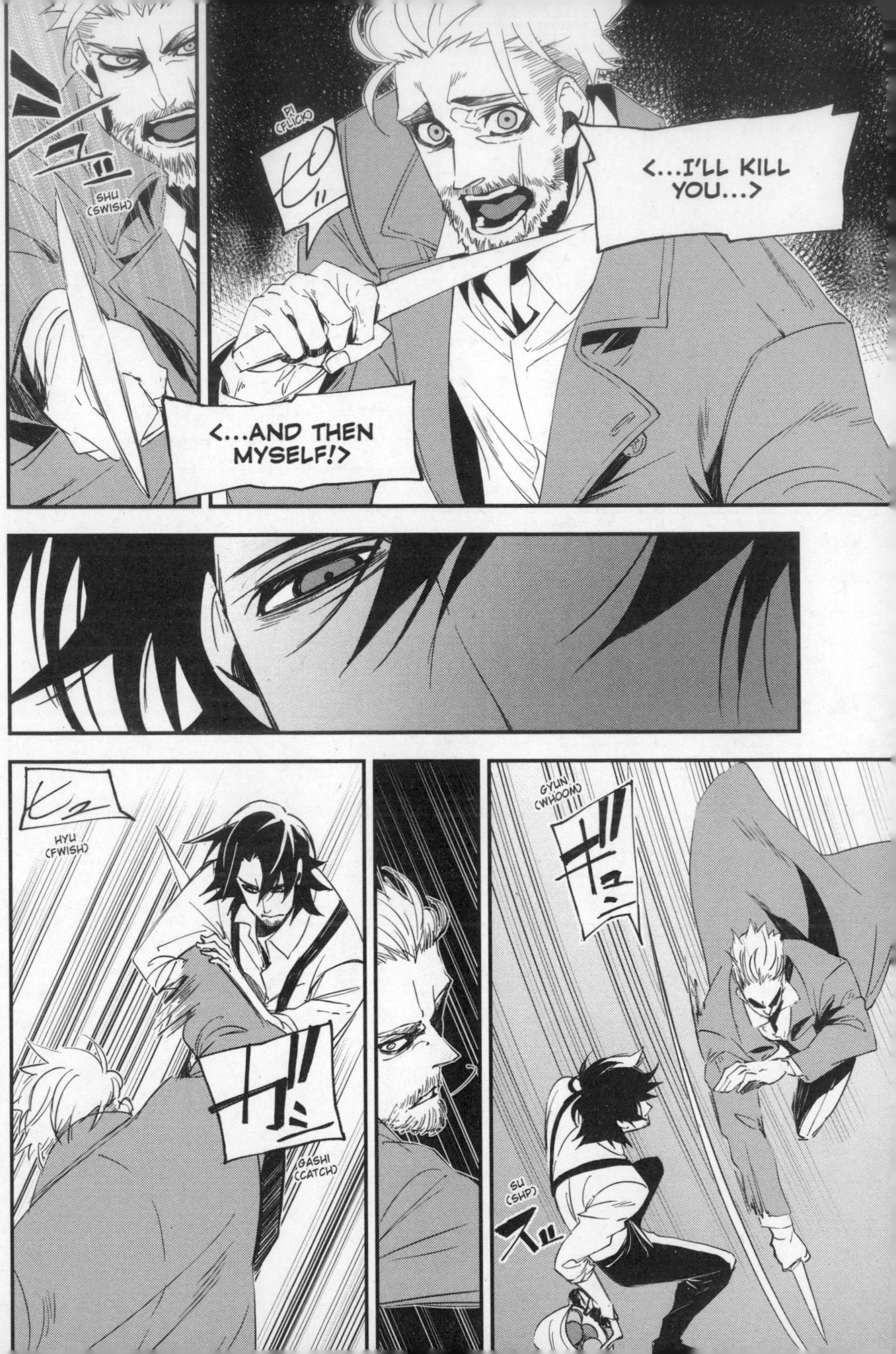
PI (FLICK)
<...I'LL KILL YOU...>
<...AND THEN MYSELF!>
SHU (SWISH)
GYUN (WHOOM)
SU (SHP)
HYU (FWISH)
GASHI (CATCH)

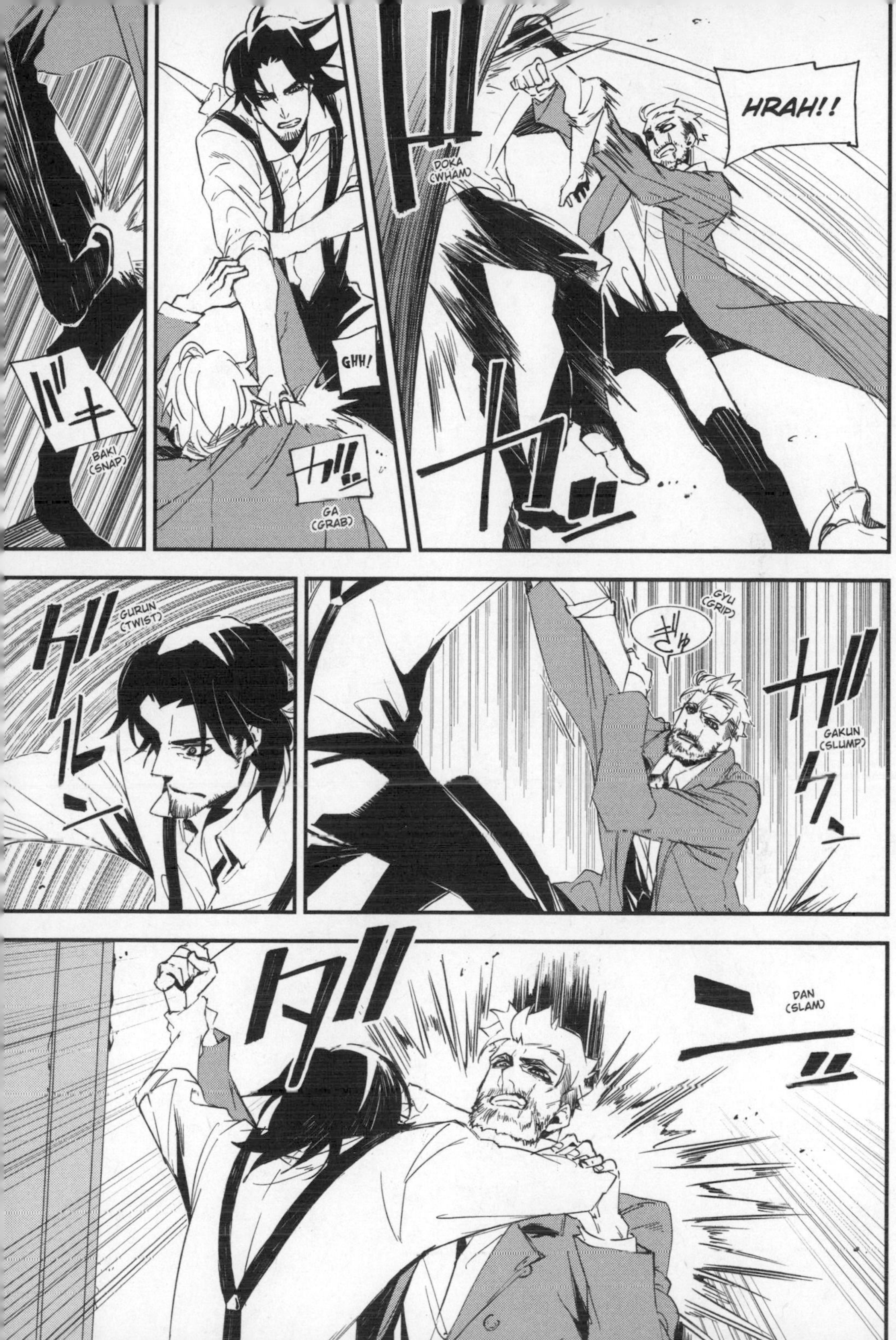
HRAH!!
DOKA (WHAM)
GHH!
GA (GRAB)
BAKI (SNAP)
GYU (GRIP)
ぎゅ
GAKUN (SLUMP)
GURUN (TWIST)
DAN (SLAM)

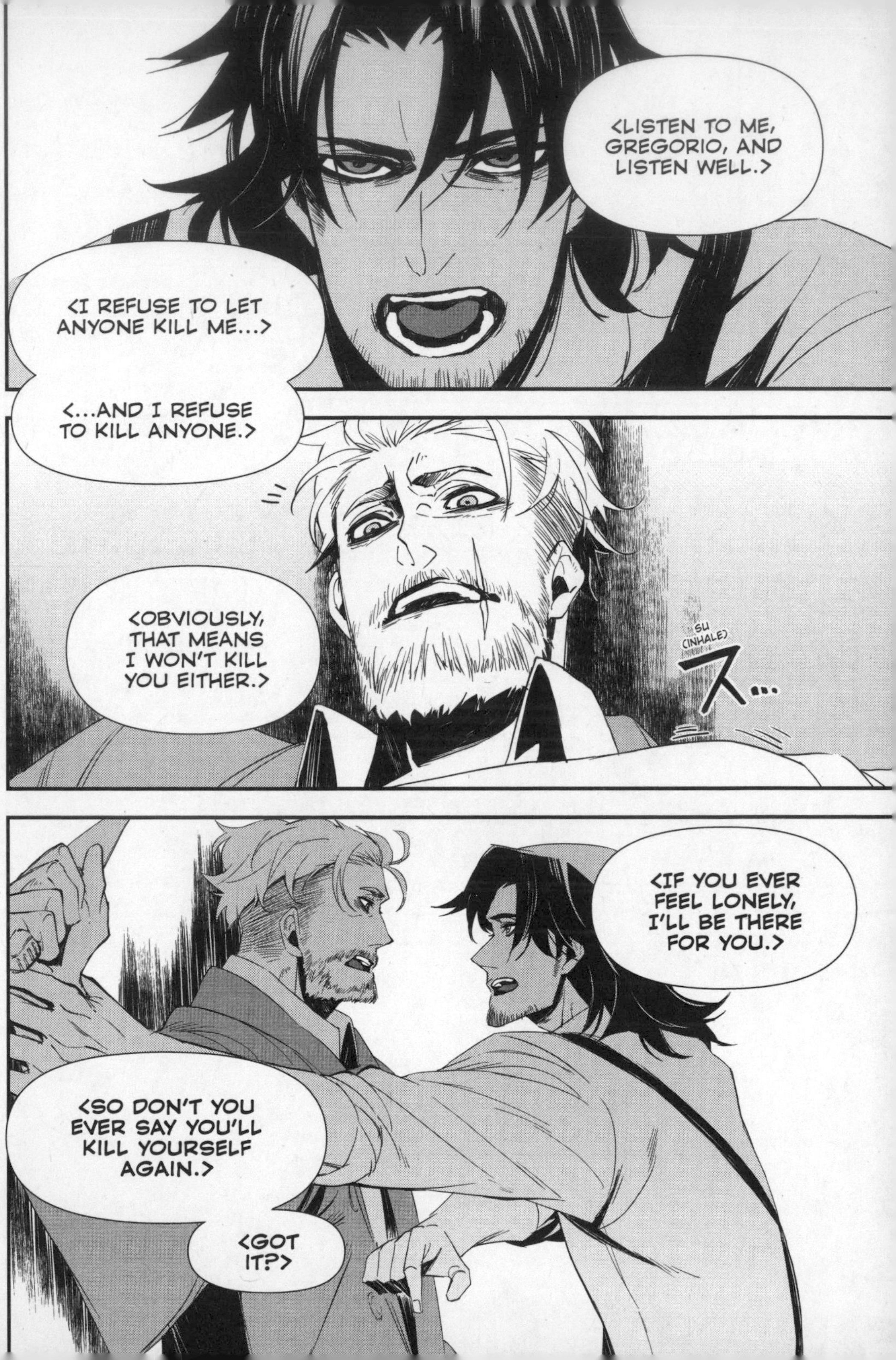
<LISTEN TO ME, GREGORIO, AND LISTEN WELL.>
<I REFUSE TO LET ANYONE KILL ME...>
<...AND I REFUSE TO KILL ANYONE.>
<OBVIOUSLY, THAT MEANS I WON'T KILL YOU EITHER.>
SU (INHALE)
ス...
<IF YOU EVER FEEL LONELY, I'LL BE THERE FOR YOU.>
<SO DON'T YOU EVER SAY YOU'LL KILL YOURSELF AGAIN.>
<GOT IT?>

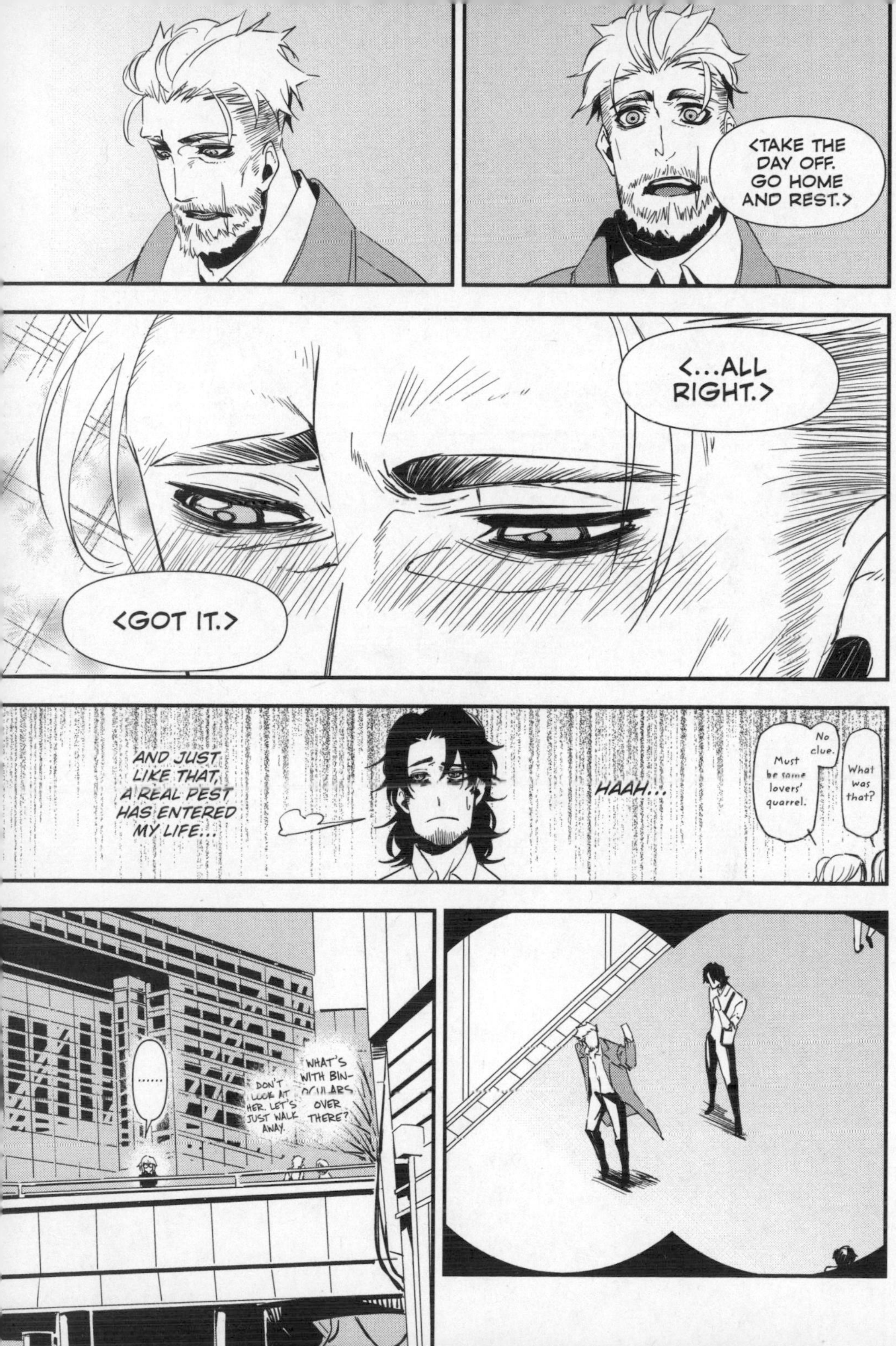
<TAKE THE DAY OFF. GO HOME AND REST.>
<...ALL RIGHT.>
<GOT IT.>
What was that?
No clue.
Must be some lovers' quarrel.
HAAH...
AND JUST LIKE THAT, A REAL PEST HAS ENTERED MY LIFE...
WHAT'S WITH BINOCULARS OVER THERE?
DON'T LOOK AT HER. LET'S JUST WALK AWAY.
......

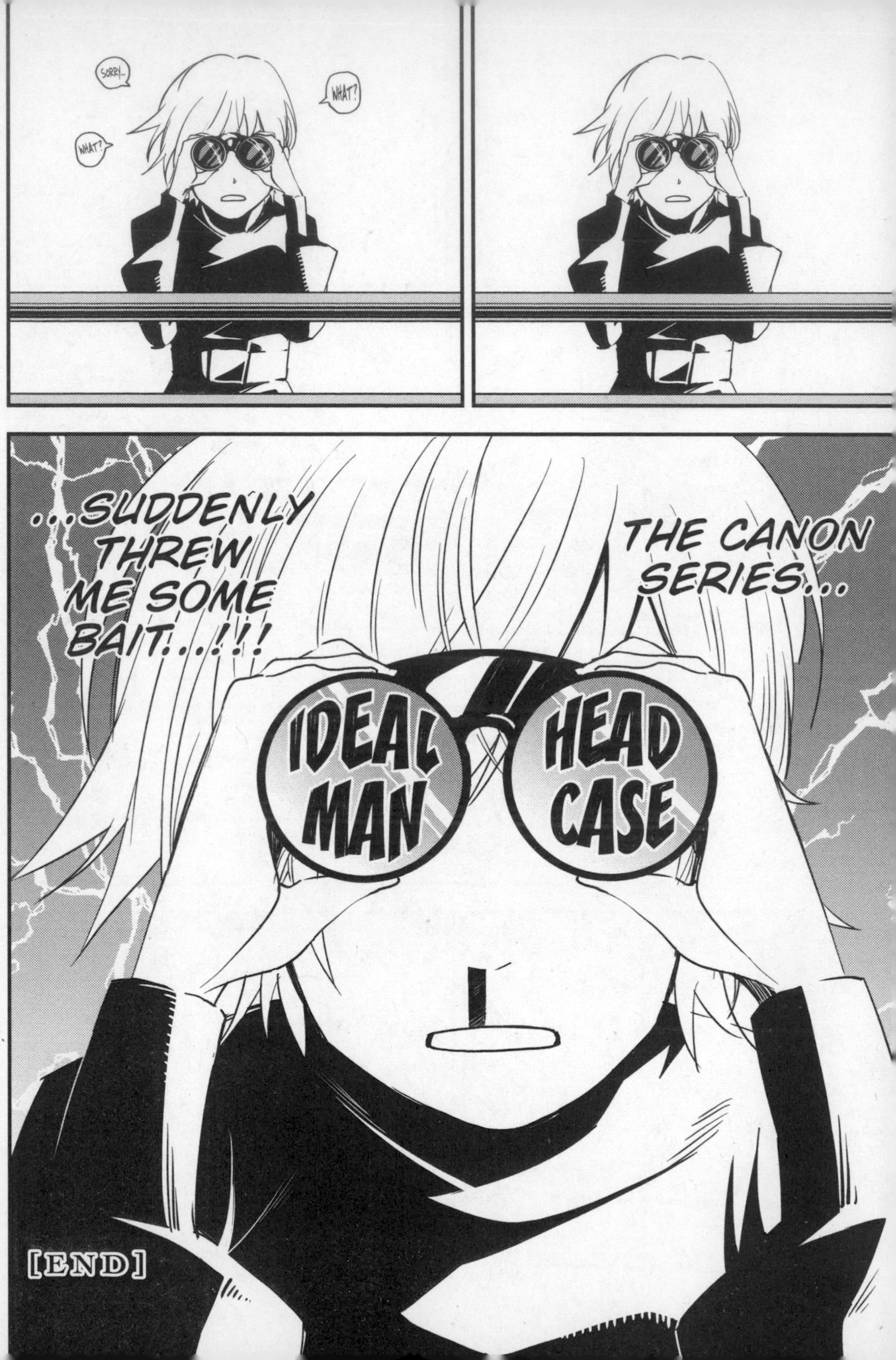
SORRY...
WHAT?
WHAT?
THE CANON SERIES...
...SUDDENLY THREW ME SOME BAIT...!!!
HEAD CASE
IDEAL MAN
[END]

Viviana was actually spying
on them the whole time.

THE GEEK EX-HITMAN

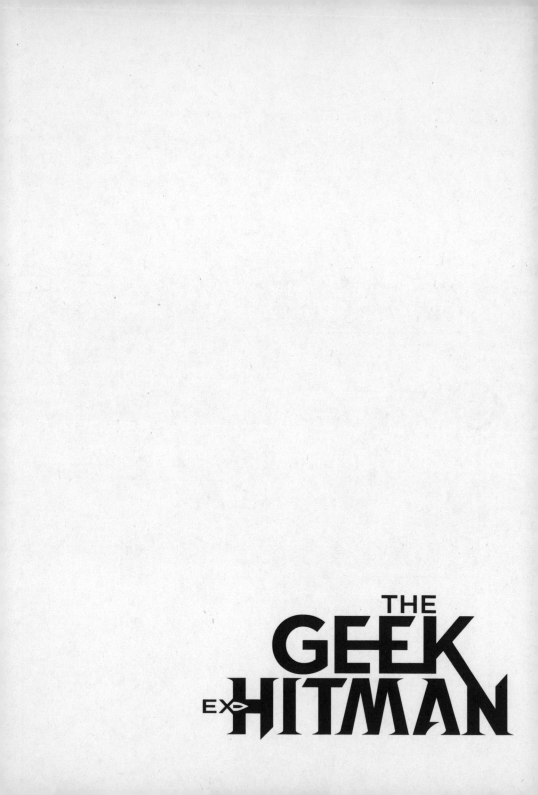

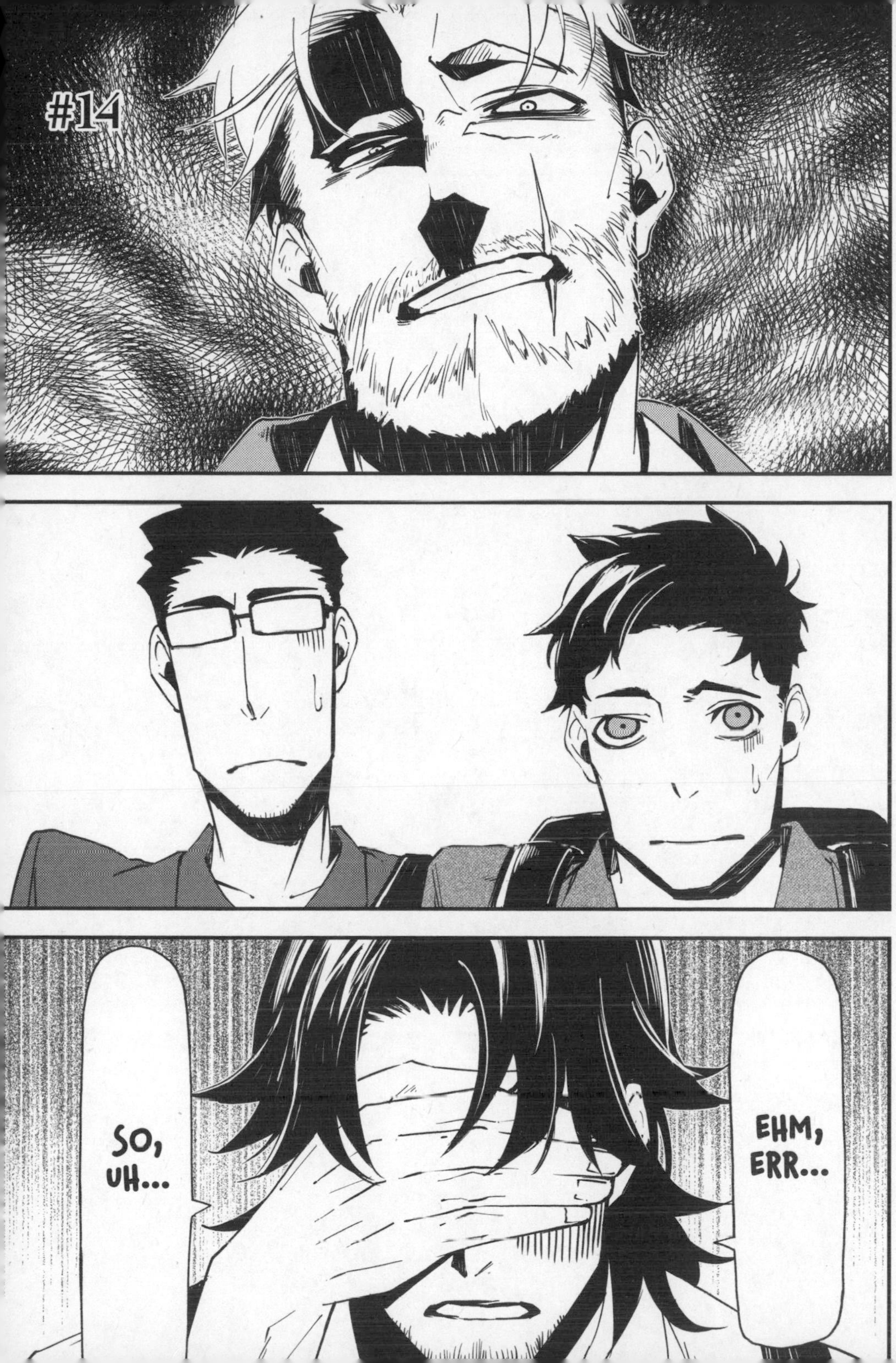
#14
EHM, ERR...
SO, UH...

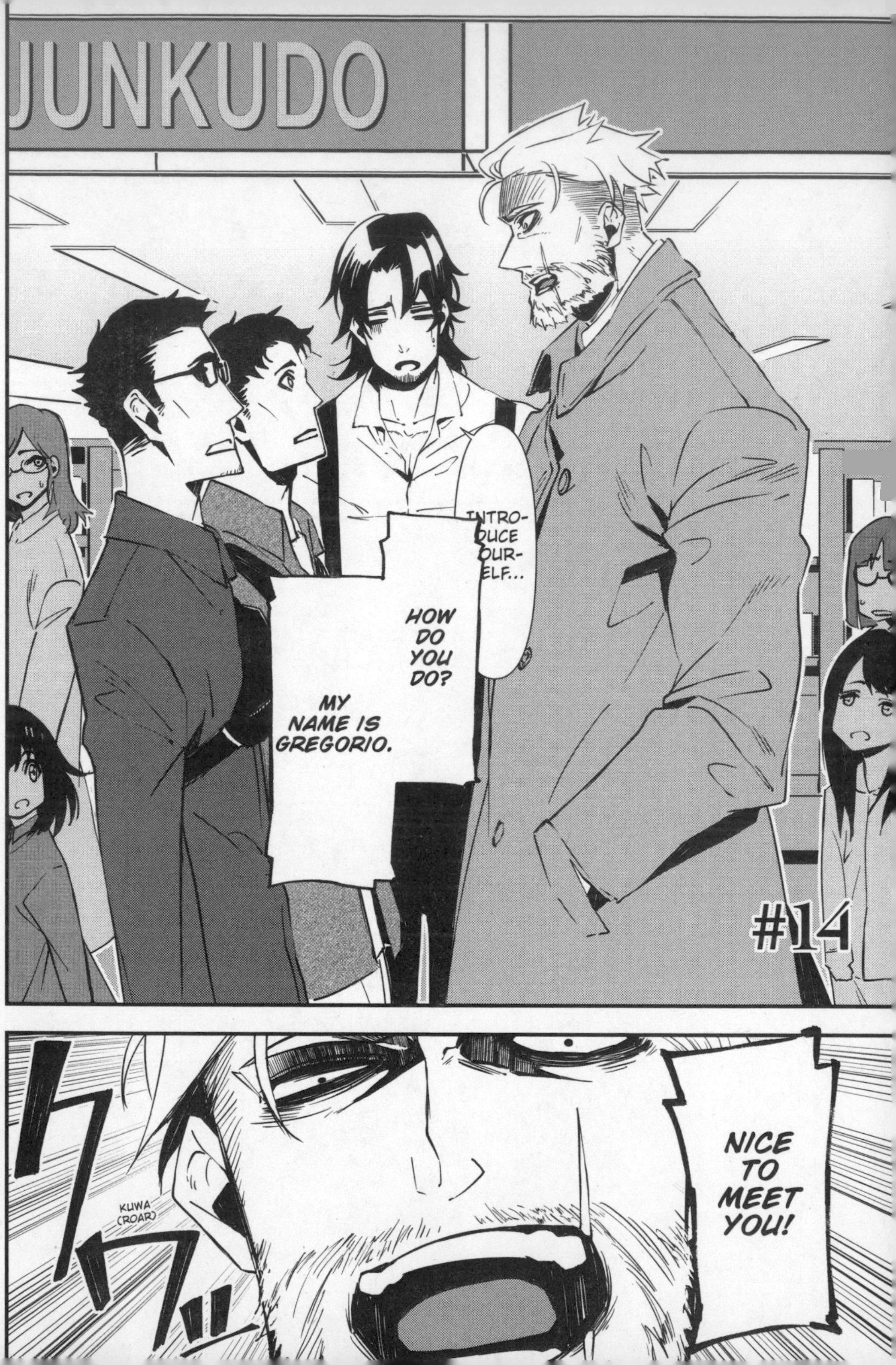
JUNKUDO
INTRO-DUCE OUR-ELF...
HOW DO YOU DO?
MY NAME IS GREGORIO.
#14
NICE TO MEET YOU!
KUWA (ROAR)

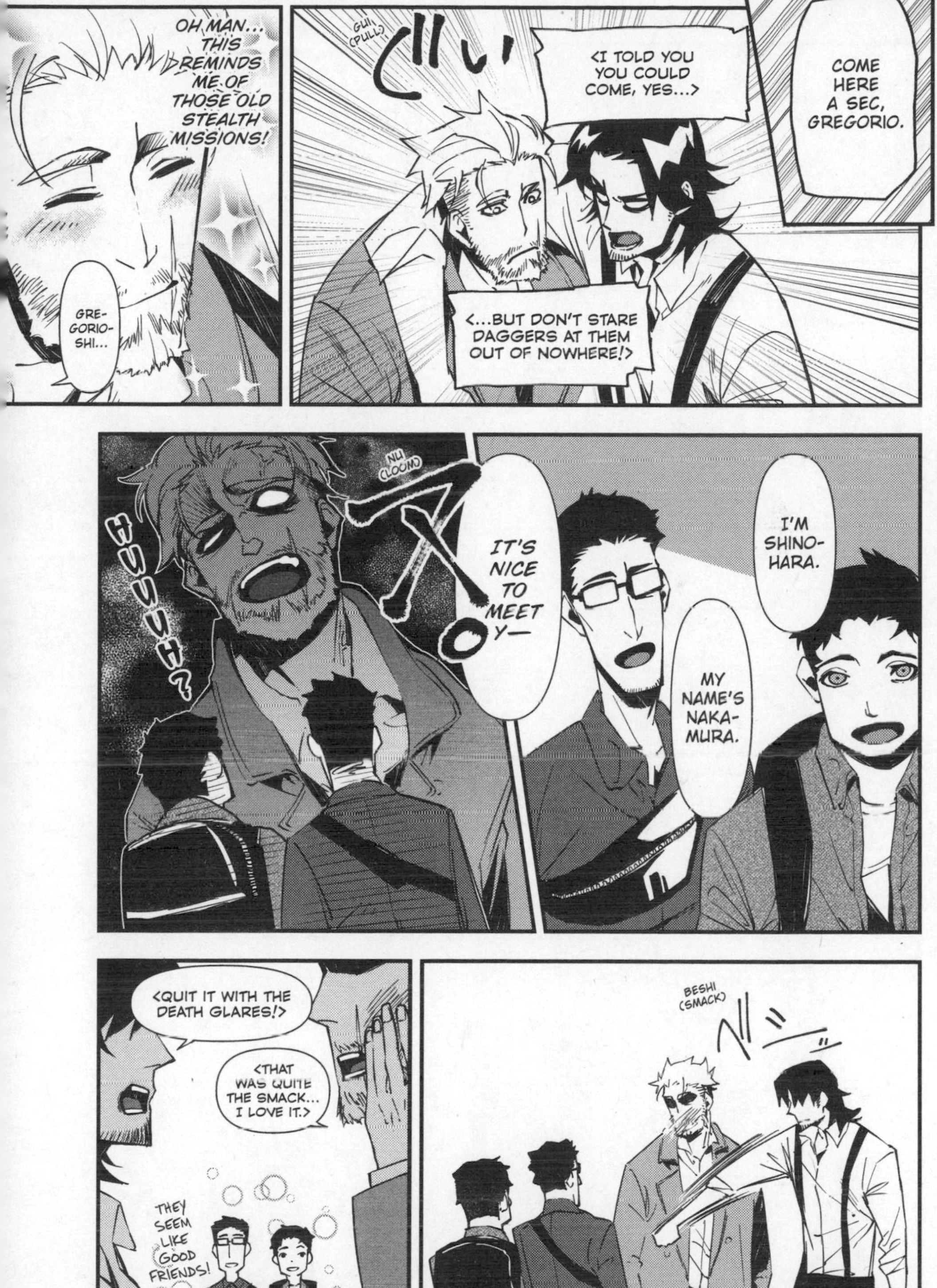
COME HERE A SEC, GREGORIO.
GUI (PULL)
<I TOLD YOU YOU COULD COME, YES...>
<...BUT DON'T STARE DAGGERS AT THEM OUT OF NOWHERE!>
OH MAN... THIS REMINDS ME OF THOSE OLD STEALTH MISSIONS!
GREGORIO-SHI...
I'M SHINOHARA.
MY NAME'S NAKAMURA.
IT'S NICE TO MEET Y—
NU (LOOM)
HUUUUH?
BESHI (SMACK)
<QUIT IT WITH THE DEATH GLARES!>
<THAT WAS QUITE THE SMACK... I LOVE IT.>
THEY SEEM LIKE GOOD FRIENDS!

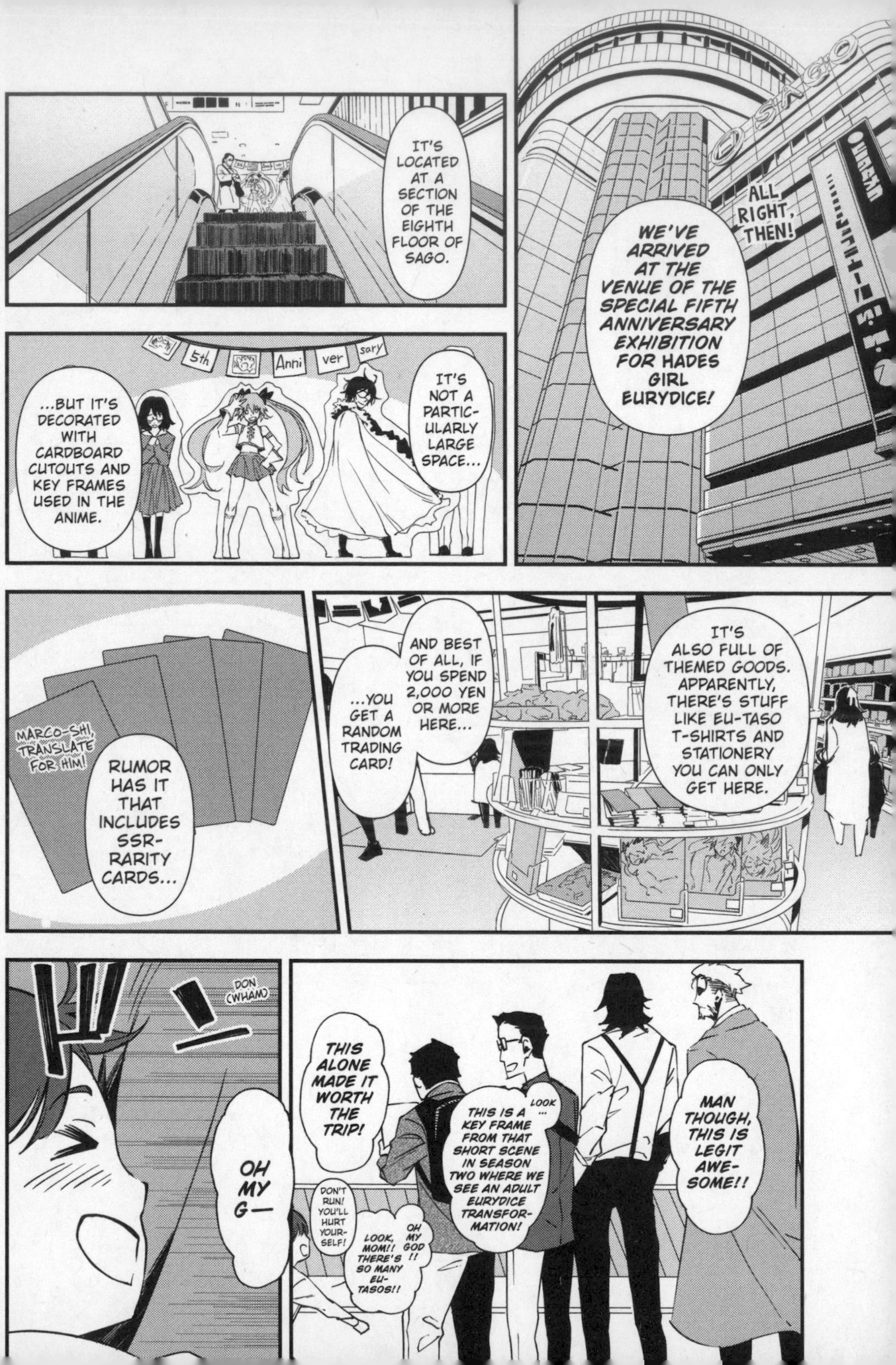
ALL RIGHT, THEN!
WE'VE ARRIVED AT THE VENUE OF THE SPECIAL FIFTH ANNIVERSARY EXHIBITION FOR HADES GIRL EURYDICE!
SAGO
IT'S LOCATED AT A SECTION OF THE EIGHTH FLOOR OF SAGO.
5th Anni ver sary
IT'S NOT A PARTICULARLY LARGE SPACE...
...BUT IT'S DECORATED WITH CARDBOARD CUTOUTS AND KEY FRAMES USED IN THE ANIME.
IT'S ALSO FULL OF THEMED GOODS. APPARENTLY, THERE'S STUFF LIKE EU-TASO T-SHIRTS AND STATIONERY YOU CAN ONLY GET HERE.
AND BEST OF ALL, IF YOU SPEND 2,000 YEN OR MORE HERE...
...YOU GET A RANDOM TRADING CARD!
RUMOR HAS IT THAT INCLUDES SSR-RARITY CARDS...
MARCO-SHI, TRANSLATE FOR HIM!
MAN THOUGH, THIS IS LEGIT AWESOME!!
LOOK...
THIS IS A KEY FRAME FROM THAT SHORT SCENE IN SEASON TWO WHERE WE SEE AN ADULT EURYDICE TRANSFORMATION!
THIS ALONE MADE IT WORTH THE TRIP!
OH MY GOD!!
LOOK, MOM!! THERE'S SO MANY EU-TASOS!!
DON'T RUN! YOU'LL HURT YOURSELF!
DON (WHAM)
OH MY G—

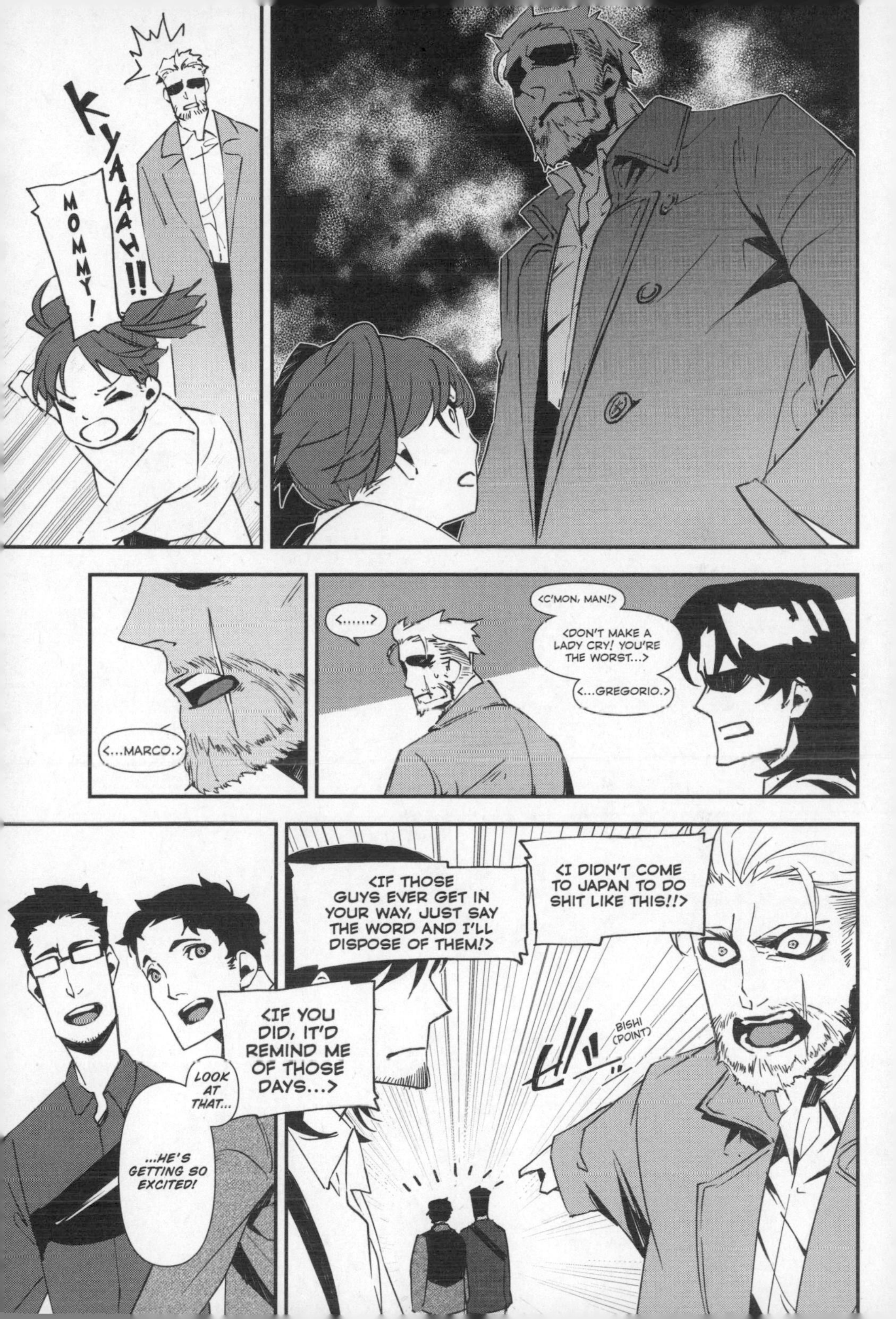
KYAAAH!!
MOMMY!
<C'MON, MAN!>
<DON'T MAKE A LADY CRY! YOU'RE THE WORST...>
<...GREGORIO.>
<......>
<...MARCO.>
<I DIDN'T COME TO JAPAN TO DO SHIT LIKE THIS!!>
<IF THOSE GUYS EVER GET IN YOUR WAY, JUST SAY THE WORD AND I'LL DISPOSE OF THEM!>
BISHI (POINT)
<IF YOU DID, IT'D REMIND ME OF THOSE DAYS...>
LOOK AT THAT...
...HE'S GETTING SO EXCITED!

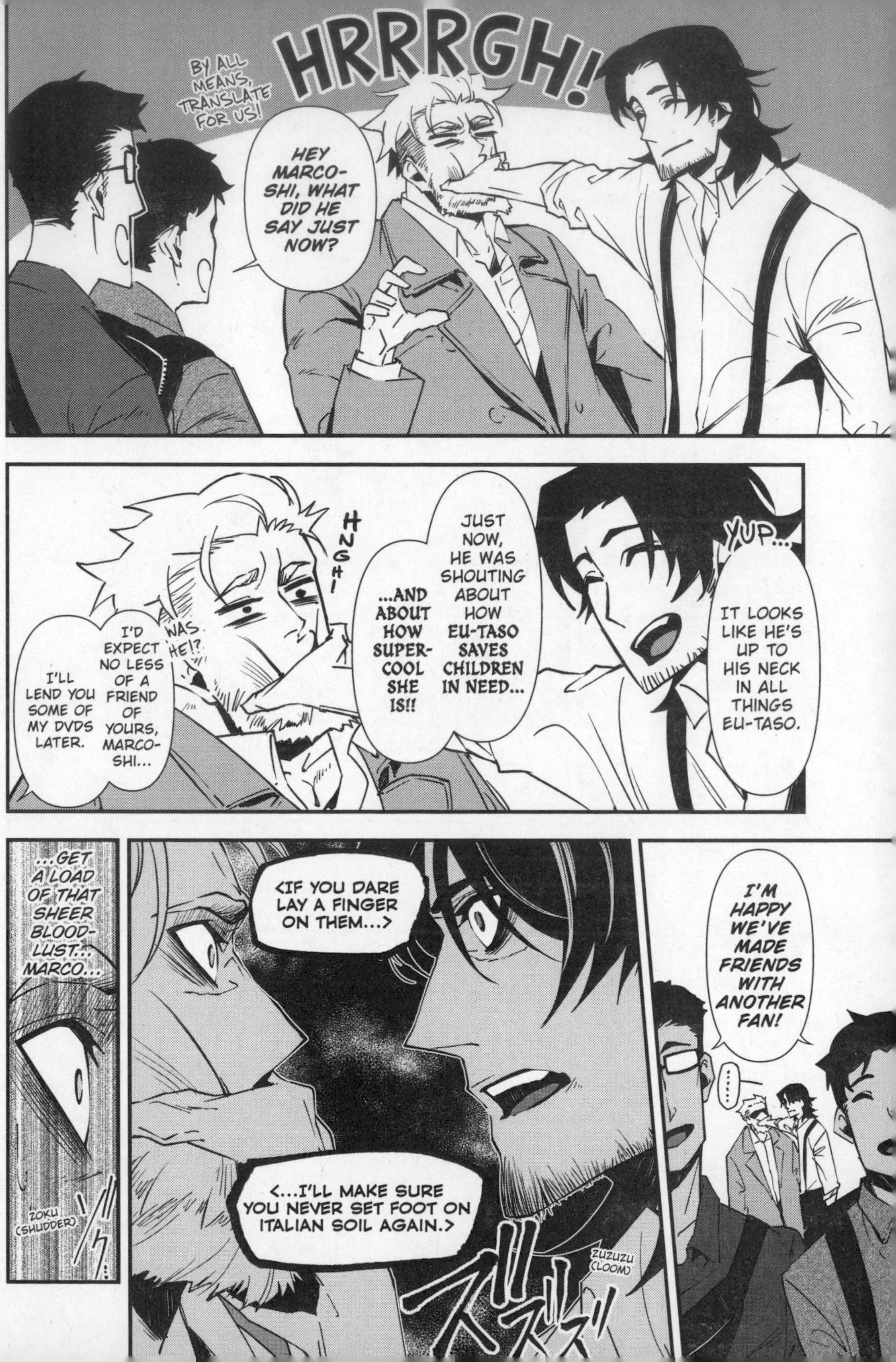
HRRRGH!
BY ALL MEANS, TRANSLATE FOR US!
HEY MARCO-SHI, WHAT DID HE SAY JUST NOW?
YUP...
IT LOOKS LIKE HE'S UP TO HIS NECK IN ALL THINGS EU-TASO.
JUST NOW, HE WAS SHOUTING ABOUT HOW EU-TASO SAVES CHILDREN IN NEED...
...AND ABOUT HOW SUPER-COOL SHE IS!!
HNGH!
WAS HE!?
I'D EXPECT NO LESS OF A FRIEND OF YOURS, MARCO-SHI...
I'LL LEND YOU SOME OF MY DVDS LATER.
I'M HAPPY WE'VE MADE FRIENDS WITH ANOTHER FAN!
......
<IF YOU DARE LAY A FINGER ON THEM...>
<...I'LL MAKE SURE YOU NEVER SET FOOT ON ITALIAN SOIL AGAIN.>
ZUZUZU (LOOM)
...GET A LOAD OF THAT SHEER BLOOD-LUST... MARCO...
ZOKU (SHUDDER)

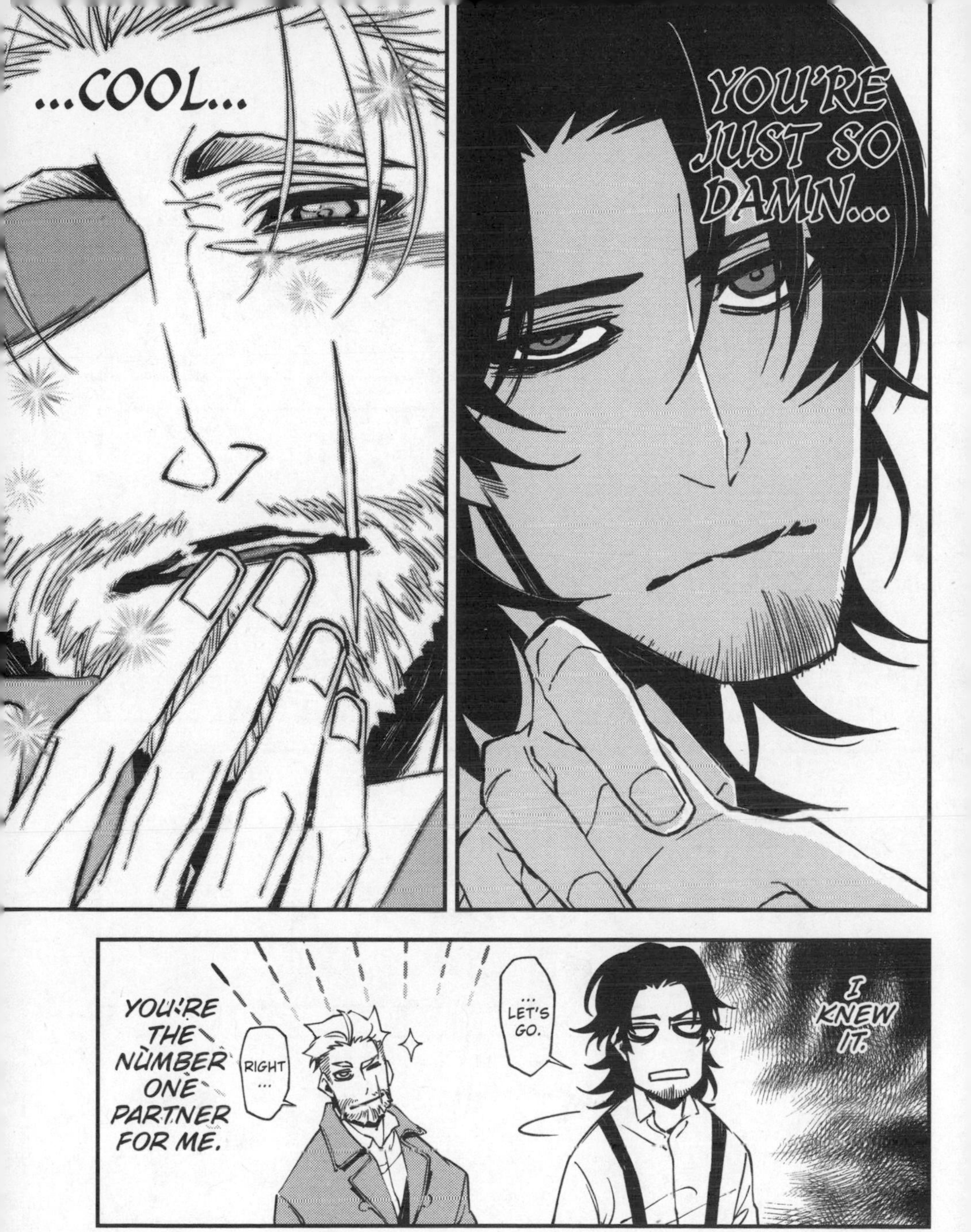
YOU'RE JUST SO DAMN...
...COOL...
I KNEW IT.
...LET'S GO.
RIGHT...
YOU'RE THE NUMBER ONE PARTNER FOR ME.

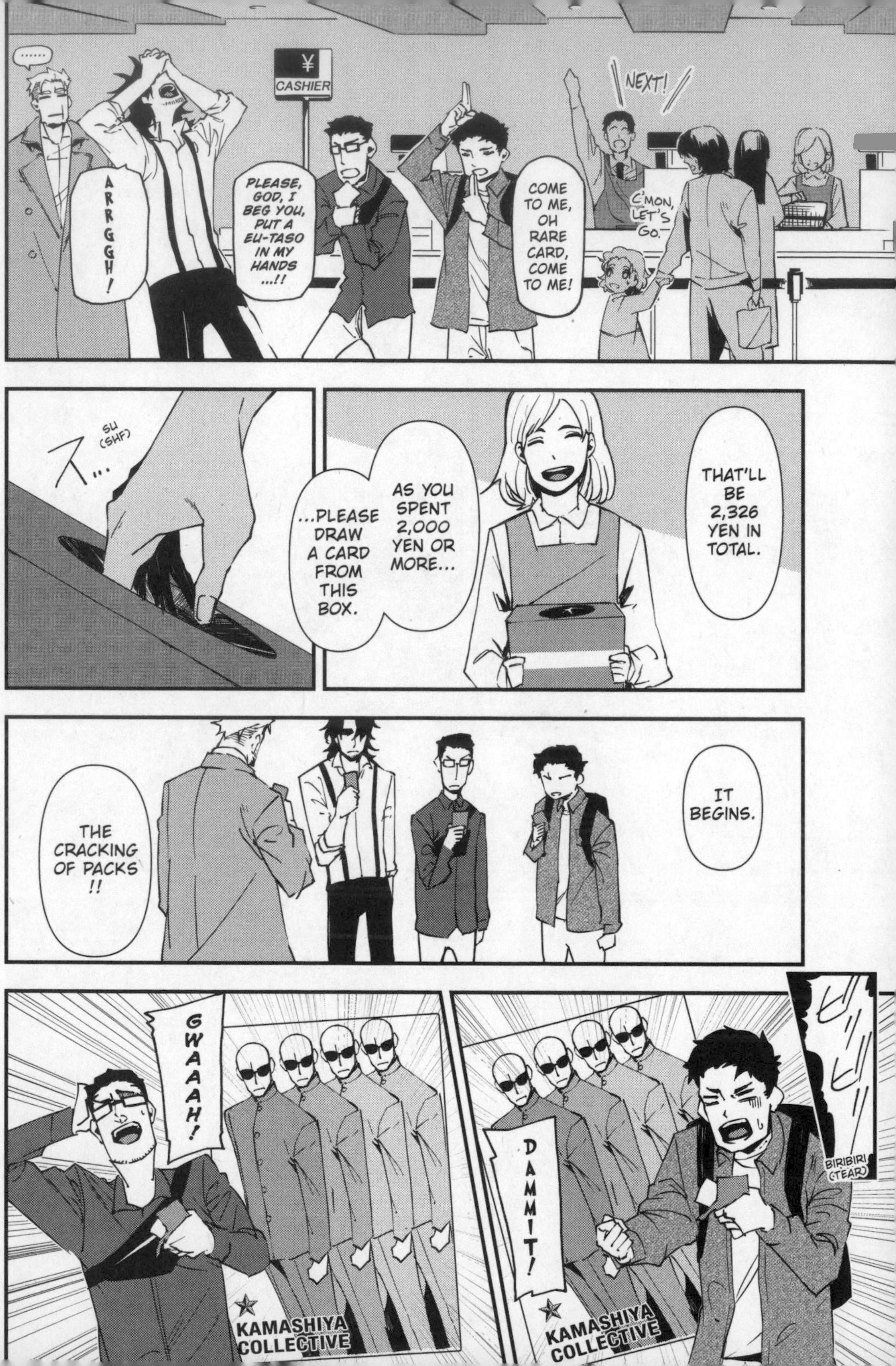
NEXT!
C'MON, LET'S GO.
COME TO ME, OH RARE CARD, COME TO ME!
PLEASE, GOD, I BEG YOU, PUT A EU-TASO IN MY HANDS ...!!
¥
CASHIER
ARRGGH!
......
THAT'LL BE 2,326 YEN IN TOTAL.
AS YOU SPENT 2,000 YEN OR MORE...
...PLEASE DRAW A CARD FROM THIS BOX.
ス...
SU (SHF)
IT BEGINS.
THE CRACKING OF PACKS!!
BIRIBIRI (TEAR)
DAMMIT!
KAMASHIYA COLLECTIVE
GWAAAAH!
KAMASHIYA COLLECTIVE

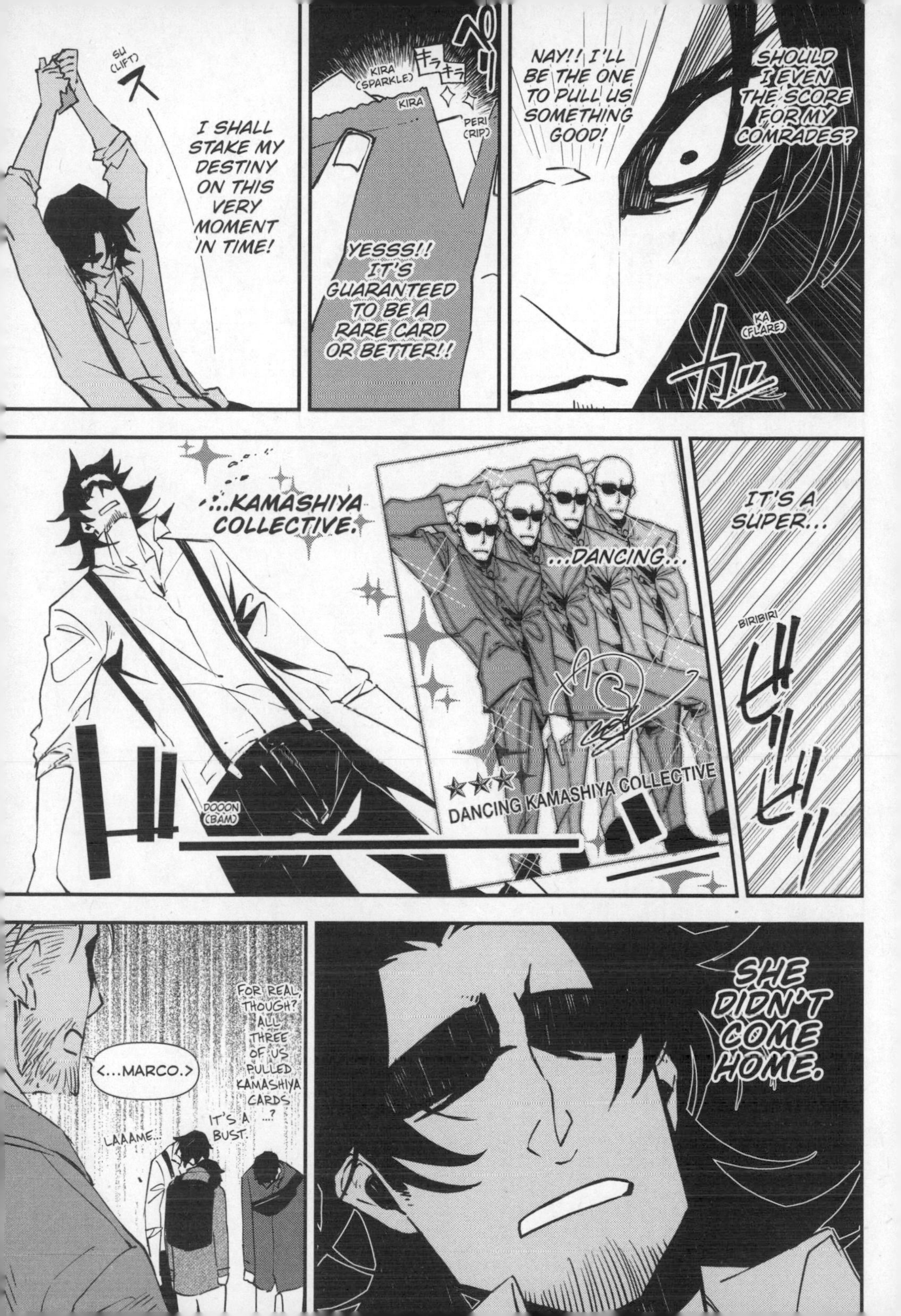
SHOULD I EVEN THE SCORE FOR MY COMRADES?
KA (FLARE)
NAY!! I'LL BE THE ONE TO PULL US SOMETHING GOOD!
KIRA (SPARKLE)
KIRA
PERI (RIP)
YESSS!! IT'S GUARANTEED TO BE A RARE CARD OR BETTER!!
SU (LIFT)
I SHALL STAKE MY DESTINY ON THIS VERY MOMENT IN TIME!
IT'S A SUPER...
BIRIBIRI
...DANCING...
DANCING KAMASHIYA COLLECTIVE
...KAMASHIYA COLLECTIVE.
DOOON (BAM)
SHE DIDN'T COME HOME.
FOR REAL, THOUGH? ALL THREE OF US PULLED KAMASHIYA CARDS...?
<...MARCO.>
IT'S A BUST.
LAAAME...

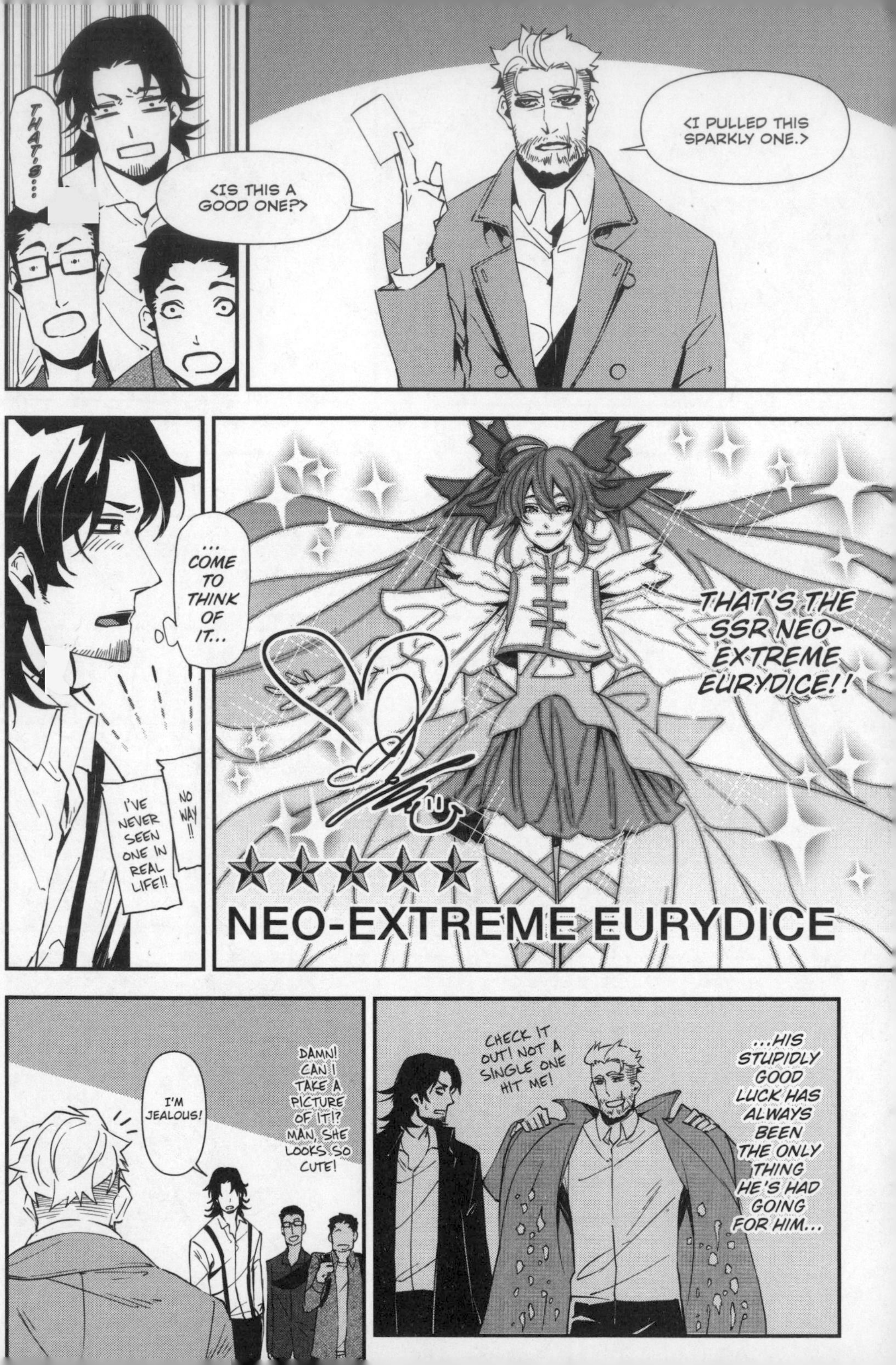
<I PULLED THIS SPARKLY ONE.>
<IS THIS A GOOD ONE?>
THAT'S...
THAT'S THE SSR NEO-EXTREME EURYDICE!!
NEO-EXTREME EURYDICE
...COME TO THINK OF IT...
NO WAY!!
I'VE NEVER SEEN ONE IN REAL LIFE!!
...HIS STUPIDLY GOOD LUCK HAS ALWAYS BEEN THE ONLY THING HE'S HAD GOING FOR HIM...
CHECK IT OUT! NOT A SINGLE ONE HIT ME!
DAMN! CAN I TAKE A PICTURE OF IT!? MAN, SHE LOOKS SO CUTE!
I'M JEALOUS!

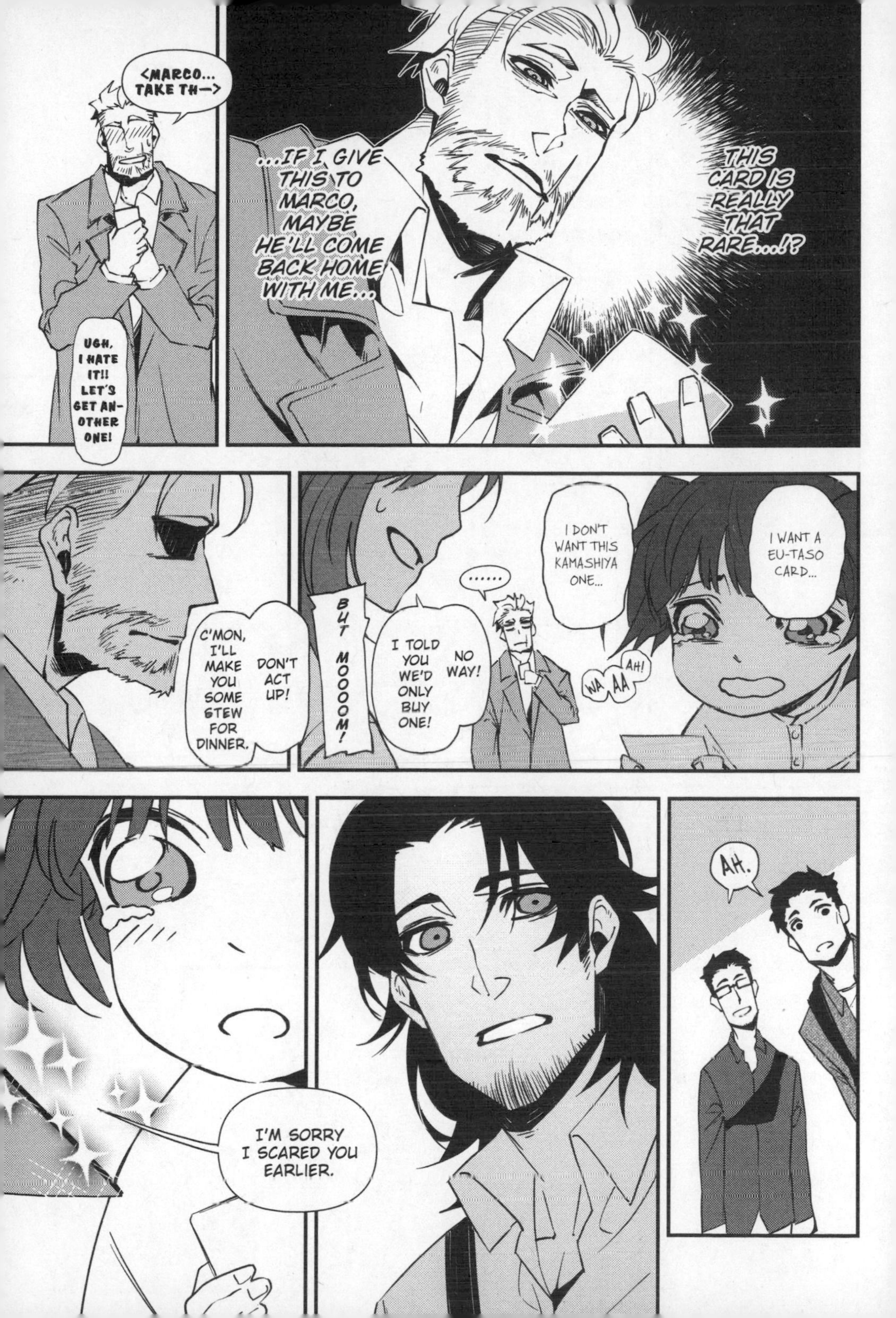
THIS CARD IS REALLY THAT RARE...!?
...IF I GIVE THIS TO MARCO, MAYBE HE'LL COME BACK HOME WITH ME...
<MARCO... TAKE TH—>
UGH, I HATE IT!! LET'S GET ANOTHER ONE!
I WANT A EU-TASO CARD...
I DON'T WANT THIS KAMASHIYA ONE...
WA AA AH!
......
NO WAY!
I TOLD YOU WE'D ONLY BUY ONE!
BUT MOOOOOM!
DON'T ACT UP!
C'MON, I'LL MAKE YOU SOME STEW FOR DINNER.
AH.
I'M SORRY I SCARED YOU EARLIER.

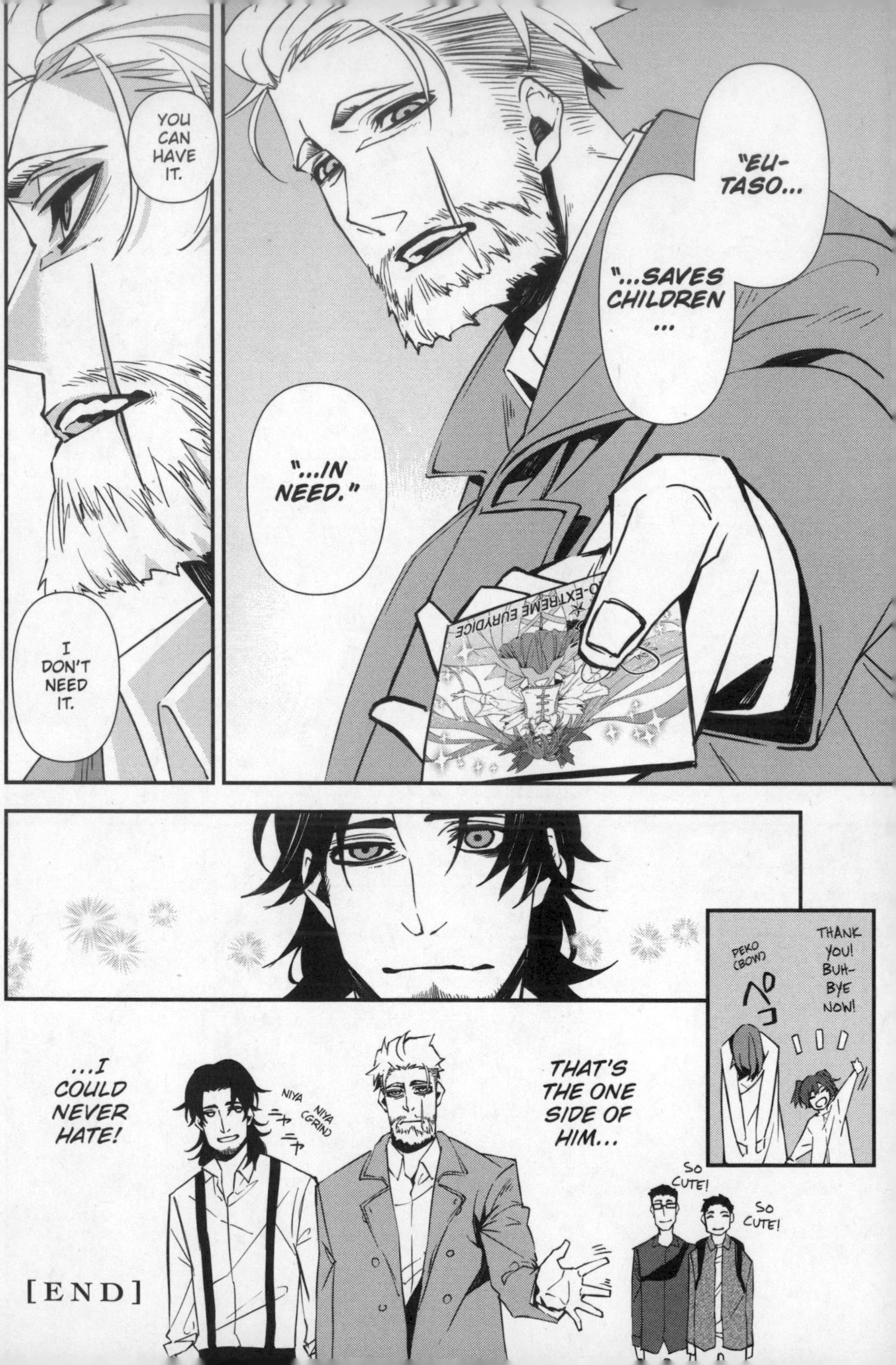
"EU-TASO...
"...SAVES CHILDREN...
"...IN NEED."
EXTREME EURYDICE
YOU CAN HAVE IT.
I DON'T NEED IT.
THANK YOU! BUH-BYE NOW!
PEKO (BOW)
THAT'S THE ONE SIDE OF HIM...
NIYA NIYA (GRIN)
...I COULD NEVER HATE!
SO CUTE!
SO CUTE!

[END]

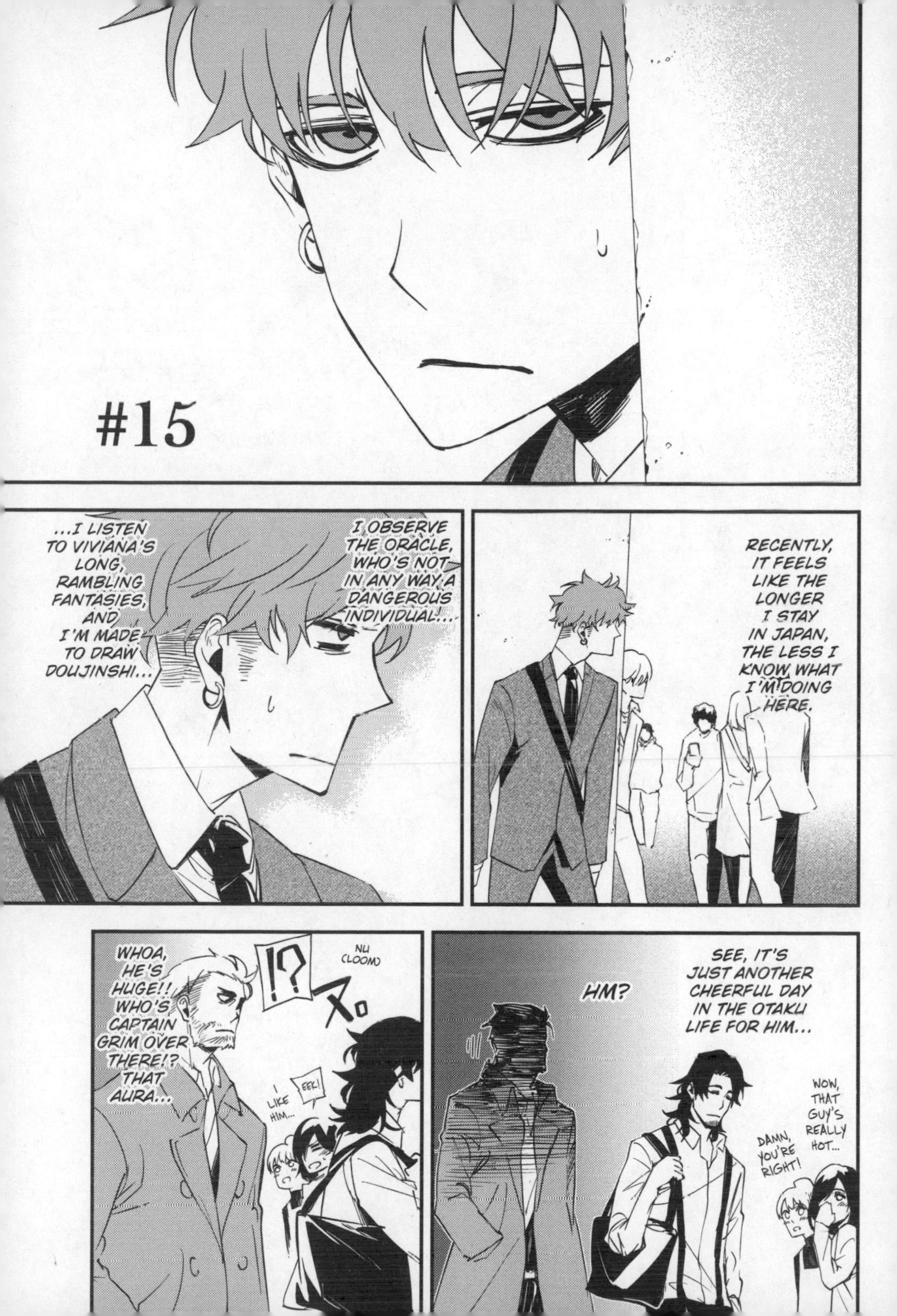
#15
…
RECENTLY, IT FEELS LIKE THE LONGER I STAY IN JAPAN, THE LESS I KNOW WHAT I'M DOING HERE.
I OBSERVE THE ORACLE, WHO'S NOT IN ANY WAY A DANGEROUS INDIVIDUAL…
…I LISTEN TO VIVIANA'S LONG, RAMBLING FANTASIES, AND I'M MADE TO DRAW DOUJINSHI…
SEE, IT'S JUST ANOTHER CHEERFUL DAY IN THE OTAKU LIFE FOR HIM…
HM?
WOW, THAT GUY'S REALLY HOT…
DAMN, YOU'RE RIGHT!
NU (LOOM)
!?
WHOA, HE'S HUGE!! WHO'S CAPTAIN GRIM OVER THERE!? THAT AURA…
EEK!
I LIKE HIM…

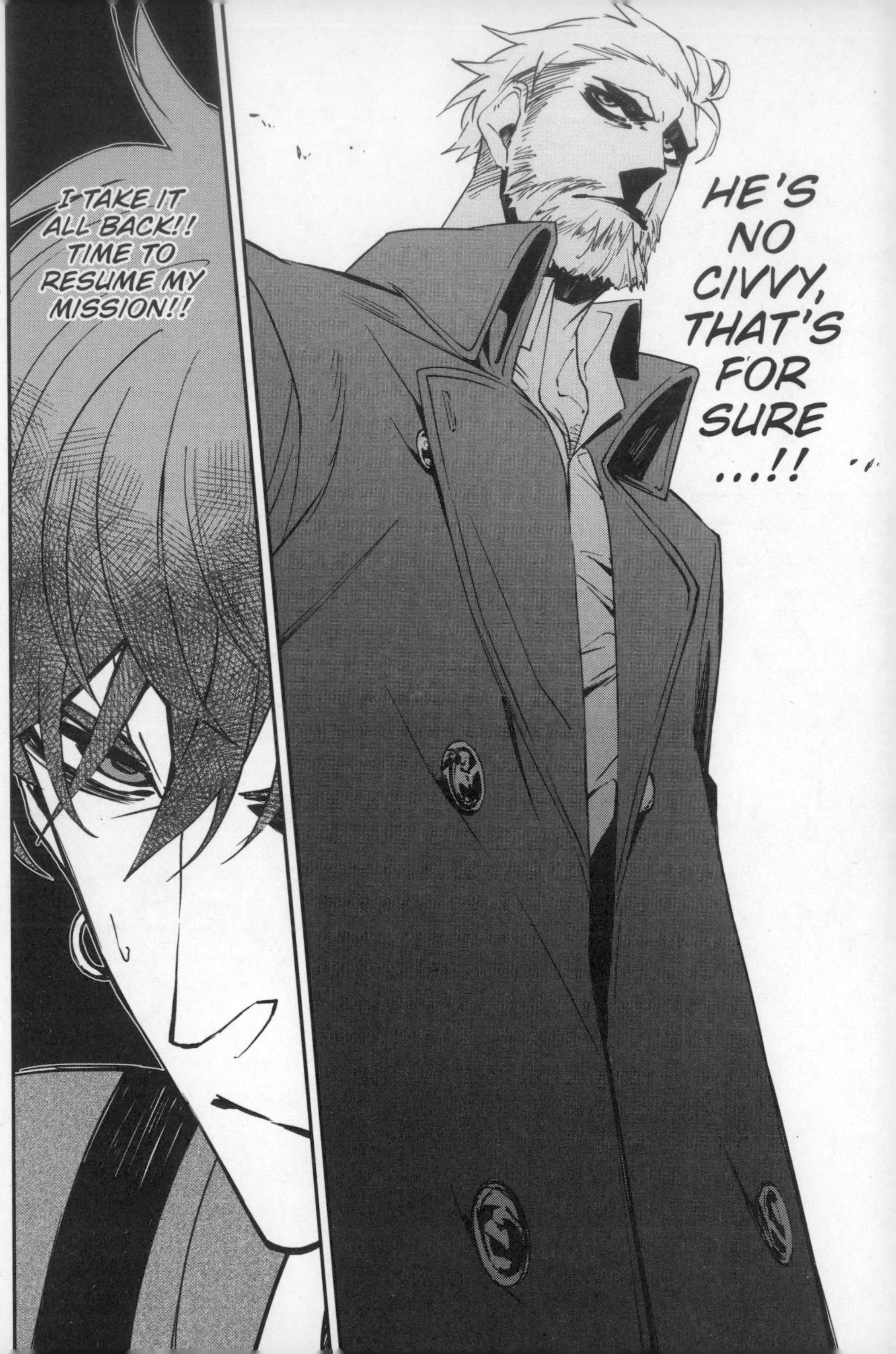
HE'S NO CIVVY, THAT'S FOR SURE ...!!
I TAKE IT ALL BACK!! TIME TO RESUME MY MISSION!!

FIRST, I'LL REFER TO THE ITALIAN GOVERNMENT'S PERSONAL INFO DATABASE.

PIPI (BEEP)

PASHA (FLASH)

THOUGH AS EXPECTED, TAKING PICTURES OF THE ORACLE'S NOT SO EASY!

...I SNAPPED SOME PHOTOS OF HIM WITHOUT A HITCH...

PON (BLIP)

KATA KATA KATA KATA KATA KATA (CLACK)

PAKA (POP)

NOW THEN, WHAT INTEL AWAITS ME...?

LET'S SEE HERE...

...THERE'S A LOT OF PHOTOS OF HIM...

...HUH...

BUT NOTHING OF THE SORT WAS WRITTEN IN VIVIANA'S REPO—

Report_124.word

king inside Oomiya Station when
aded toward the anime goods store
ed buying multiple gacha capsules
and one for the Hades Girl Eurydice
even Forms Throughout the Seasons
ed in his tracks. For fifteen minutes,
the man with whom he had relations
his set of rubber straps and departed
.O. proceeded not to say a single word
don't come back, I'll kill you and then
a physical altercation, after which T.O.
onely, I'll be there for you, so don't say
hen the two men's faces grew closer and
sic "ideal man x head case"

BUT MORE IMPORTANTLY, THERE'S THE FACT HE'S HERE IN JAPAN NOW... COULD HE BE HERE TO GIVE HIM MORE ASSASSINATION WORK....!?

"GREGORIO, FORMER PARTNER OF THE ORACLE OF FLORENCE"... TO THINK THERE WAS A GUY LIKE THAT... I SHOULD'VE DONE MORE RESEARCH.

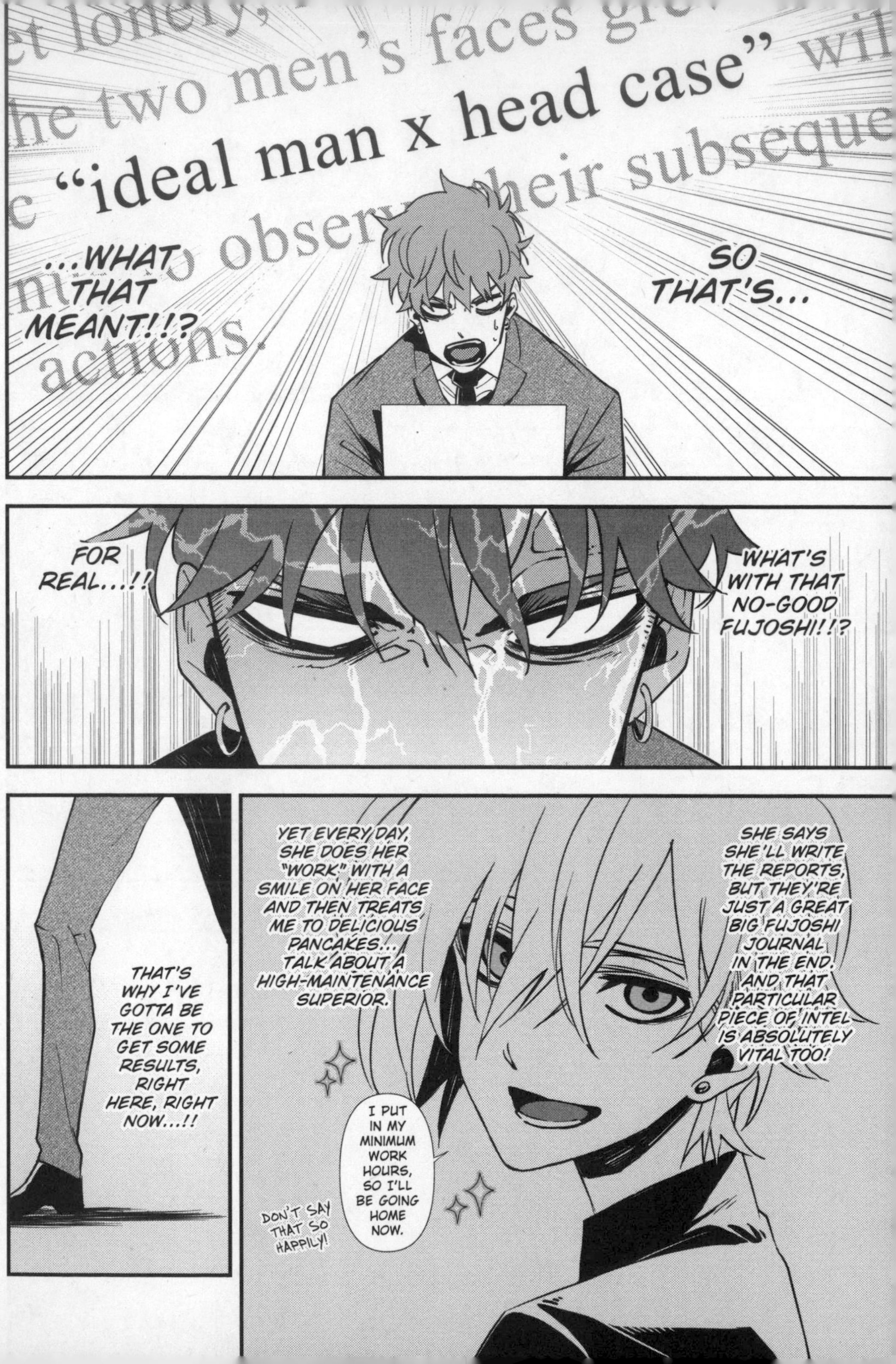
the two men's faces gre
“ideal man x head case” wil
observ heir subseque
actions.
SO THAT'S...
...WHAT THAT MEANT!!?
WHAT'S WITH THAT NO-GOOD FUJOSHI!!?
FOR REAL...!!
SHE SAYS SHE'LL WRITE THE REPORTS, BUT THEY'RE JUST A GREAT BIG FUJOSHI JOURNAL IN THE END. AND THAT PARTICULAR PIECE OF INTEL IS ABSOLUTELY VITAL TOO!
YET EVERY DAY, SHE DOES HER "WORK" WITH A SMILE ON HER FACE AND THEN TREATS ME TO DELICIOUS PANCAKES... TALK ABOUT A HIGH-MAINTENANCE SUPERIOR.
I PUT IN MY MINIMUM WORK HOURS, SO I'LL BE GOING HOME NOW.
DON'T SAY THAT SO HAPPILY!
THAT'S WHY I'VE GOTTA BE THE ONE TO GET SOME RESULTS, RIGHT HERE, RIGHT NOW...!!

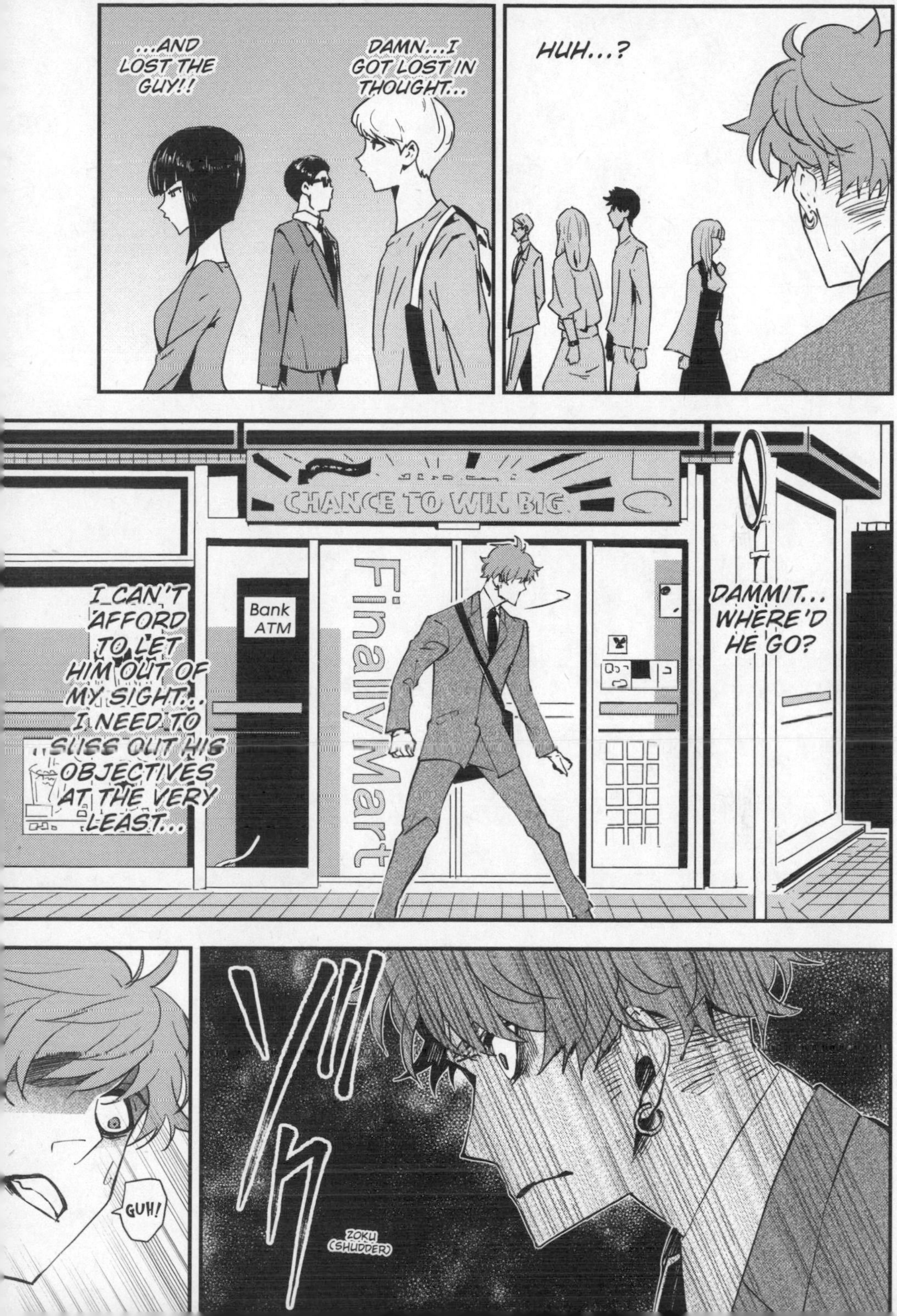
HUH...?
DAMN...I GOT LOST IN THOUGHT...
...AND LOST THE GUY!!
CHANCE TO WIN BIG
DAMMIT... WHERE'D HE GO?
FinallyMart
Bank ATM
I CAN'T AFFORD TO LET HIM OUT OF MY SIGHT... I NEED TO SUSS OUT HIS OBJECTIVES AT THE VERY LEAST...
ZOKU (SHUDDER)
GUH!

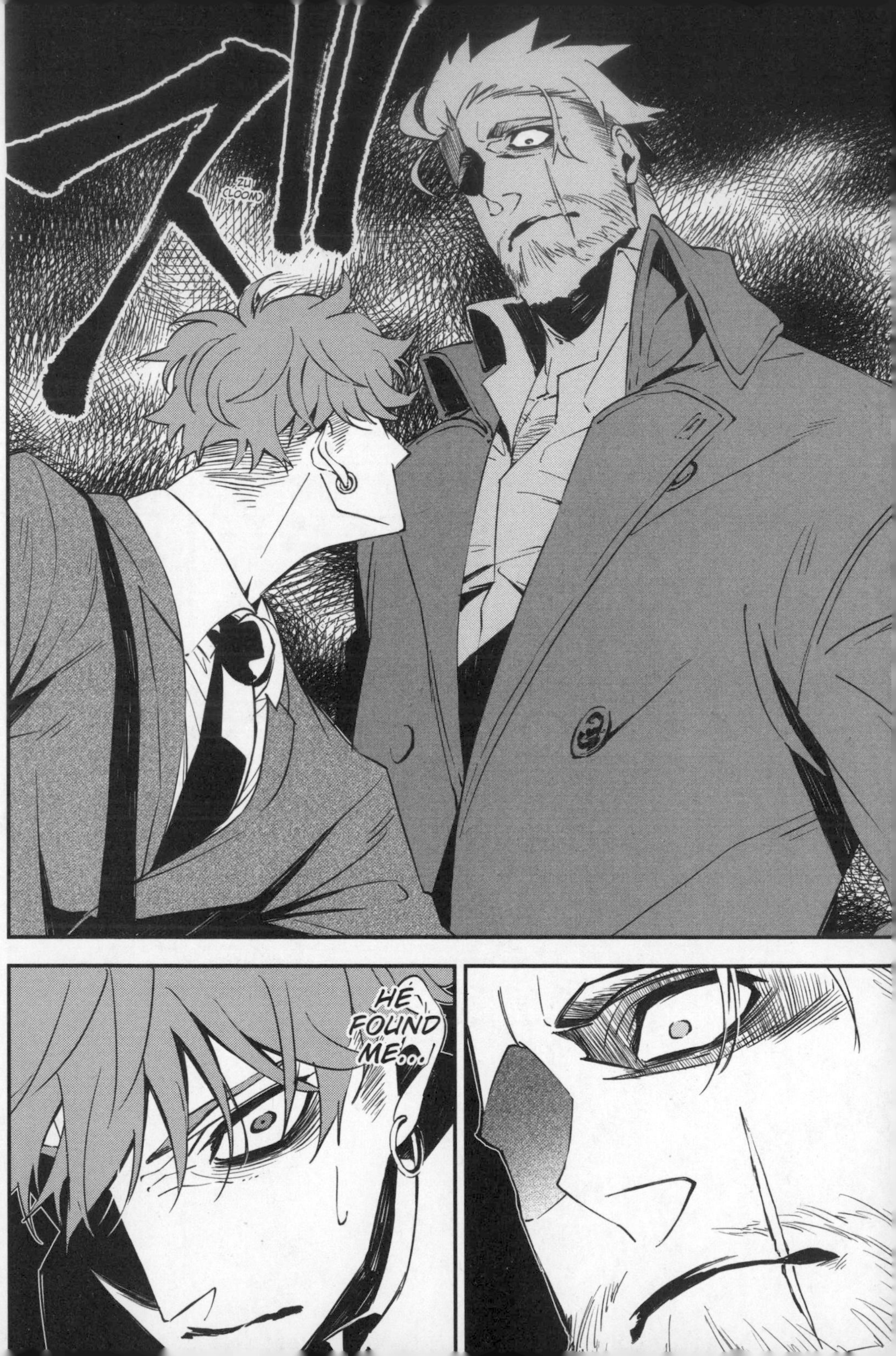
ZU
(LOOM)
HE FOUND ME...

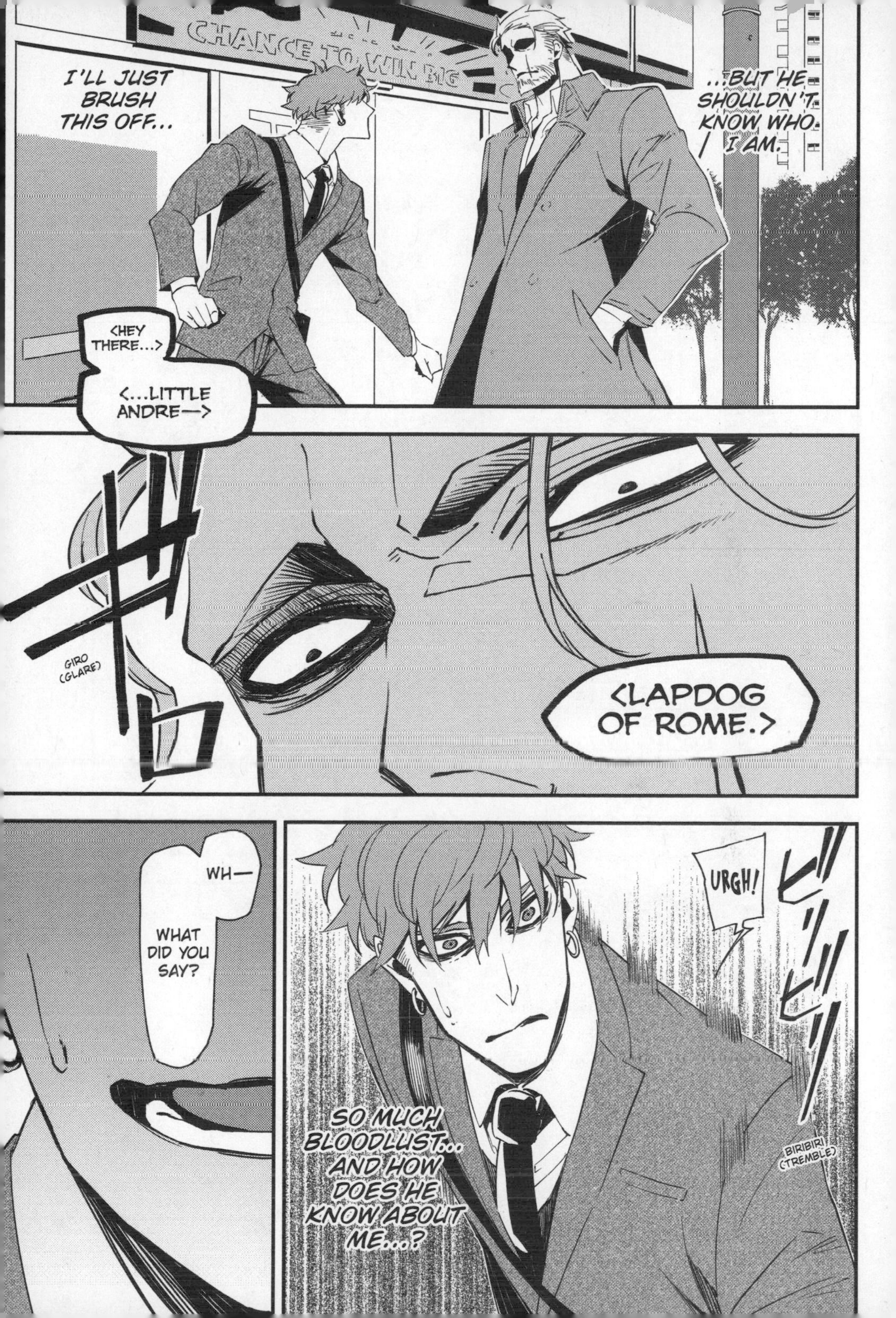
CHANCE TO WIN BIG
I'LL JUST BRUSH THIS OFF...
...BUT HE SHOULDN'T KNOW WHO I AM.
<HEY THERE...>
<...LITTLE ANDRE—>
GIRO (GLARE)
<LAPDOG OF ROME.>
URGH!
BIRIBIRI (TREMBLE)
SO MUCH BLOODLUST... AND HOW DOES HE KNOW ABOUT ME...?
WH—
WHAT DID YOU SAY?

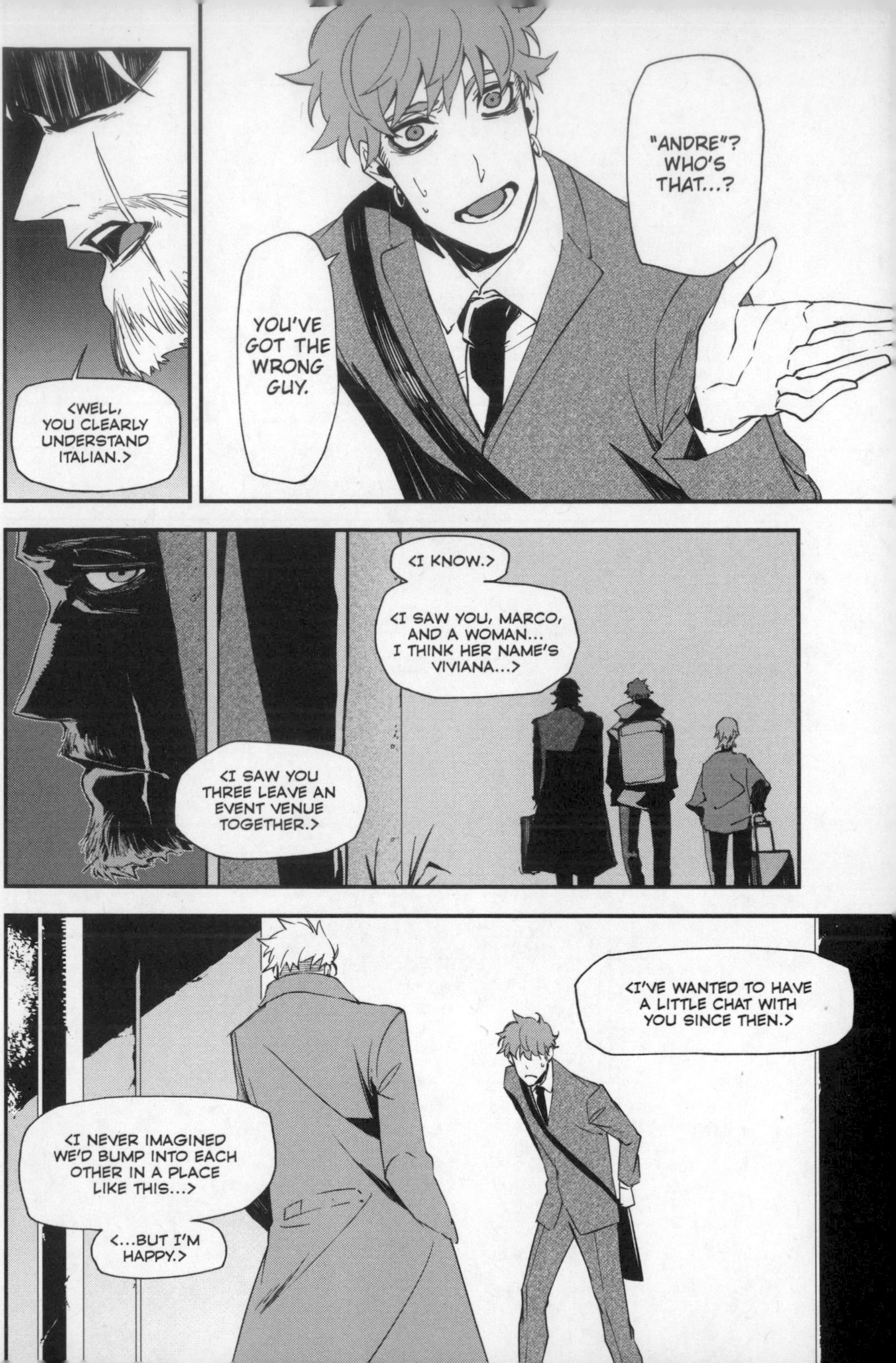
"ANDRE"? WHO'S THAT...?
YOU'VE GOT THE WRONG GUY.
<WELL, YOU CLEARLY UNDERSTAND ITALIAN.>
<I KNOW.>
<I SAW YOU, MARCO, AND A WOMAN... I THINK HER NAME'S VIVIANA...>
<I SAW YOU THREE LEAVE AN EVENT VENUE TOGETHER.>
<I'VE WANTED TO HAVE A LITTLE CHAT WITH YOU SINCE THEN.>
<I NEVER IMAGINED WE'D BUMP INTO EACH OTHER IN A PLACE LIKE THIS...>
<...BUT I'M HAPPY.>

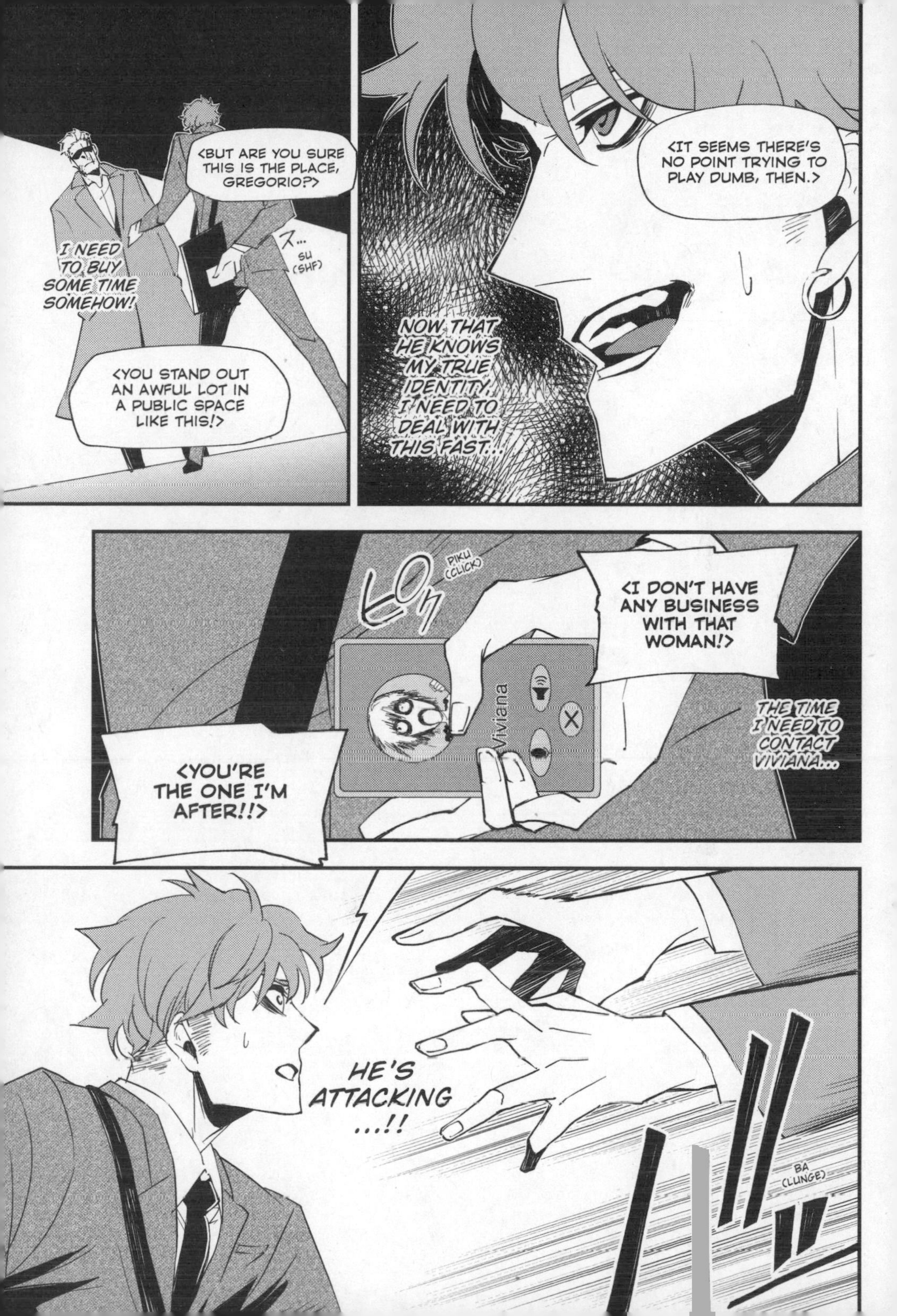

<IT SEEMS THERE'S NO POINT TRYING TO PLAY DUMB, THEN.>
NOW THAT HE KNOWS MY TRUE IDENTITY, I NEED TO DEAL WITH THIS FAST...
<BUT ARE YOU SURE THIS IS THE PLACE, GREGORIO?>
ス…
SU (SHF)
I NEED TO BUY SOME TIME SOMEHOW!
<YOU STAND OUT AN AWFUL LOT IN A PUBLIC SPACE LIKE THIS!>
<I DON'T HAVE ANY BUSINESS WITH THAT WOMAN!>
PIKU (CLICK)
Viviana
THE TIME I NEED TO CONTACT VIVIANA...
<YOU'RE THE ONE I'M AFTER!!>
HE'S ATTACKING ...!!
BA (LUNGE)

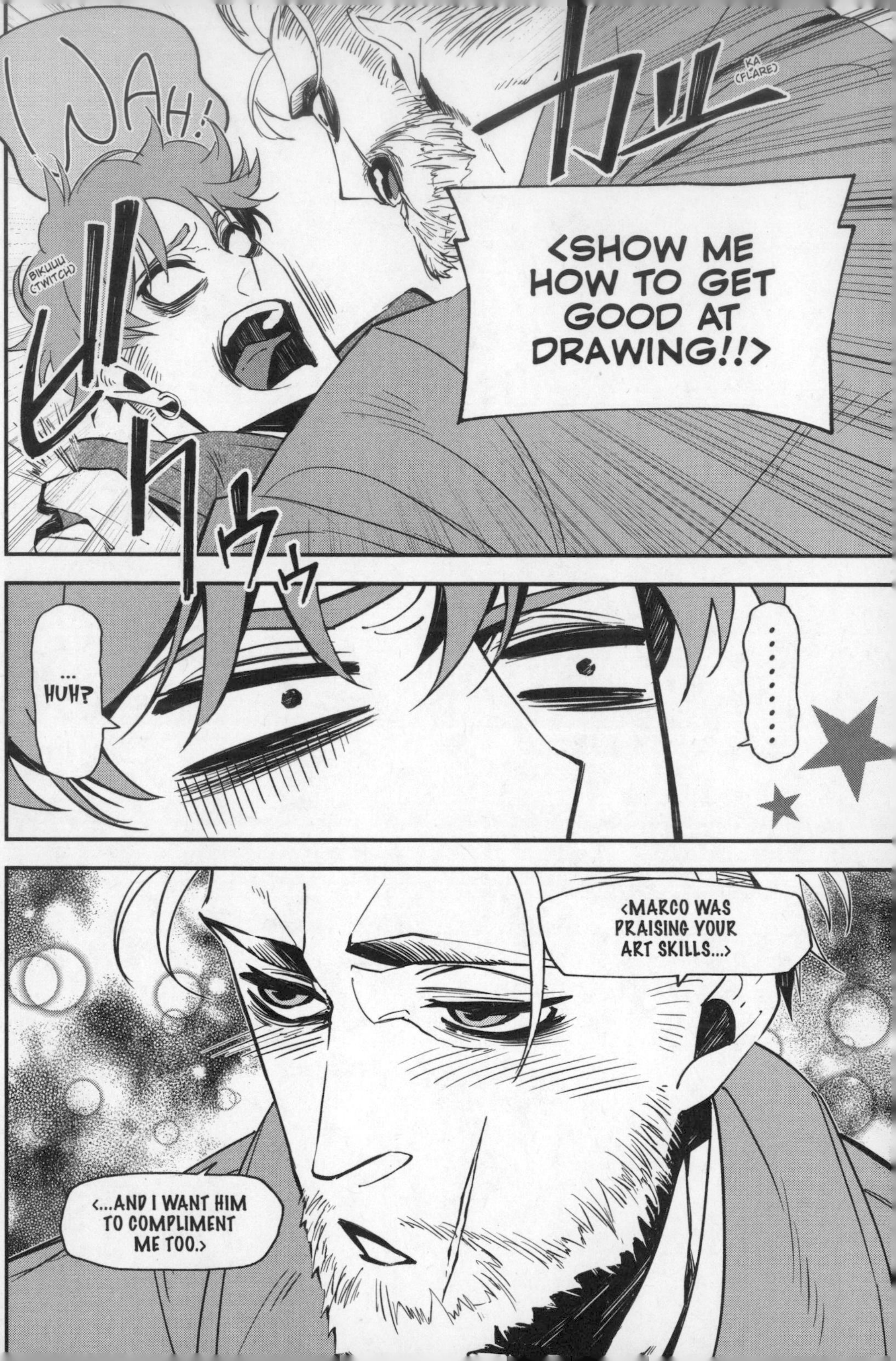
KA (FLARE)
<SHOW ME HOW TO GET GOOD AT DRAWING!!>
WAH!
BIKUUU (TWITCH)
....
... HUH?
<MARCO WAS PRAISING YOUR ART SKILLS...>
<...AND I WANT HIM TO COMPLIMENT ME TOO.>

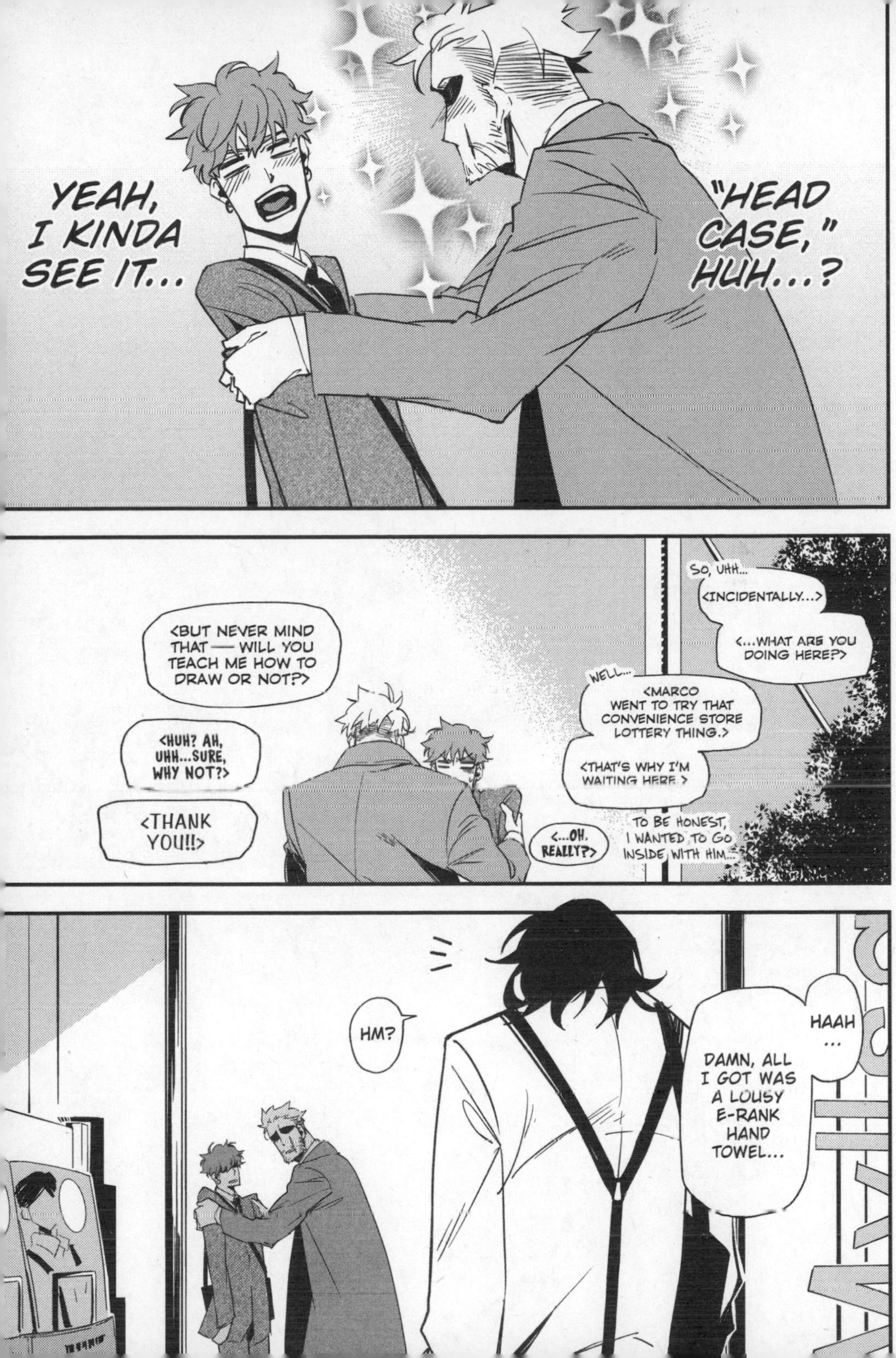
"HEAD CASE," HUH...?
YEAH, I KINDA SEE IT...
SO, UHH...
<INCIDENTALLY...>
<...WHAT ARE YOU DOING HERE?>
WELL...
<MARCO WENT TO TRY THAT CONVENIENCE STORE LOTTERY THING.>
<THAT'S WHY I'M WAITING HERE.>
TO BE HONEST, I WANTED TO GO INSIDE WITH HIM...
<...OH, REALLY?>
<BUT NEVER MIND THAT — WILL YOU TEACH ME HOW TO DRAW OR NOT?>
<HUH? AH, UHH...SURE, WHY NOT?>
<THANK YOU!!>
HAAH...
DAMN, ALL I GOT WAS A LOUSY E-RANK HAND TOWEL...
HM?

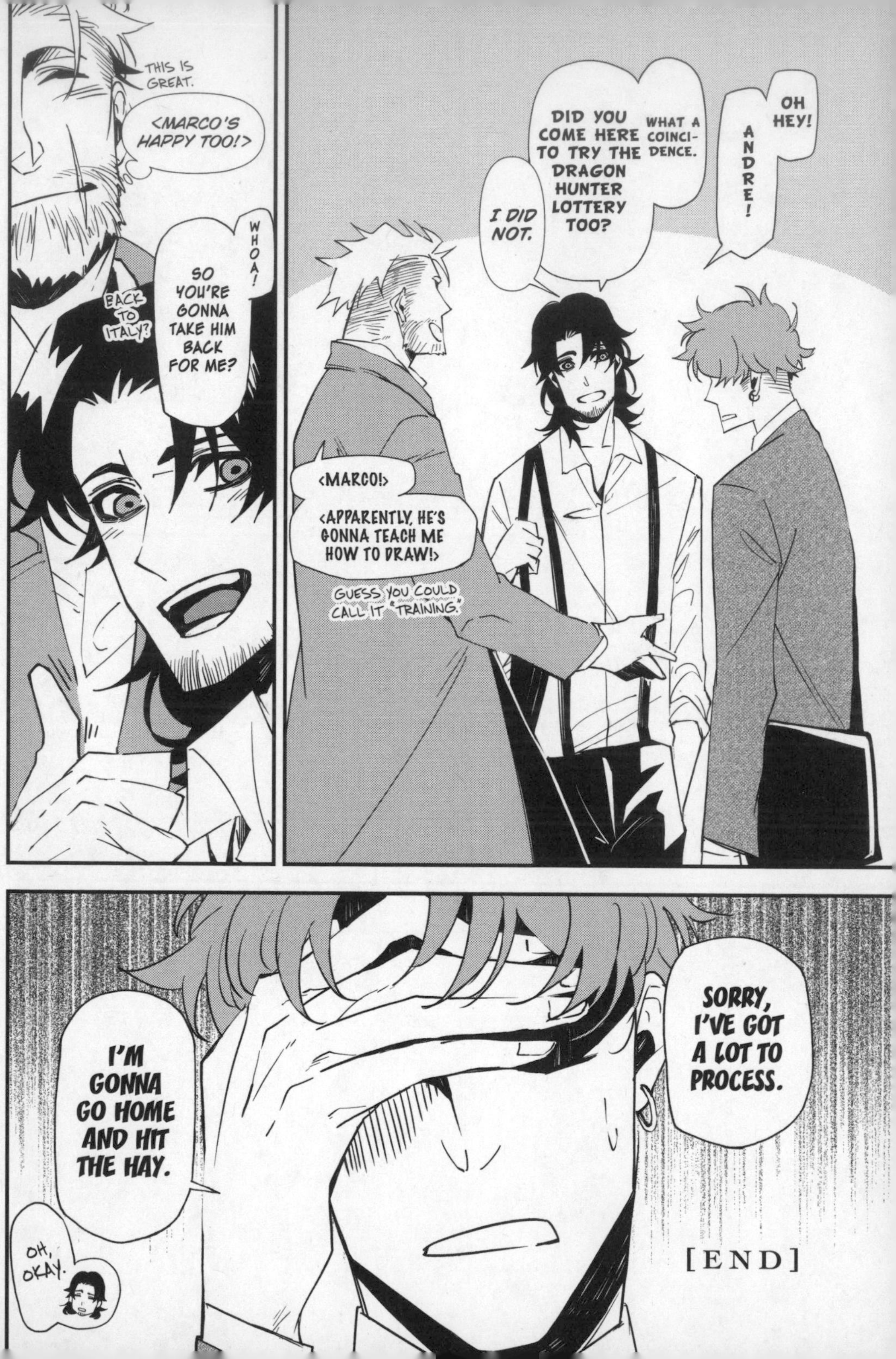
OH HEY!
ANDRE!
WHAT A COINCIDENCE.
DID YOU COME HERE TO TRY THE DRAGON HUNTER LOTTERY TOO?
I DID NOT.
<MARCO!>
<APPARENTLY, HE'S GONNA TEACH ME HOW TO DRAW!>
GUESS YOU COULD CALL IT "TRAINING."
THIS IS GREAT.
<MARCO'S HAPPY TOO!>
WHOA!
SO YOU'RE GONNA TAKE HIM BACK FOR ME?
BACK TO ITALY?
SORRY, I'VE GOT A LOT TO PROCESS.
I'M GONNA GO HOME AND HIT THE HAY.
OH, OKAY.
[END]

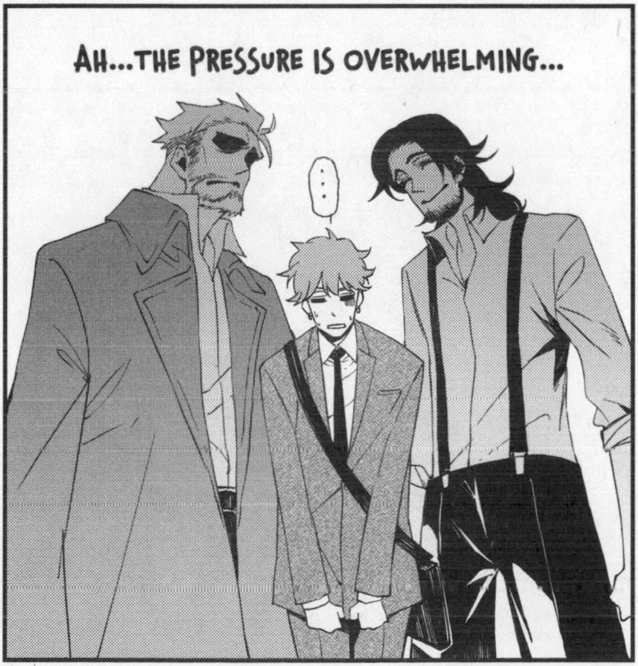
AH...THE PRESSURE IS OVERWHELMING...
...

THE GEEK EX-HITMAN

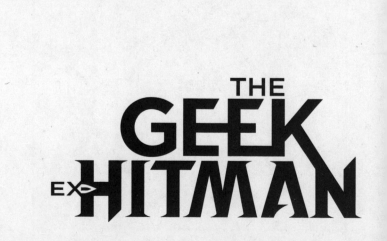

#16

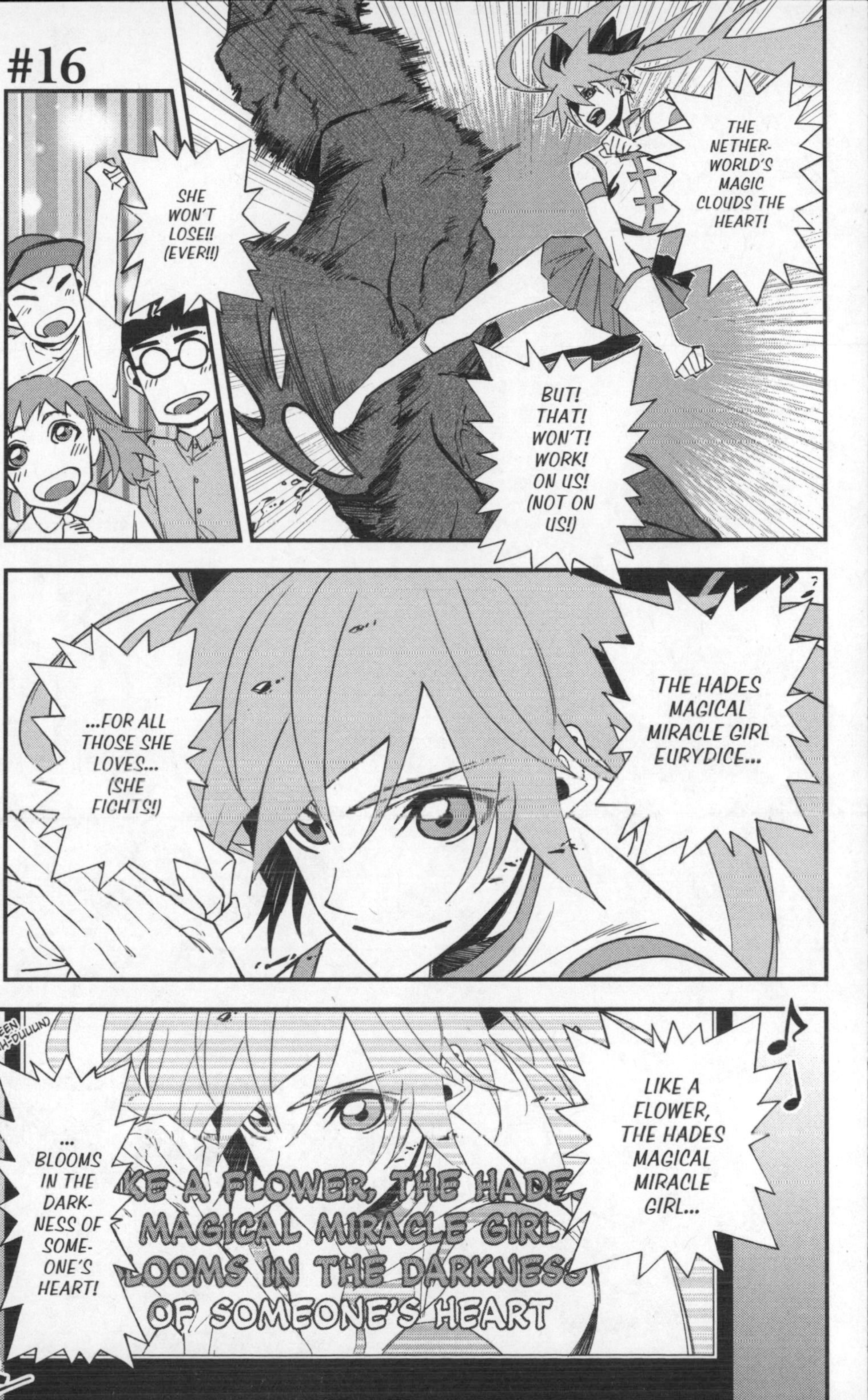
THE NETHER-WORLD'S MAGIC CLOUDS THE HEART!
SHE WON'T LOSE!! (EVER!!)
BUT! THAT! WON'T! WORK! ON US! (NOT ON US!)
THE HADES MAGICAL MIRACLE GIRL EURYDICE...
...FOR ALL THOSE SHE LOVES... (SHE FIGHTS!)
LIKE A FLOWER, THE HADES MAGICAL MIRACLE GIRL...
KE A FLOWER, THE HADE MAGICAL MIRACLE GIRL LOOMS IN THE DARKNES OF SOMEONE'S HEART
... BLOOMS IN THE DARK-NESS OF SOME-ONE'S HEART!
DEREDEDEEN (DUN-DUH-DUH-DUUUN)

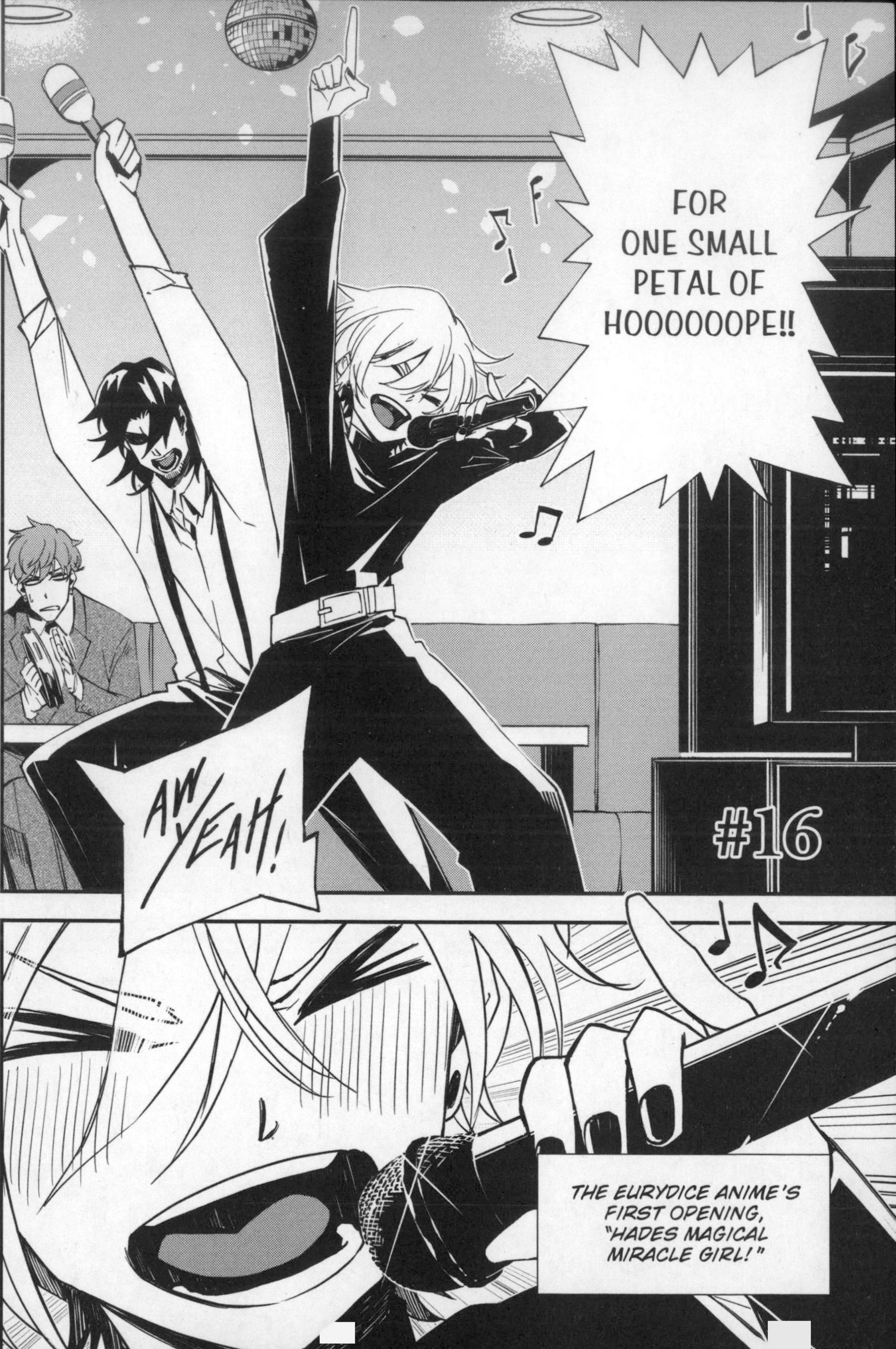
FOR ONE SMALL PETAL OF HOOOOOOPE!!
#16
AW YEAH!
THE EURYDICE ANIME'S FIRST OPENING, "HADES MAGICAL MIRACLE GIRL!"

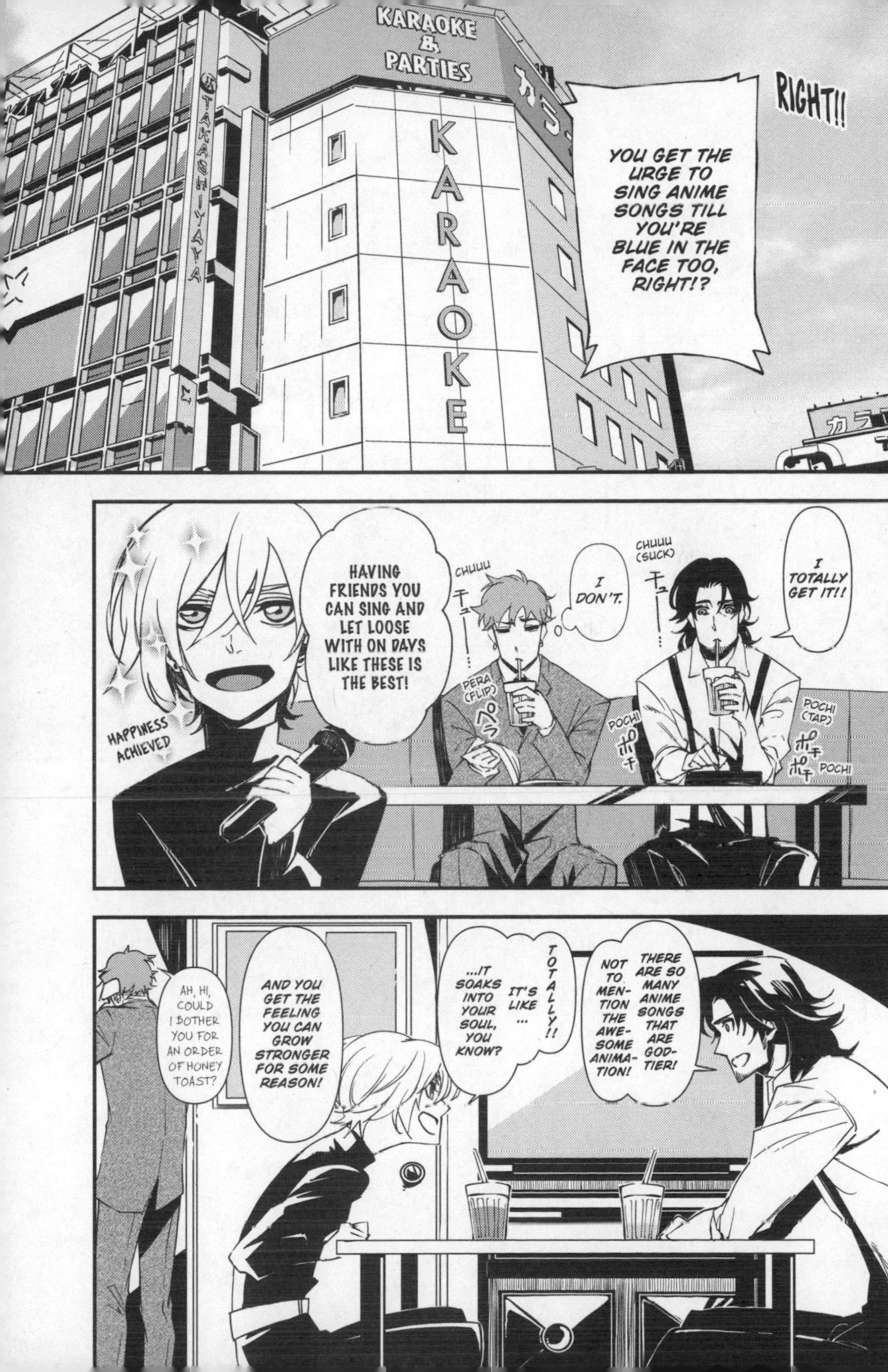
KARAOKE & PARTIES
KARAOKE
TAKASHIYAYA
YOU GET THE URGE TO SING ANIME SONGS TILL YOU'RE BLUE IN THE FACE TOO, RIGHT!?
RIGHT!!
I TOTALLY GET IT!!
CHUUU (SUCK)
I DON'T.
CHUUU
POCHI (TAP)
POCHI
POCHI
PERA (FLIP)
HAVING FRIENDS YOU CAN SING AND LET LOOSE WITH ON DAYS LIKE THESE IS THE BEST!
HAPPINESS ACHIEVED
THERE ARE SO MANY ANIME SONGS THAT ARE GOD-TIER!
NOT TO MEN-TION THE AWE-SOME ANIMA-TION!
TOTALLY!!
IT'S LIKE ...
...IT SOAKS INTO YOUR SOUL, YOU KNOW?
AND YOU GET THE FEELING YOU CAN GROW STRONGER FOR SOME REASON!
AH, HI, COULD I BOTHER YOU FOR AN ORDER OF HONEY TOAST?

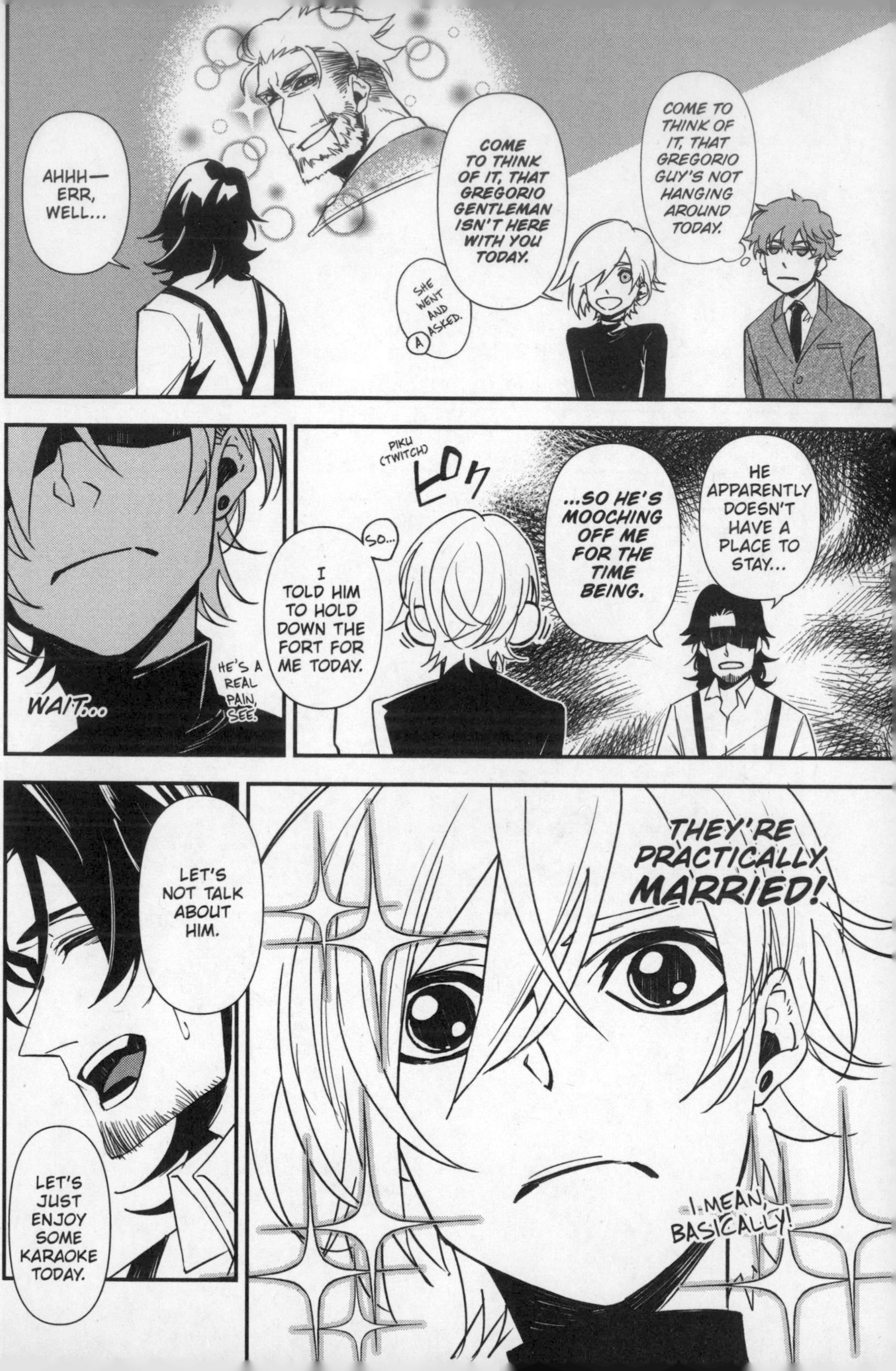
COME TO THINK OF IT, THAT GREGORIO GUY'S NOT HANGING AROUND TODAY.
COME TO THINK OF IT, THAT GREGORIO GENTLEMAN ISN'T HERE WITH YOU TODAY.
SHE WENT AND ASKED.
A
AHHH— ERR, WELL...
HE APPARENTLY DOESN'T HAVE A PLACE TO STAY...
...SO HE'S MOOCHING OFF ME FOR THE TIME BEING.
PIKU (TWITCH)
SO...
I TOLD HIM TO HOLD DOWN THE FORT FOR ME TODAY.
HE'S A REAL PAIN, SEE.
WAIT...
THEY'RE PRACTICALLY MARRIED!
I MEAN, BASICALLY!
LET'S NOT TALK ABOUT HIM.
LET'S JUST ENJOY SOME KARAOKE TODAY.

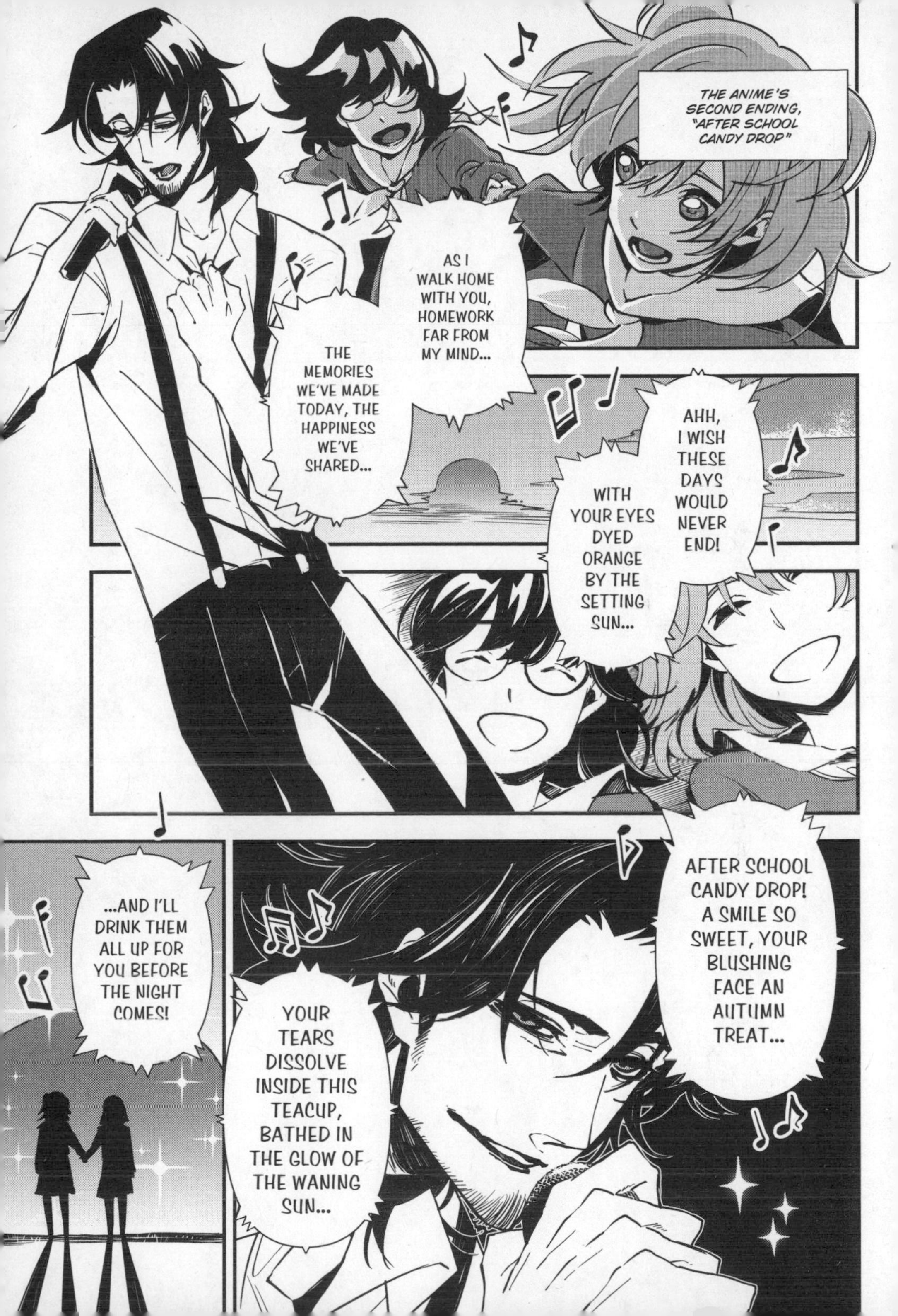
THE ANIME'S SECOND ENDING, "AFTER SCHOOL CANDY DROP"
AS I WALK HOME WITH YOU, HOMEWORK FAR FROM MY MIND...
THE MEMORIES WE'VE MADE TODAY, THE HAPPINESS WE'VE SHARED...
AHH, I WISH THESE DAYS WOULD NEVER END!
WITH YOUR EYES DYED ORANGE BY THE SETTING SUN...
AFTER SCHOOL CANDY DROP! A SMILE SO SWEET, YOUR BLUSHING FACE AN AUTUMN TREAT...
YOUR TEARS DISSOLVE INSIDE THIS TEACUP, BATHED IN THE GLOW OF THE WANING SUN...
...AND I'LL DRINK THEM ALL UP FOR YOU BEFORE THE NIGHT COMES!

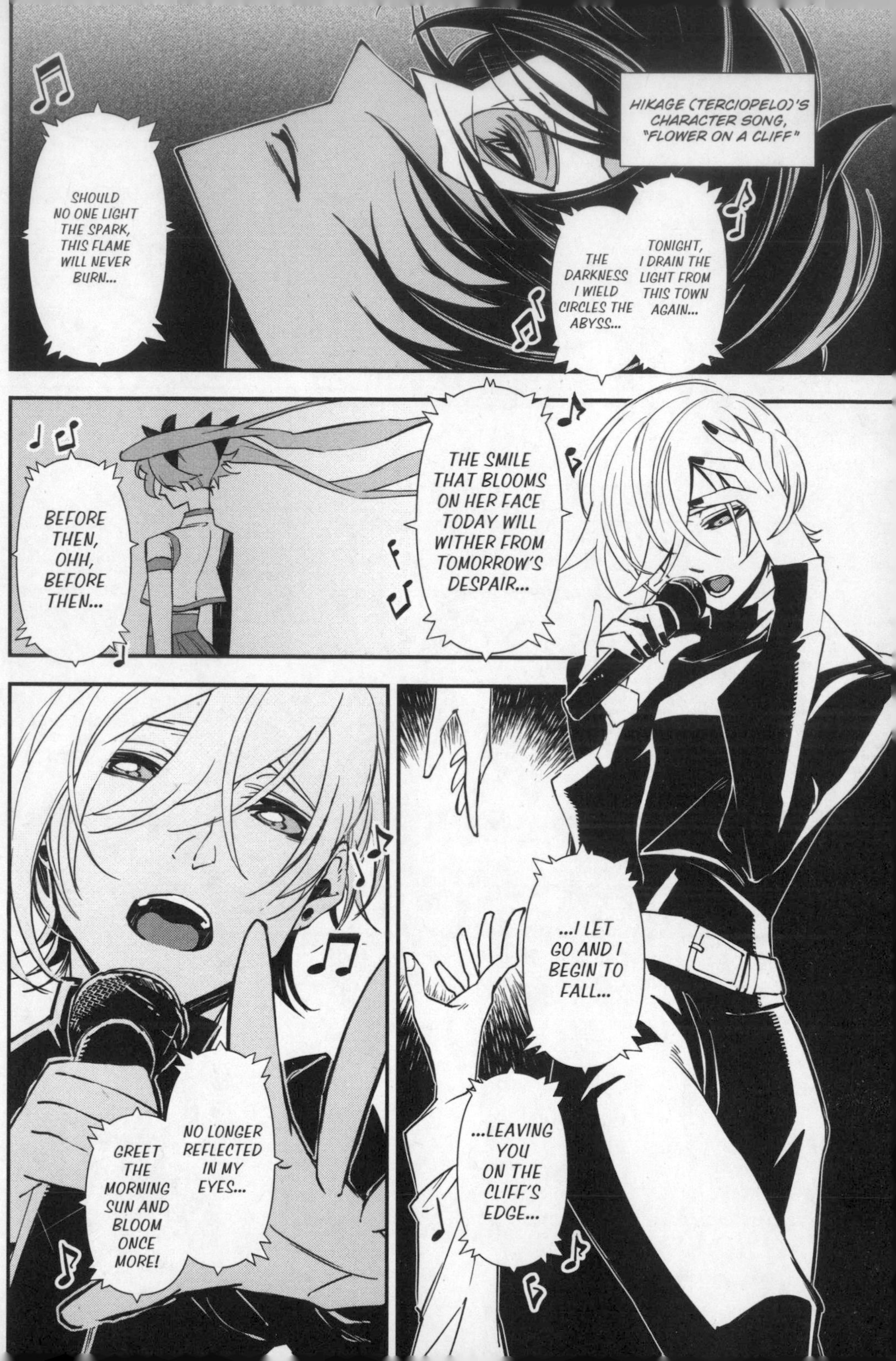
HIKAGE (TERCIOPELO)'S CHARACTER SONG, "FLOWER ON A CLIFF"
TONIGHT, I DRAIN THE LIGHT FROM THIS TOWN AGAIN...
THE DARKNESS I WIELD CIRCLES THE ABYSS...
SHOULD NO ONE LIGHT THE SPARK, THIS FLAME WILL NEVER BURN...
THE SMILE THAT BLOOMS ON HER FACE TODAY WILL WITHER FROM TOMORROW'S DESPAIR...
BEFORE THEN, OHH, BEFORE THEN...
...I LET GO AND I BEGIN TO FALL...
...LEAVING YOU ON THE CLIFF'S EDGE...
NO LONGER REFLECTED IN MY EYES...
GREET THE MORNING SUN AND BLOOM ONCE MORE!

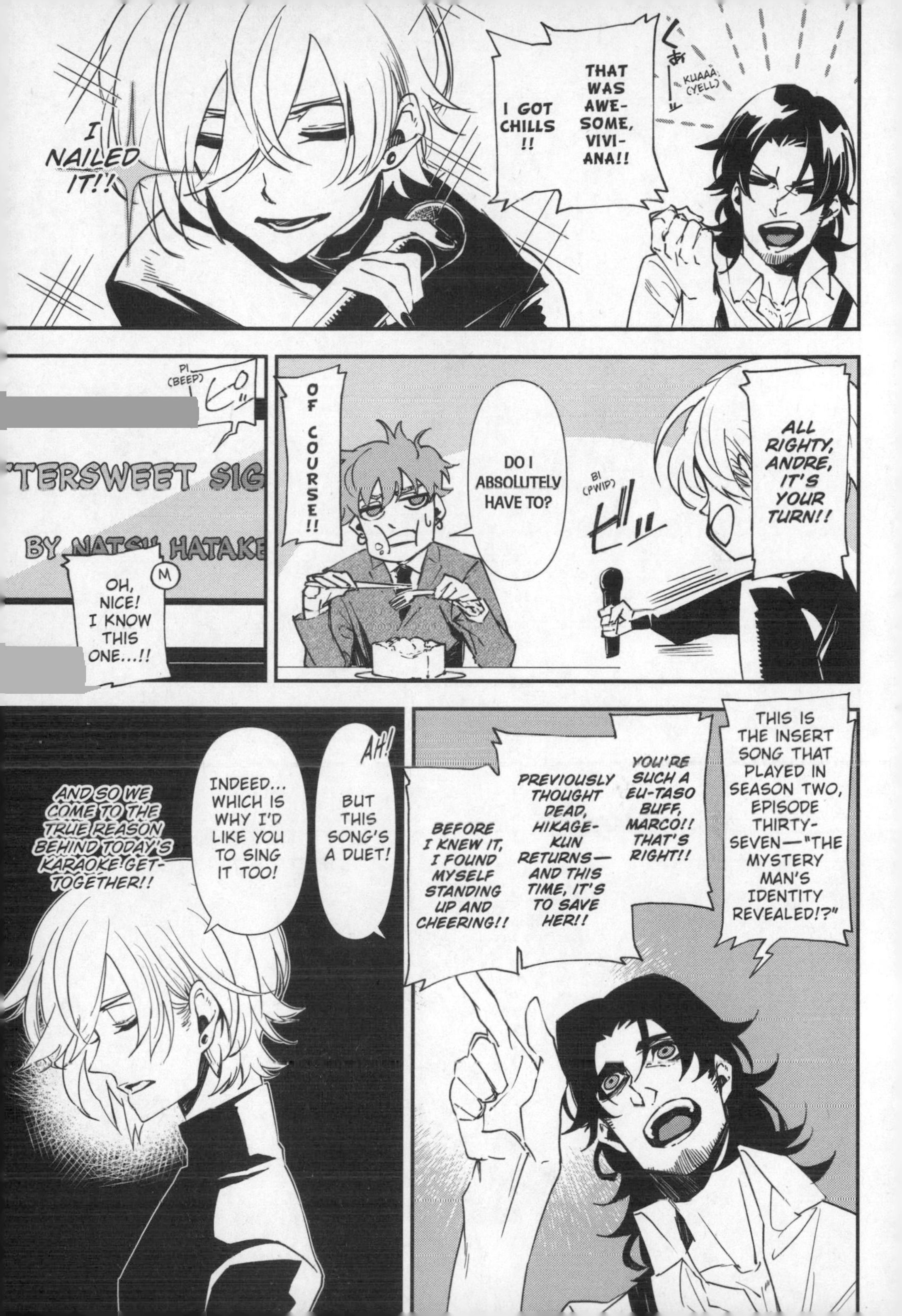

KUAAA (YELL)
THAT WAS AWESOME, VIVIANA!!
I GOT CHILLS!!
I NAILED IT!!
ALL RIGHTY, ANDRE, IT'S YOUR TURN!!
BI (PWIP)
DO I ABSOLUTELY HAVE TO?
OF COURSE!!
PI (BEEP)
TERSWEET SIG
BY NATSU HATAKE
M
OH, NICE! I KNOW THIS ONE...!!
THIS IS THE INSERT SONG THAT PLAYED IN SEASON TWO, EPISODE THIRTY-SEVEN—"THE MYSTERY MAN'S IDENTITY REVEALED!?"
YOU'RE SUCH A EU-TASO BUFF, MARCO!! THAT'S RIGHT!!
PREVIOUSLY THOUGHT DEAD, HIKAGE-KUN RETURNS—AND THIS TIME, IT'S TO SAVE HER!!
BEFORE I KNEW IT, I FOUND MYSELF STANDING UP AND CHEERING!!
AH!
BUT THIS SONG'S A DUET!
INDEED... WHICH IS WHY I'D LIKE YOU TO SING IT TOO!
AND SO WE COME TO THE TRUE REASON BEHIND TODAY'S KARAOKE GET-TOGETHER!!

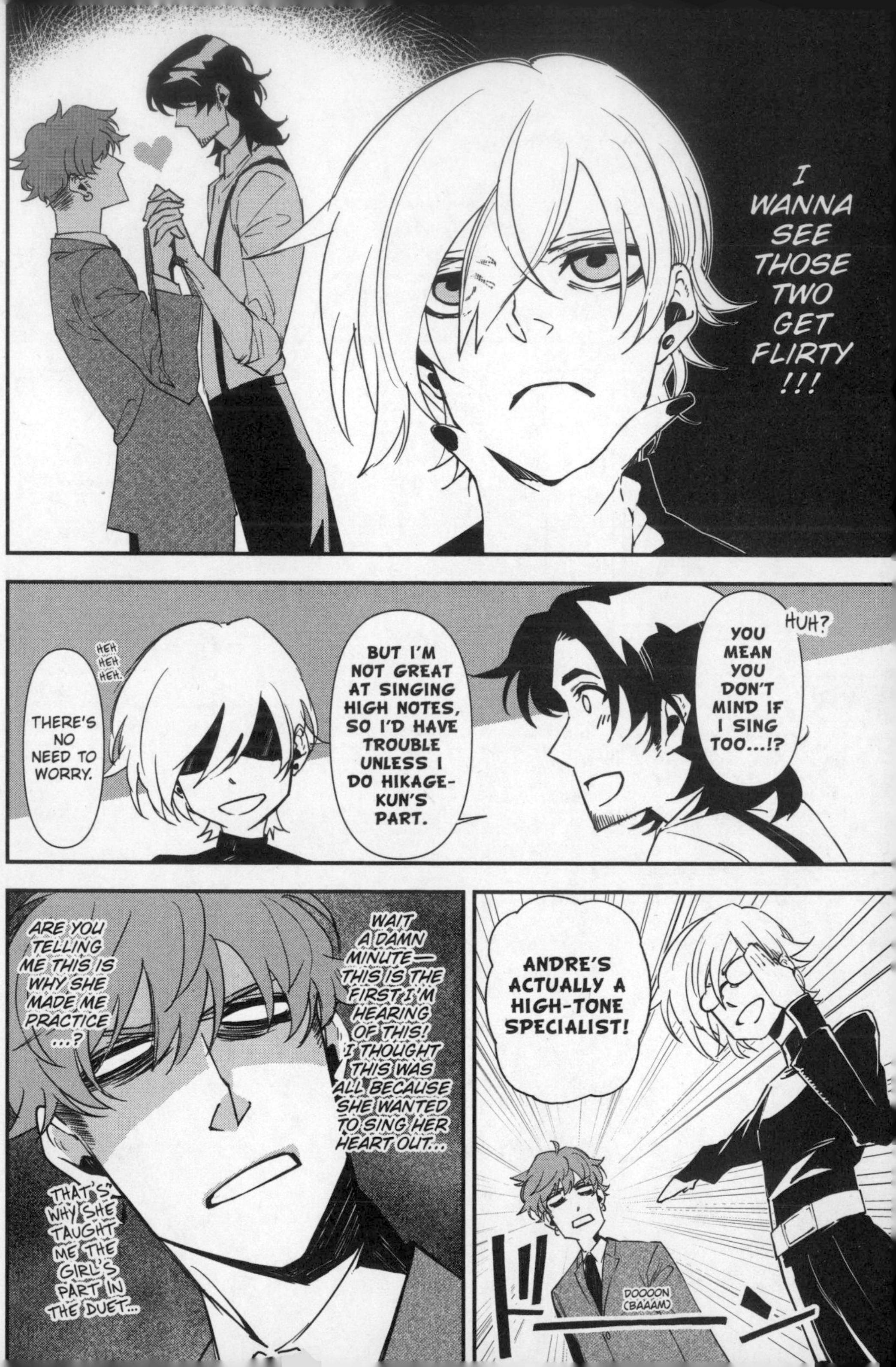
I WANNA SEE THOSE TWO GET FLIRTY!!!
HUH?
YOU MEAN YOU DON'T MIND IF I SING TOO...!?
BUT I'M NOT GREAT AT SINGING HIGH NOTES, SO I'D HAVE TROUBLE UNLESS I DO HIKAGE-KUN'S PART.
HEH HEH HEH.
THERE'S NO NEED TO WORRY.
ANDRE'S ACTUALLY A HIGH-TONE SPECIALIST!
DOOOON (BAAAM)
WAIT A DAMN MINUTE— THIS IS THE FIRST I'M HEARING OF THIS! I THOUGHT THIS WAS ALL BECAUSE SHE WANTED TO SING HER HEART OUT...
ARE YOU TELLING ME THIS IS WHY SHE MADE ME PRACTICE...?
THAT'S WHY SHE TAUGHT ME THE GIRL'S PART IN THE DUET...

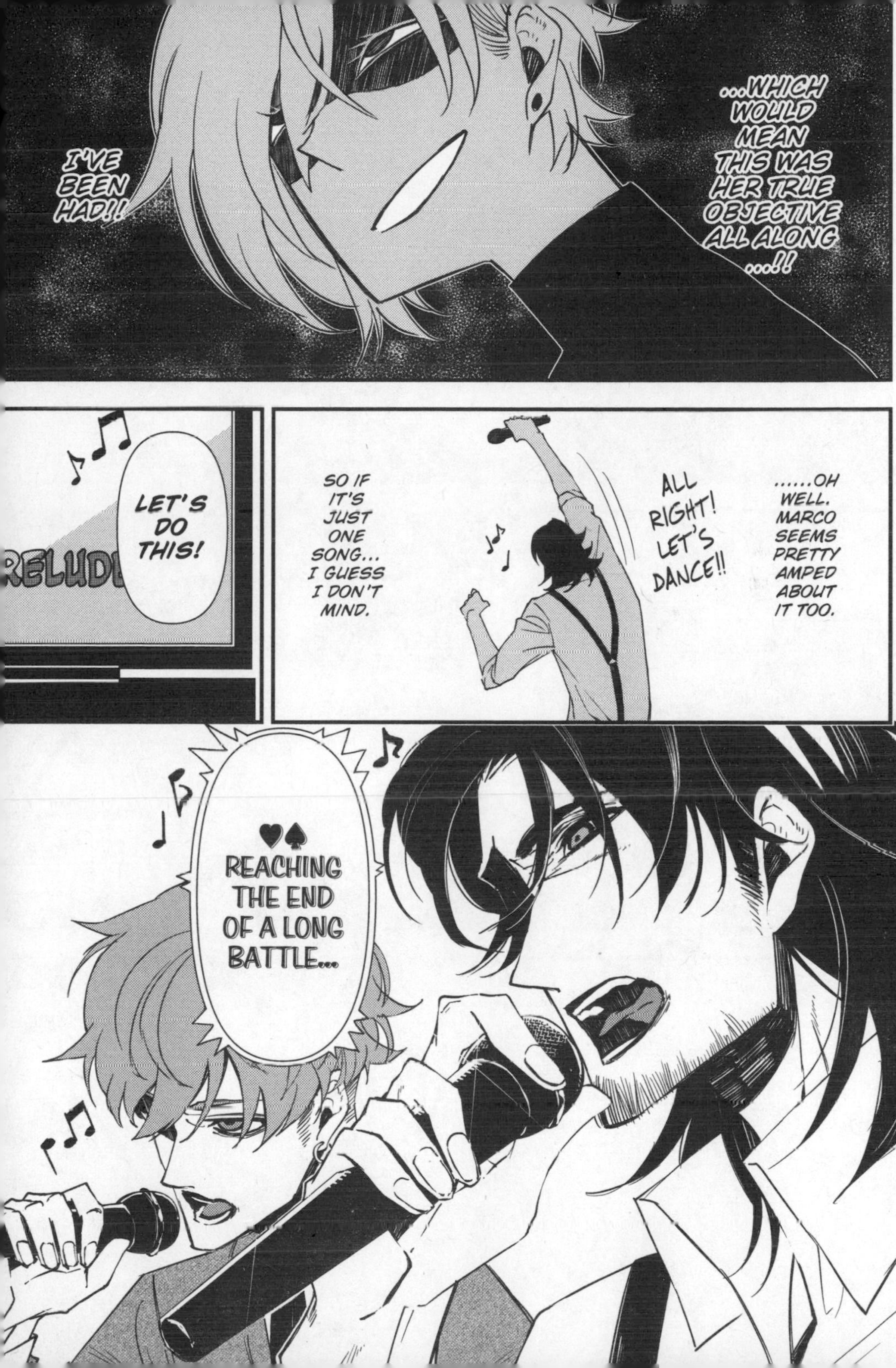
...WHICH WOULD MEAN THIS WAS HER TRUE OBJECTIVE ALL ALONG ...!!
I'VE BEEN HAD!!
......OH WELL. MARCO SEEMS PRETTY AMPED ABOUT IT TOO.
ALL RIGHT! LET'S DANCE!!
SO IF IT'S JUST ONE SONG... I GUESS I DON'T MIND.
LET'S DO THIS!
♥♠ REACHING THE END OF A LONG BATTLE...

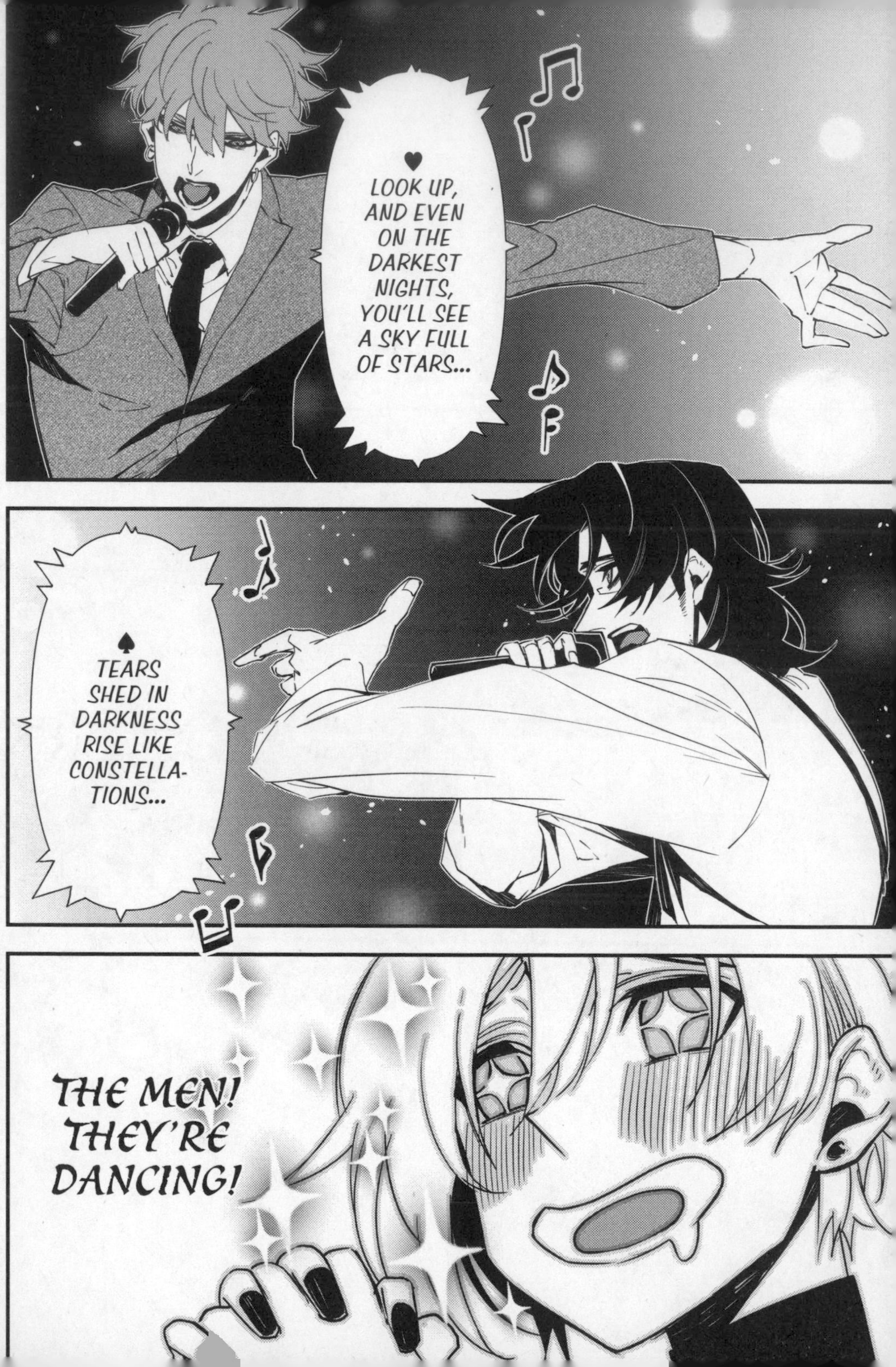
♥ LOOK UP, AND EVEN ON THE DARKEST NIGHTS, YOU'LL SEE A SKY FULL OF STARS...
♠ TEARS SHED IN DARKNESS RISE LIKE CONSTELLATIONS...
THE MEN! THEY'RE DANCING!

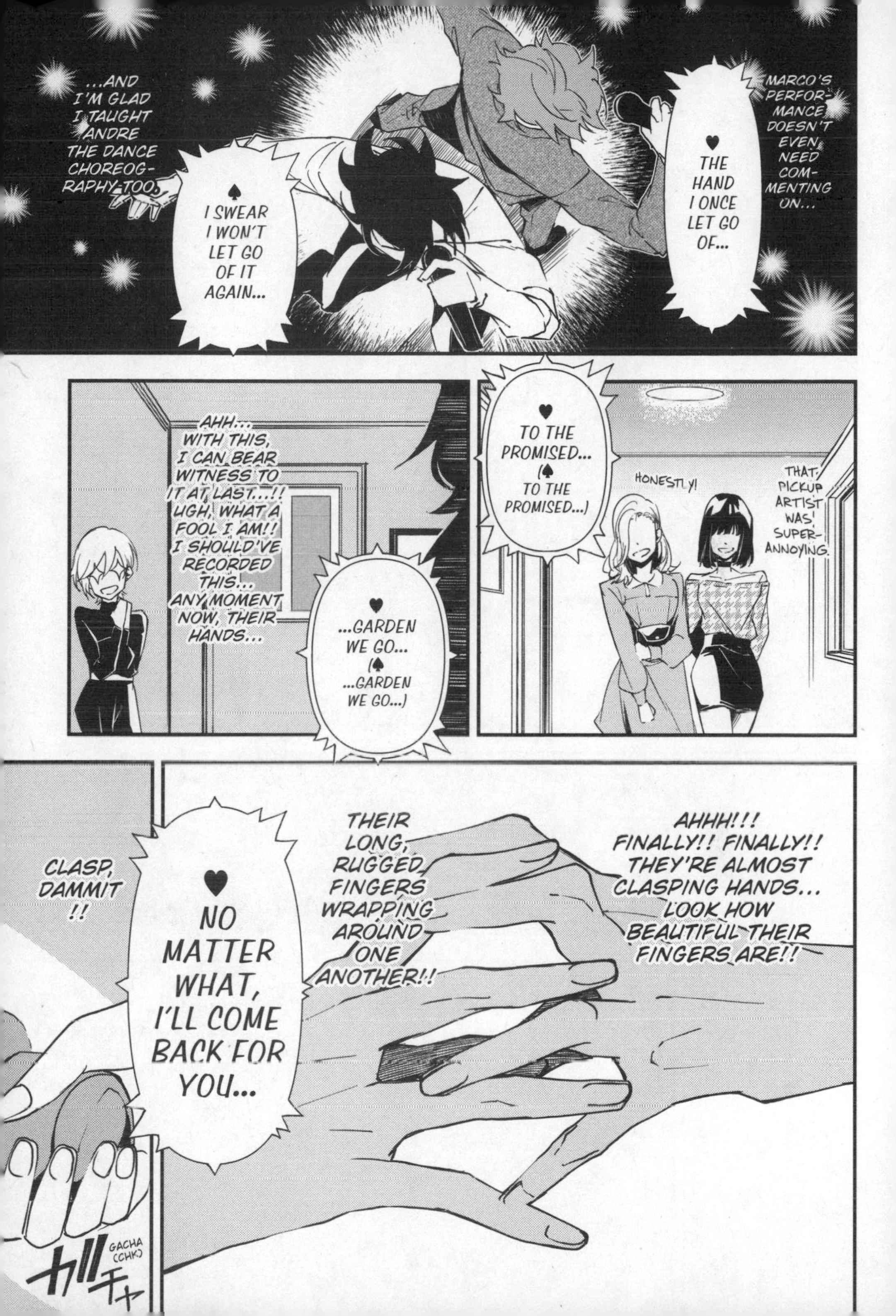
MARCO'S PERFORMANCE DOESN'T EVEN NEED COMMENTING ON...
♥ THE HAND I ONCE LET GO OF...
♠ I SWEAR I WON'T LET GO OF IT AGAIN...
...AND I'M GLAD I TAUGHT ANDRE THE DANCE CHOREOGRAPHY TOO.
THAT PICKUP ARTIST WAS SUPER-ANNOYING.
HONESTLY!
♥ TO THE PROMISED... (♠ TO THE PROMISED...)
♥ ...GARDEN WE GO... (♠ ...GARDEN WE GO...)
AHH... WITH THIS, I CAN BEAR WITNESS TO IT AT LAST...!! UGH, WHAT A FOOL I AM!! I SHOULD'VE RECORDED THIS... ANY MOMENT NOW, THEIR HANDS...
AHHH!!! FINALLY!! FINALLY!! THEY'RE ALMOST CLASPING HANDS... LOOK HOW BEAUTIFUL THEIR FINGERS ARE!!
THEIR LONG, RUGGED FINGERS WRAPPING AROUND ONE ANOTHER!!
♥ NO MATTER WHAT, I'LL COME BACK FOR YOU...
CLASP, DAMMIT!!
GACHA (CHK)
ガチャ

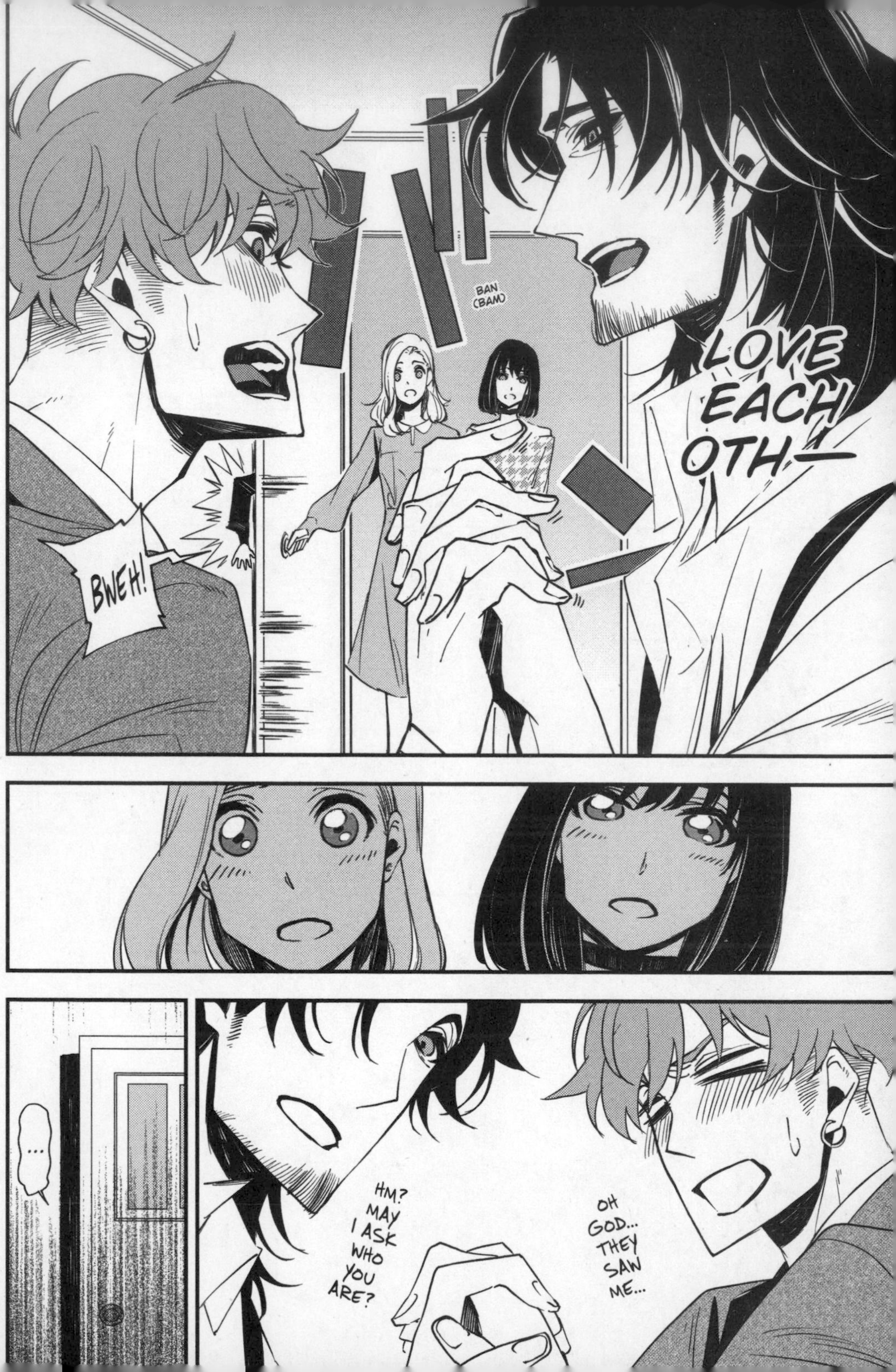
LOVE EACH OTH—
BAN (BAM)
BWEH!
OH GOD... THEY SAW ME...
HM? MAY I ASK WHO YOU ARE?
...

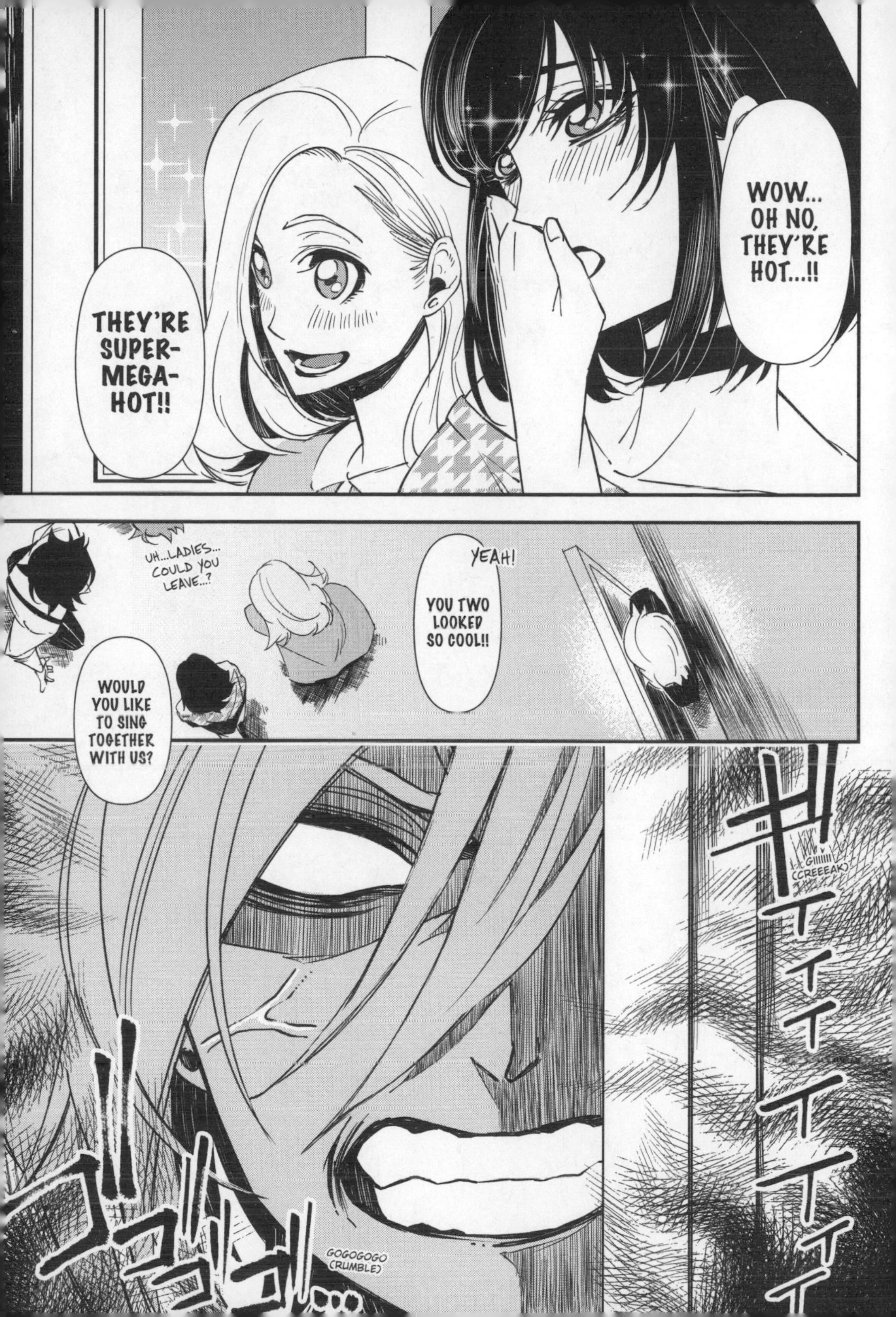
WOW... OH NO, THEY'RE HOT...!!
THEY'RE SUPER-MEGA-HOT!!
YEAH!
YOU TWO LOOKED SO COOL!!
UH...LADIES... COULD YOU LEAVE...?
WOULD YOU LIKE TO SING TOGETHER WITH US?
(CREEEAK)
GOGOGOGO (RUMBLE)

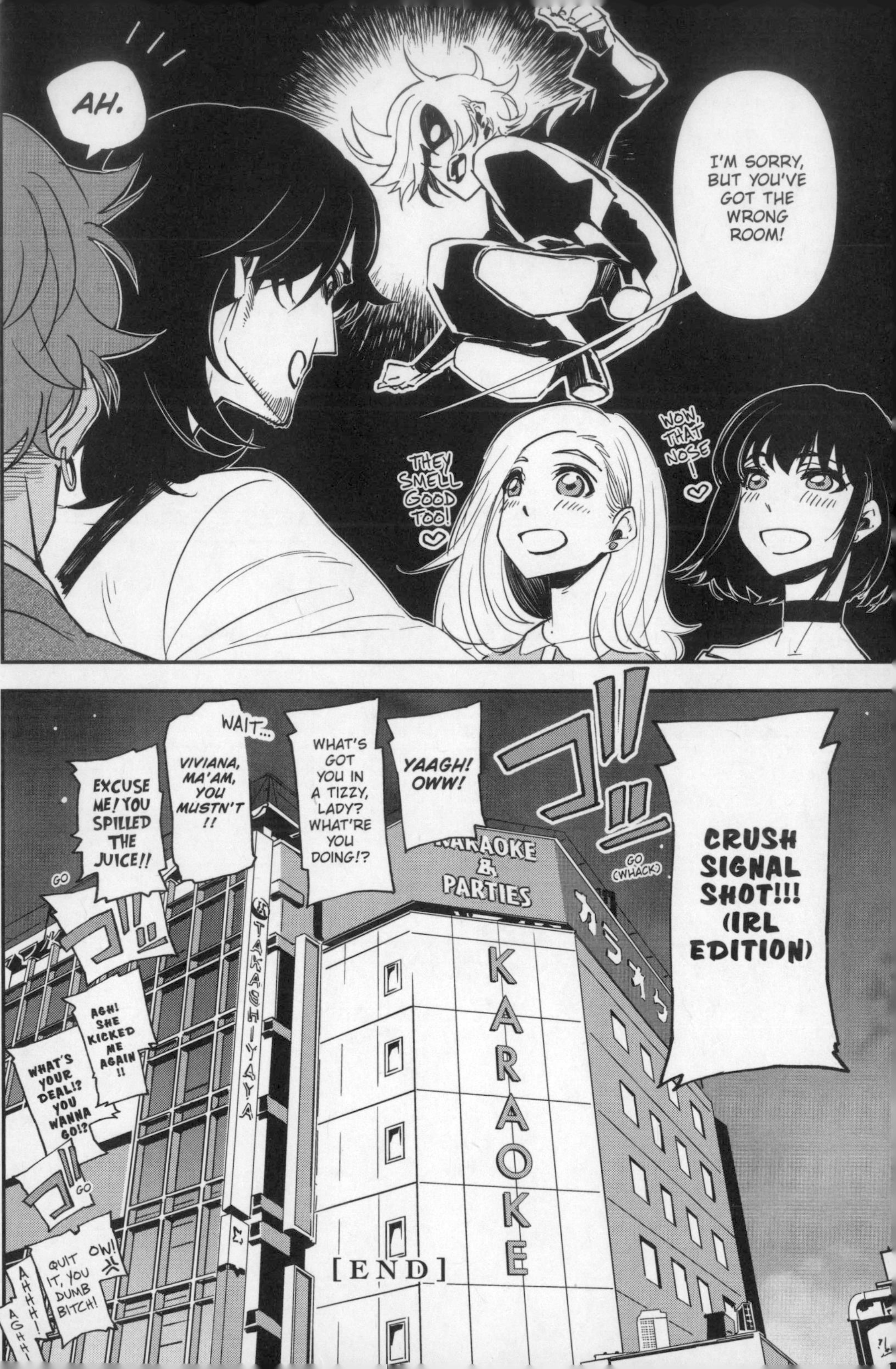
I'M SORRY, BUT YOU'VE GOT THE WRONG ROOM!
AH.
WOW, THAT NOSE!
THEY SMELL GOOD TOO!
CRUSH SIGNAL SHOT!!! (IRL EDITION)
GO (WHACK)
YAAGH! OWW!
WHAT'S GOT YOU IN A TIZZY, LADY? WHAT'RE YOU DOING!?
WAIT...
VIVIANA, MA'AM, YOU MUSTN'T!!
EXCUSE ME! YOU SPILLED THE JUICE!!
KARAOKE & PARTIES
KARAOKE
GO
AGH! SHE KICKED ME AGAIN!!
WHAT'S YOUR DEAL!? YOU WANNA GO!?
GO
OW!
QUIT IT, YOU DUMB BITCH!
AHHH!
AGHH!
[END]

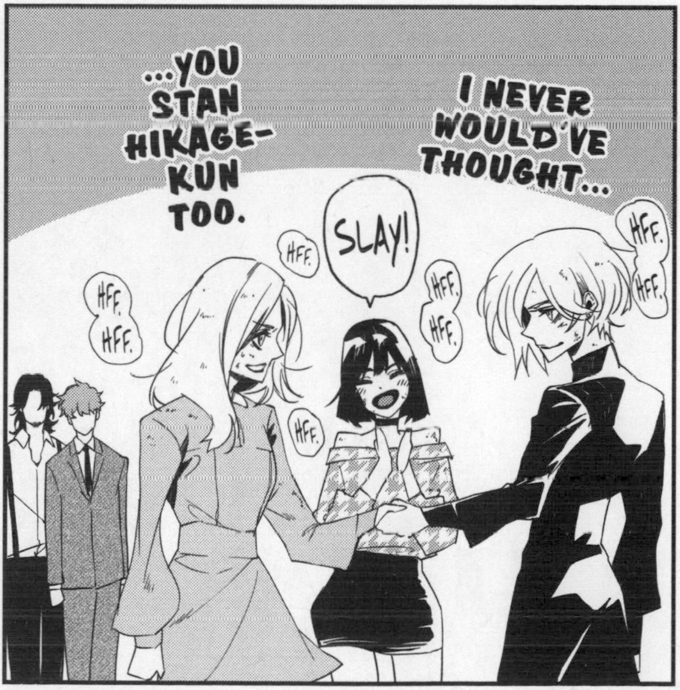
I NEVER WOULD'VE THOUGHT...
HFF. HFF.
...YOU STAN HIKAGE-KUN TOO.
SLAY!
HFF. HFF.
HFF.
HFF.
HFF. HFF.
HFF.

THE GEEK EX-HITMAN

#17

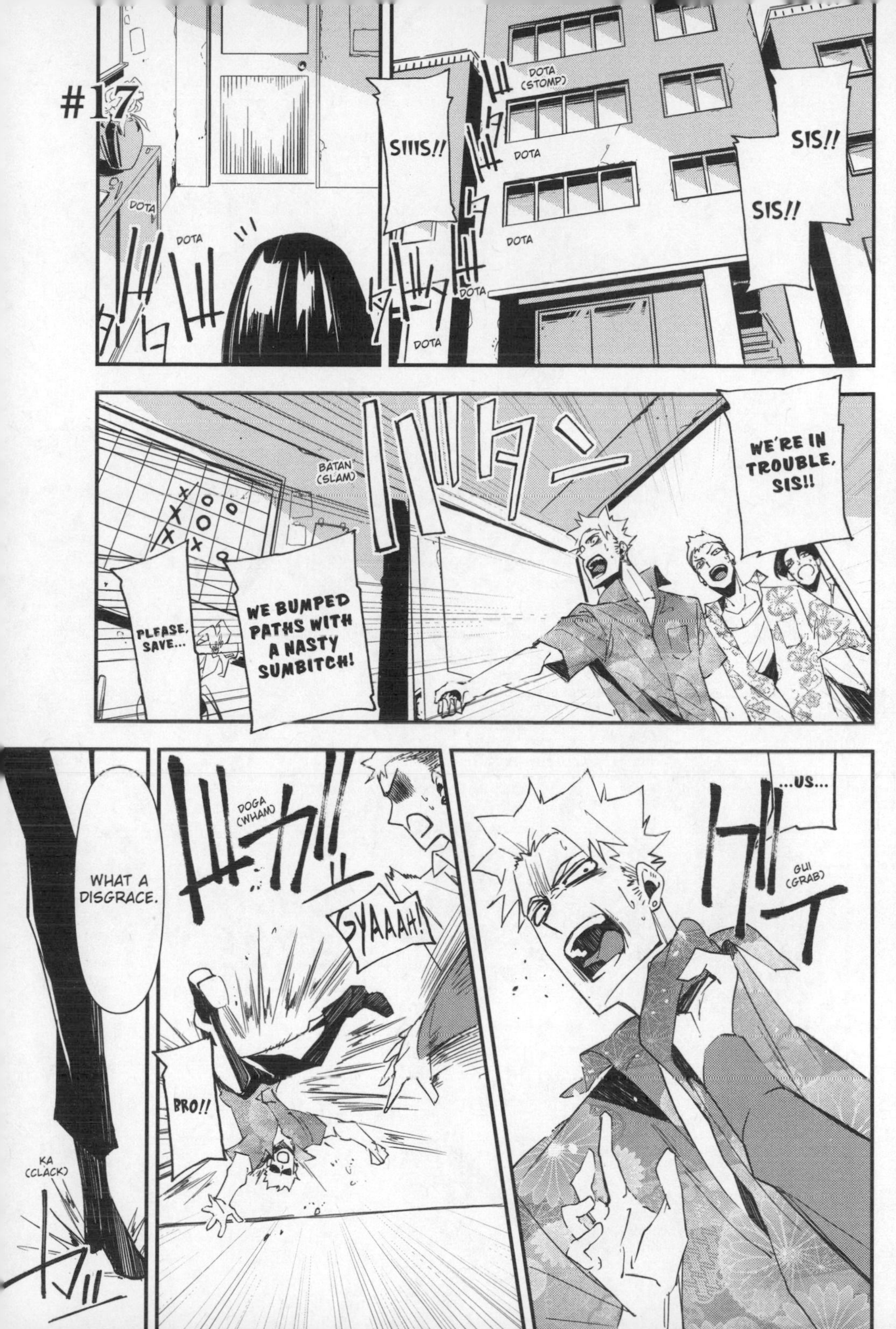
SIS!!
SIS!!
DOTA (STOMP)
DOTA
DOTA
SIIIS!!
DOTA
DOTA
DOTA
DOTA
WE'RE IN TROUBLE, SIS!!
BATAN (SLAM)
WE BUMPED PATHS WITH A NASTY SUMBITCH!
PLEASE, SAVE...
...US...
GUI (GRAB)
DOGA (WHAM)
GYAAAH!
BRO!!
WHAT A DISGRACE.
KA (CLACK)

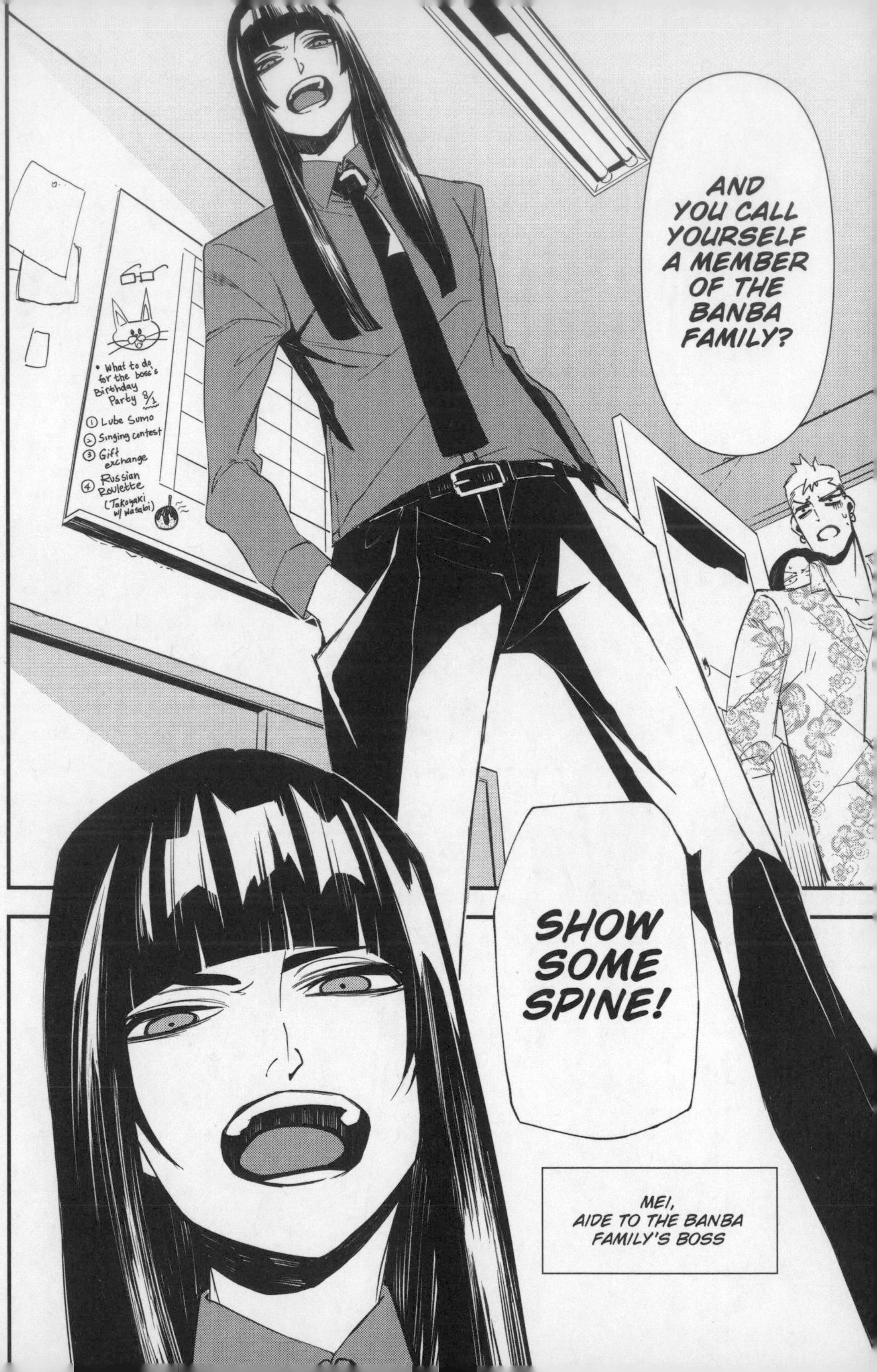
AND YOU CALL YOURSELF A MEMBER OF THE BANBA FAMILY?
• What to do for the boss's Birthday Party 8/1
① Lube Sumo
② Singing contest
③ Gift exchange
④ Russian Roulette (Takoyaki w/ Wasabi)
SHOW SOME SPINE!
MEI, AIDE TO THE BANBA FAMILY'S BOSS

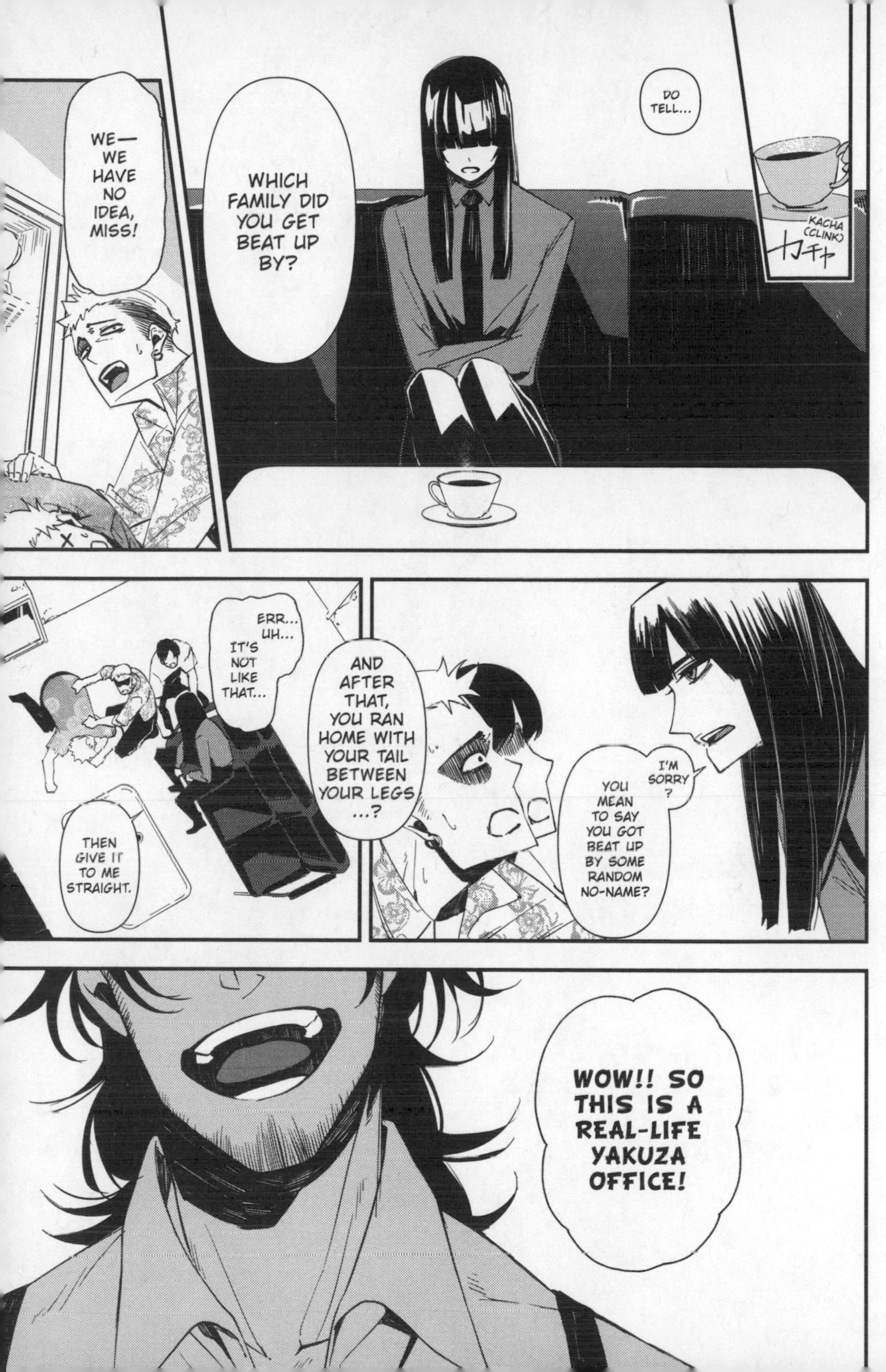
DO TELL...
KACHA (CLINK)
カチャ
WHICH FAMILY DID YOU GET BEAT UP BY?
WE— WE HAVE NO IDEA, MISS!
I'M SORRY?
YOU MEAN TO SAY YOU GOT BEAT UP BY SOME RANDOM NO-NAME?
AND AFTER THAT, YOU RAN HOME WITH YOUR TAIL BETWEEN YOUR LEGS...?
ERR... UH...
IT'S NOT LIKE THAT...
THEN GIVE IT TO ME STRAIGHT.
WOW!! SO THIS IS A REAL-LIFE YAKUZA OFFICE!

#17

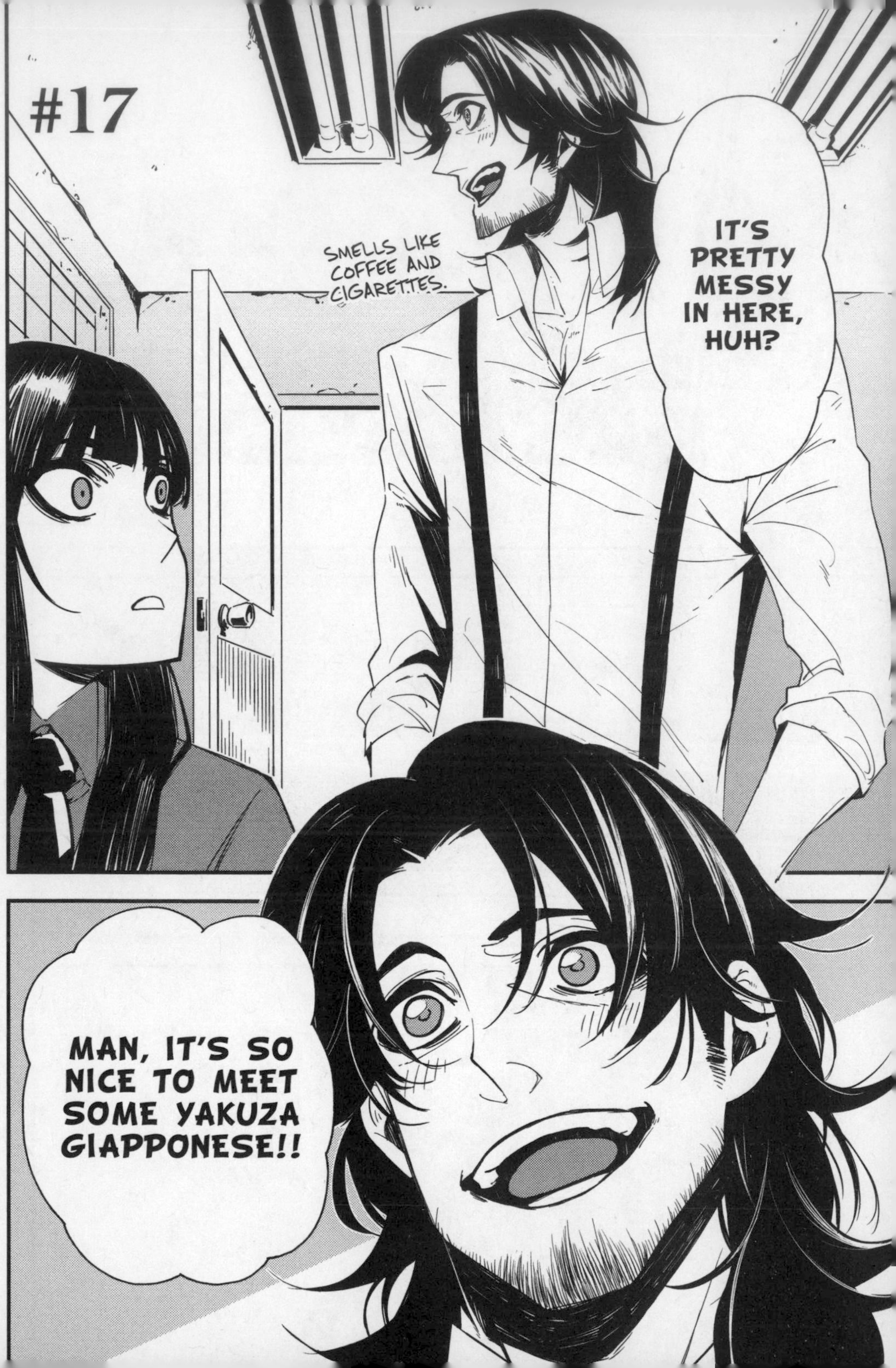
IT'S PRETTY MESSY IN HERE, HUH?
SMELLS LIKE COFFEE AND CIGARETTES.
MAN, IT'S SO NICE TO MEET SOME YAKUZA GIAPPONESE!!

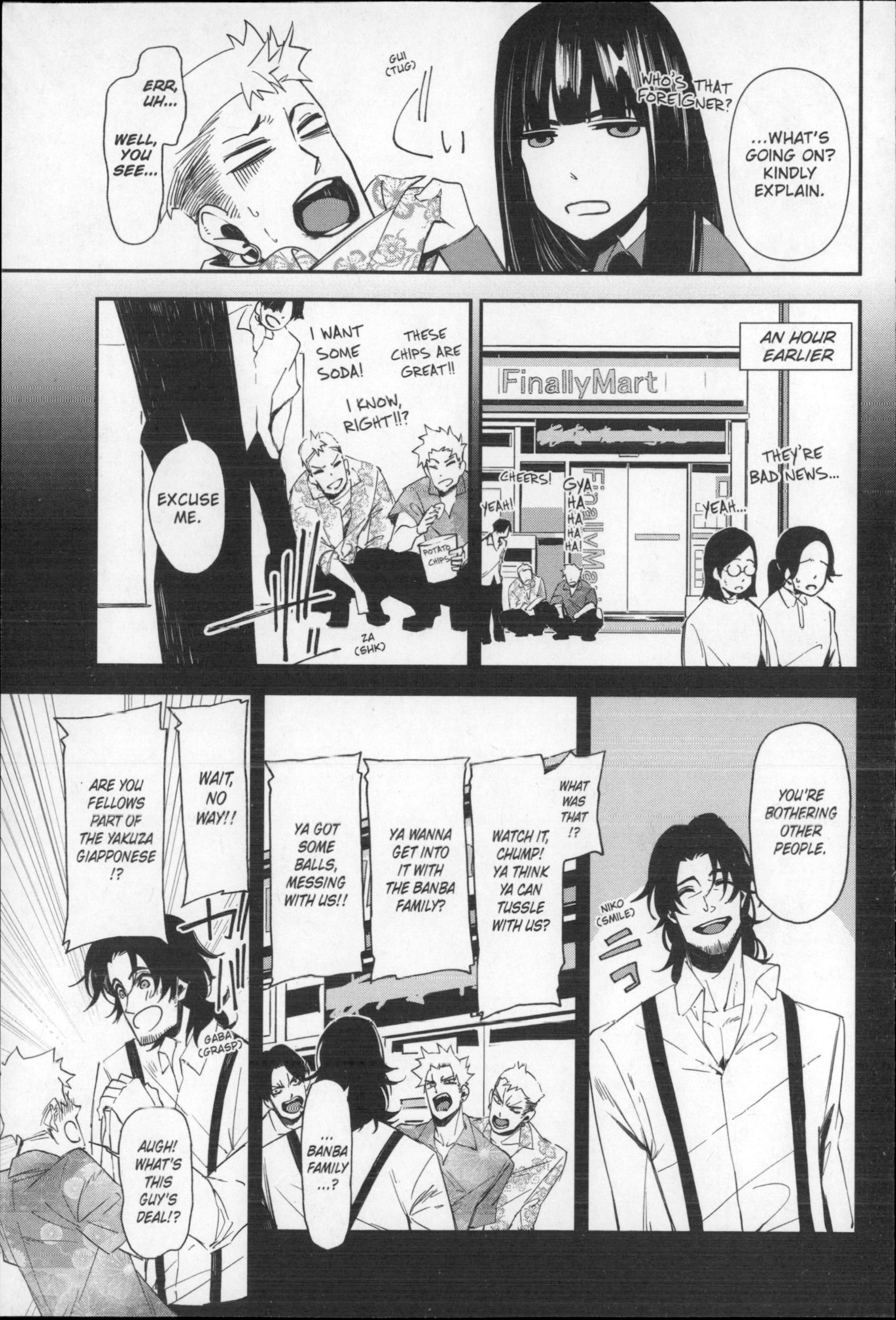
...WHAT'S GOING ON? KINDLY EXPLAIN.
WHO'S THAT FOREIGNER?
GUI (TUG)
ERR, UH...
WELL, YOU SEE...
AN HOUR EARLIER
THEY'RE BAD NEWS...
YEAH...
FinallyMart
CHEERS!
GYA HA HA HA HA!
YEAH!
THESE CHIPS ARE GREAT!!
I WANT SOME SODA!
I KNOW, RIGHT!!?
EXCUSE ME.
POTATO CHIPS
ZA (SHK)
YOU'RE BOTHERING OTHER PEOPLE.
NIKO (SMILE)
WHAT WAS THAT!?
WATCH IT, CHUMP! YA THINK YA CAN TUSSLE WITH US?
YA WANNA GET INTO IT WITH THE BANBA FAMILY?
YA GOT SOME BALLS, MESSING WITH US!!
...BANBA FAMILY...?
WAIT, NO WAY!!
ARE YOU FELLOWS PART OF THE YAKUZA GIAPPONESE!?
GABA (GRASP)
AUGH! WHAT'S THIS GUY'S DEAL!?

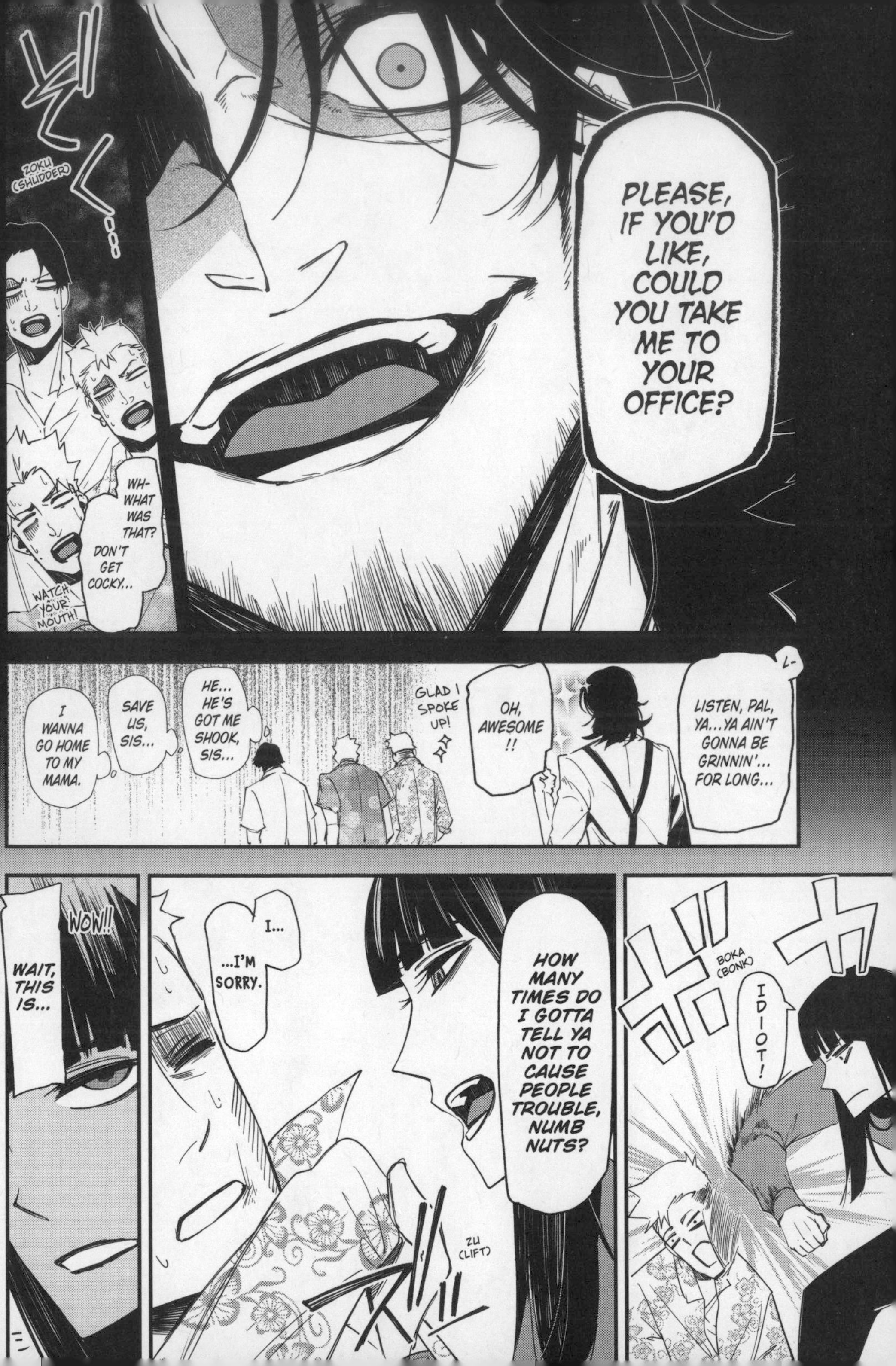
PLEASE, IF YOU'D LIKE, COULD YOU TAKE ME TO YOUR OFFICE?
ZOKU (SHUDDER)
WH-WHAT WAS THAT?
DON'T GET COCKY...
WATCH YOUR MOUTH!
LISTEN, PAL, YA...YA AIN'T GONNA BE GRINNIN'... FOR LONG...
OH, AWESOME!!
GLAD I SPOKE UP!
HE... HE'S GOT ME SHOOK, SIS...
SAVE US, SIS...
I WANNA GO HOME TO MY MAMA.
BOKA (BONK)
IDIOT!
HOW MANY TIMES DO I GOTTA TELL YA NOT TO CAUSE PEOPLE TROUBLE, NUMB NUTS?
I...
...I'M SORRY.
ZU (LIFT)
WOW!!
WAIT, THIS IS...

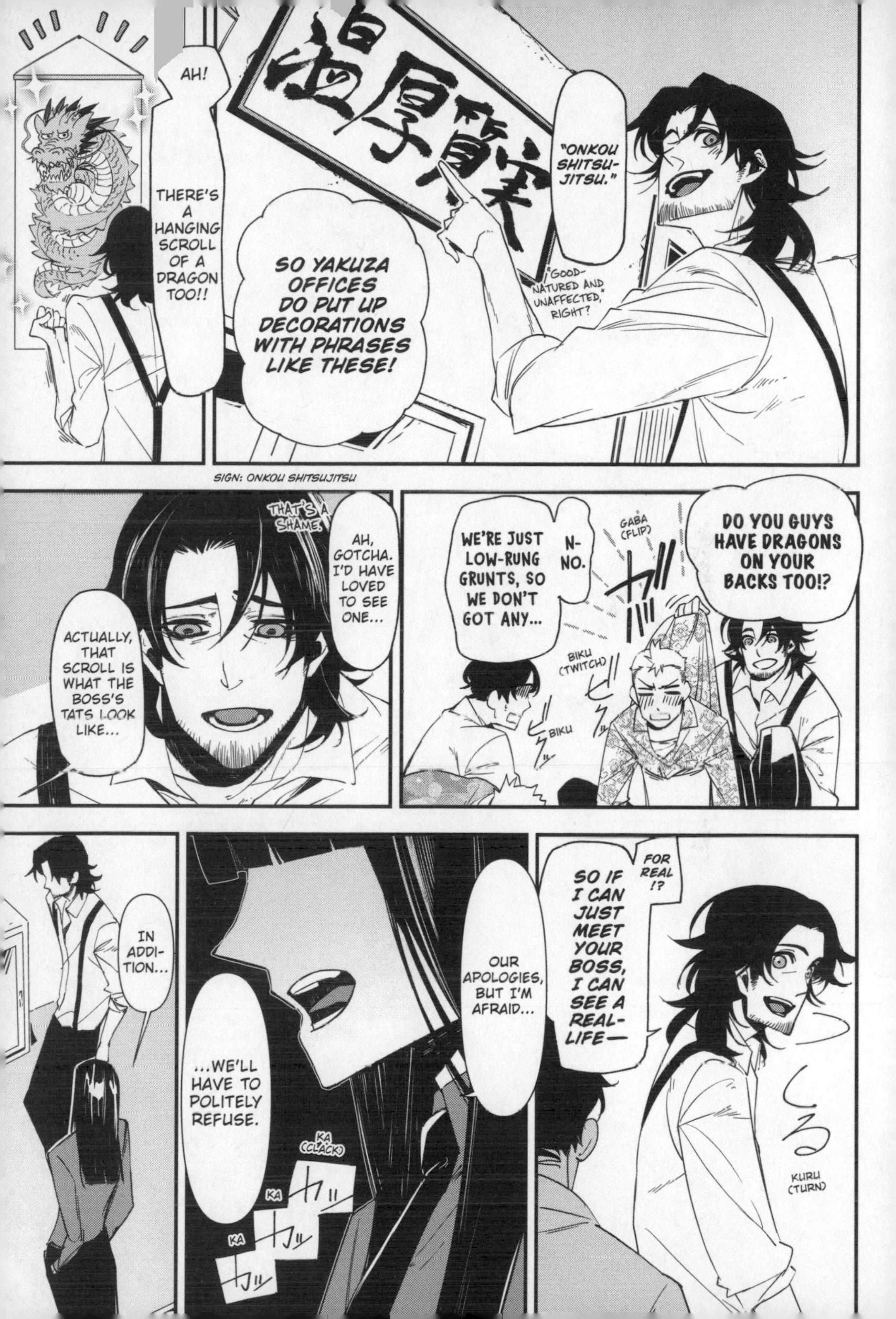
"ONKOU SHITSU-JITSU."
"GOOD-NATURED AND UNAFFECTED," RIGHT?
SO YAKUZA OFFICES DO PUT UP DECORATIONS WITH PHRASES LIKE THESE!
AH!
THERE'S A HANGING SCROLL OF A DRAGON TOO!!
SIGN: ONKOU SHITSUJITSU
DO YOU GUYS HAVE DRAGONS ON YOUR BACKS TOO!?
GABA (FLIP)
N-NO.
WE'RE JUST LOW-RUNG GRUNTS, SO WE DON'T GOT ANY...
BIKU (TWITCH)
BIKU
AH, GOTCHA. I'D HAVE LOVED TO SEE ONE...
THAT'S A SHAME.
ACTUALLY, THAT SCROLL IS WHAT THE BOSS'S TATS LOOK LIKE...
FOR REAL!?
SO IF I CAN JUST MEET YOUR BOSS, I CAN SEE A REAL-LIFE—
KURU (TURN)
OUR APOLOGIES, BUT I'M AFRAID...
...WE'LL HAVE TO POLITELY REFUSE.
KA (CLACK)
KA
KA
IN ADDITION...

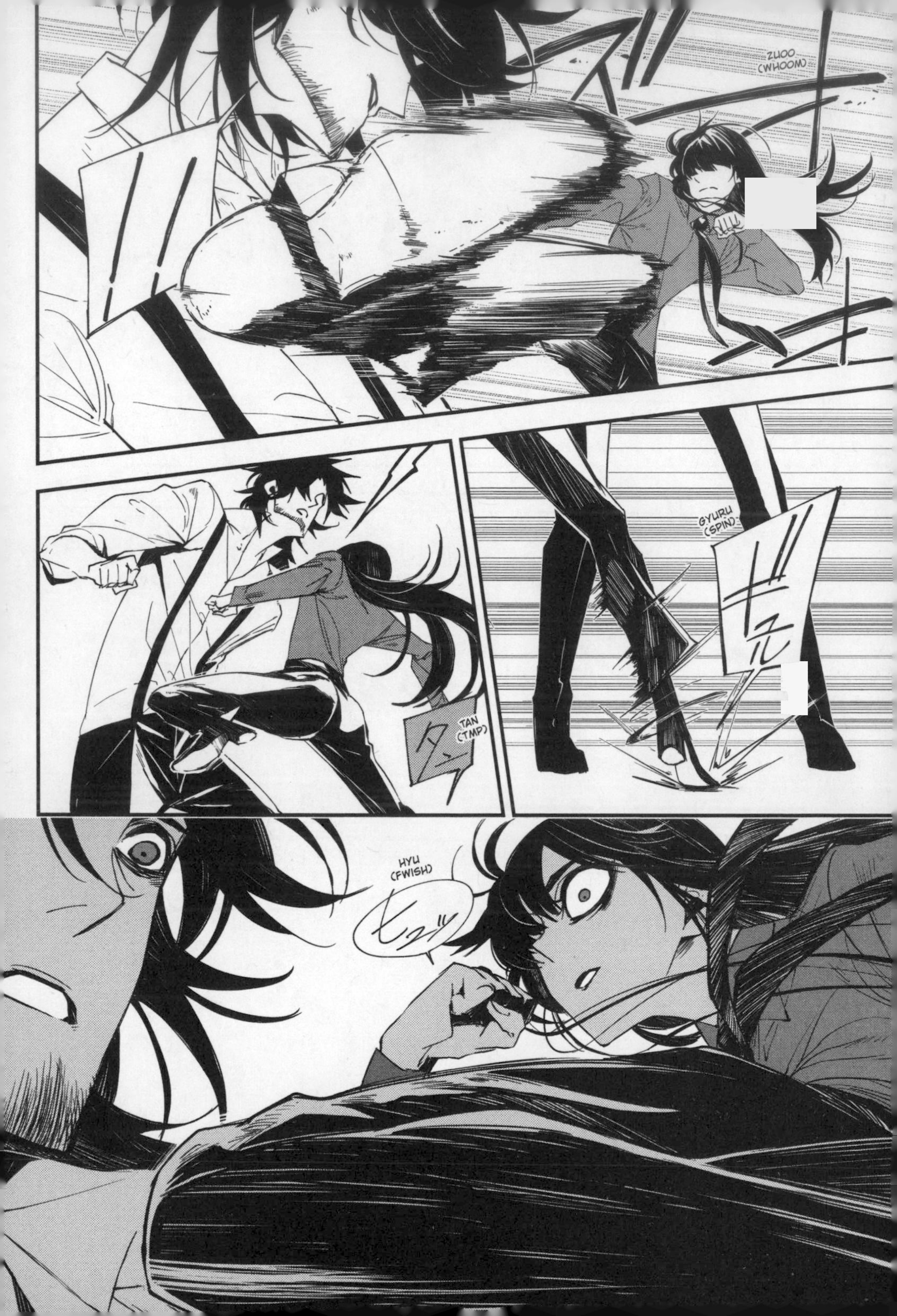
ZUOO
(WHOOM)
GYURU
(SPIN)
TAN
(TMP)
HYU
(FWISH)

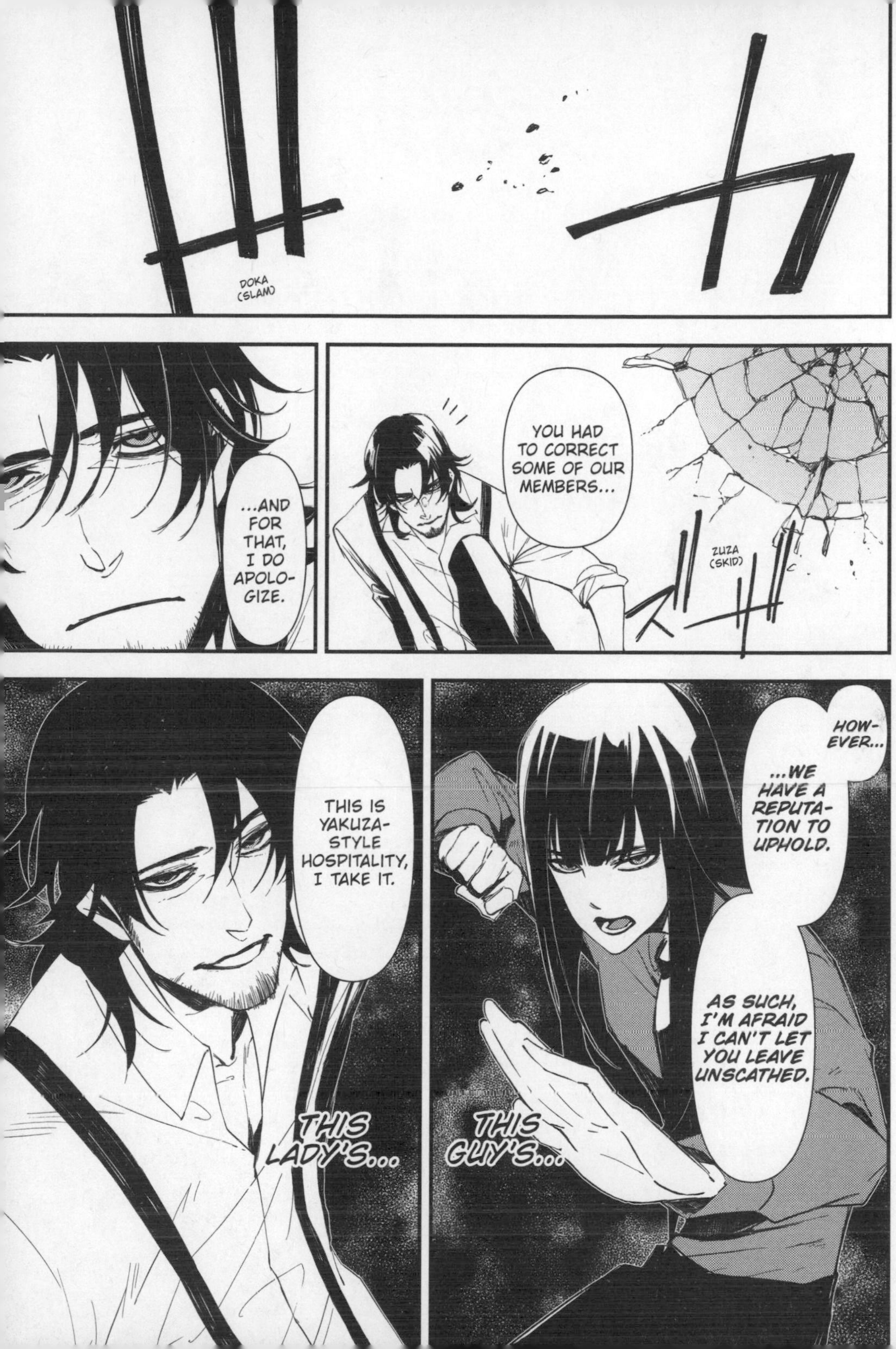
DOKA (SLAM)
ZUZA (SKID)
YOU HAD TO CORRECT SOME OF OUR MEMBERS...
...AND FOR THAT, I DO APOLOGIZE.
HOW-EVER...
...WE HAVE A REPUTATION TO UPHOLD.
AS SUCH, I'M AFRAID I CAN'T LET YOU LEAVE UNSCATHED.
THIS GUY'S...
THIS IS YAKUZA-STYLE HOSPITALITY, I TAKE IT.
THIS LADY'S...

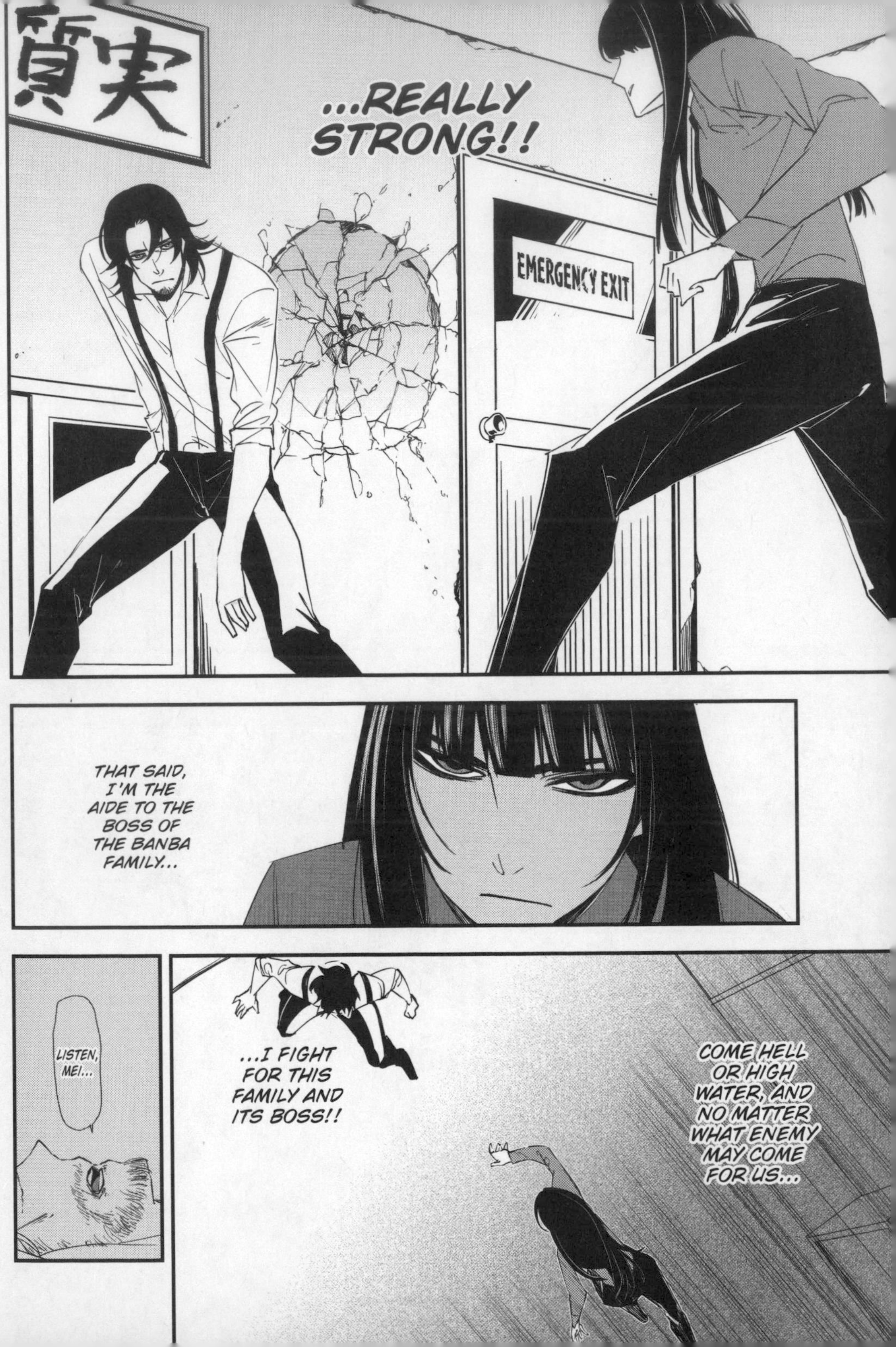
質実
...REALLY STRONG!!
EMERGENCY EXIT
THAT SAID, I'M THE AIDE TO THE BOSS OF THE BANBA FAMILY...
COME HELL OR HIGH WATER, AND NO MATTER WHAT ENEMY MAY COME FOR US...
...I FIGHT FOR THIS FAMILY AND ITS BOSS!!
LISTEN, MEI...

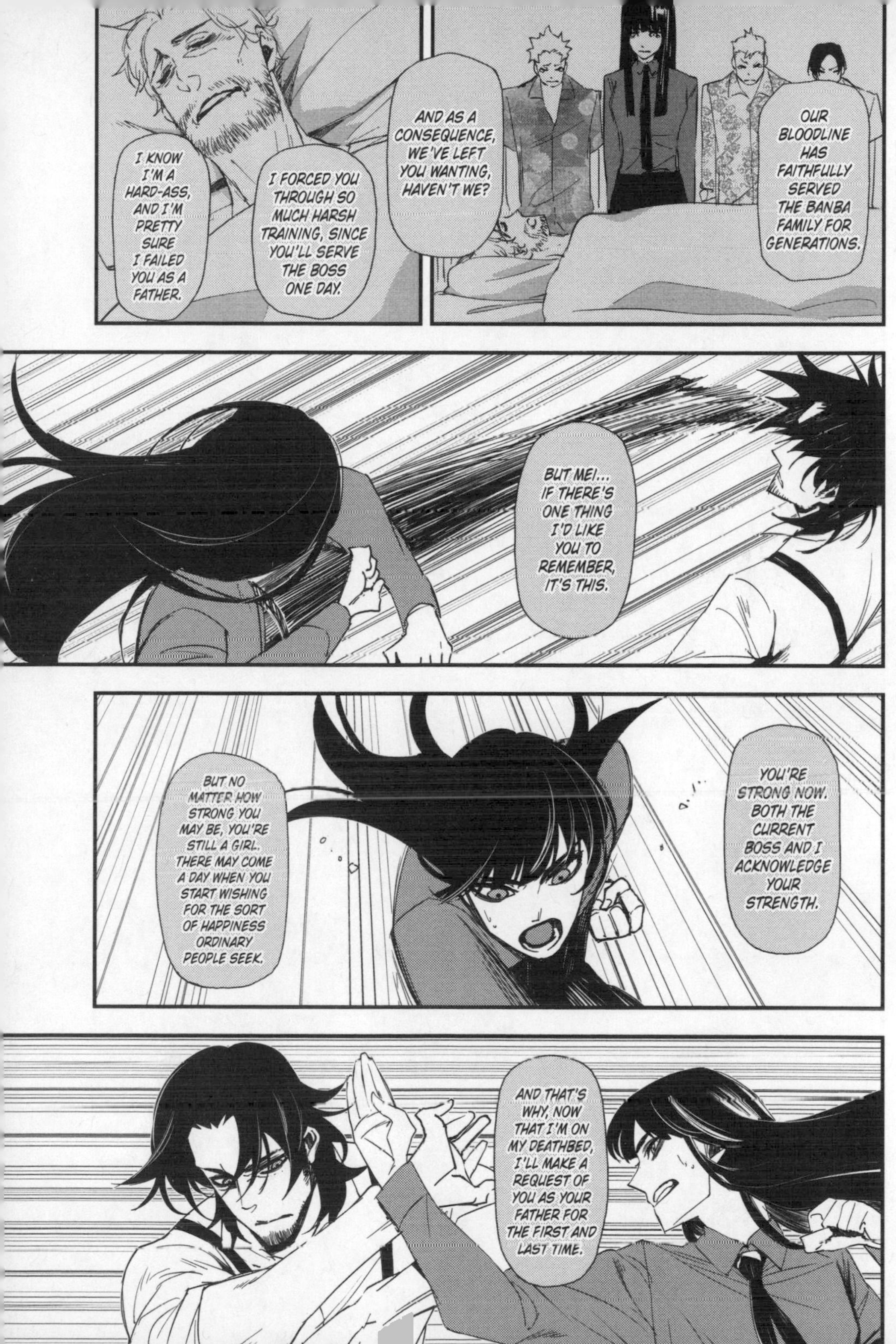
OUR BLOODLINE HAS FAITHFULLY SERVED THE BANBA FAMILY FOR GENERATIONS.
AND AS A CONSEQUENCE, WE'VE LEFT YOU WANTING, HAVEN'T WE?
I FORCED YOU THROUGH SO MUCH HARSH TRAINING, SINCE YOU'LL SERVE THE BOSS ONE DAY.
I KNOW I'M A HARD-ASS, AND I'M PRETTY SURE I FAILED YOU AS A FATHER.
BUT MEI... IF THERE'S ONE THING I'D LIKE YOU TO REMEMBER, IT'S THIS.
YOU'RE STRONG NOW. BOTH THE CURRENT BOSS AND I ACKNOWLEDGE YOUR STRENGTH.
BUT NO MATTER HOW STRONG YOU MAY BE, YOU'RE STILL A GIRL. THERE MAY COME A DAY WHEN YOU START WISHING FOR THE SORT OF HAPPINESS ORDINARY PEOPLE SEEK.
AND THAT'S WHY, NOW THAT I'M ON MY DEATHBED, I'LL MAKE A REQUEST OF YOU AS YOUR FATHER FOR THE FIRST AND LAST TIME.

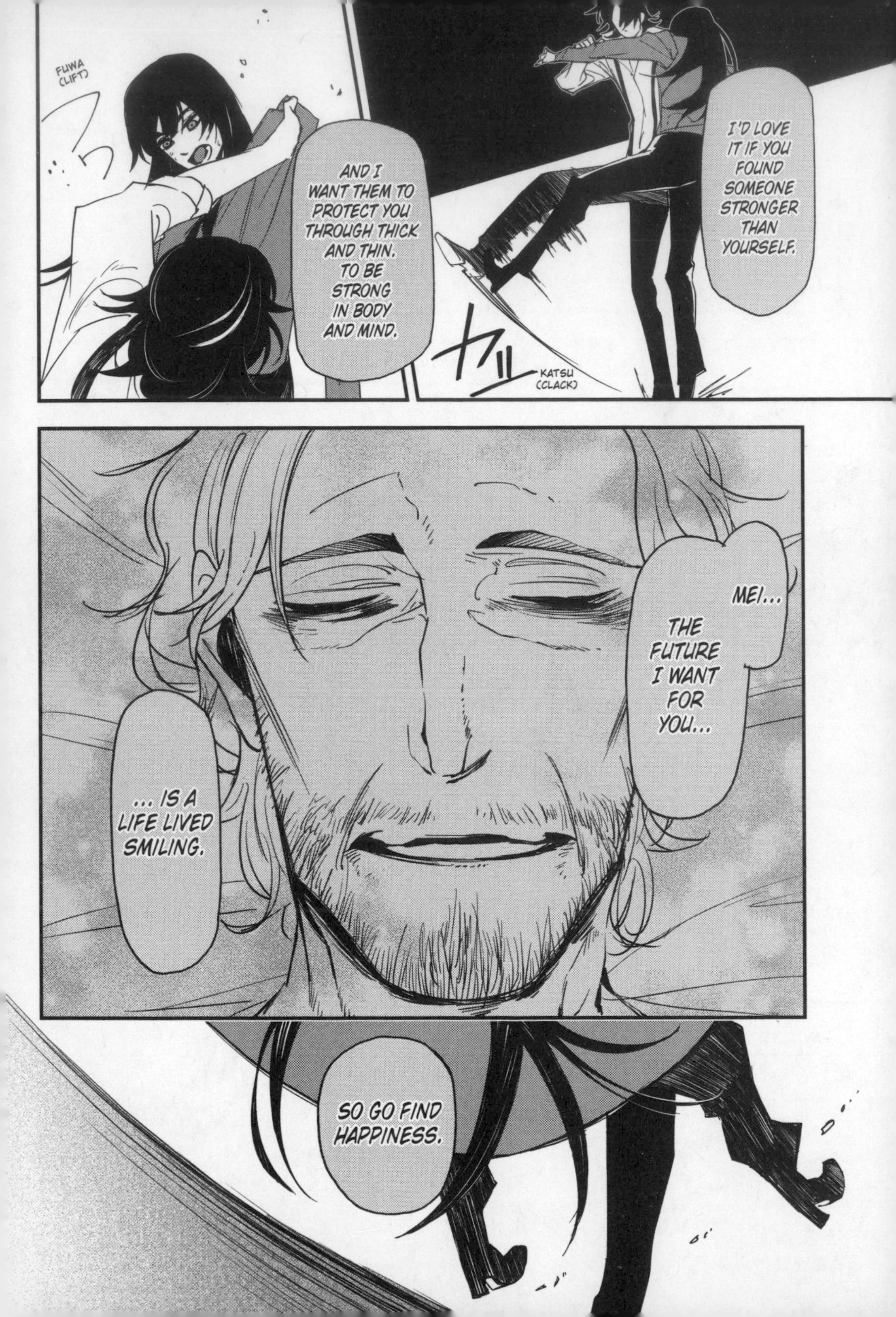
I'D LOVE IT IF YOU FOUND SOMEONE STRONGER THAN YOURSELF.
KATSU (CLACK)
FUWA (LIFT)
AND I WANT THEM TO PROTECT YOU THROUGH THICK AND THIN. TO BE STRONG IN BODY AND MIND.
MEI...
THE FUTURE I WANT FOR YOU...
... IS A LIFE LIVED SMILING.
SO GO FIND HAPPINESS.

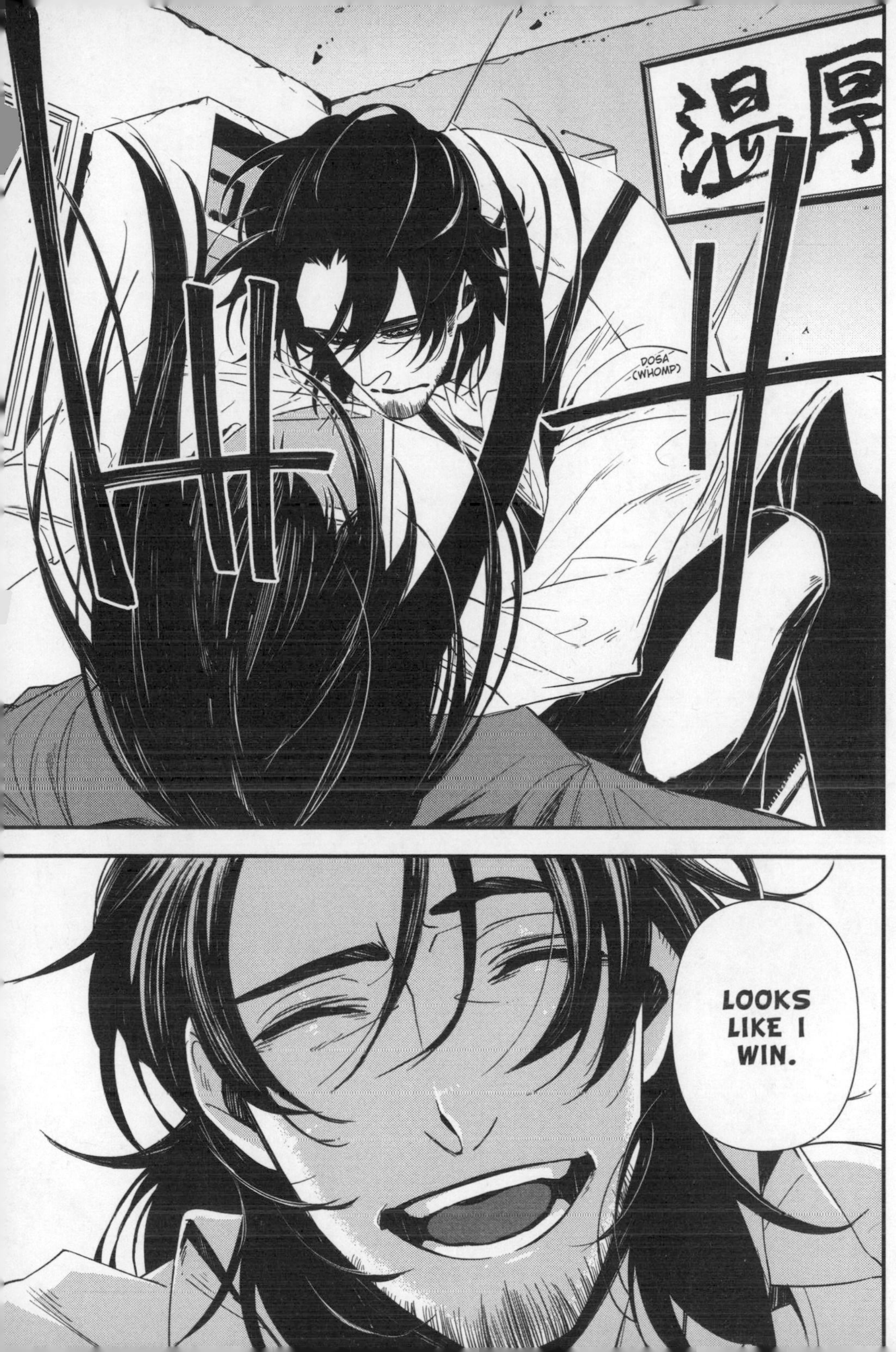
DOSA
(WHOMP)
LOOKS LIKE I WIN.

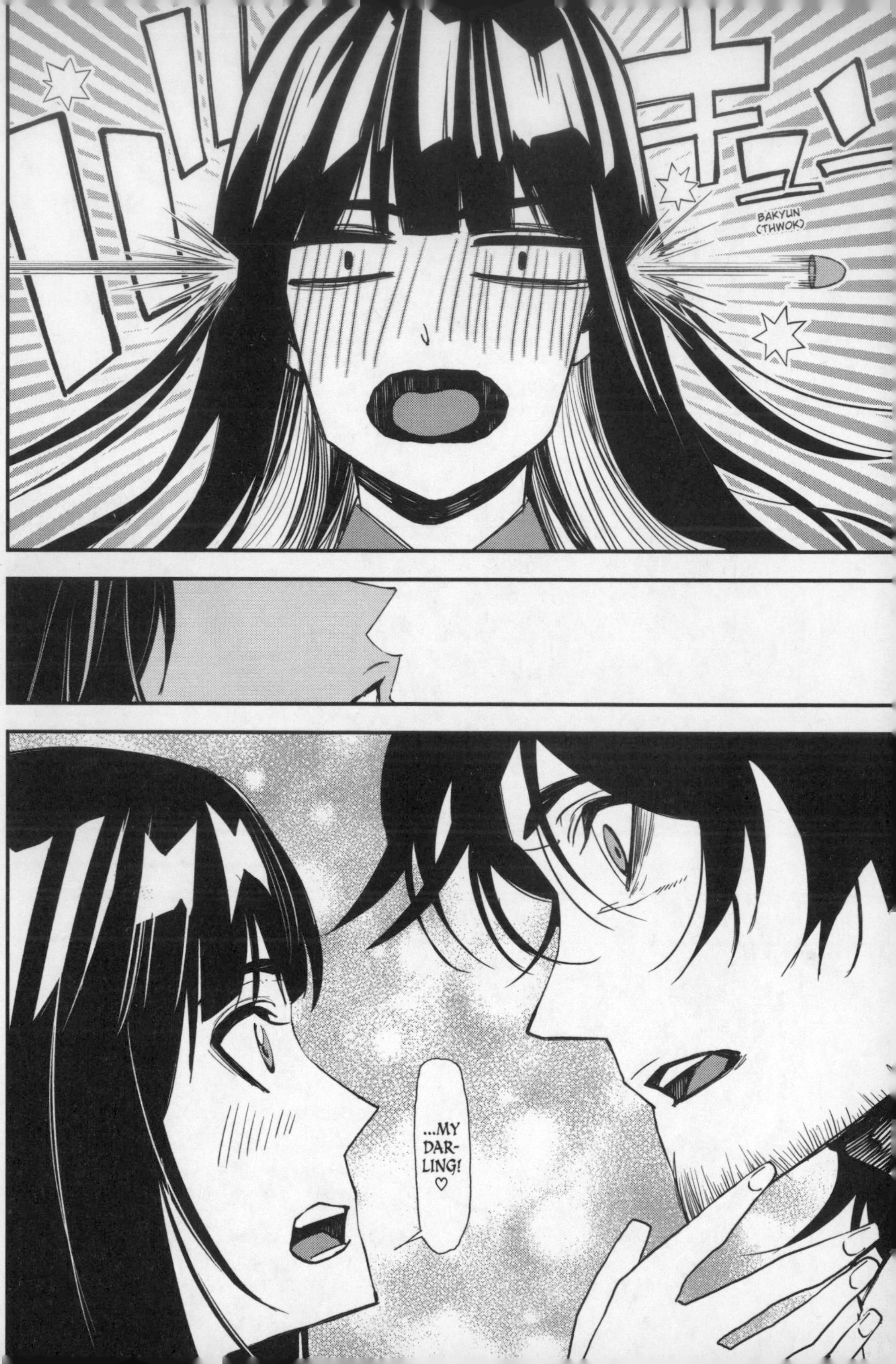
BAKYUN (THWOK)
...MY DAR-LING! ♡

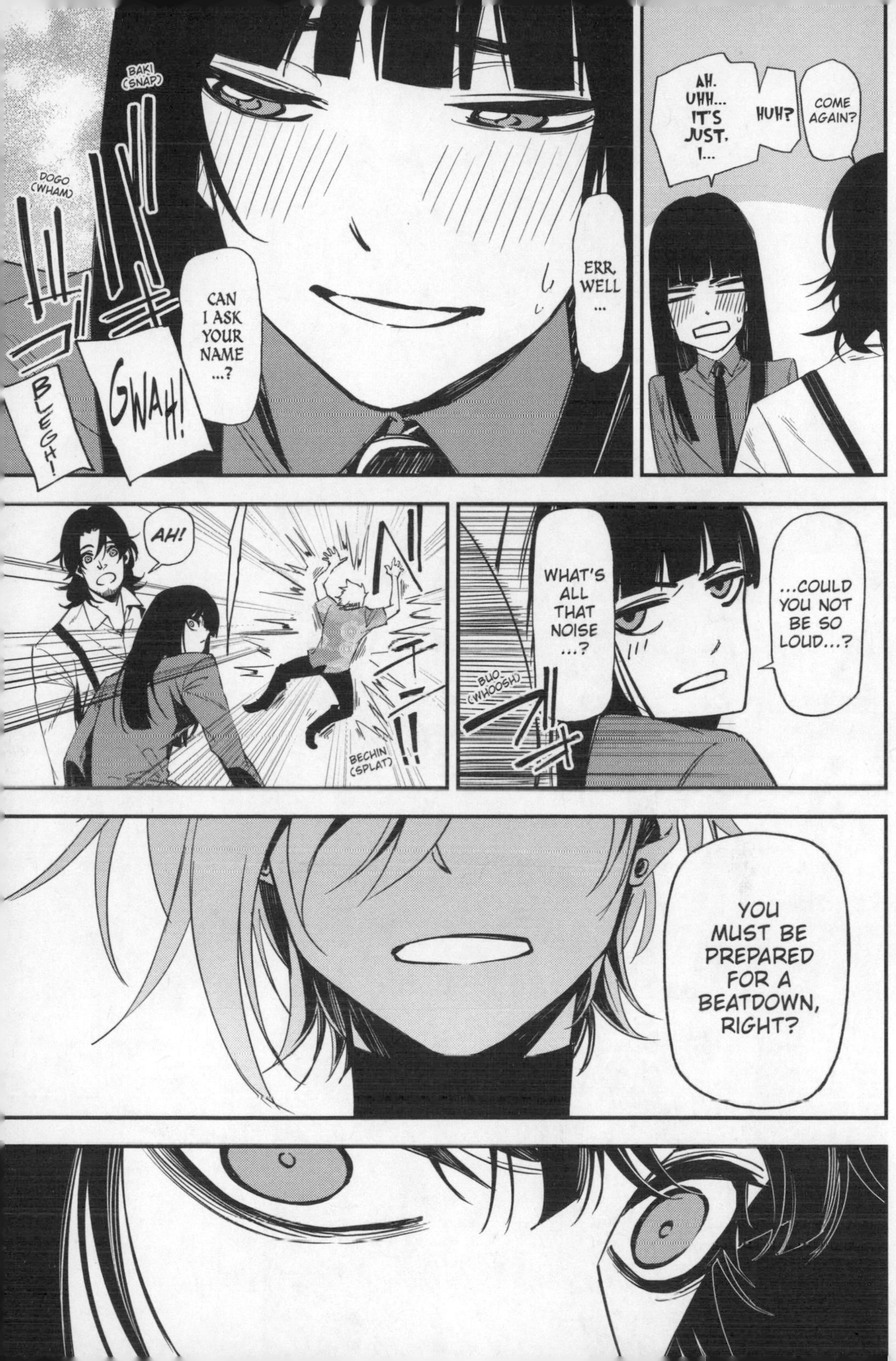
COME AGAIN?
HUH?
AH. UHH... IT'S JUST, I...
ERR, WELL ...
CAN I ASK YOUR NAME ...?
BAKI (SNAP)
DOGO (WHAM)
GWAH!
BLEGH!
...COULD YOU NOT BE SO LOUD...?
WHAT'S ALL THAT NOISE ...?
BUO (WHOOSH)
AH!
BECHIN (SPLAT)
YOU MUST BE PREPARED FOR A BEATDOWN, RIGHT?

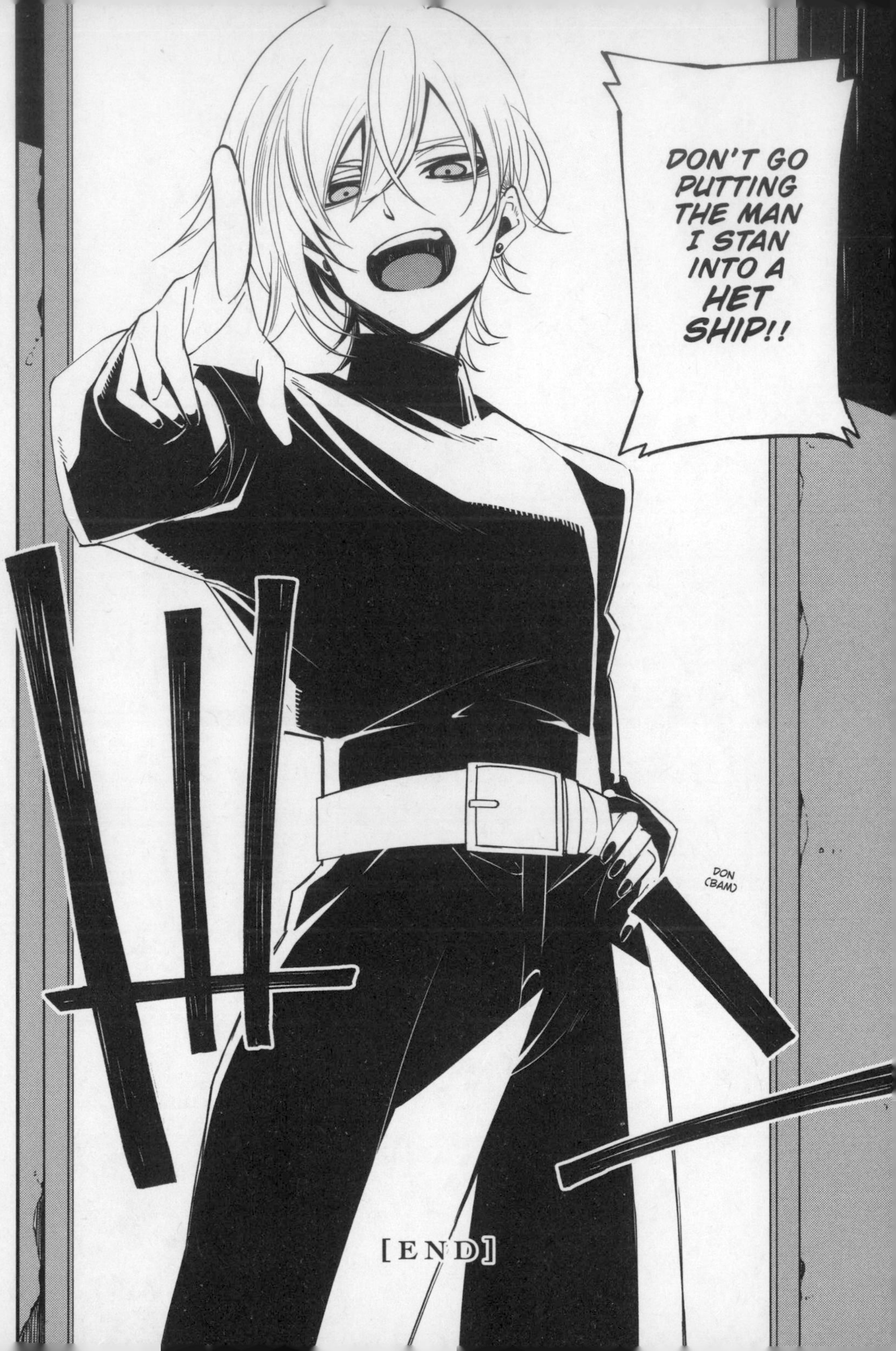
DON'T GO PUTTING THE MAN I STAN INTO A HET SHIP!!
DON (BAM)
[END]

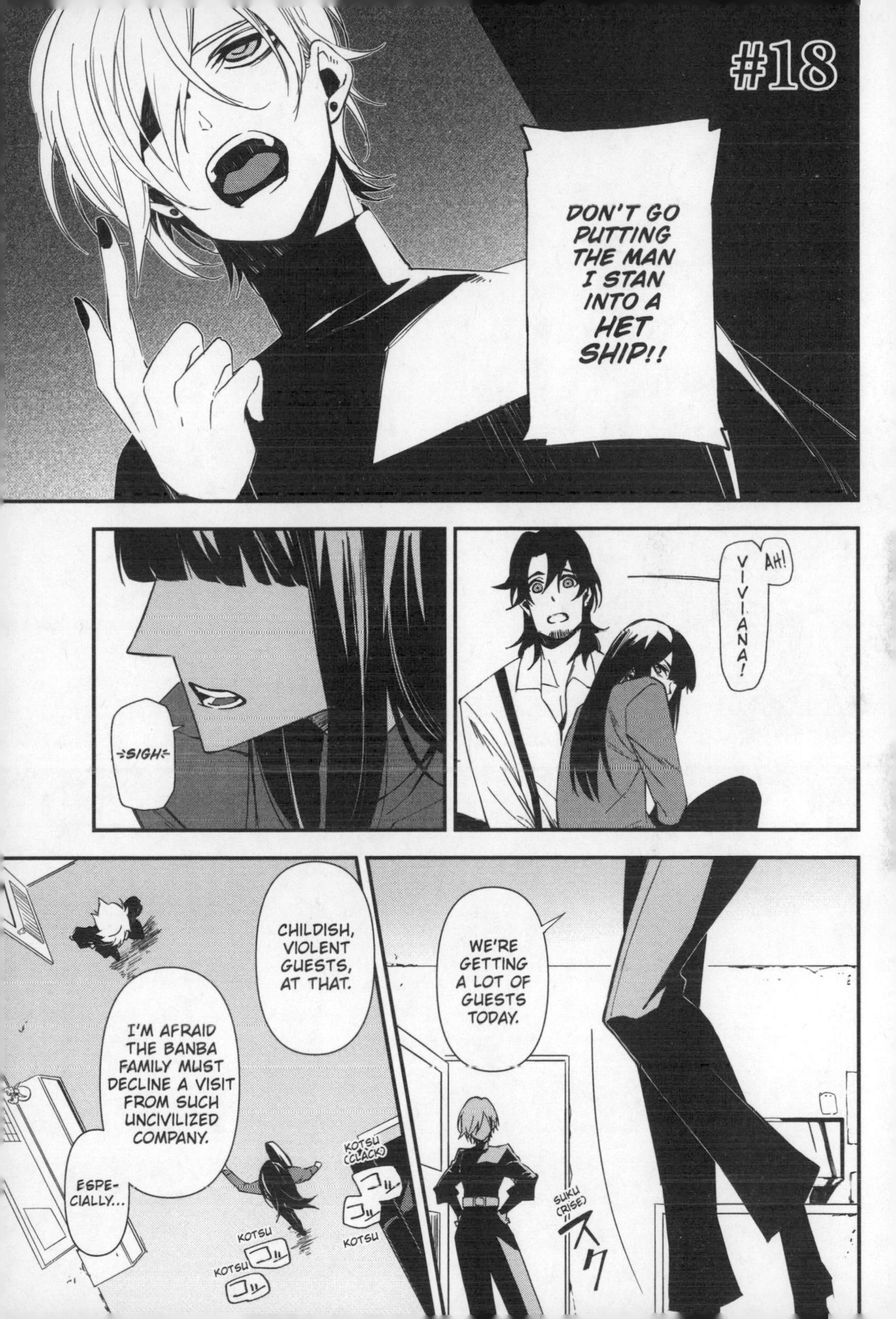
#18
DON'T GO PUTTING THE MAN I STAN INTO A HET SHIP!!
AH!
VIVIANA!
≈SIGH≈
WE'RE GETTING A LOT OF GUESTS TODAY.
SUKU (RISE)
スク
CHILDISH, VIOLENT GUESTS, AT THAT.
I'M AFRAID THE BANBA FAMILY MUST DECLINE A VISIT FROM SUCH UNCIVILIZED COMPANY.
ESPE-CIALLY...
KOTSU (CLACK)
コツ
コツ
KOTSU
KOTSU
コツ
KOTSU
コツ

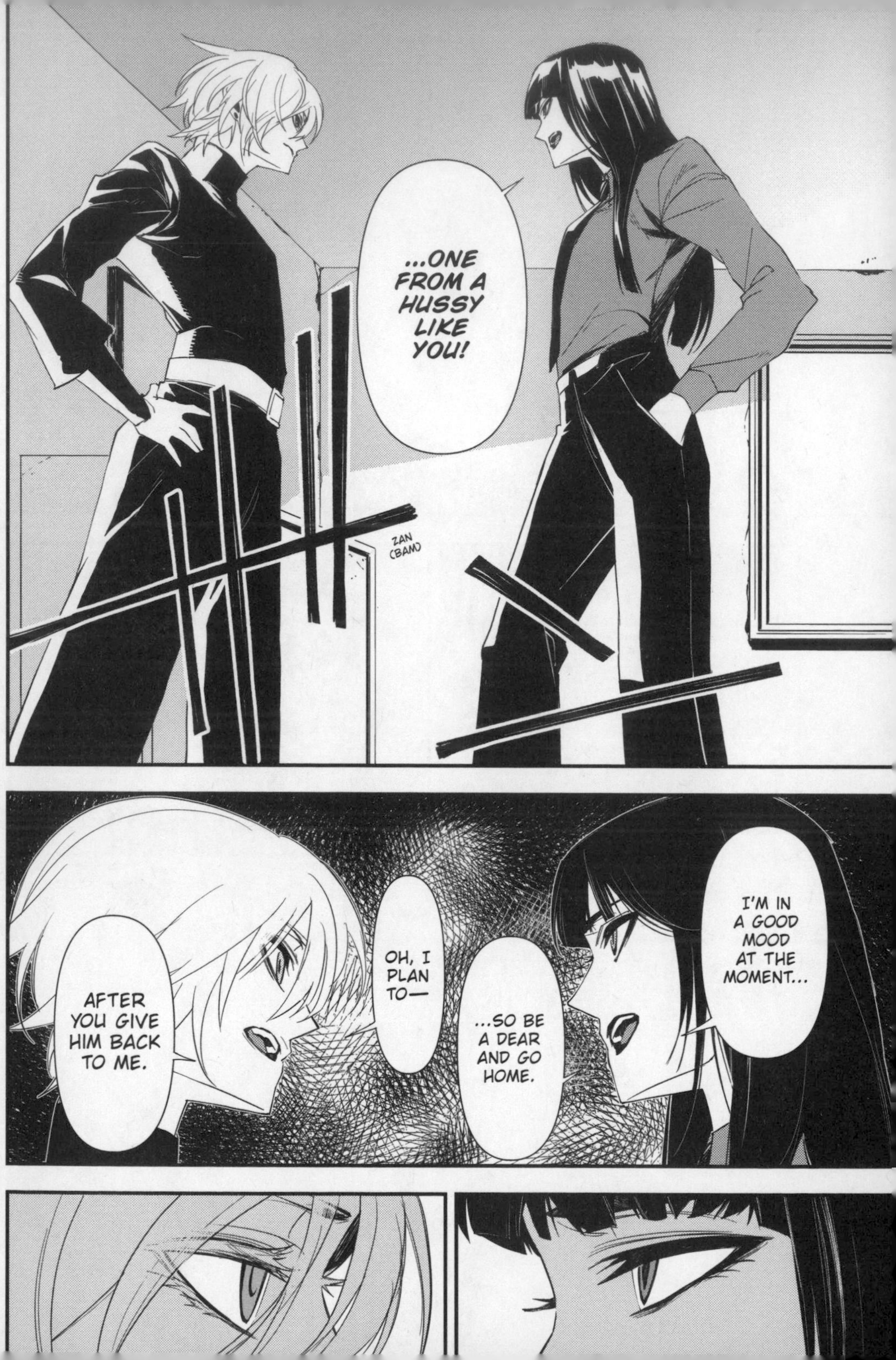
...ONE FROM A HUSSY LIKE YOU!
ZAN (BAM)
I'M IN A GOOD MOOD AT THE MOMENT...
...SO BE A DEAR AND GO HOME.
OH, I PLAN TO—
AFTER YOU GIVE HIM BACK TO ME.

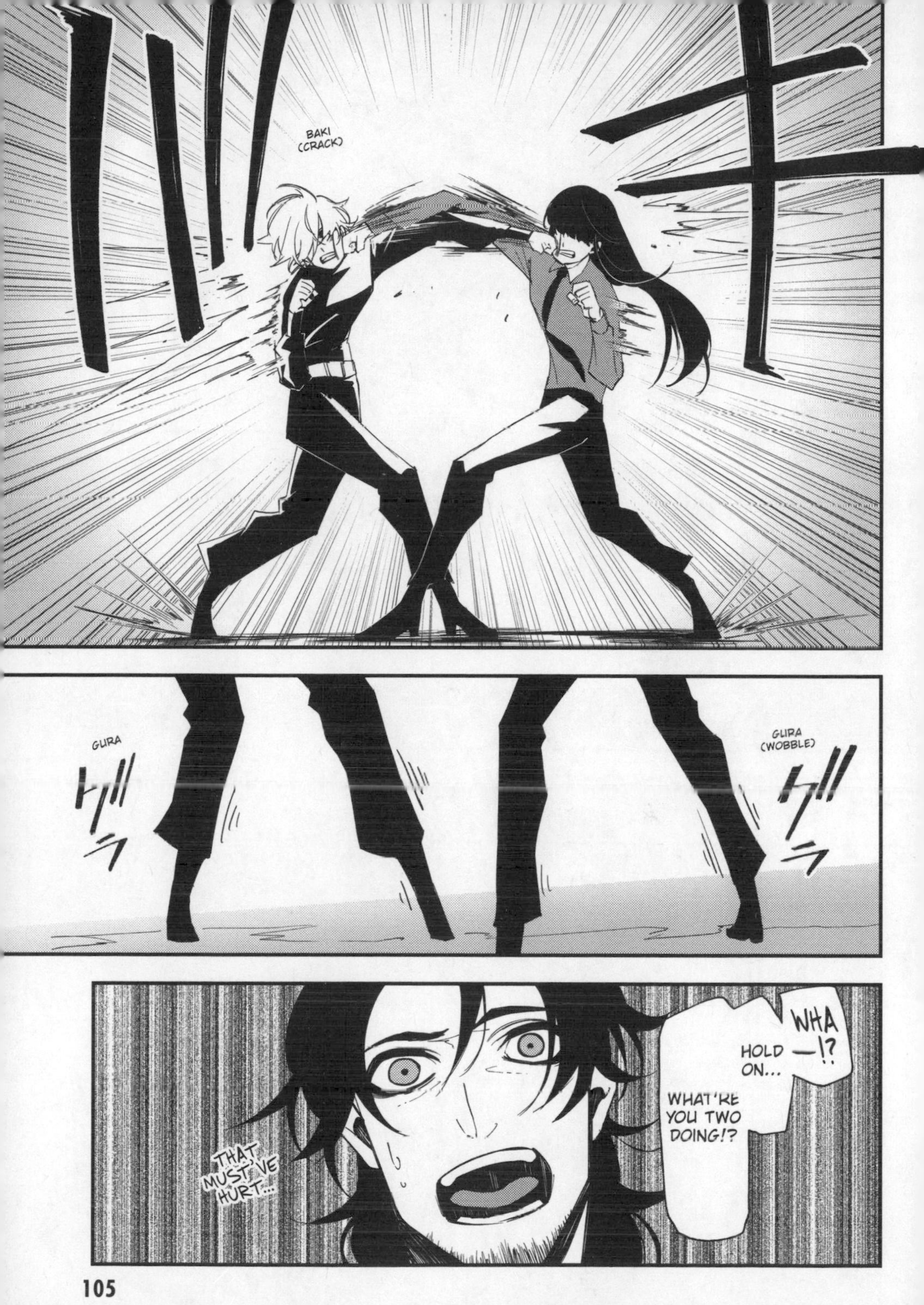
BAKI (CRACK)
GURA (WOBBLE)
GURA
WHA—!?
HOLD ON...
WHAT'RE YOU TWO DOING!?
THAT MUST'VE HURT...

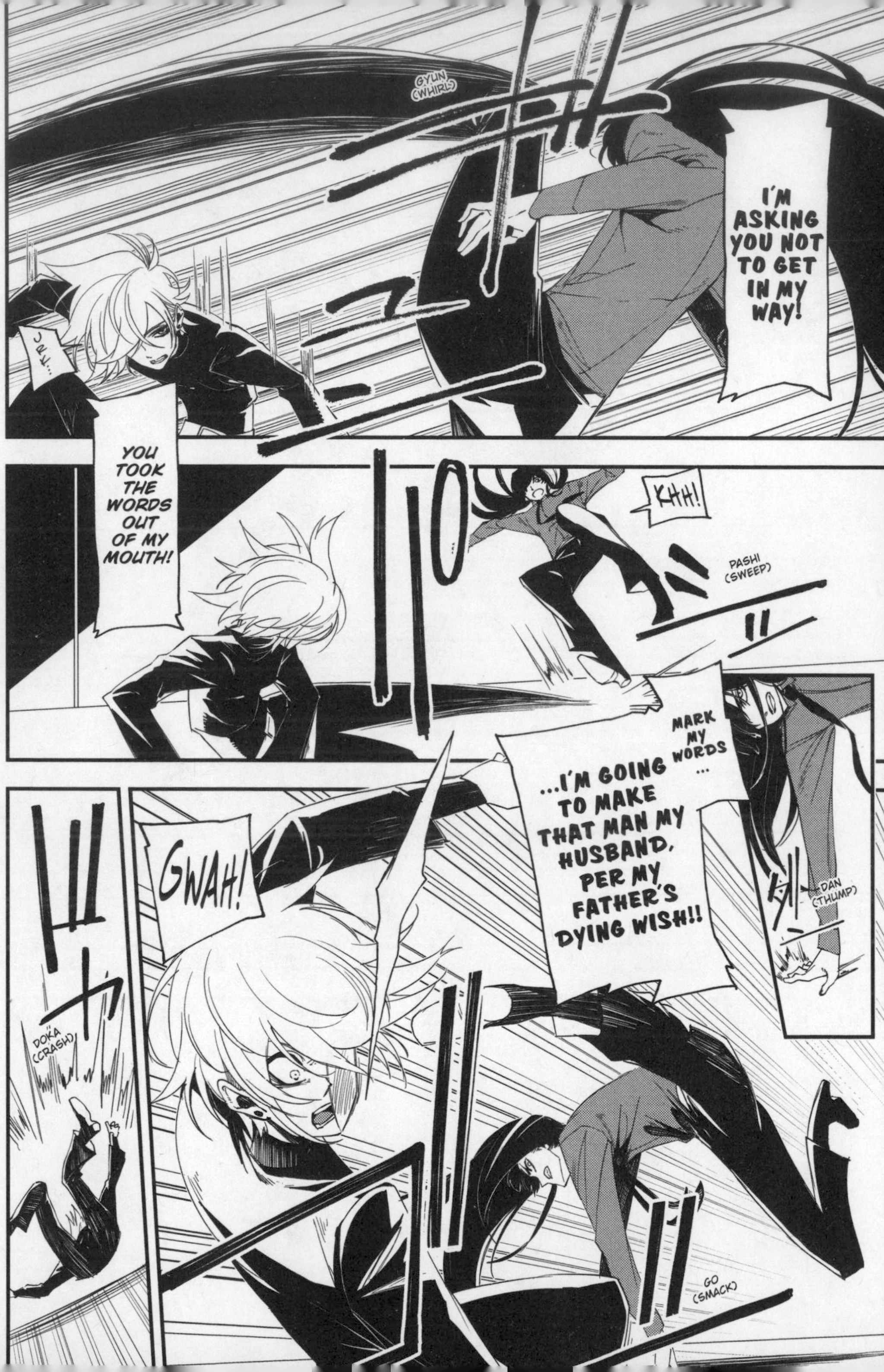
I'M ASKING YOU NOT TO GET IN MY WAY!
GYUN (WHIRL)
URK...
PASHI (SWEEP)
KHH!
YOU TOOK THE WORDS OUT OF MY MOUTH!
DAN (THUMP)
MARK MY WORDS...
...I'M GOING TO MAKE THAT MAN MY HUSBAND, PER MY FATHER'S DYING WISH!!
GWAH!
GO (SMACK)
DOKA (CRASH)

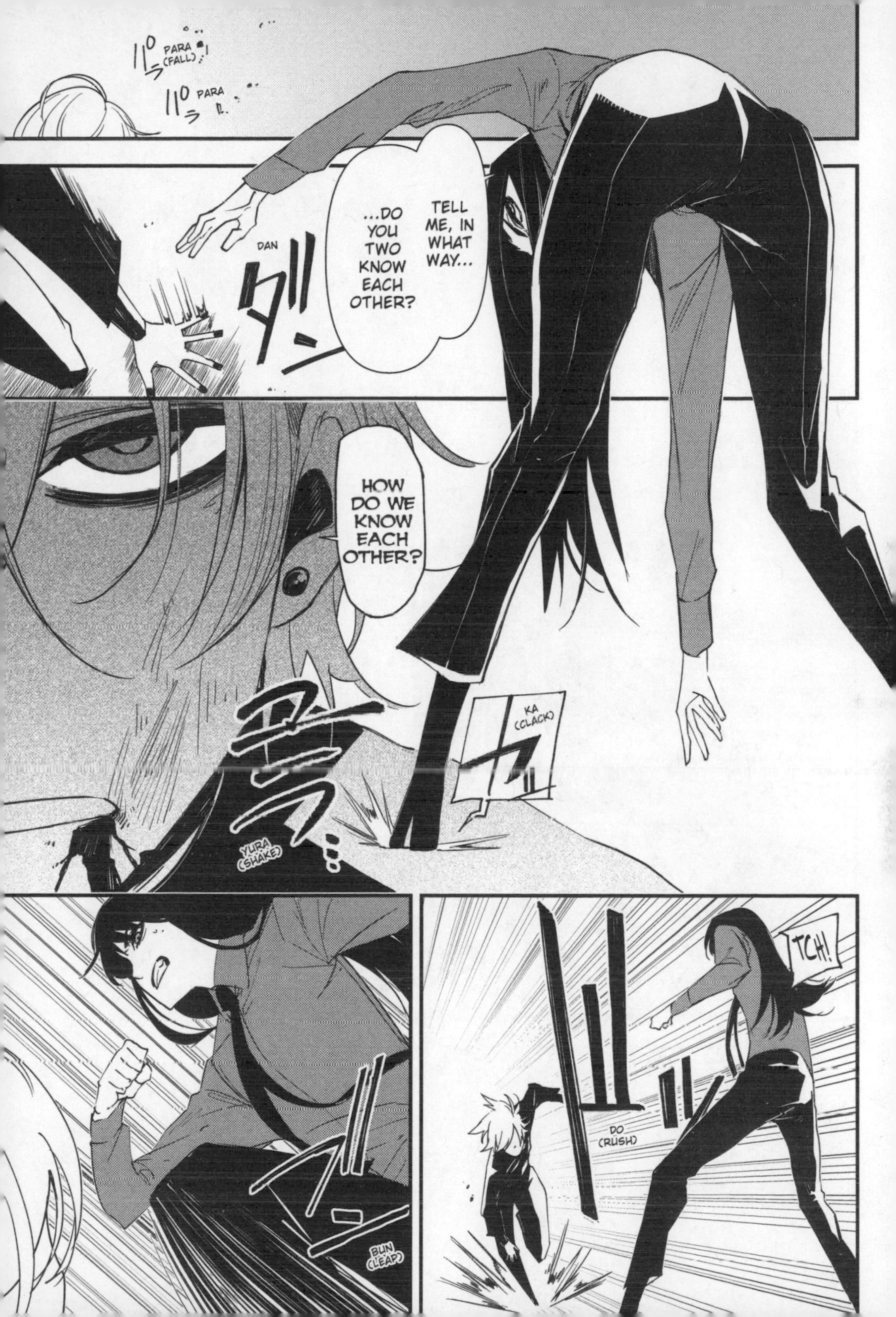
PARA (FALL)
PARA
TELL ME, IN WHAT WAY...
...DO YOU TWO KNOW EACH OTHER?
DAN
HOW DO WE KNOW EACH OTHER?
KA (CLACK)
YURA (SHAKE)
TCH!
DO (RUSH)
BUN (LEAP)

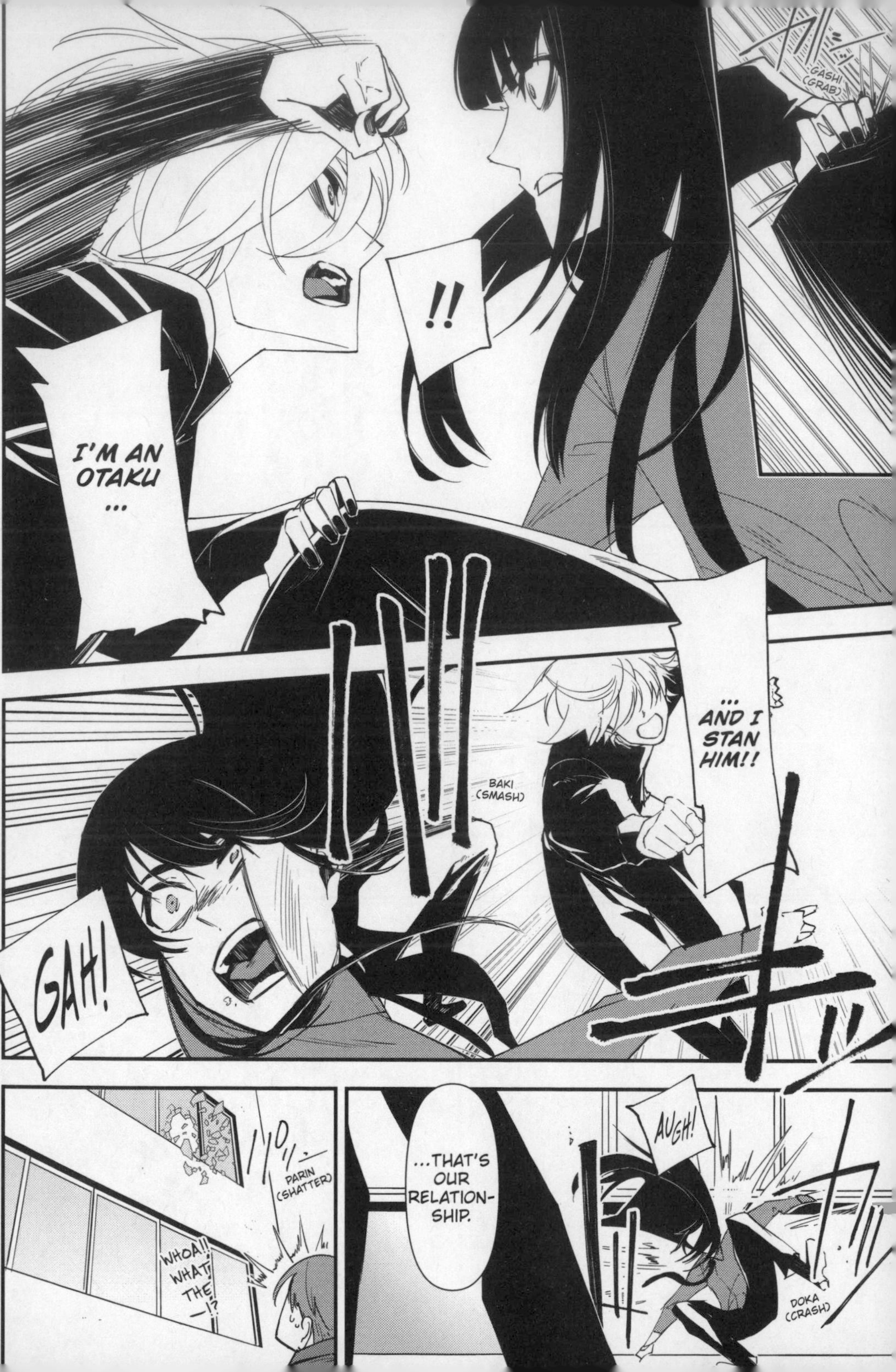

GASHI (GRAB)
!!
I'M AN OTAKU ...
... AND I STAN HIM!!
BAKI (SMASH)
GAH!
AUGH!
DOKA (CRASH)
...THAT'S OUR RELATIONSHIP.
PARIN (SHATTER)
WHOA!! WHAT THE —!?

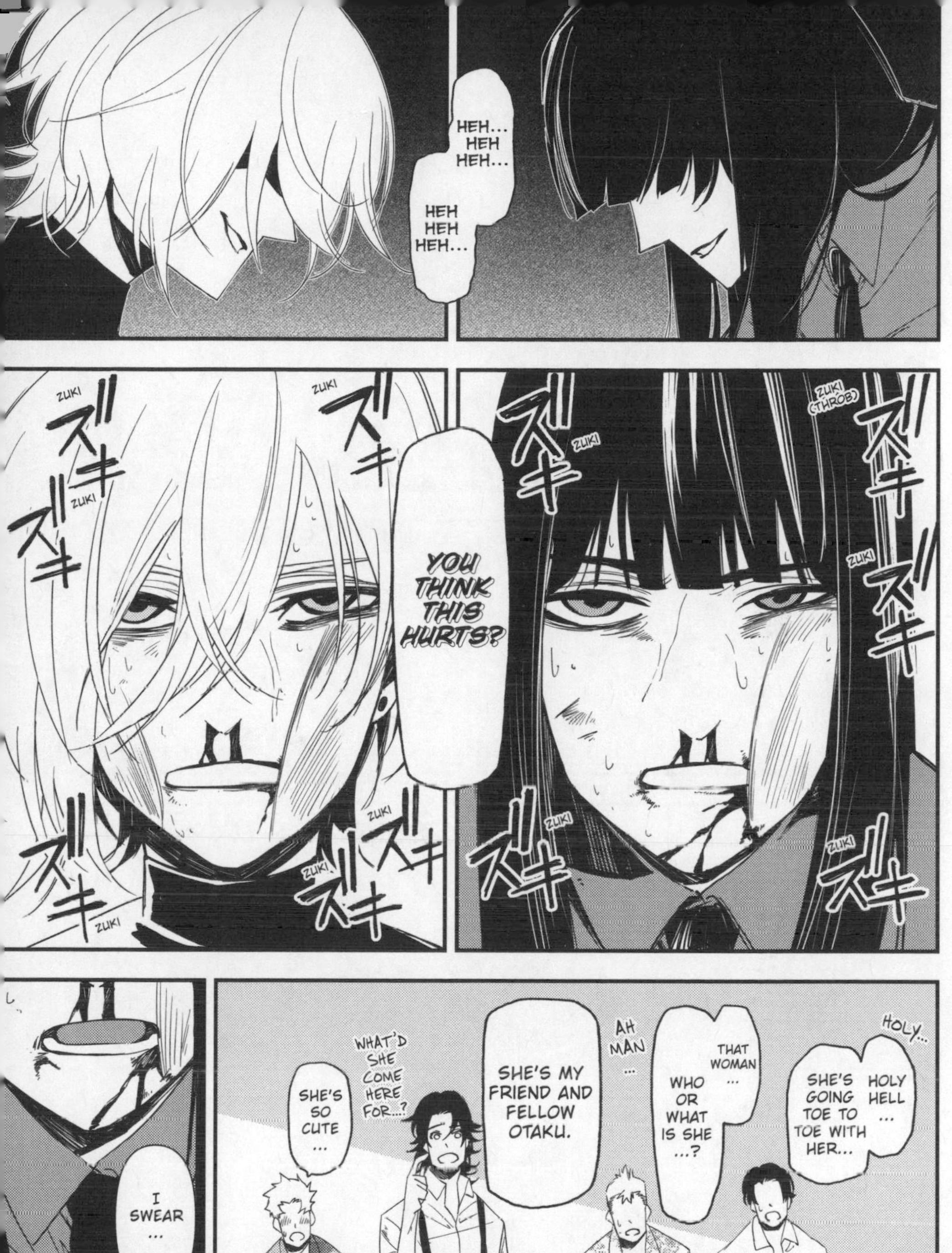
HEH... HEH HEH...
HEH HEH HEH...
ズキ ZUKI (THROB)
ズキ ZUKI
ズキ ZUKI
ズキ ZUKI
ズキ ZUKI
YOU THINK THIS HURTS?
ズキ ZUKI
ズキ ZUKI
ズキ ZUKI
ズキ ZUKI
ズキ ZUKI
ズキ ZUKI
HOLY...
HOLY HELL...
SHE'S GOING TOE TO TOE WITH HER...
THAT WOMAN...
WHO OR WHAT IS SHE...?
AH MAN...
SHE'S MY FRIEND AND FELLOW OTAKU.
WHAT'D SHE COME HERE FOR...?
SHE'S SO CUTE...
I SWEAR...

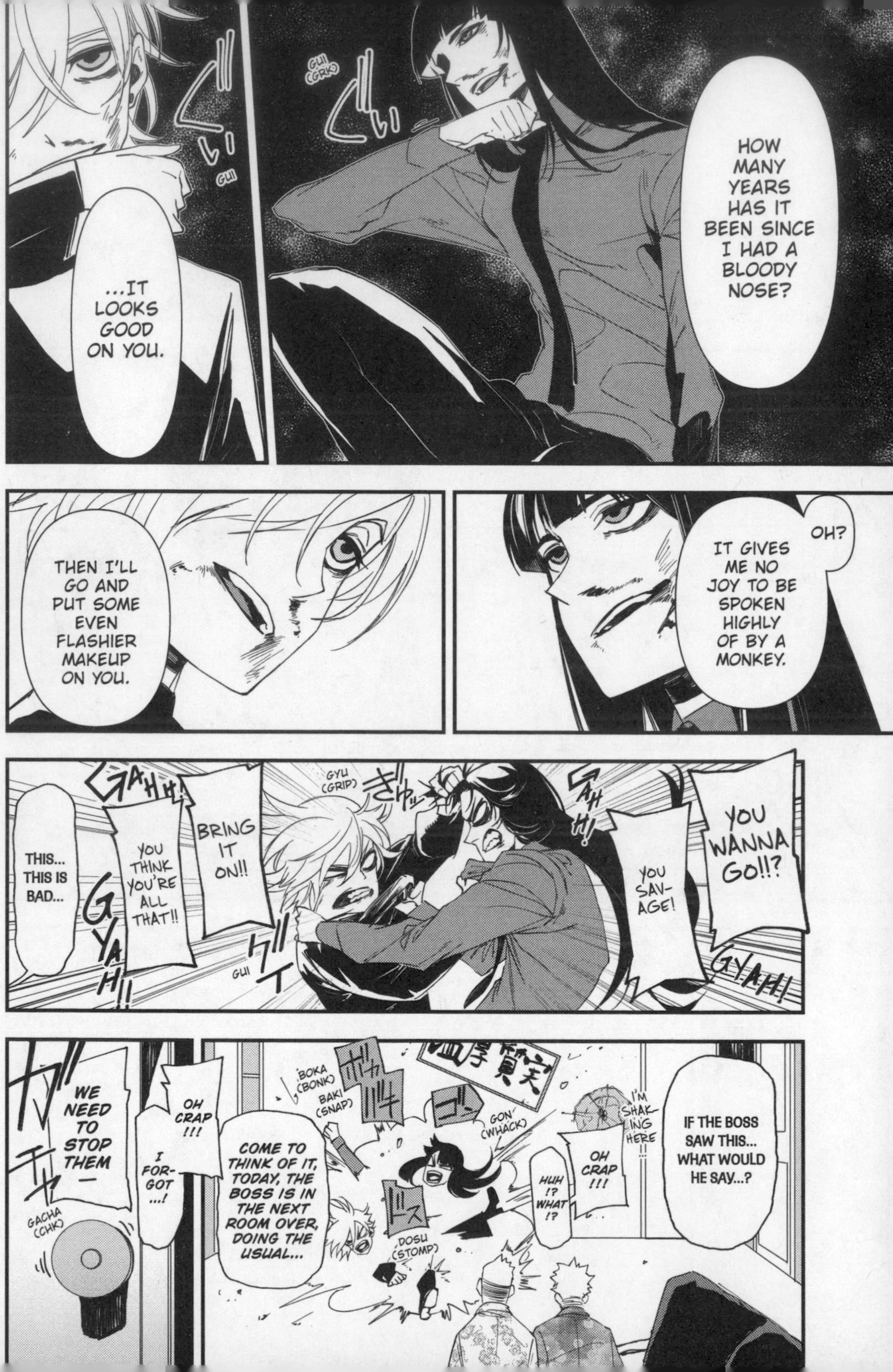
GUI (GRK)
HOW MANY YEARS HAS IT BEEN SINCE I HAD A BLOODY NOSE?
GUI
...IT LOOKS GOOD ON YOU.
OH?
IT GIVES ME NO JOY TO BE SPOKEN HIGHLY OF BY A MONKEY.
THEN I'LL GO AND PUT SOME EVEN FLASHIER MAKEUP ON YOU.
YOU WANNA GO!!?
GYAH!
GAHH!
YOU SAVAGE!
GYU (GRIP)
BRING IT ON!!
YOU THINK YOU'RE ALL THAT!!
GAHH!
GYAH!!
GUI
THIS... THIS IS BAD...
IF THE BOSS SAW THIS... WHAT WOULD HE SAY...?
I'M SHAKING HERE!!
OH CRAP!!!
HUH!? WHAT!?
GON (WHACK)
BOKA (BONK)
BAKI (SNAP)
COME TO THINK OF IT, TODAY, THE BOSS IS IN THE NEXT ROOM OVER, DOING THE USUAL...
DOSU (STOMP)
I FORGOT...!
OH CRAP!!!
WE NEED TO STOP THEM—
GACHA (CHK)

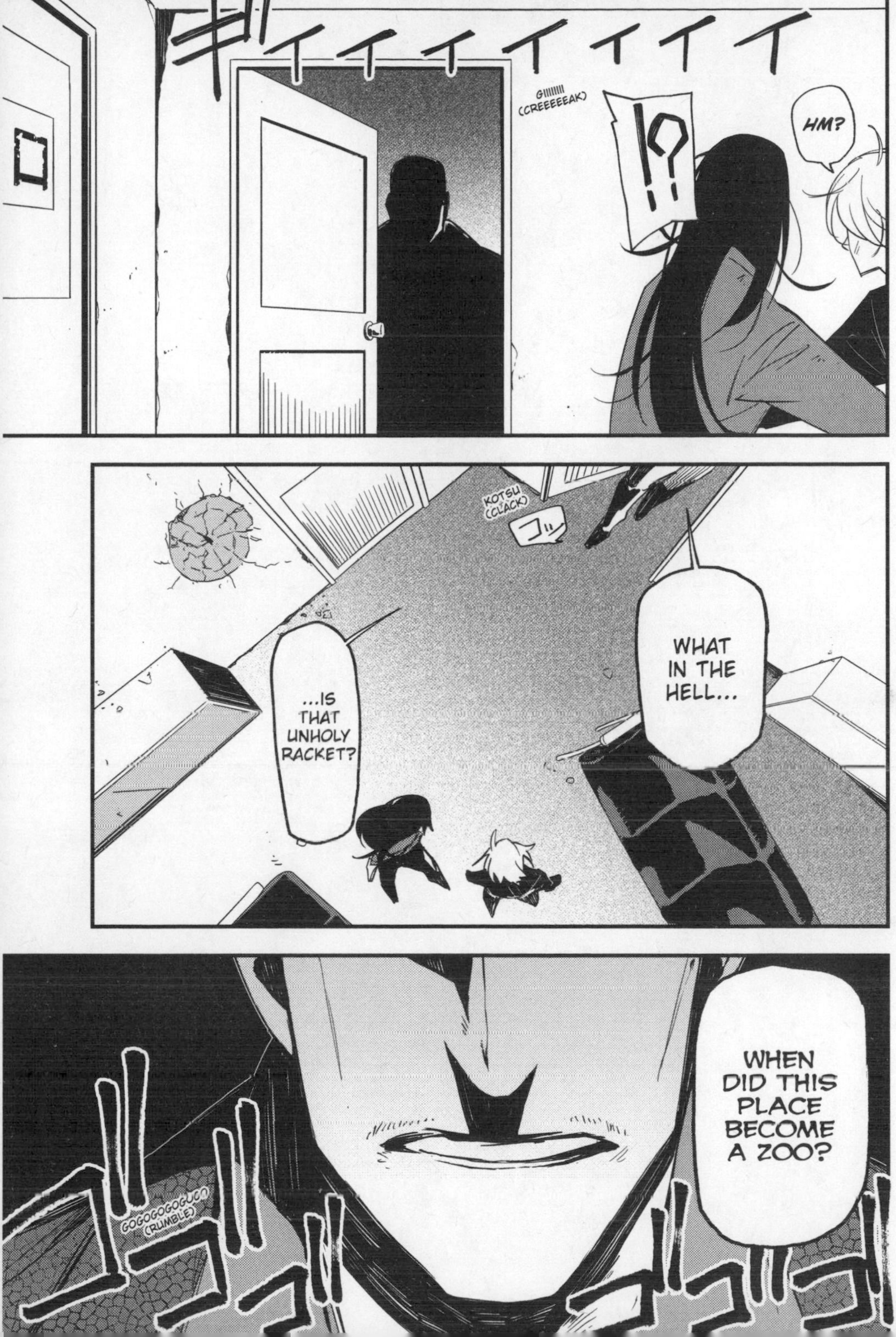
HM?
!?
GIIIIIIIII
(CREEEEEEAK)
KOTSU
(CLACK)
WHAT IN THE HELL...
...IS THAT UNHOLY RACKET?
WHEN DID THIS PLACE BECOME A ZOO?
GOGOGOGOGUCN
(RUMBLE)

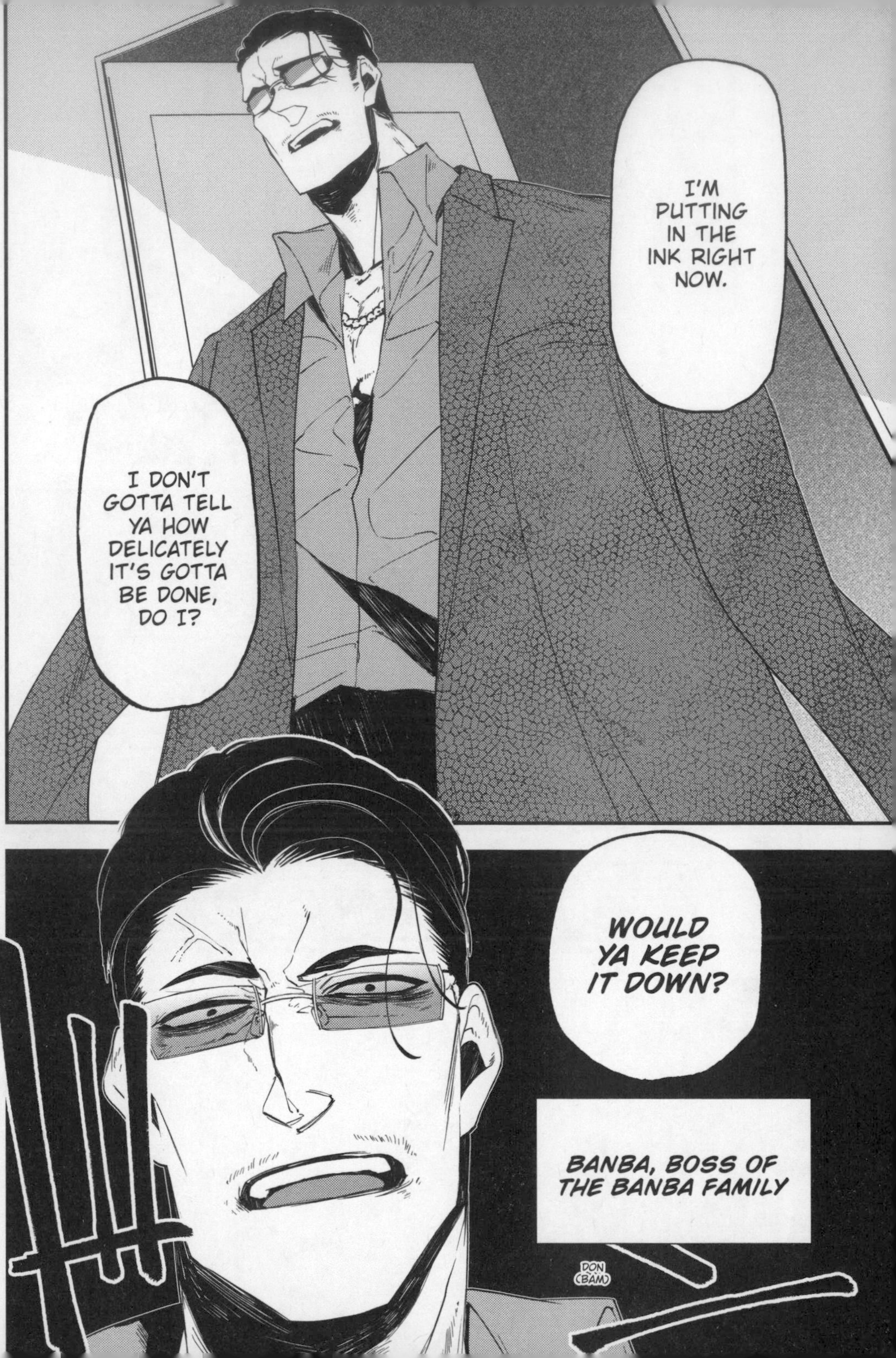
I'M PUTTING IN THE INK RIGHT NOW.
I DON'T GOTTA TELL YA HOW DELICATELY IT'S GOTTA BE DONE, DO I?
WOULD YA KEEP IT DOWN?
BANBA, BOSS OF THE BANBA FAMILY
DON (BAM)

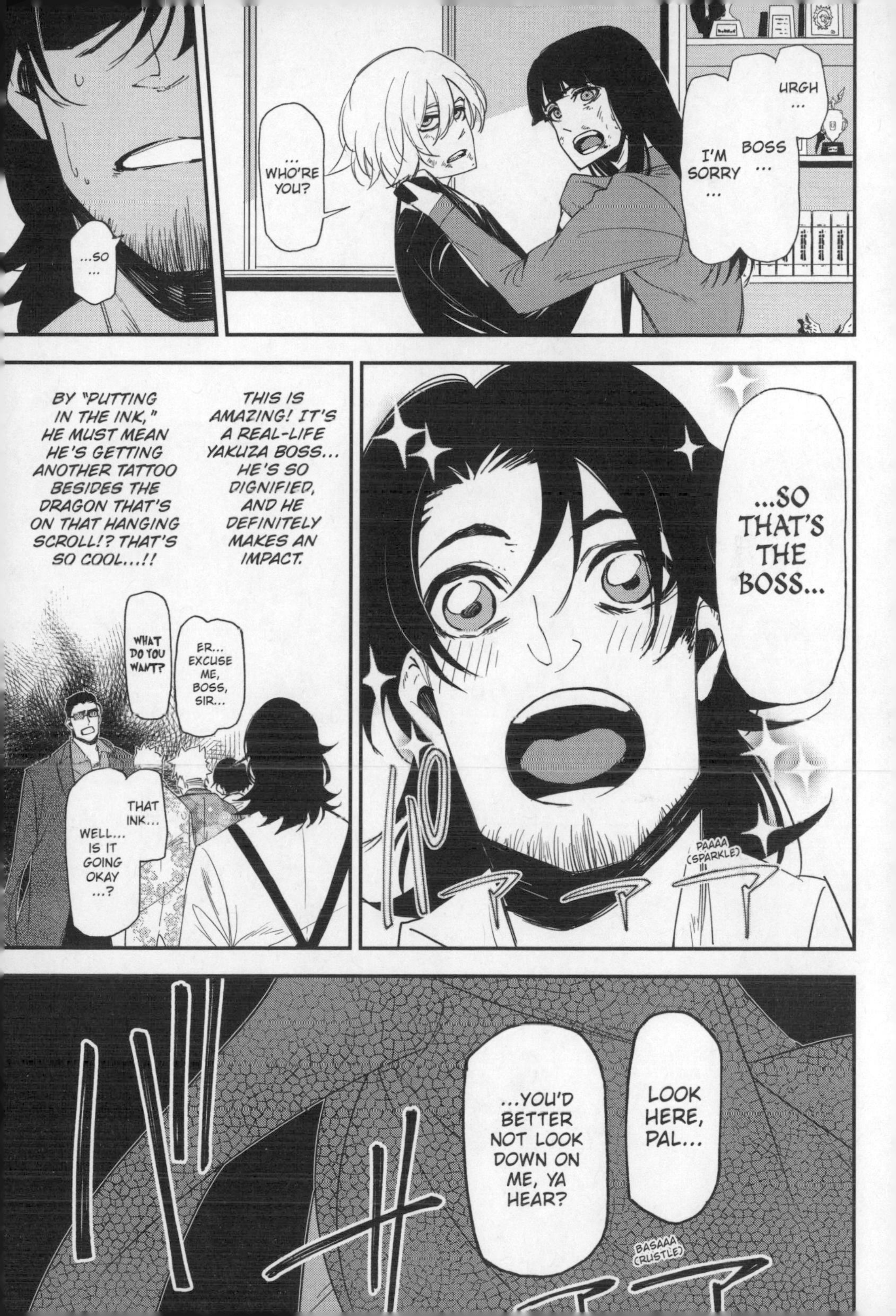
URGH ... BOSS ... I'M SORRY ...
... WHO'RE YOU?
...SO ...
...SO THAT'S THE BOSS...
PAAAA (SPARKLE)
THIS IS AMAZING! IT'S A REAL-LIFE YAKUZA BOSS... HE'S SO DIGNIFIED, AND HE DEFINITELY MAKES AN IMPACT.
BY "PUTTING IN THE INK," HE MUST MEAN HE'S GETTING ANOTHER TATTOO BESIDES THE DRAGON THAT'S ON THAT HANGING SCROLL!? THAT'S SO COOL...!!
ER... EXCUSE ME, BOSS, SIR...
WHAT DO YOU WANT?
THAT INK... WELL... IS IT GOING OKAY ...?
LOOK HERE, PAL...
...YOU'D BETTER NOT LOOK DOWN ON ME, YA HEAR?
BASAAA (RUSTLE)

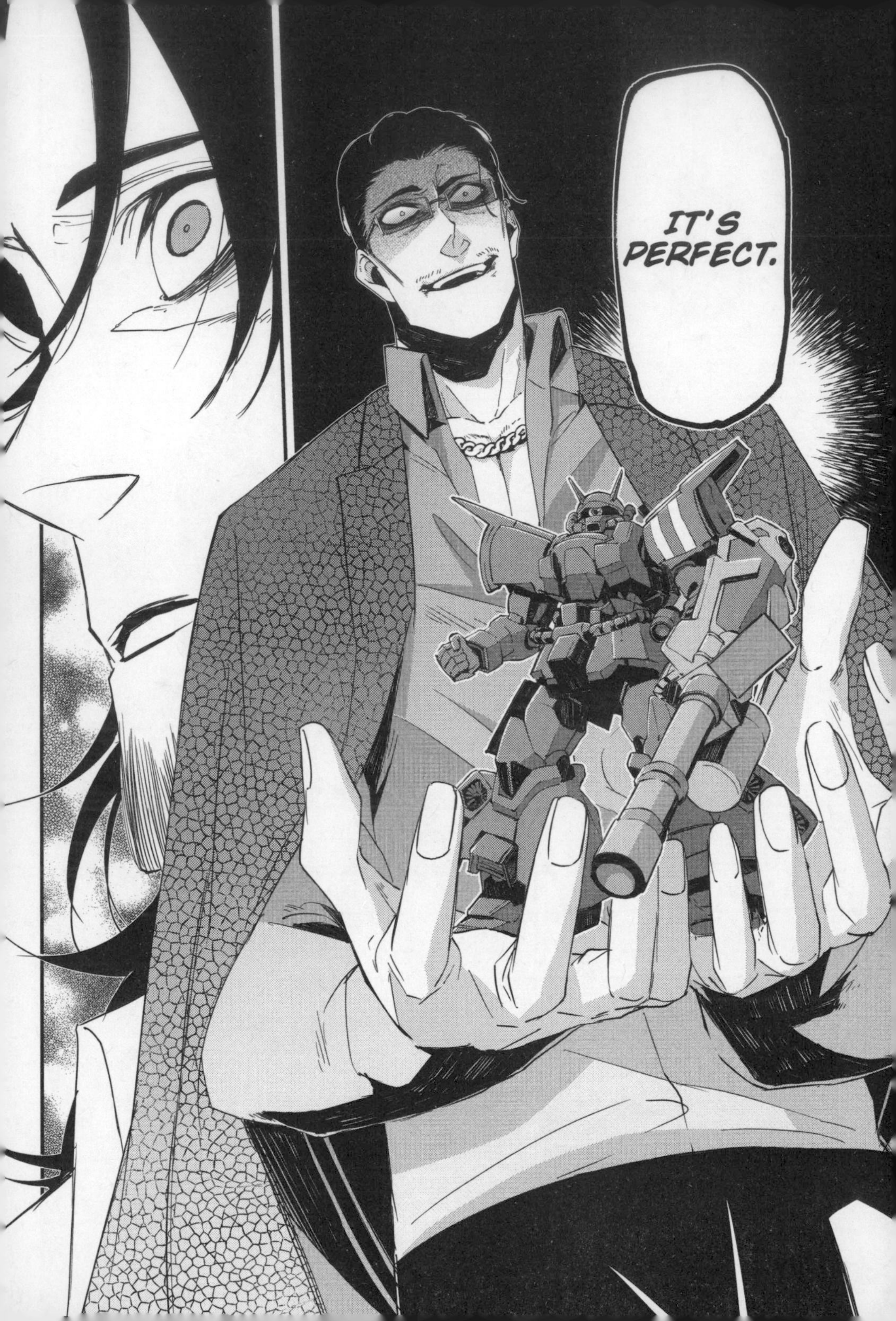
IT'S PERFECT.

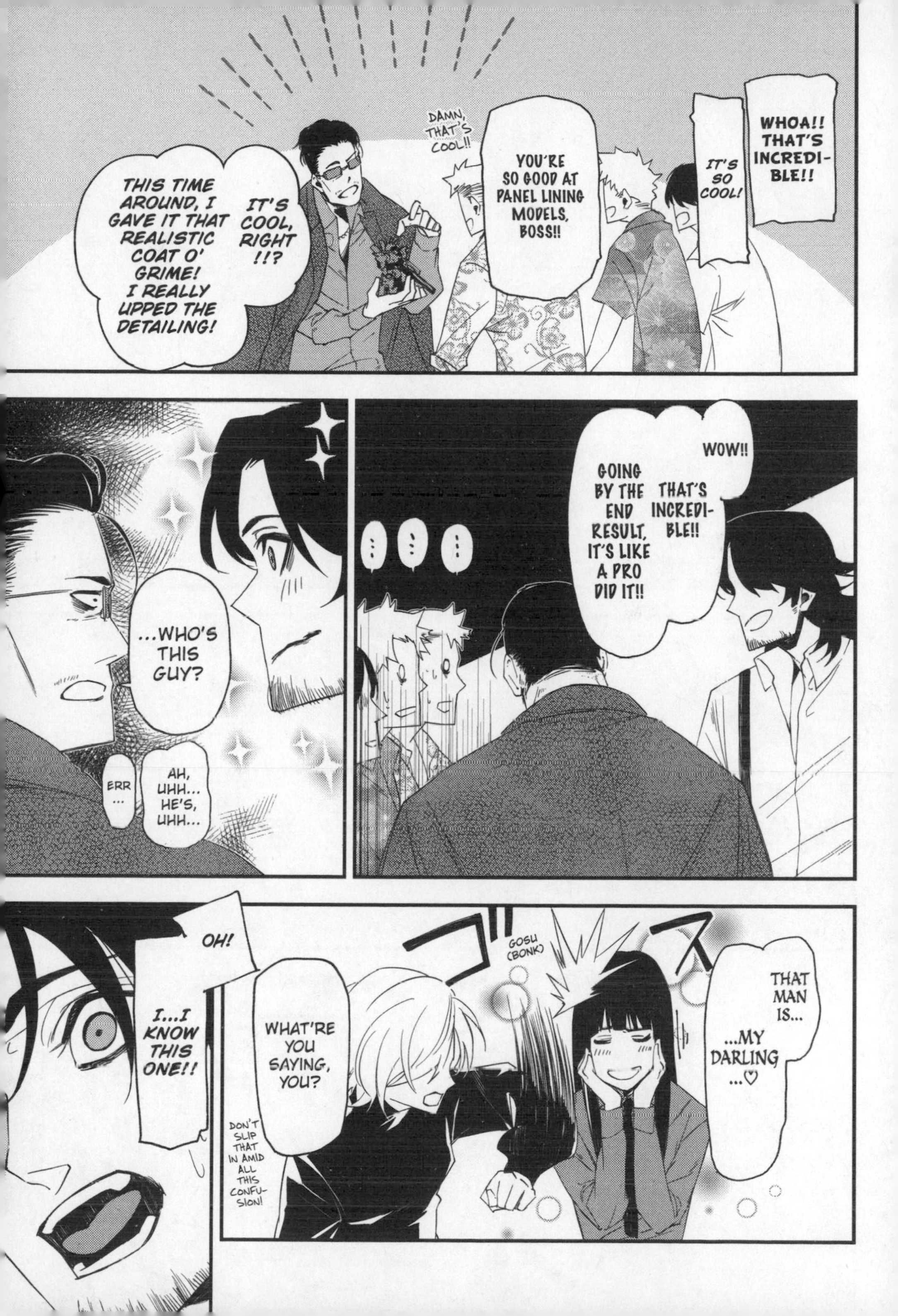
WHOA!! THAT'S INCREDI-BLE!!
IT'S SO COOL!
YOU'RE SO GOOD AT PANEL LINING MODELS, BOSS!!
DAMN, THAT'S COOL!!
IT'S COOL, RIGHT!!?
THIS TIME AROUND, I GAVE IT THAT REALISTIC COAT O' GRIME! I REALLY UPPED THE DETAILING!
WOW!! THAT'S INCREDI-BLE!!
GOING BY THE END RESULT, IT'S LIKE A PRO DID IT!!
...
...
...
...WHO'S THIS GUY?
AH, UHH... HE'S, UHH...
ERR...
THAT MAN IS...
...MY DARLING ...♡
GOSU (BONK)
WHAT'RE YOU SAYING, YOU?
DON'T SLIP THAT IN AMID ALL THIS CONFU-SION!
OH!
I...I KNOW THIS ONE!!

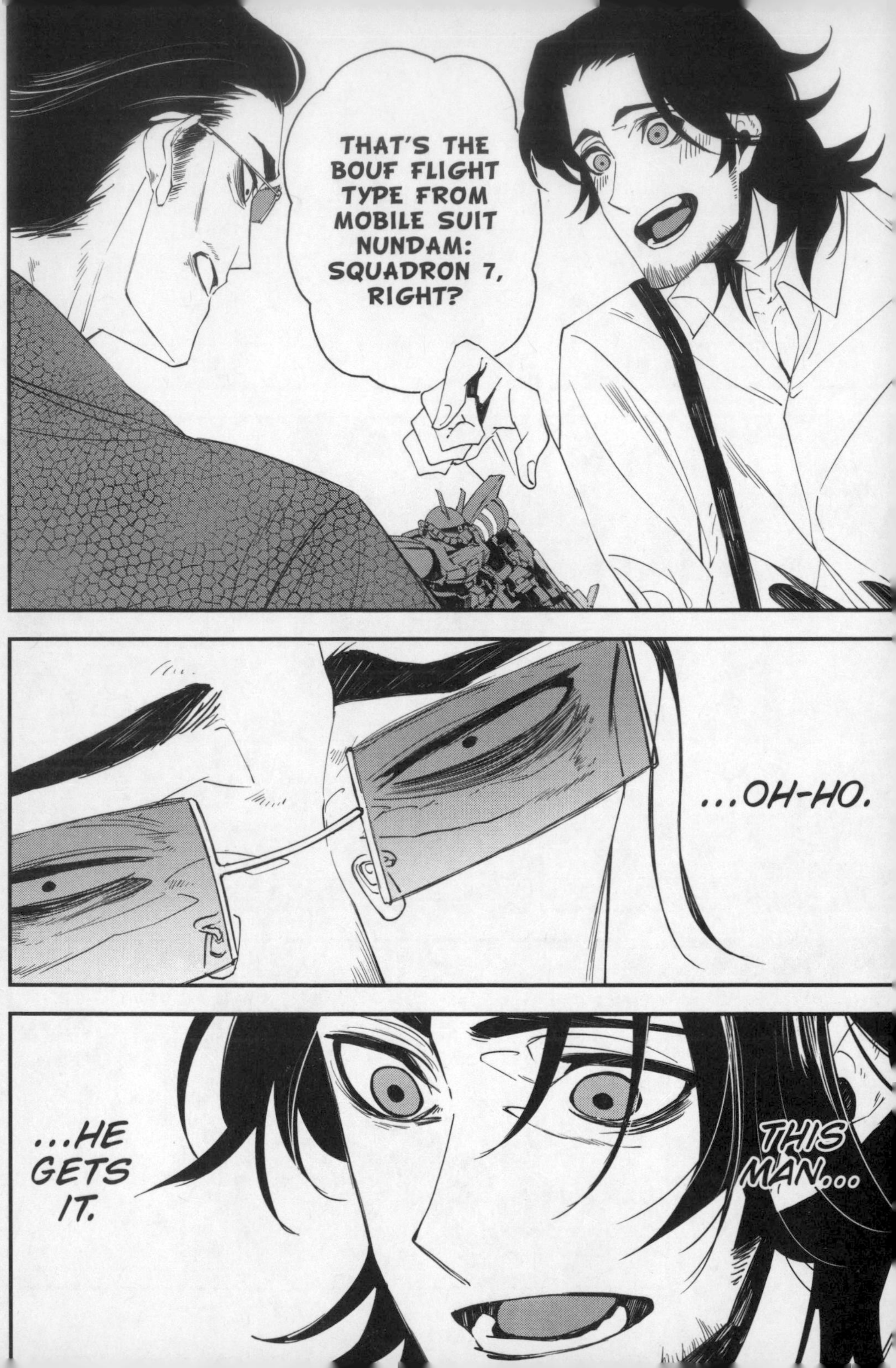
THAT'S THE BOUF FLIGHT TYPE FROM MOBILE SUIT NUNDAM: SQUADRON 7, RIGHT?
...OH-HO.
THIS MAN...
...HE GETS IT.

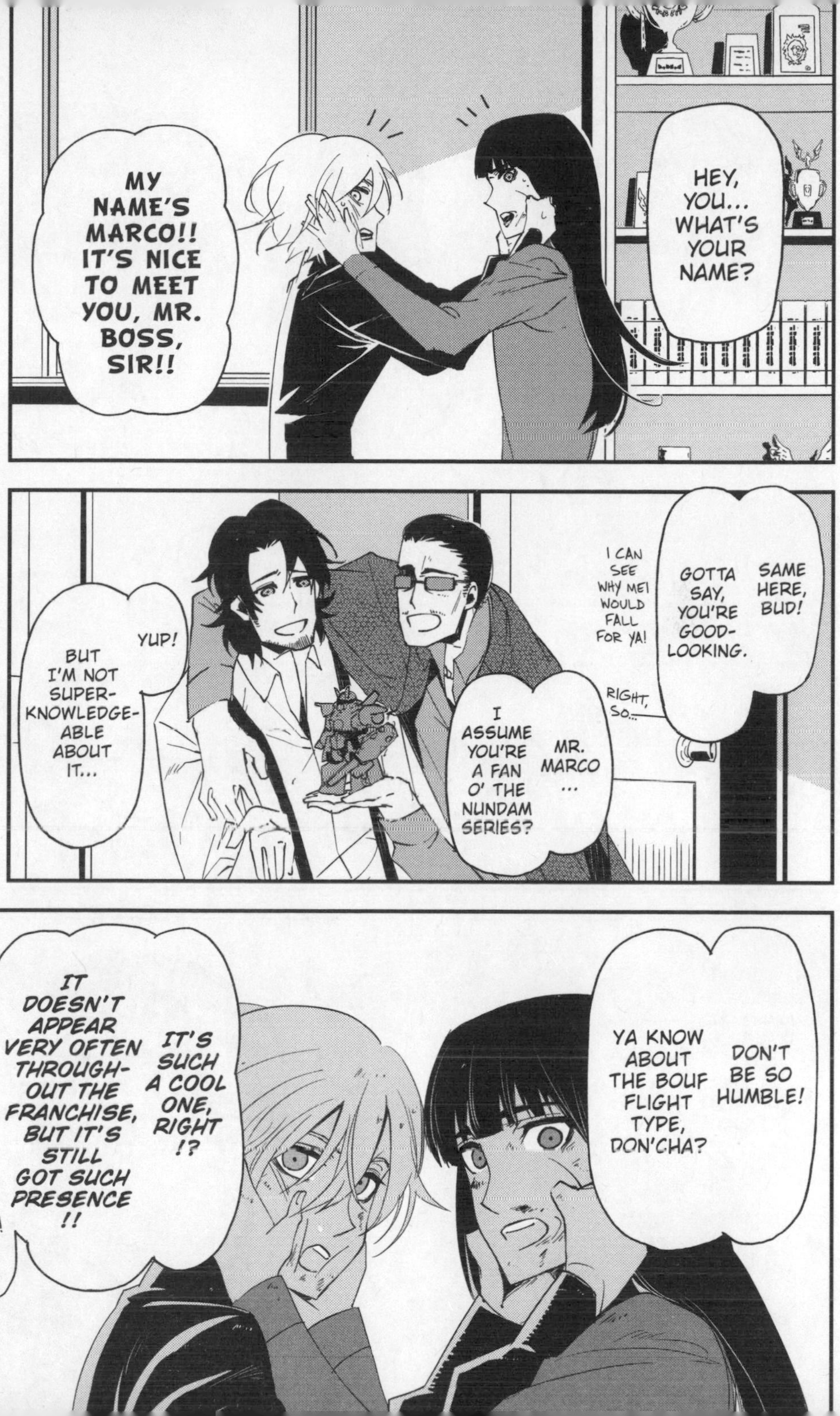
HEY, YOU... WHAT'S YOUR NAME?
MY NAME'S MARCO!! IT'S NICE TO MEET YOU, MR. BOSS, SIR!!
SAME HERE, BUD!
GOTTA SAY, YOU'RE GOOD-LOOKING.
I CAN SEE WHY MEI WOULD FALL FOR YA!
RIGHT, SO...
MR. MARCO...
I ASSUME YOU'RE A FAN O' THE NUNDAM SERIES?
YUP!
BUT I'M NOT SUPER-KNOWLEDGE-ABLE ABOUT IT...
DON'T BE SO HUMBLE!
YA KNOW ABOUT THE BOUF FLIGHT TYPE, DON'CHA?
IT'S SUCH A COOL ONE, RIGHT!?
IT DOESN'T APPEAR VERY OFTEN THROUGH-OUT THE FRANCHISE, BUT IT'S STILL GOT SUCH PRESENCE!!
IT'S SO BAD-ASS!!

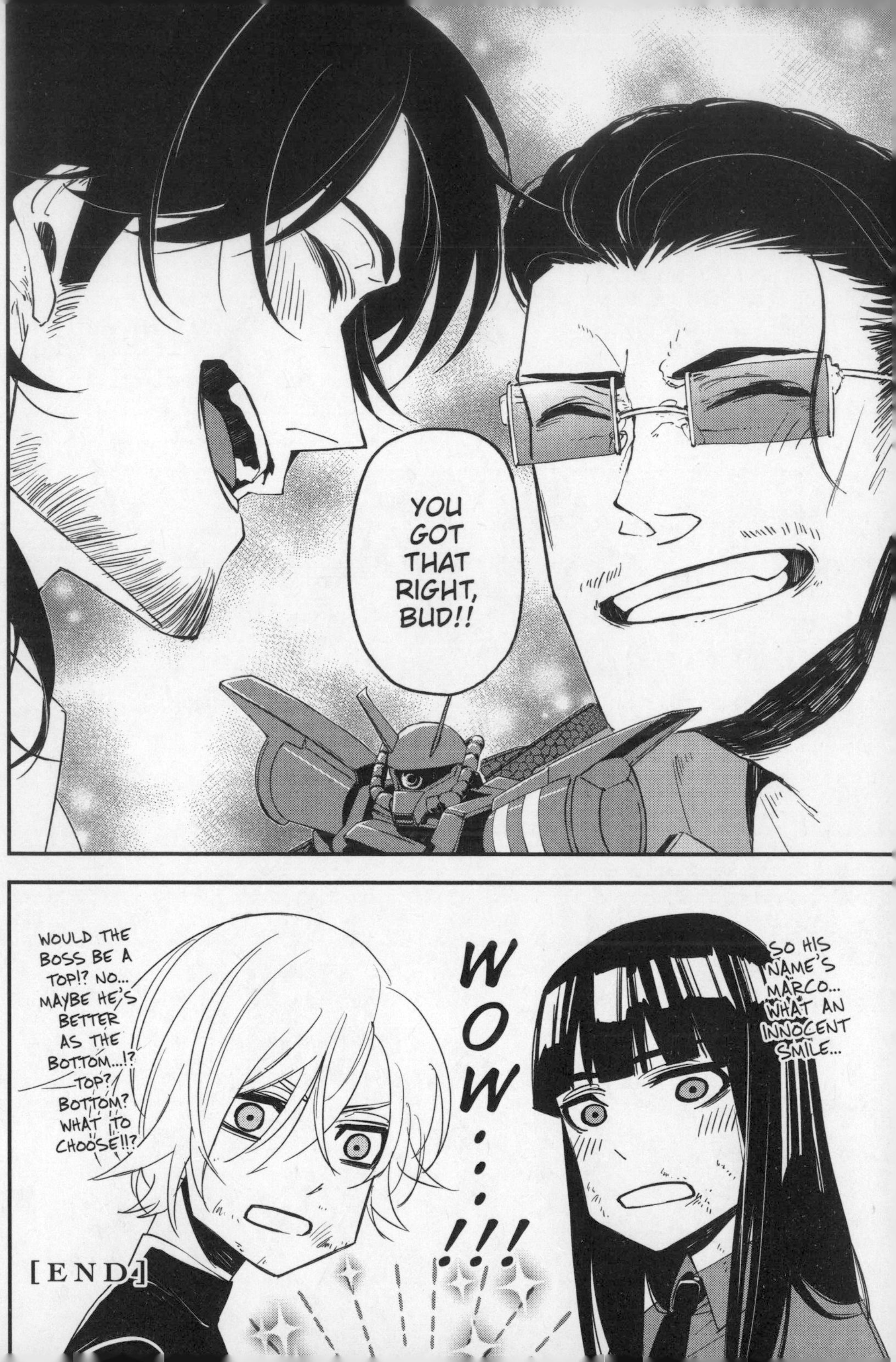
YOU GOT THAT RIGHT, BUD!!
SO HIS NAME'S MARCO... WHAT AN INNOCENT SMILE...
WOW...!!!
WOULD THE BOSS BE A TOP!? NO... MAYBE HE'S BETTER AS THE BOTTOM...!?
TOP? BOTTOM? WHAT TO CHOOSE!!?
[END]

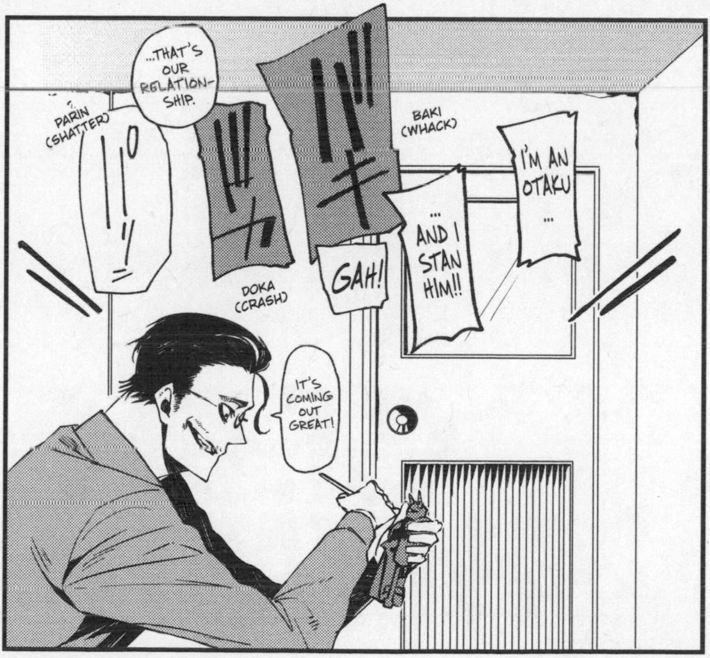
I'M AN OTAKU ...
BAKI (WHACK)
... AND I STAN HIM!!
GAH!
...THAT'S OUR RELATION-SHIP.
PARIN (SHATTER)
DOKA (CRASH)
IT'S COMING OUT GREAT!

THE GEEK EX-HITMAN

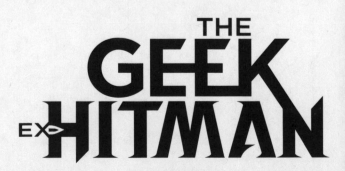

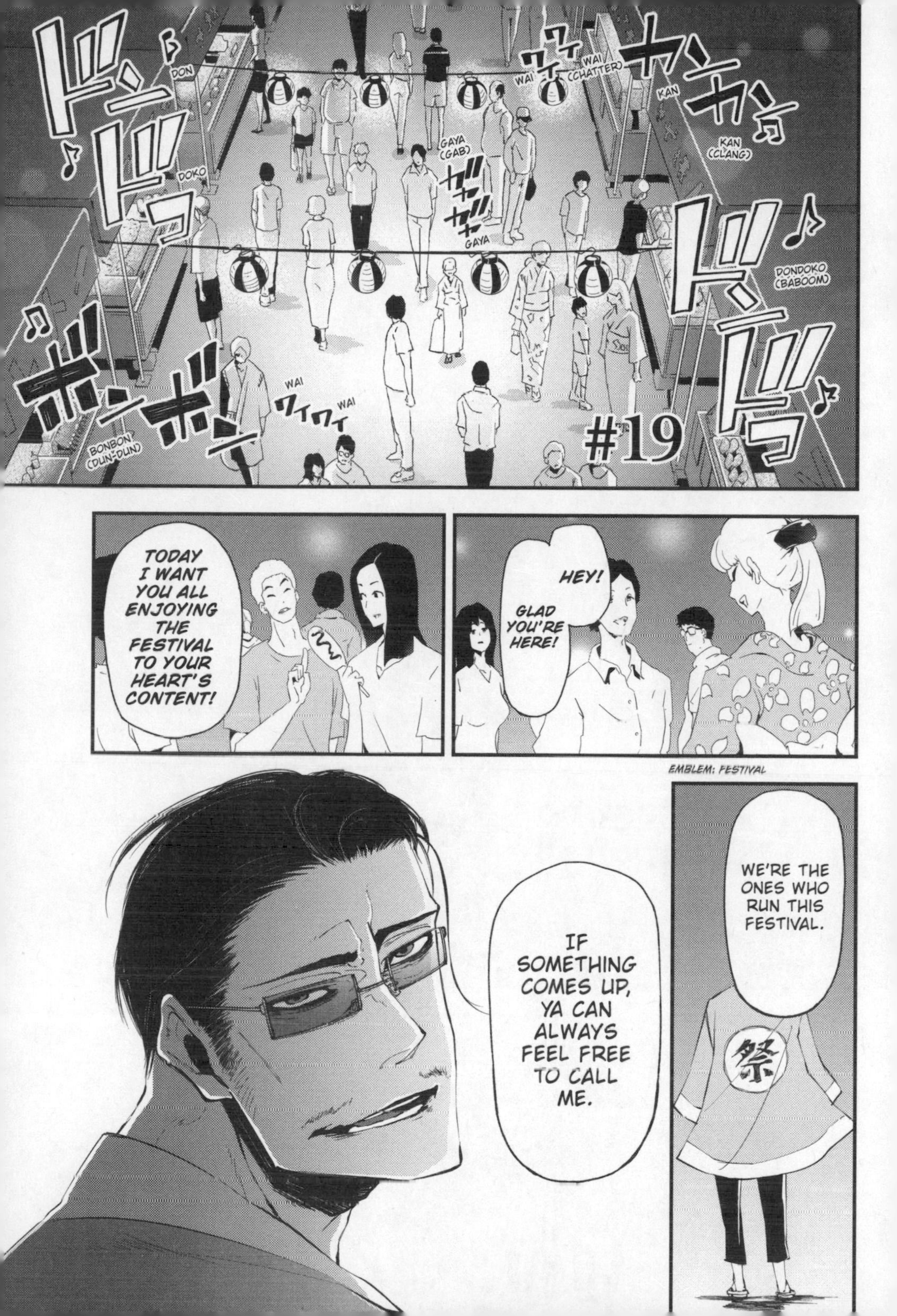
WAI WAI (CHATTER)
KAN KAN (CLANG)
DONDOKO (BABOOM)
GAYA (GAB) GAYA
DON DOKO
WAI WAI
BONBON (DUN-DUN)
#19
HEY!
GLAD YOU'RE HERE!
TODAY I WANT YOU ALL ENJOYING THE FESTIVAL TO YOUR HEART'S CONTENT!
EMBLEM: FESTIVAL
WE'RE THE ONES WHO RUN THIS FESTIVAL.
祭
IF SOMETHING COMES UP, YA CAN ALWAYS FEEL FREE TO CALL ME.

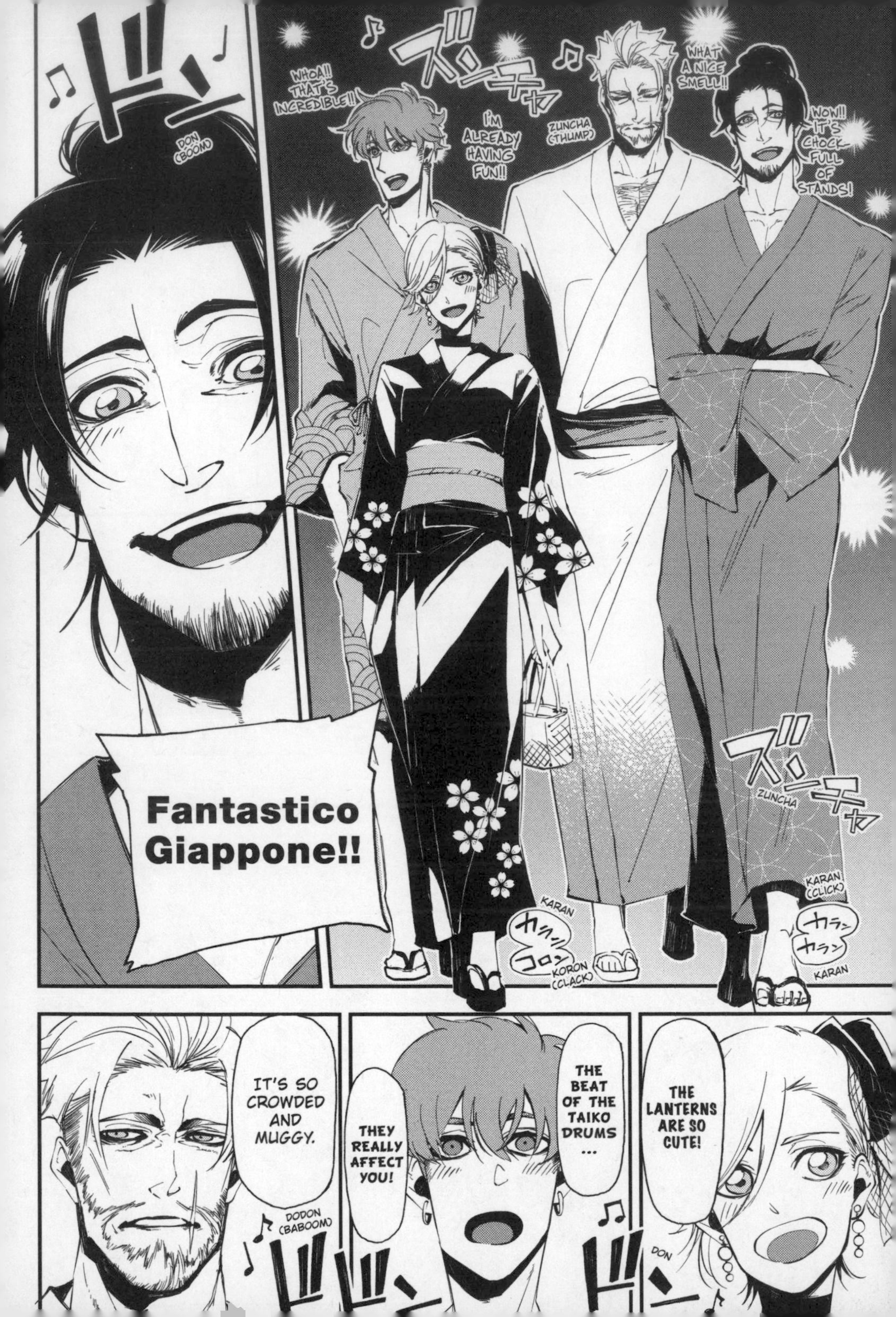

WOW!! IT'S CHOCK-FULL OF STANDS!
WHAT A NICE SMELL!!
ズンチャ
ZUNCHA (THUMP)
I'M ALREADY HAVING FUN!!
WHOA!! THAT'S INCREDIBLE!!
ズンチャ
ZUNCHA
KARAN (CLICK)
カラン カラン
KARAN
KARAN
カラン コロン
KORON (CLACK)
ドン
DON (BOOM)
Fantastico Giappone!!
THE LANTERNS ARE SO CUTE!
DON
THE BEAT OF THE TAIKO DRUMS...
THEY REALLY AFFECT YOU!
IT'S SO CROWDED AND MUGGY.
DODON (BABOOM)

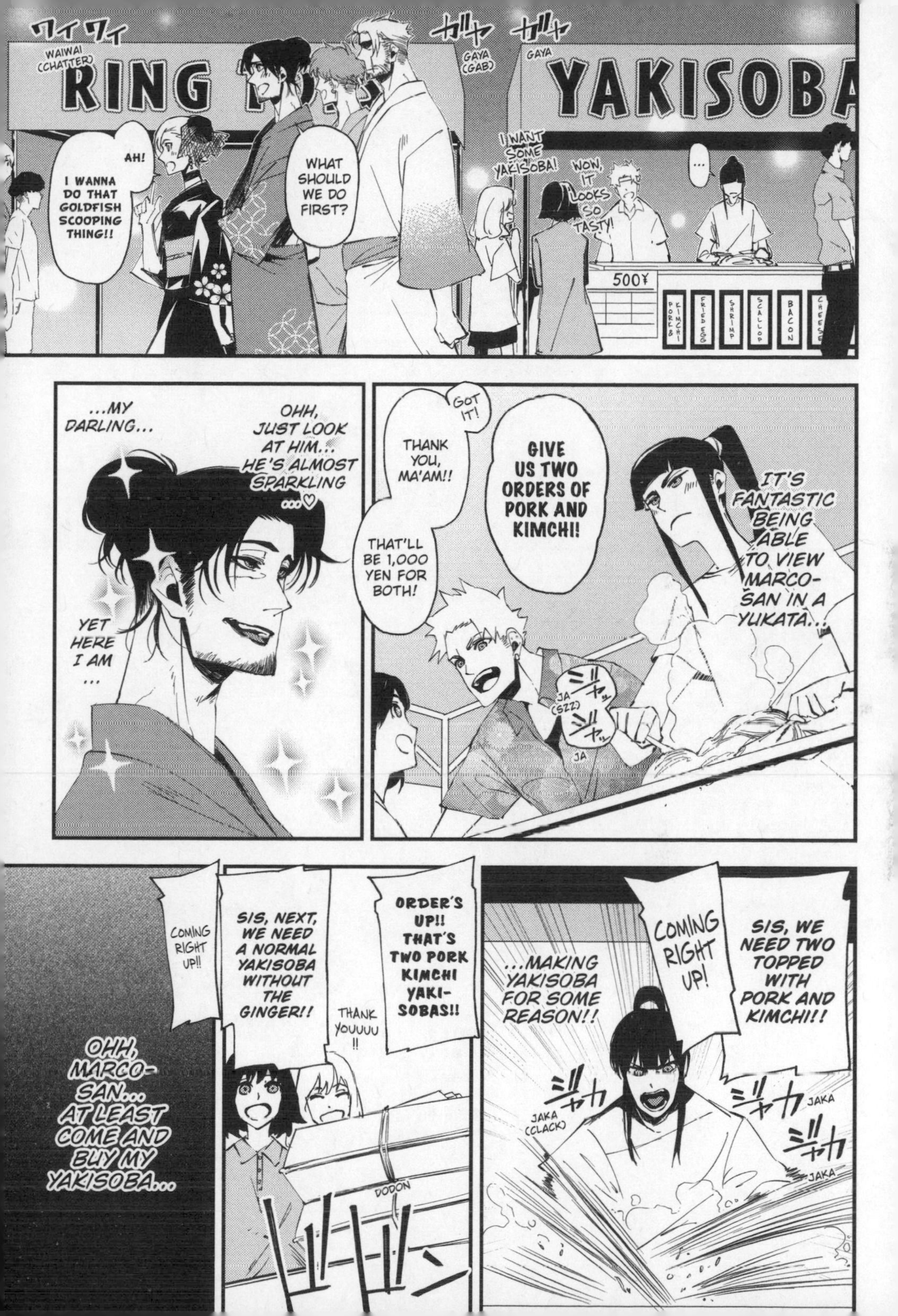
ガヤ ガヤ
GAYA (GAB)
GAYA
YAKISOBA
...
WOW, IT LOOKS SO TASTY!
I WANT SOME YAKISOBA!
500¥
PORK & KIMCHI
FRIED EGG
SHRIMP
SCALLOP
BACON
CHEESE
WHAT SHOULD WE DO FIRST?
AH! I WANNA DO THAT GOLDFISH SCOOPING THING!!
ワイワイ
WAIWAI (CHATTER)
RING TOS
IT'S FANTASTIC BEING ABLE TO VIEW MARCO-SAN IN A YUKATA...
GIVE US TWO ORDERS OF PORK AND KIMCHI!
GOT IT!
THANK YOU, MA'AM!!
THAT'LL BE 1,000 YEN FOR BOTH!
ジャッ
JA (SZZ)
ジャッ
JA
OHH, JUST LOOK AT HIM... HE'S ALMOST SPARKLING ...♡
...MY DARLING...
YET HERE I AM ...
SIS, WE NEED TWO TOPPED WITH PORK AND KIMCHI!!
COMING RIGHT UP!
...MAKING YAKISOBA FOR SOME REASON!!
ジャカ
JAKA
ジャカ
JAKA
ジャカ
JAKA (CLACK)
ORDER'S UP!! THAT'S TWO PORK KIMCHI YAKI-SOBAS!!
THANK YOUUUU!!
SIS, NEXT, WE NEED A NORMAL YAKISOBA WITHOUT THE GINGER!!
COMING RIGHT UP!!
DODON
OHH, MARCO-SAN... AT LEAST COME AND BUY MY YAKISOBA...

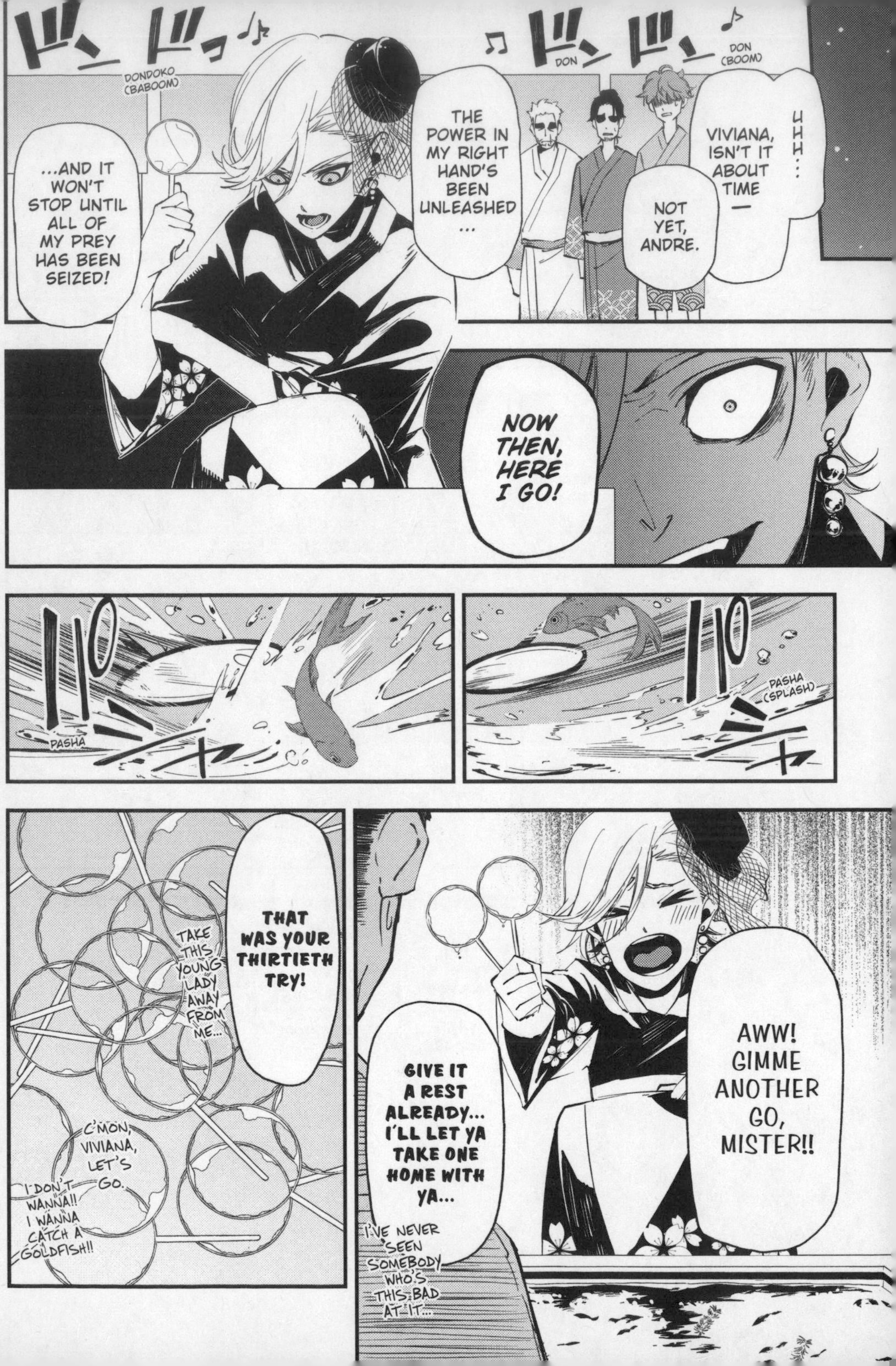
DON (BOOM)
DON
UHH...
VIVIANA, ISN'T IT ABOUT TIME—
NOT YET, ANDRE.
THE POWER IN MY RIGHT HAND'S BEEN UNLEASHED...
DONDOKO (BABOOM)
...AND IT WON'T STOP UNTIL ALL OF MY PREY HAS BEEN SEIZED!
NOW THEN, HERE I GO!
PASHA (SPLASH)
PASHA
AWW! GIMME ANOTHER GO, MISTER!!
GIVE IT A REST ALREADY... I'LL LET YA TAKE ONE HOME WITH YA...
I'VE NEVER SEEN SOMEBODY WHO'S THIS BAD AT IT...
THAT WAS YOUR THIRTIETH TRY!
TAKE THIS YOUNG LADY AWAY FROM ME...
C'MON, VIVIANA, LET'S GO.
I DON'T WANNA!! I WANNA CATCH A GOLDFISH!!

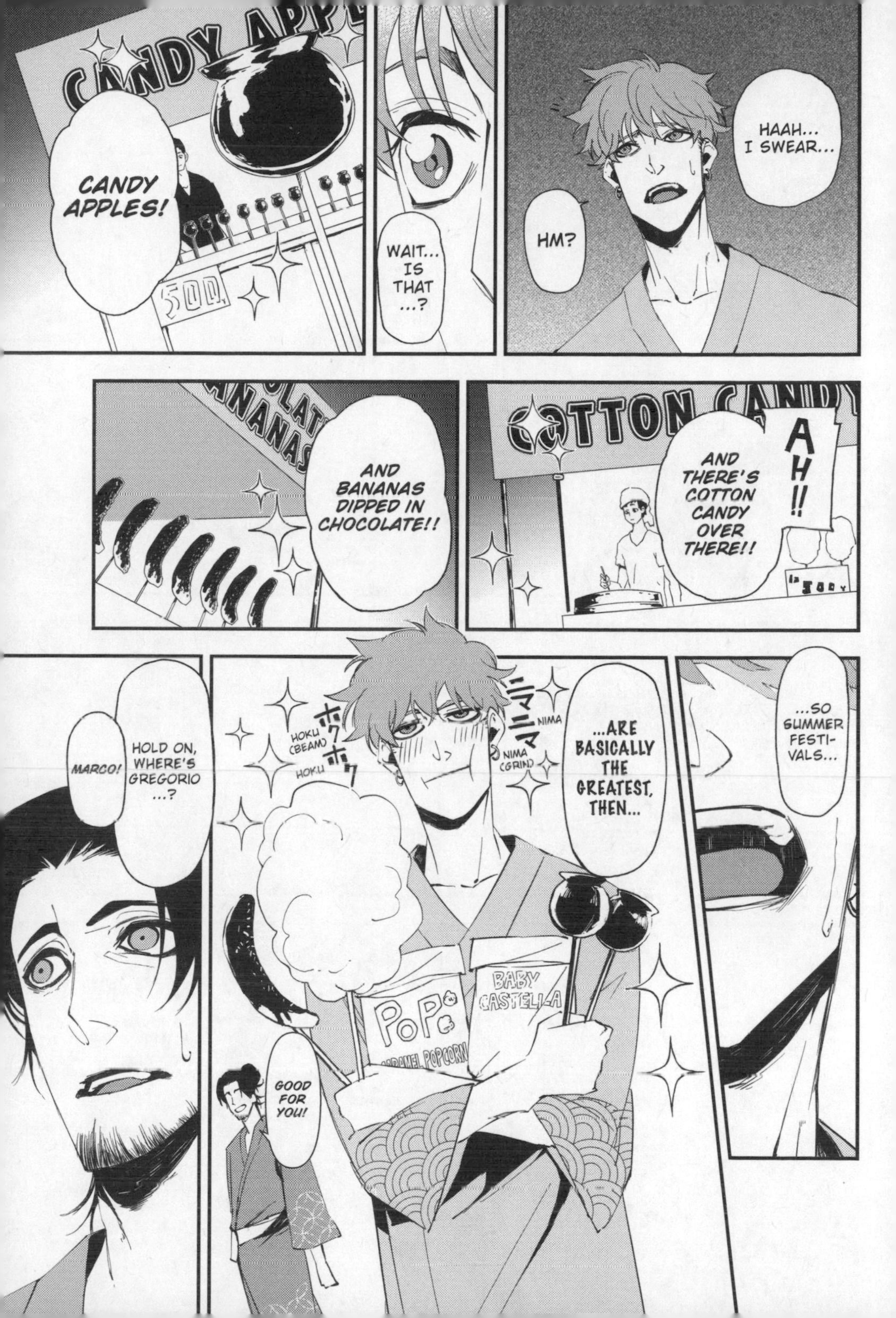
HAAH... I SWEAR...
HM?
WAIT... IS THAT ...?
CANDY APPLE
CANDY APPLES!
500
COTTON CANDY
AH!!
AND THERE'S COTTON CANDY OVER THERE!!
ANANAS
AND BANANAS DIPPED IN CHOCOLATE!!
...SO SUMMER FESTI-VALS...
...ARE BASICALLY THE GREATEST, THEN...
NIMA NIMA (GRIN)
HOKU (BEAM) HOKU
BABY CASTELLA
POP
CARAMEL POPCORN
GOOD FOR YOU!
HOLD ON, WHERE'S GREGORIO ...?
MARCO!

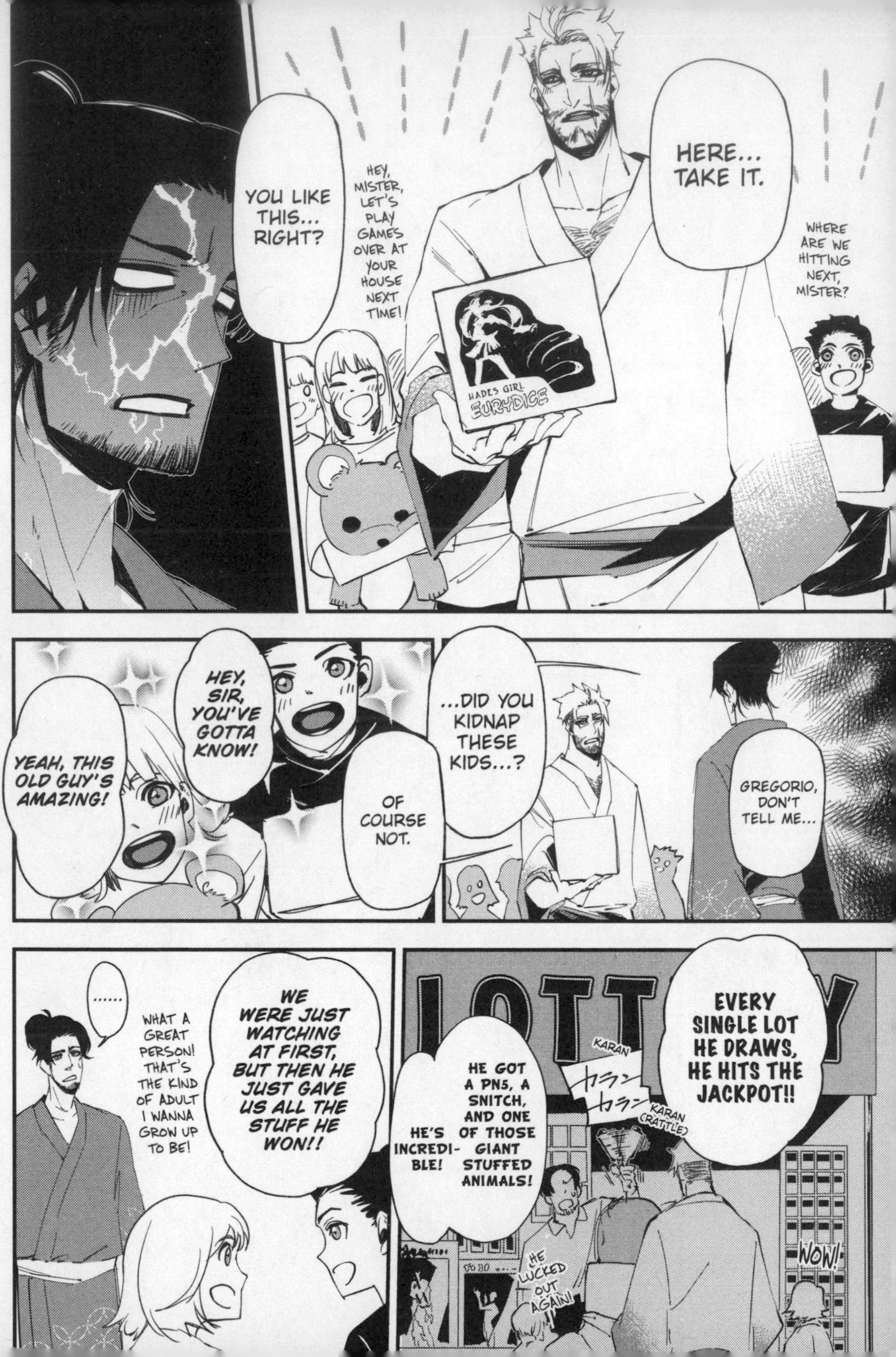
HERE... TAKE IT.
WHERE ARE WE HITTING NEXT, MISTER?
HEY, MISTER, LET'S PLAY GAMES OVER AT YOUR HOUSE NEXT TIME!
YOU LIKE THIS... RIGHT?
HADES GIRL EURYDICE
GREGORIO, DON'T TELL ME...
...DID YOU KIDNAP THESE KIDS...?
OF COURSE NOT.
HEY, SIR, YOU'VE GOTTA KNOW!
YEAH, THIS OLD GUY'S AMAZING!
EVERY SINGLE LOT HE DRAWS, HE HITS THE JACKPOT!!
カラン KARAN
カラン KARAN (RATTLE)
HE GOT A PN5, A SNITCH, AND ONE OF THOSE GIANT STUFFED ANIMALS!
HE'S INCREDI-BLE!
WOW!
HE LUCKED OUT AGAIN!
WE WERE JUST WATCHING AT FIRST, BUT THEN HE JUST GAVE US ALL THE STUFF HE WON!!
WHAT A GREAT PERSON! THAT'S THE KIND OF ADULT I WANNA GROW UP TO BE!
......

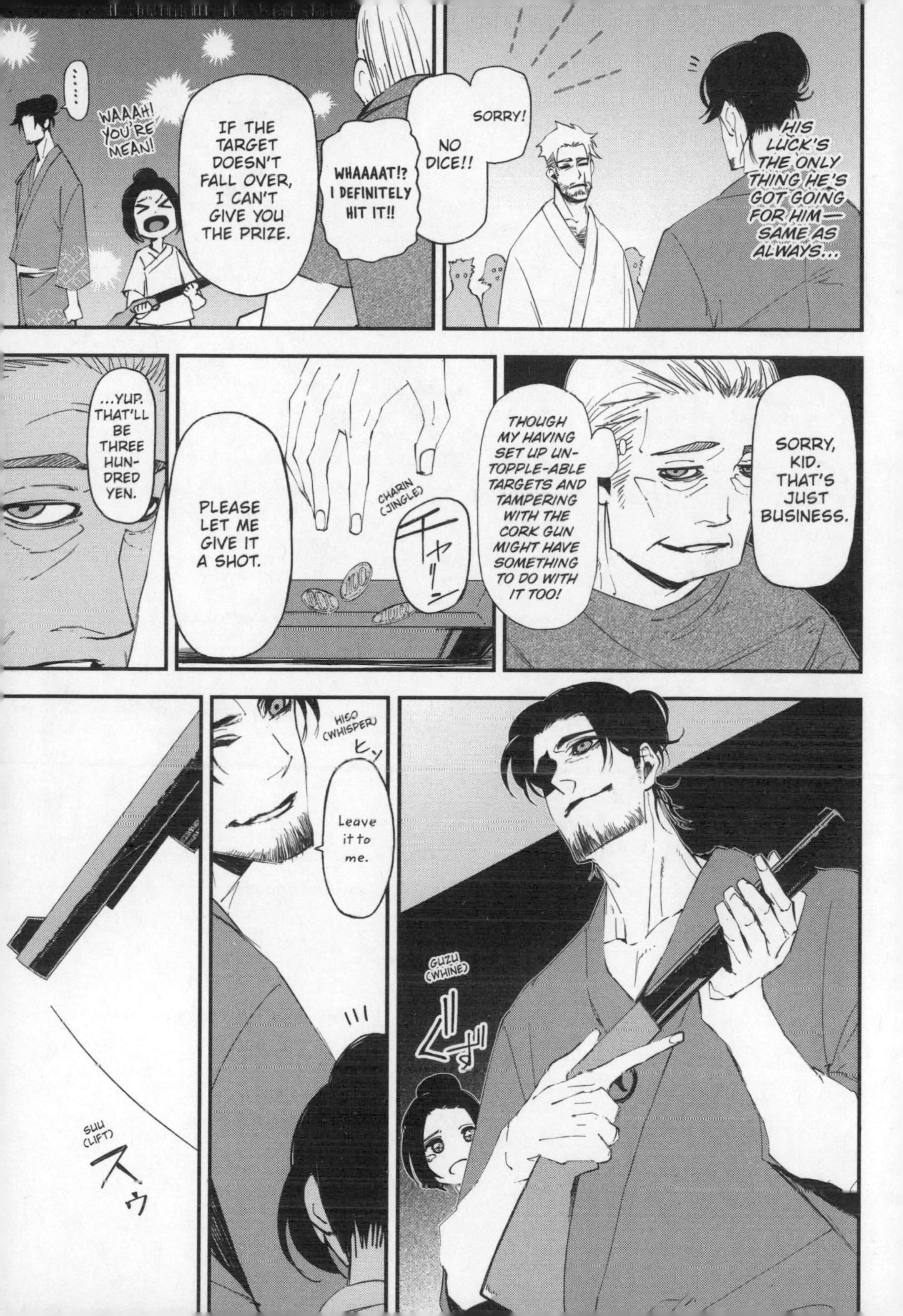
HIS LUCK'S THE ONLY THING HE'S GOT GOING FOR HIM—SAME AS ALWAYS...
SORRY!
NO DICE!!
WHAAAAT!? I DEFINITELY HIT IT!!
IF THE TARGET DOESN'T FALL OVER, I CAN'T GIVE YOU THE PRIZE.
WAAAH! YOU'RE MEAN!
......
SORRY, KID. THAT'S JUST BUSINESS.
THOUGH MY HAVING SET UP UNTOPPLE-ABLE TARGETS AND TAMPERING WITH THE CORK GUN MIGHT HAVE SOMETHING TO DO WITH IT TOO!
CHARIN (JINGLE)
チャリーン
PLEASE LET ME GIVE IT A SHOT.
...YUP. THAT'LL BE THREE HUNDRED YEN.
GUZU (WHINE)
ぐず
HISO (WHISPER)
ヒソ
Leave it to me.
SUU (LIFT)
スゥ

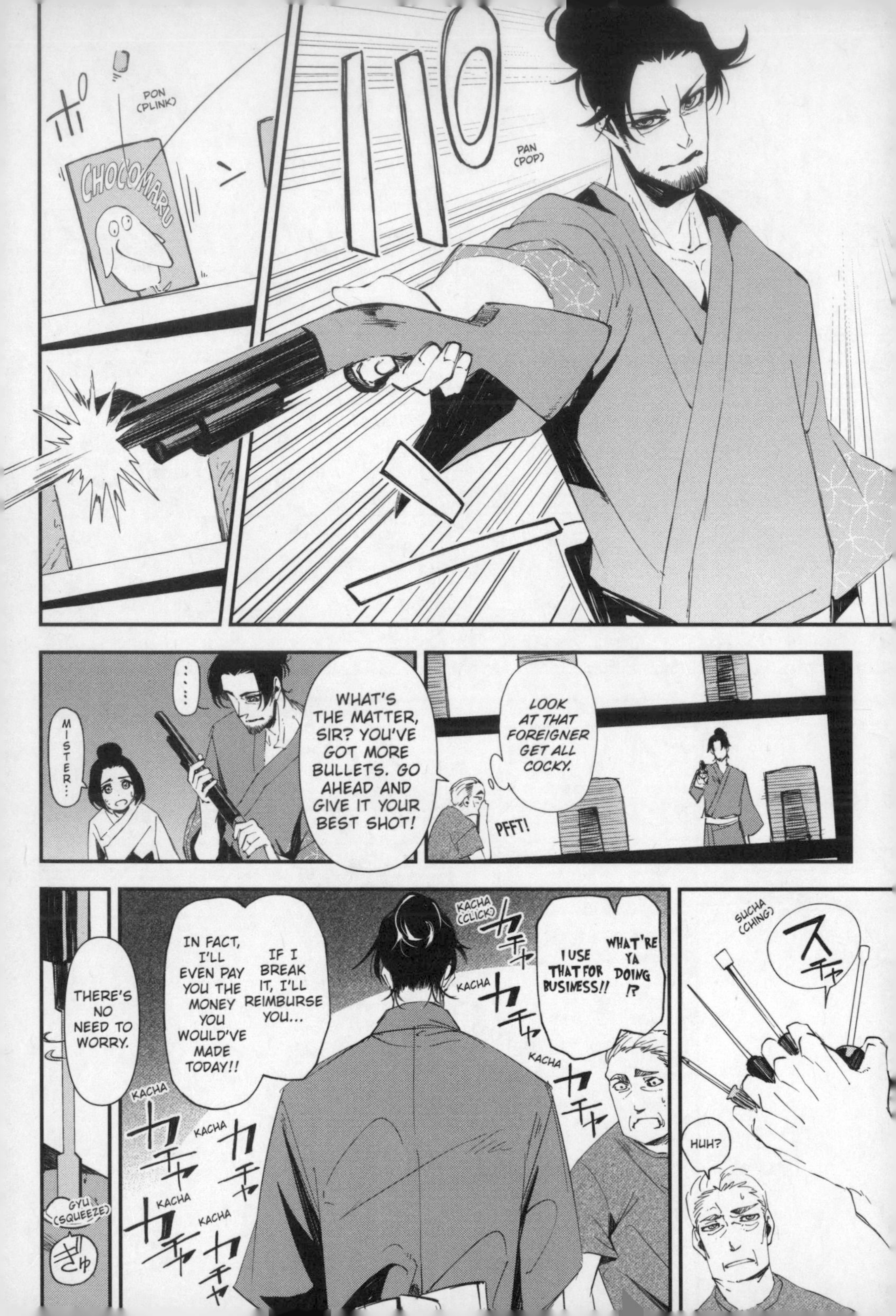
PAN (POP)
PON (PLINK)
CHOCOMARU
LOOK AT THAT FOREIGNER GET ALL COCKY.
PFFT!
WHAT'S THE MATTER, SIR? YOU'VE GOT MORE BULLETS. GO AHEAD AND GIVE IT YOUR BEST SHOT!
......
MISTER...
SUCHA (CHING)
HUH?
WHAT'RE YA DOING!?
I USE THAT FOR BUSINESS!!
KACHA (CLICK)
KACHA
KACHA
IF I BREAK IT, I'LL REIMBURSE YOU...
IN FACT, I'LL EVEN PAY YOU THE MONEY YOU WOULD'VE MADE TODAY!!
THERE'S NO NEED TO WORRY.
KACHA
KACHA
KACHA
KACHA
GYU (SQUEEZE)

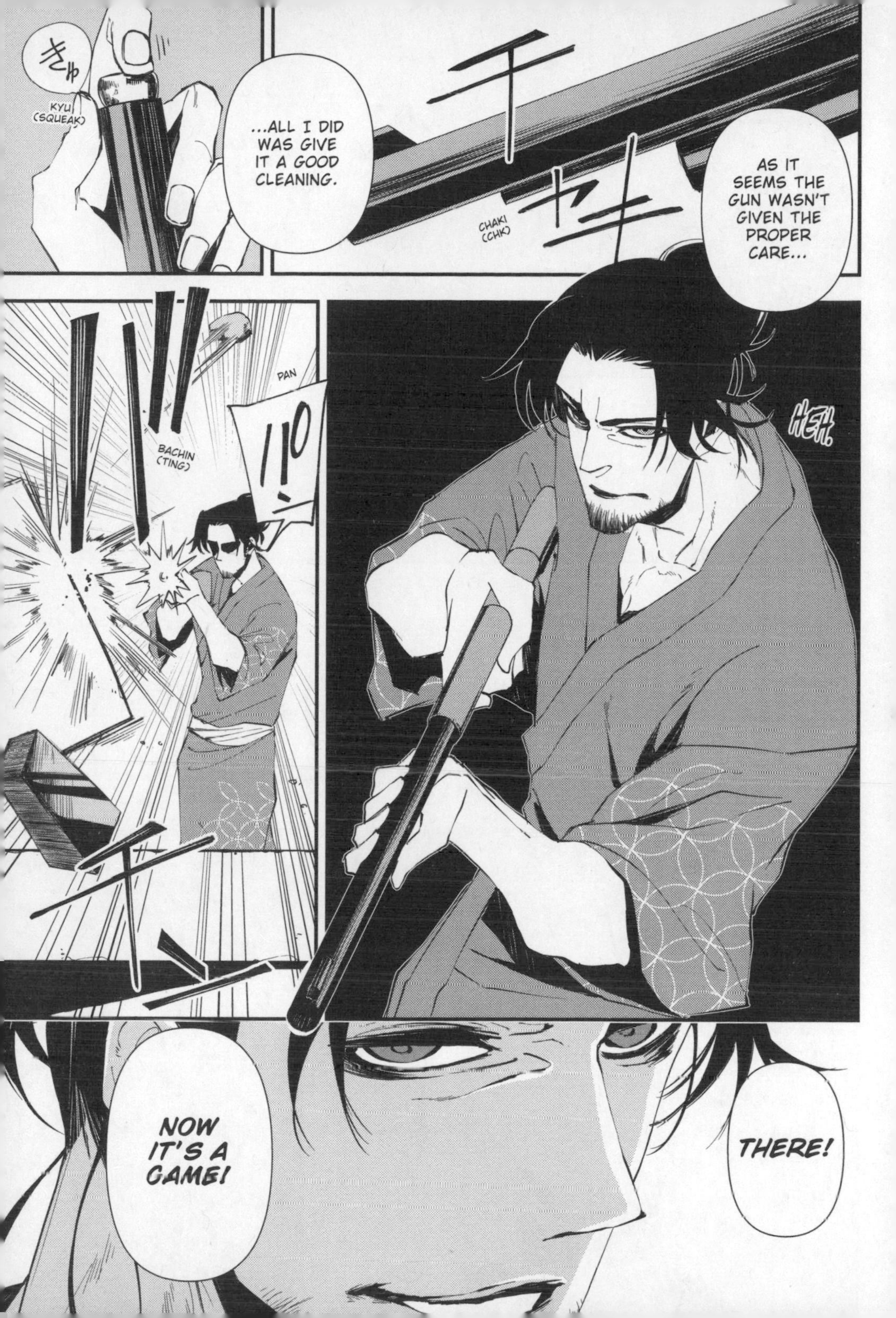

CHAKI (CHK)
AS IT SEEMS THE GUN WASN'T GIVEN THE PROPER CARE...
きゅ
KYU (SQUEAK)
...ALL I DID WAS GIVE IT A GOOD CLEANING.
HEH.
PAN
BACHIN (TING)
THERE!
NOW IT'S A GAME!

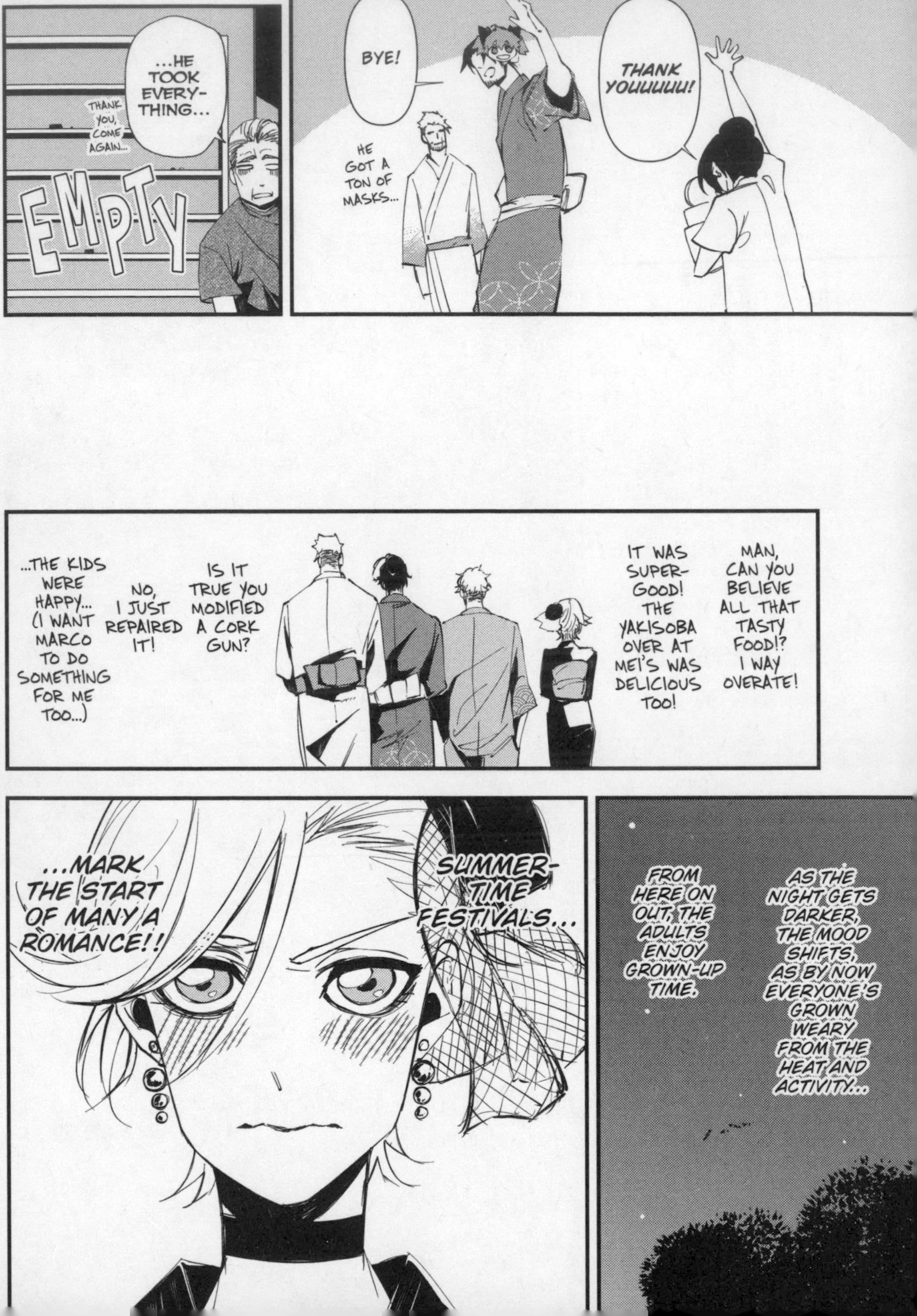
THANK YOUUUUU!
BYE!
HE GOT A TON OF MASKS...
...HE TOOK EVERY-THING...
THANK YOU, COME AGAIN...
EMPTY
MAN, CAN YOU BELIEVE ALL THAT TASTY FOOD!? I WAY OVERATE!
IT WAS SUPER-GOOD! THE YAKISOBA OVER AT MEI'S WAS DELICIOUS TOO!
IS IT TRUE YOU MODIFIED A CORK GUN?
NO, I JUST REPAIRED IT!
...THE KIDS WERE HAPPY... (I WANT MARCO TO DO SOMETHING FOR ME TOO...)
AS THE NIGHT GETS DARKER, THE MOOD SHIFTS, AS BY NOW EVERYONE'S GROWN WEARY FROM THE HEAT AND ACTIVITY...
FROM HERE ON OUT, THE ADULTS ENJOY GROWN-UP TIME.
SUMMER-TIME FESTIVALS...
...MARK THE START OF MANY A ROMANCE!!

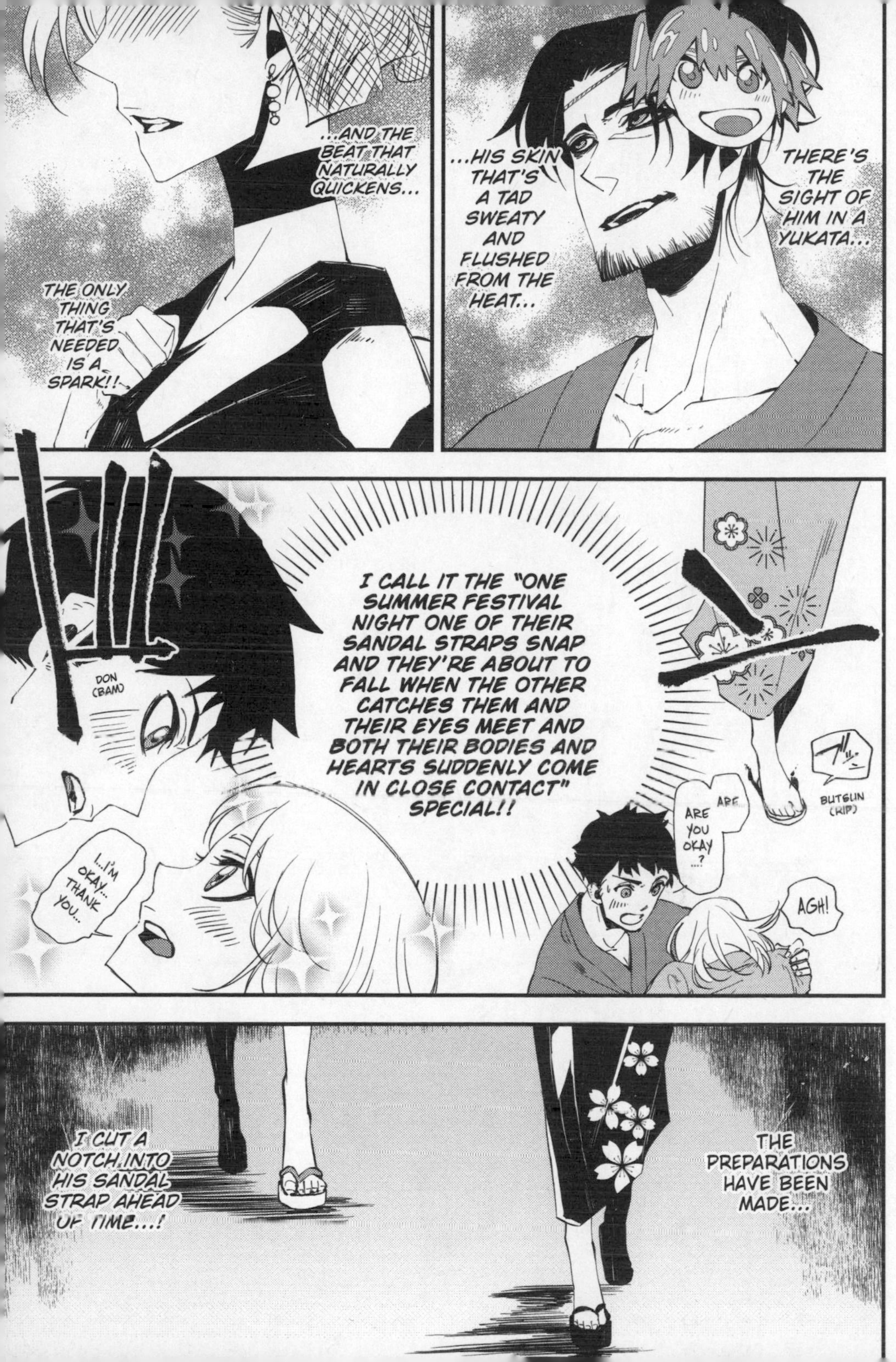
THERE'S THE SIGHT OF HIM IN A YUKATA...
...HIS SKIN THAT'S A TAD SWEATY AND FLUSHED FROM THE HEAT...
...AND THE BEAT THAT NATURALLY QUICKENS...
THE ONLY THING THAT'S NEEDED IS A SPARK!!
BUTSUN (RIP)
I CALL IT THE "ONE SUMMER FESTIVAL NIGHT ONE OF THEIR SANDAL STRAPS SNAP AND THEY'RE ABOUT TO FALL WHEN THE OTHER CATCHES THEM AND THEIR EYES MEET AND BOTH THEIR BODIES AND HEARTS SUDDENLY COME IN CLOSE CONTACT" SPECIAL!!
ARE ARE YOU OKAY ...?
AGH!
DON (BAM)
I...I'M OKAY... THANK YOU...
THE PREPARATIONS HAVE BEEN MADE...
I CUT A NOTCH INTO HIS SANDAL STRAP AHEAD OF TIME...!

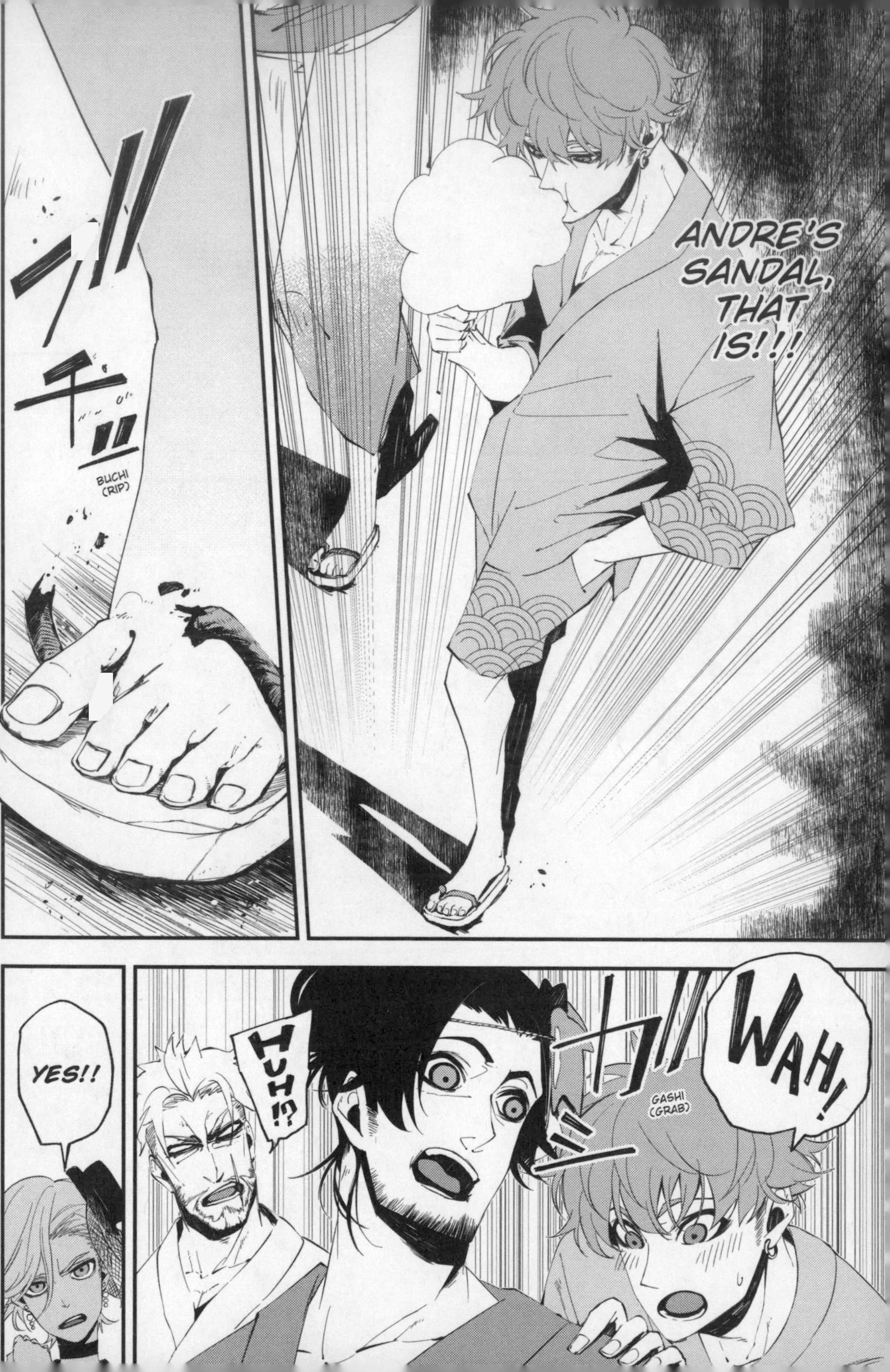
ANDRE'S SANDAL, THAT IS!!!
BUCHI (RIP)
WAH!
GASHI (GRAB)
HUH!?
YES!!

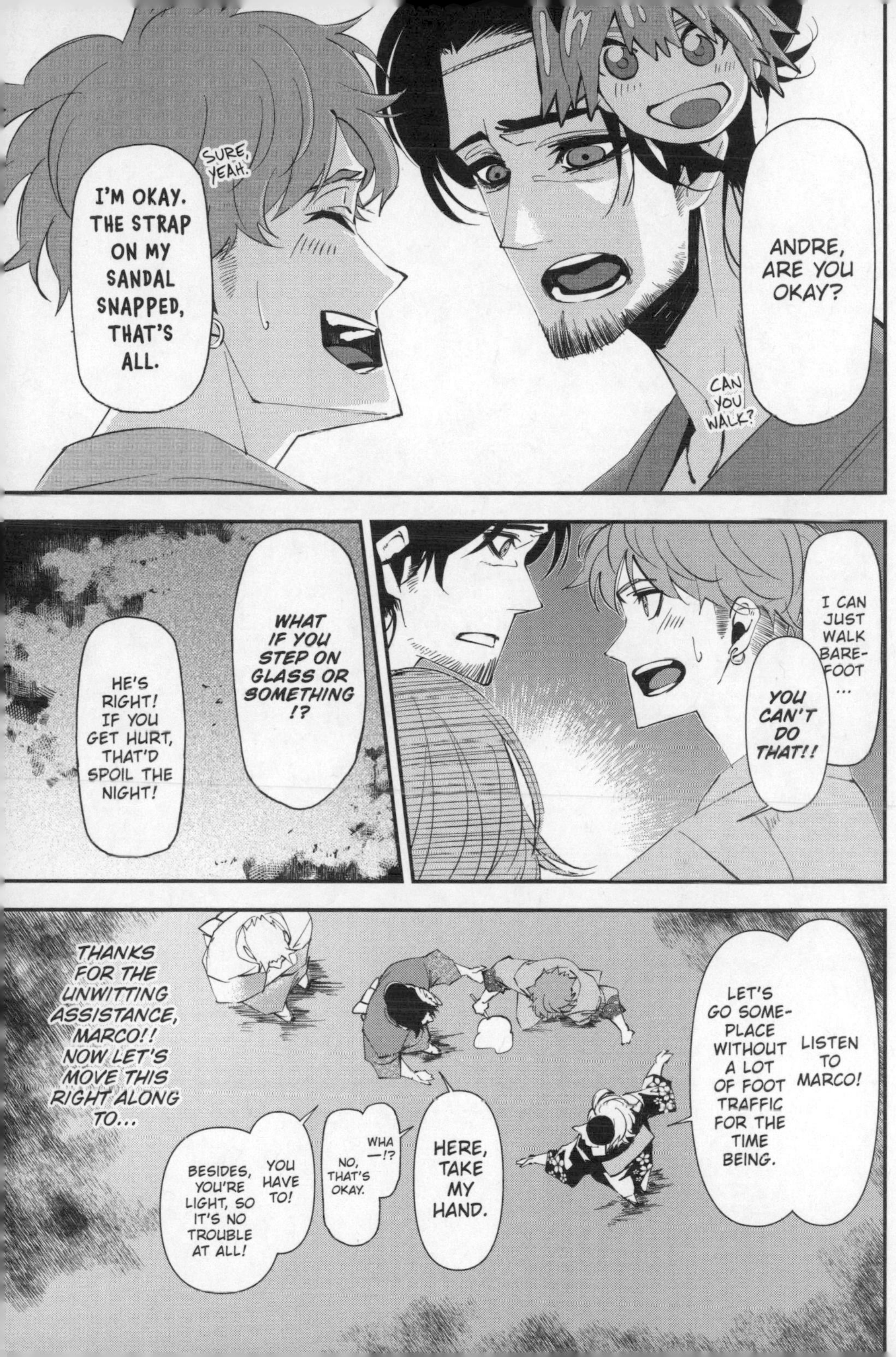
ANDRE, ARE YOU OKAY?
CAN YOU WALK?
SURE, YEAH.
I'M OKAY. THE STRAP ON MY SANDAL SNAPPED, THAT'S ALL.
I CAN JUST WALK BARE-FOOT...
YOU CAN'T DO THAT!!
WHAT IF YOU STEP ON GLASS OR SOMETHING!?
HE'S RIGHT! IF YOU GET HURT, THAT'D SPOIL THE NIGHT!
LISTEN TO MARCO!
LET'S GO SOME-PLACE WITHOUT A LOT OF FOOT TRAFFIC FOR THE TIME BEING.
HERE, TAKE MY HAND.
WHA—!?
NO, THAT'S OKAY.
YOU HAVE TO!
BESIDES, YOU'RE LIGHT, SO IT'S NO TROUBLE AT ALL!
THANKS FOR THE UNWITTING ASSISTANCE, MARCO!! NOW LET'S MOVE THIS RIGHT ALONG TO...

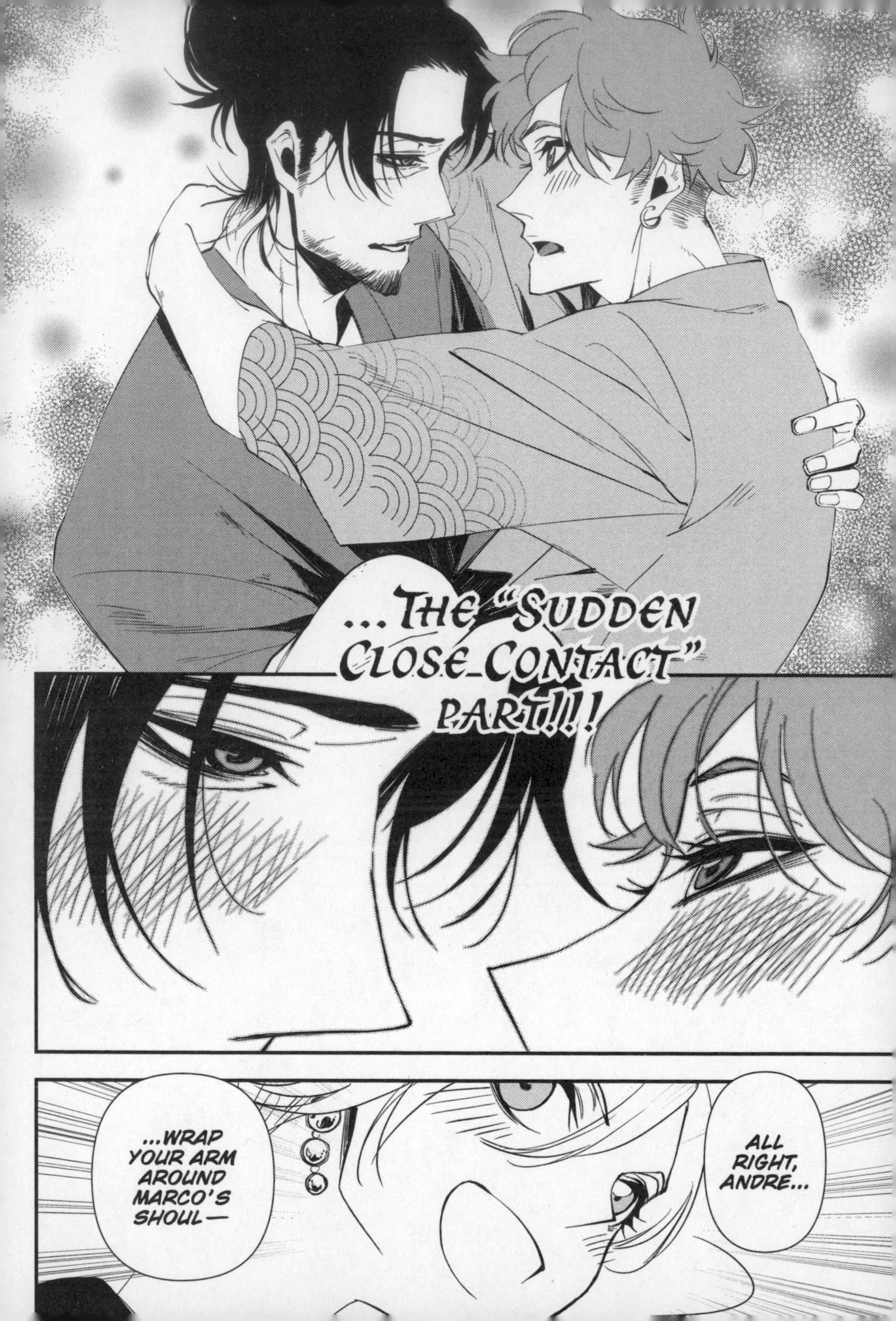
...THE "SUDDEN CLOSE CONTACT" PART!!!!
ALL RIGHT, ANDRE...
...WRAP YOUR ARM AROUND MARCO'S SHOUL—

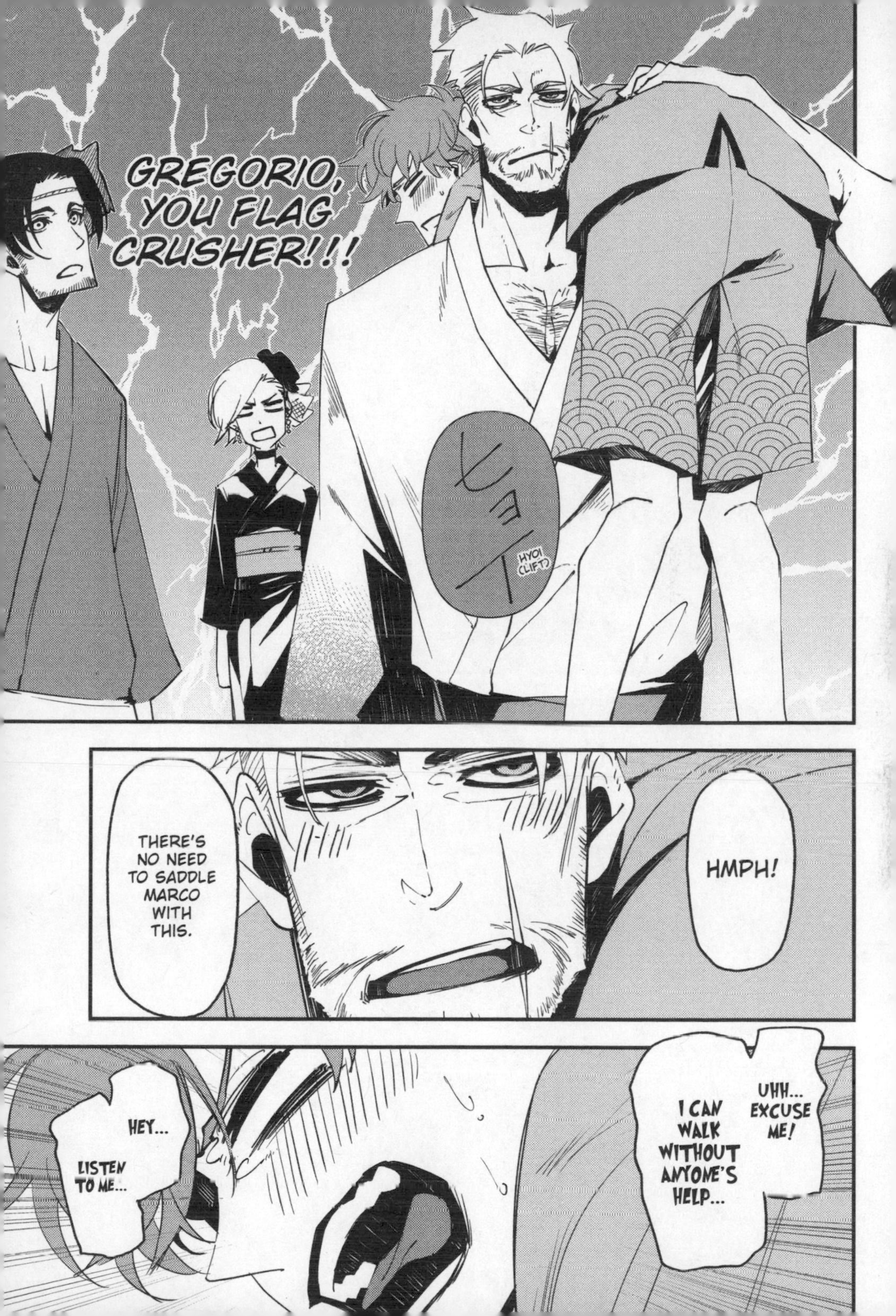
HYOI (LIFT)
GREGORIO, YOU FLAG CRUSHER!!!
HMPH!
THERE'S NO NEED TO SADDLE MARCO WITH THIS.
UHH... EXCUSE ME!
I CAN WALK WITHOUT ANYONE'S HELP...
HEY...
LISTEN TO ME...

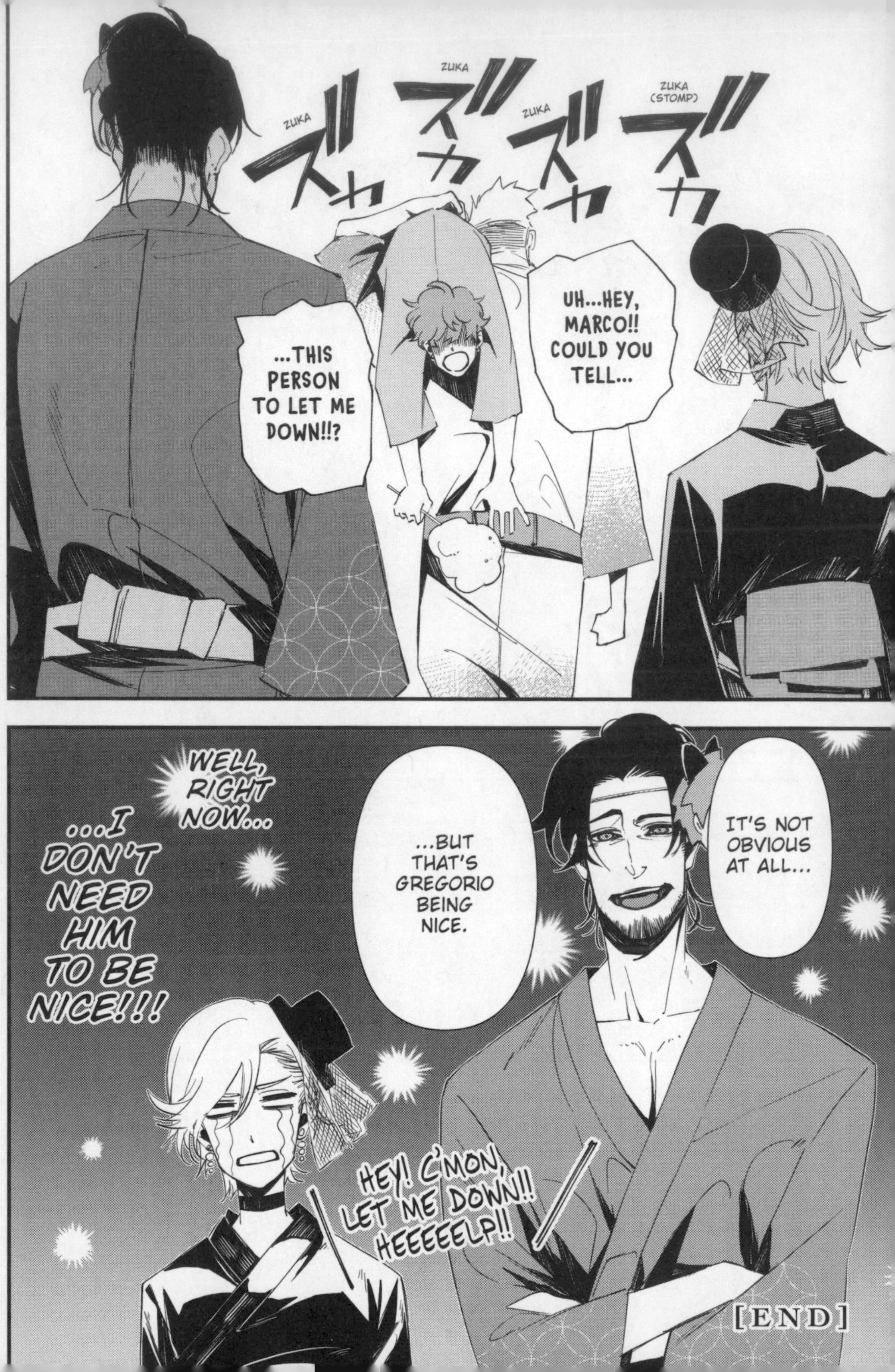
ZUKA (STOMP)
ズカ
ZUKA
ズカ
ZUKA
ズカ
ZUKA
ズカ
UH...HEY, MARCO!! COULD YOU TELL...
...THIS PERSON TO LET ME DOWN!!?
IT'S NOT OBVIOUS AT ALL...
...BUT THAT'S GREGORIO BEING NICE.
WELL, RIGHT NOW...
...I DON'T NEED HIM TO BE NICE!!!
HEY! C'MON, LET ME DOWN!! HEEEEELP!!
[END]

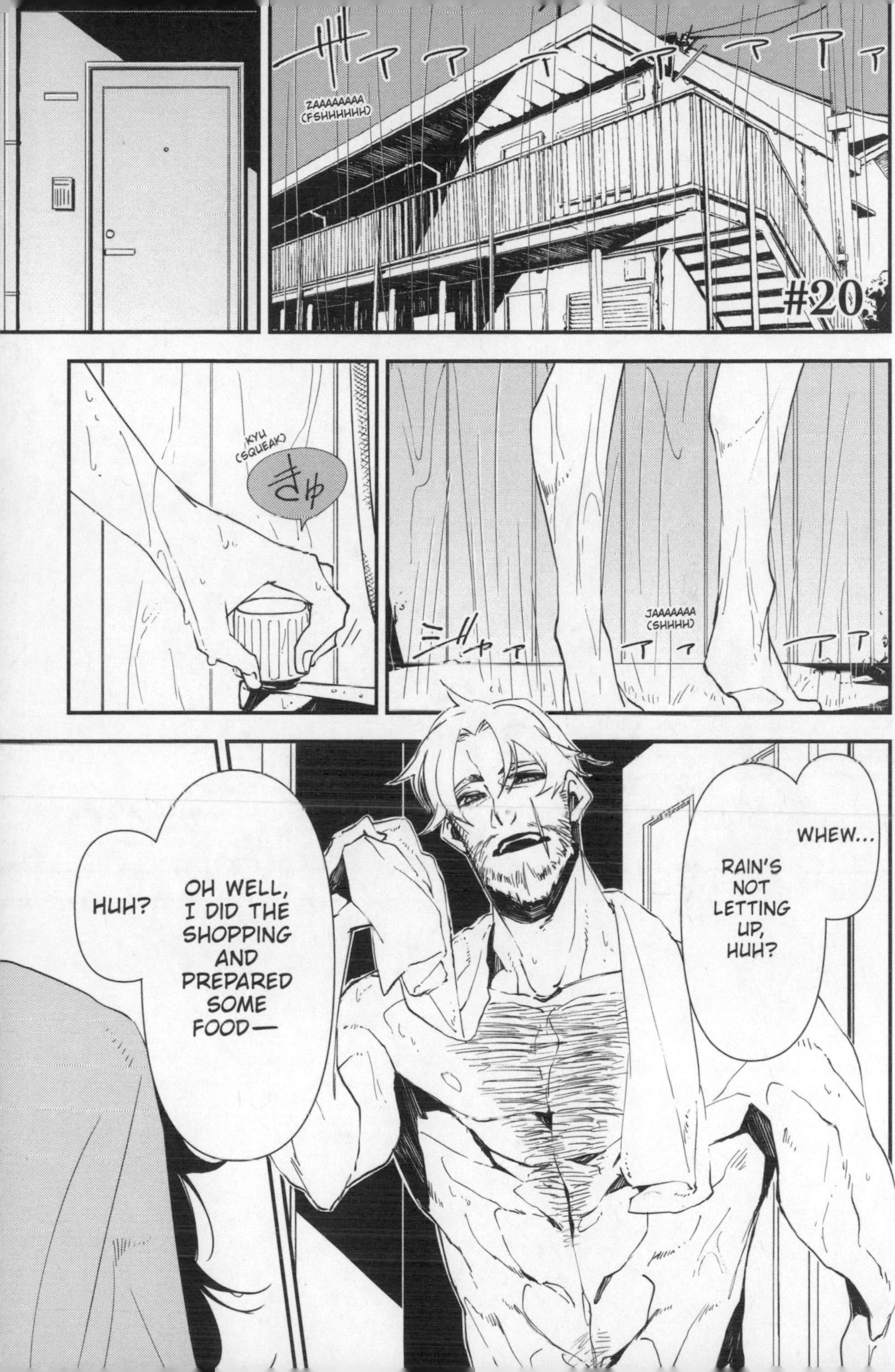
ZAAAAAAAA (FSHHHHHH)
#20
JAAAAAAA (SHHHH)
KYU (SQUEAK)
きゅ
WHEW...
RAIN'S NOT LETTING UP, HUH?
OH WELL, I DID THE SHOPPING AND PREPARED SOME FOOD—
HUH?

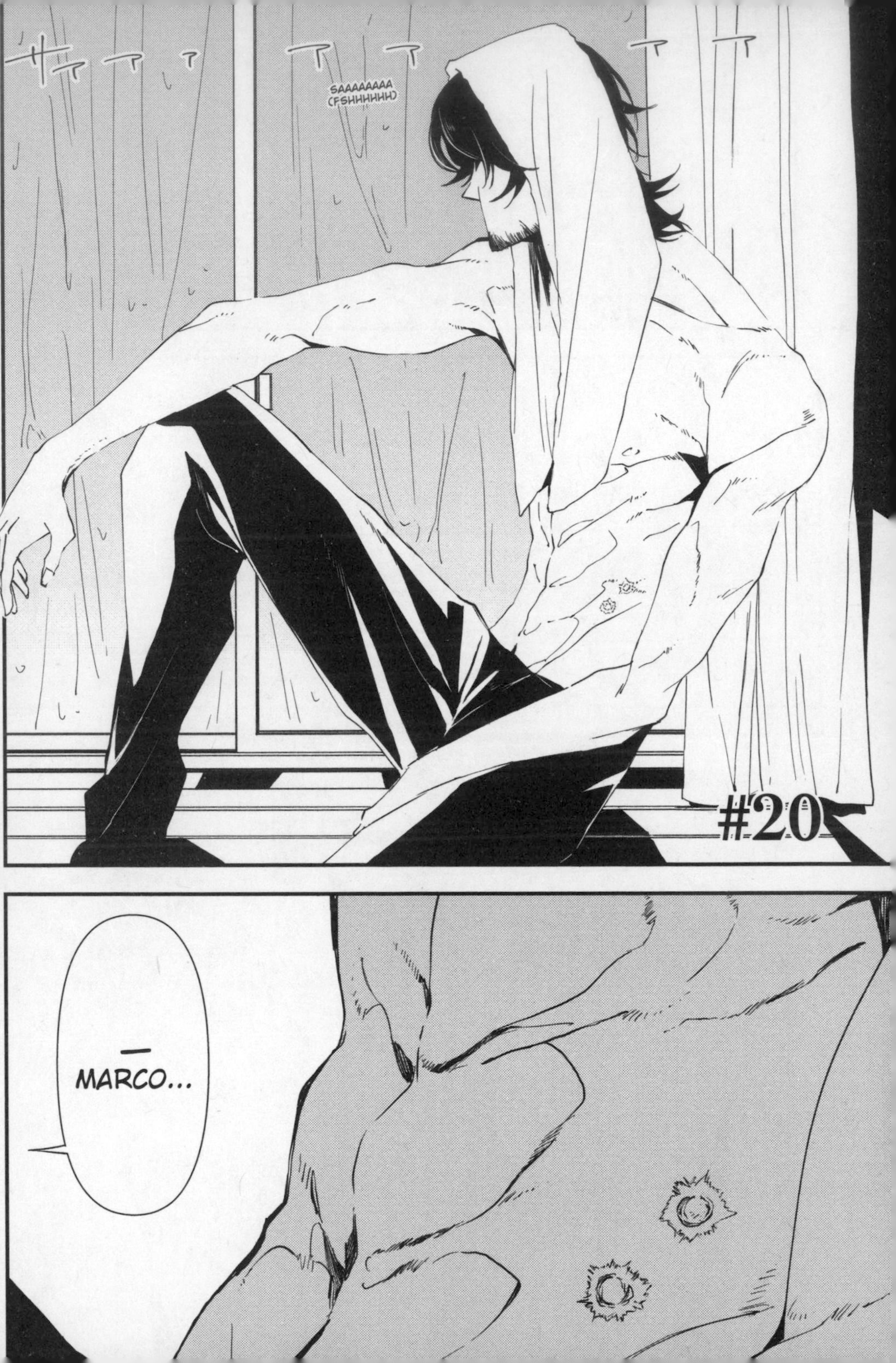
サァァァ
SAAAAAAAA (FSHHHHHH)
#20
—MARCO...

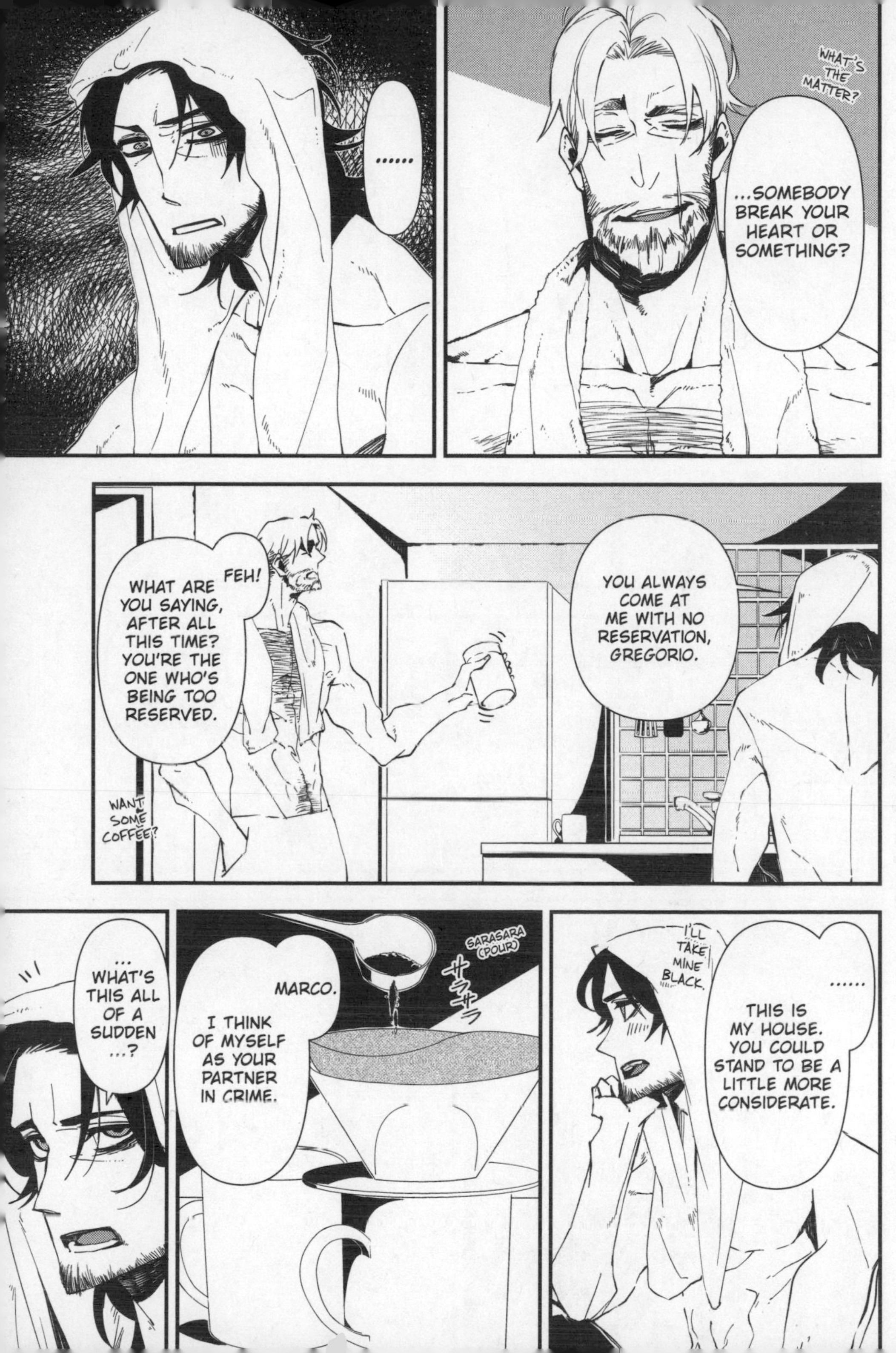
WHAT'S THE MATTER?
...SOMEBODY BREAK YOUR HEART OR SOMETHING?
......
YOU ALWAYS COME AT ME WITH NO RESERVATION, GREGORIO.
FEH!
WHAT ARE YOU SAYING, AFTER ALL THIS TIME? YOU'RE THE ONE WHO'S BEING TOO RESERVED.
WANT SOME COFFEE?
I'LL TAKE MINE BLACK.
......
THIS IS MY HOUSE. YOU COULD STAND TO BE A LITTLE MORE CONSIDERATE.
SARASARA (POUR)
サラサラ
MARCO.
I THINK OF MYSELF AS YOUR PARTNER IN CRIME.
... WHAT'S THIS ALL OF A SUDDEN ...?

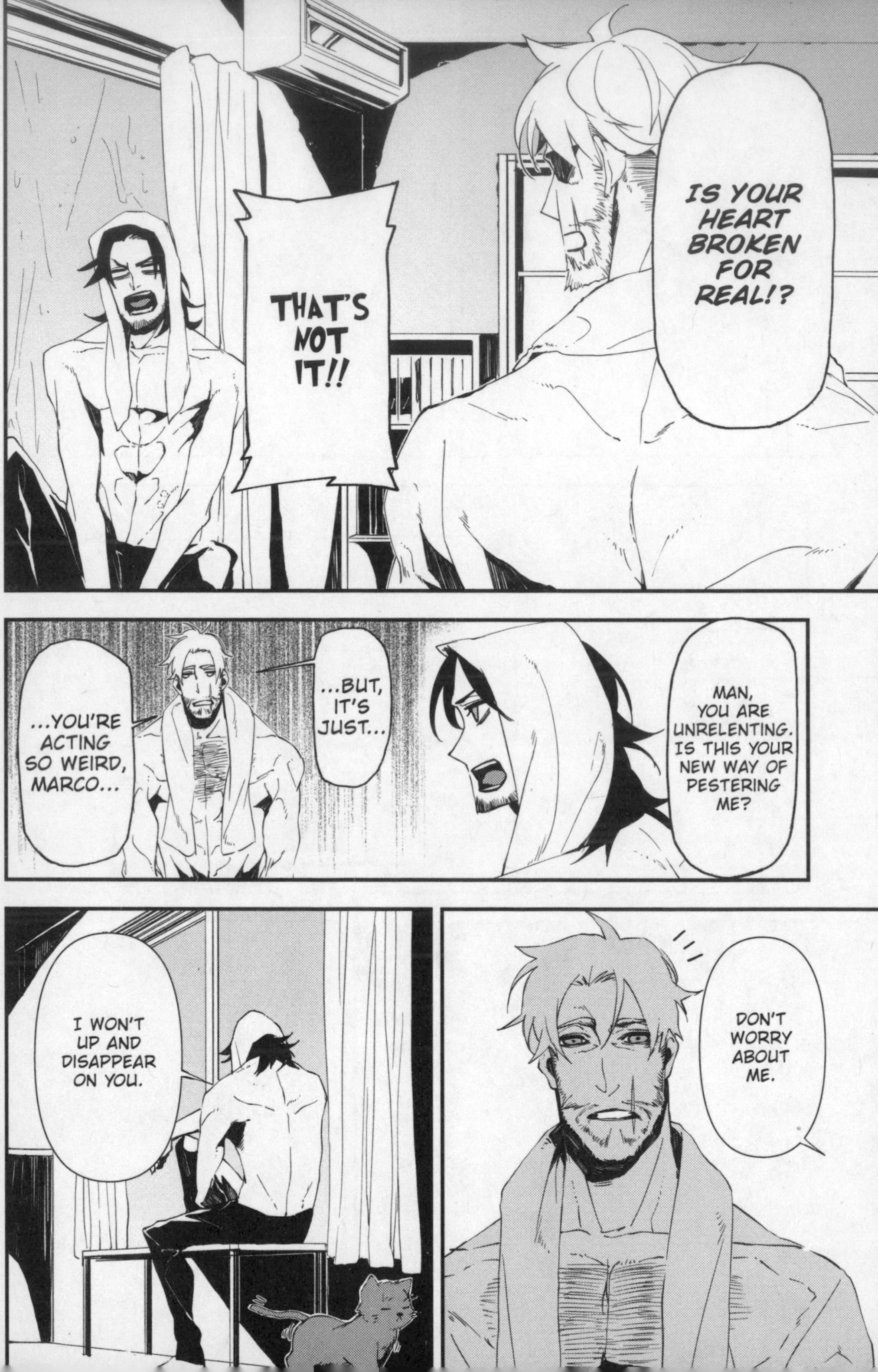
IS YOUR HEART BROKEN FOR REAL!?
THAT'S NOT IT!!
MAN, YOU ARE UNRELENTING. IS THIS YOUR NEW WAY OF PESTERING ME?
...BUT, IT'S JUST...
...YOU'RE ACTING SO WEIRD, MARCO...
DON'T WORRY ABOUT ME.
I WON'T UP AND DISAPPEAR ON YOU.

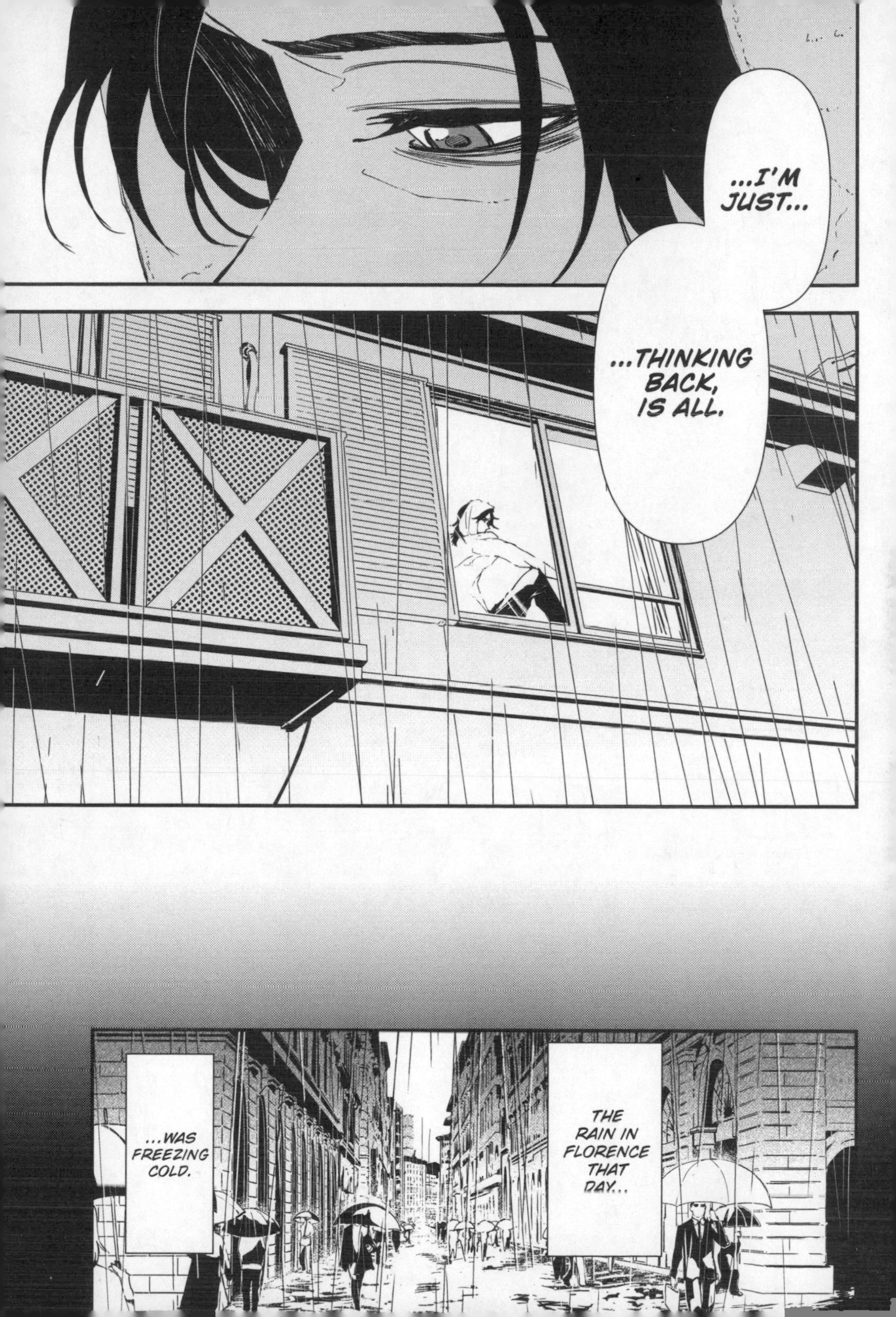
...I'M JUST...
...THINKING BACK, IS ALL.
THE RAIN IN FLORENCE THAT DAY...
...WAS FREEZING COLD.

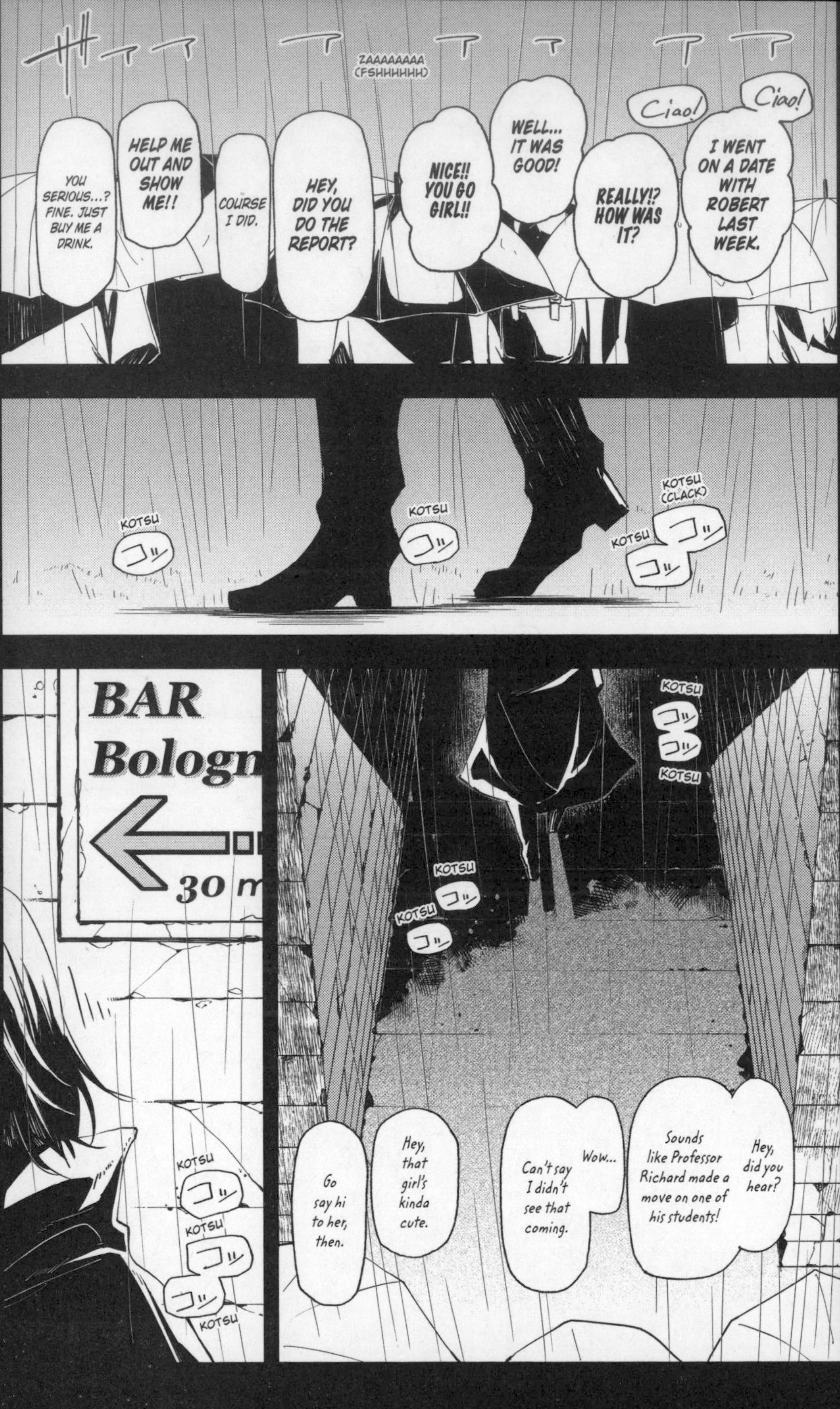
ZAAAAAAAA (FSHHHHHH)
Ciao!
Ciao!
I WENT ON A DATE WITH ROBERT LAST WEEK.
REALLY!? HOW WAS IT?
WELL... IT WAS GOOD!
NICE!! YOU GO GIRL!!
HEY, DID YOU DO THE REPORT?
COURSE I DID.
HELP ME OUT AND SHOW ME!!
YOU SERIOUS...? FINE. JUST BUY ME A DRINK.
KOTSU (CLACK)
KOTSU
KOTSU
KOTSU
KOTSU
KOTSU
KOTSU
KOTSU
Hey, did you hear?
Sounds like Professor Richard made a move on one of his students!
Wow...
Can't say I didn't see that coming.
Hey, that girl's kinda cute.
Go say hi to her, then.
BAR
Bologn
30 m
KOTSU
KOTSU
KOTSU

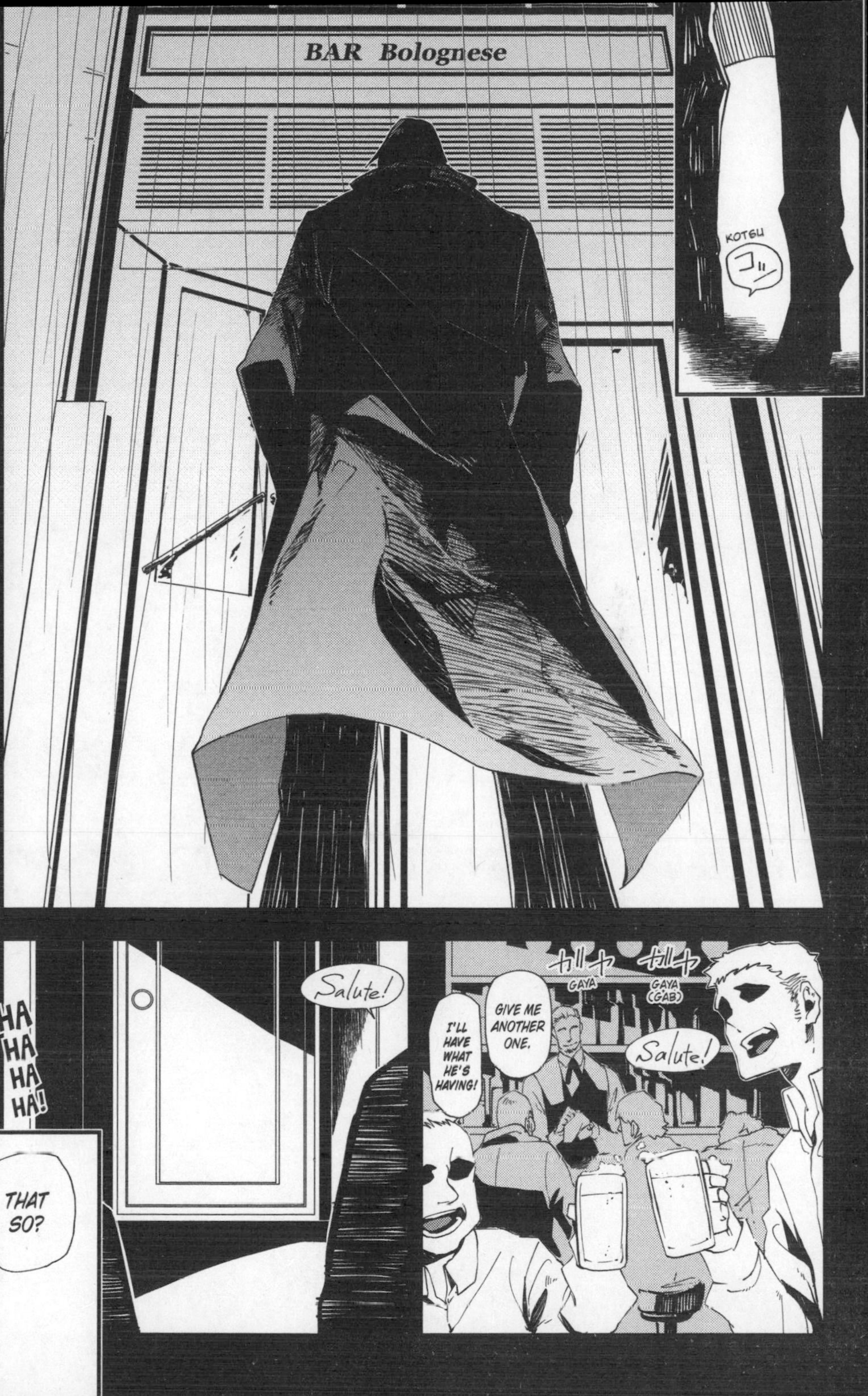
KOTSU
BAR Bolognese
GAYA (GAB)
GAYA
Salute!
GIVE ME ANOTHER ONE.
I'LL HAVE WHAT HE'S HAVING!
Salute!
HA HA HA HA!
THAT SO?

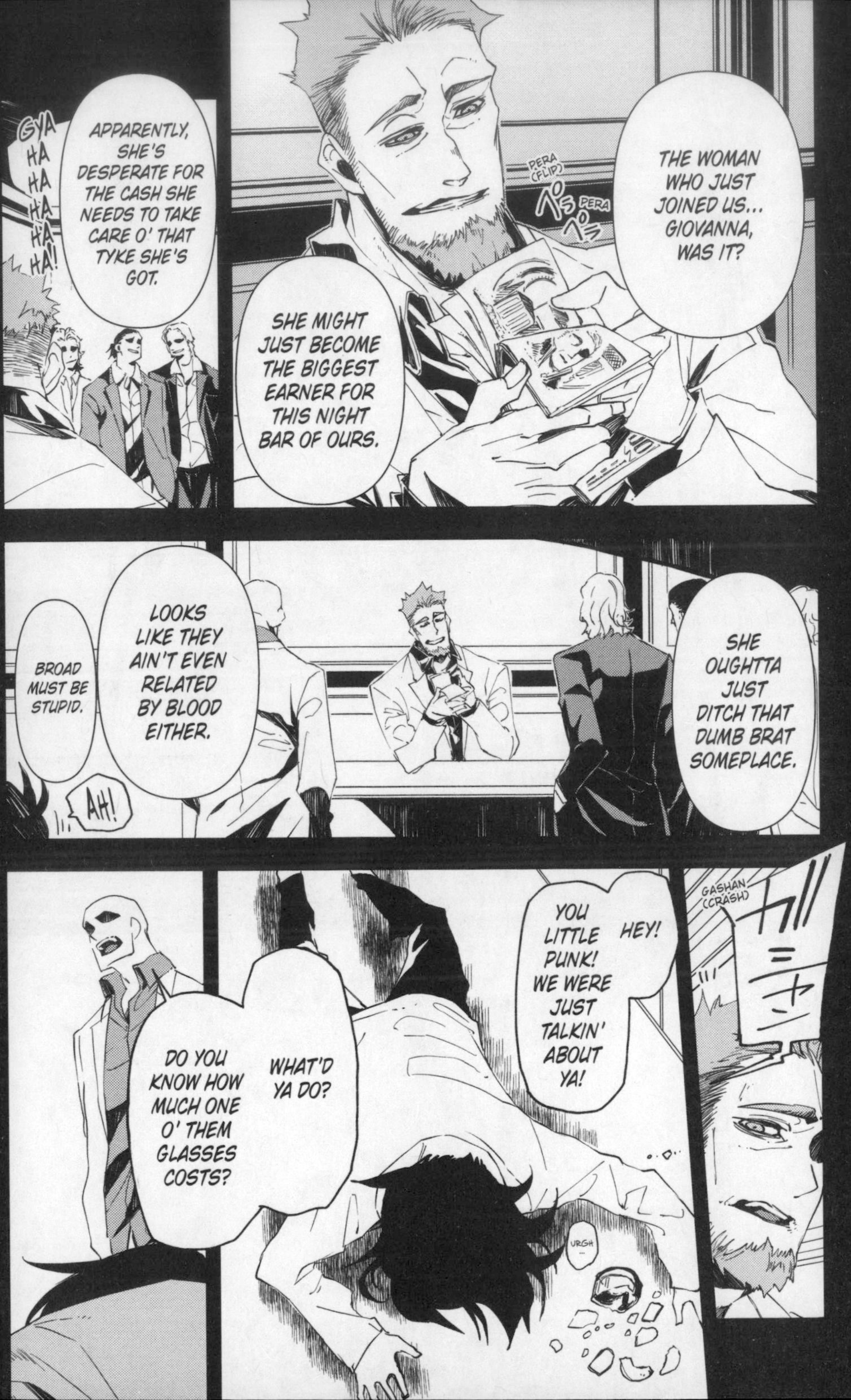
THE WOMAN WHO JUST JOINED US... GIOVANNA, WAS IT?
PERA (FLIP)
PERA
SHE MIGHT JUST BECOME THE BIGGEST EARNER FOR THIS NIGHT BAR OF OURS.
APPARENTLY, SHE'S DESPERATE FOR THE CASH SHE NEEDS TO TAKE CARE O' THAT TYKE SHE'S GOT.
GYA HA HA HA HA HA!
SHE OUGHTTA JUST DITCH THAT DUMB BRAT SOMEPLACE.
LOOKS LIKE THEY AIN'T EVEN RELATED BY BLOOD EITHER.
BROAD MUST BE STUPID.
AH!
GASHAN (CRASH)
HEY!
YOU LITTLE PUNK! WE WERE JUST TALKIN' ABOUT YA!
URGH...
WHAT'D YA DO?
DO YOU KNOW HOW MUCH ONE O' THEM GLASSES COSTS?

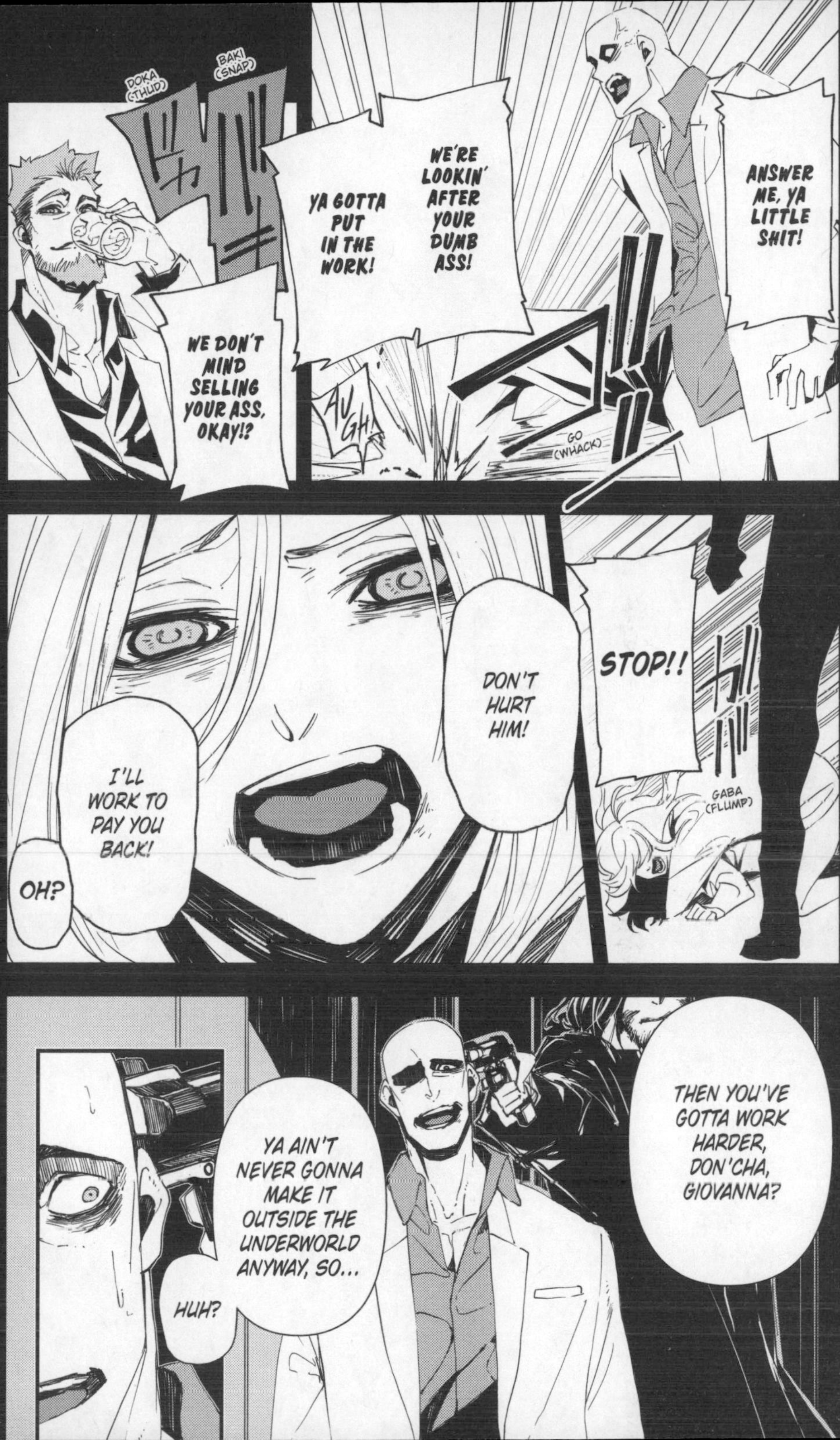
ANSWER ME, YA LITTLE SHIT!
WE'RE LOOKIN' AFTER YOUR DUMB ASS!
YA GOTTA PUT IN THE WORK!
GO (WHACK)
AUGH!
BAKI (SNAP)
DOKA (THUD)
WE DON'T MIND SELLING YOUR ASS, OKAY!?
STOP!!
GABA (FLUMP)
DON'T HURT HIM!
I'LL WORK TO PAY YOU BACK!
OH?
THEN YOU'VE GOTTA WORK HARDER, DON'CHA, GIOVANNA?
YA AIN'T NEVER GONNA MAKE IT OUTSIDE THE UNDERWORLD ANYWAY, SO...
HUH?

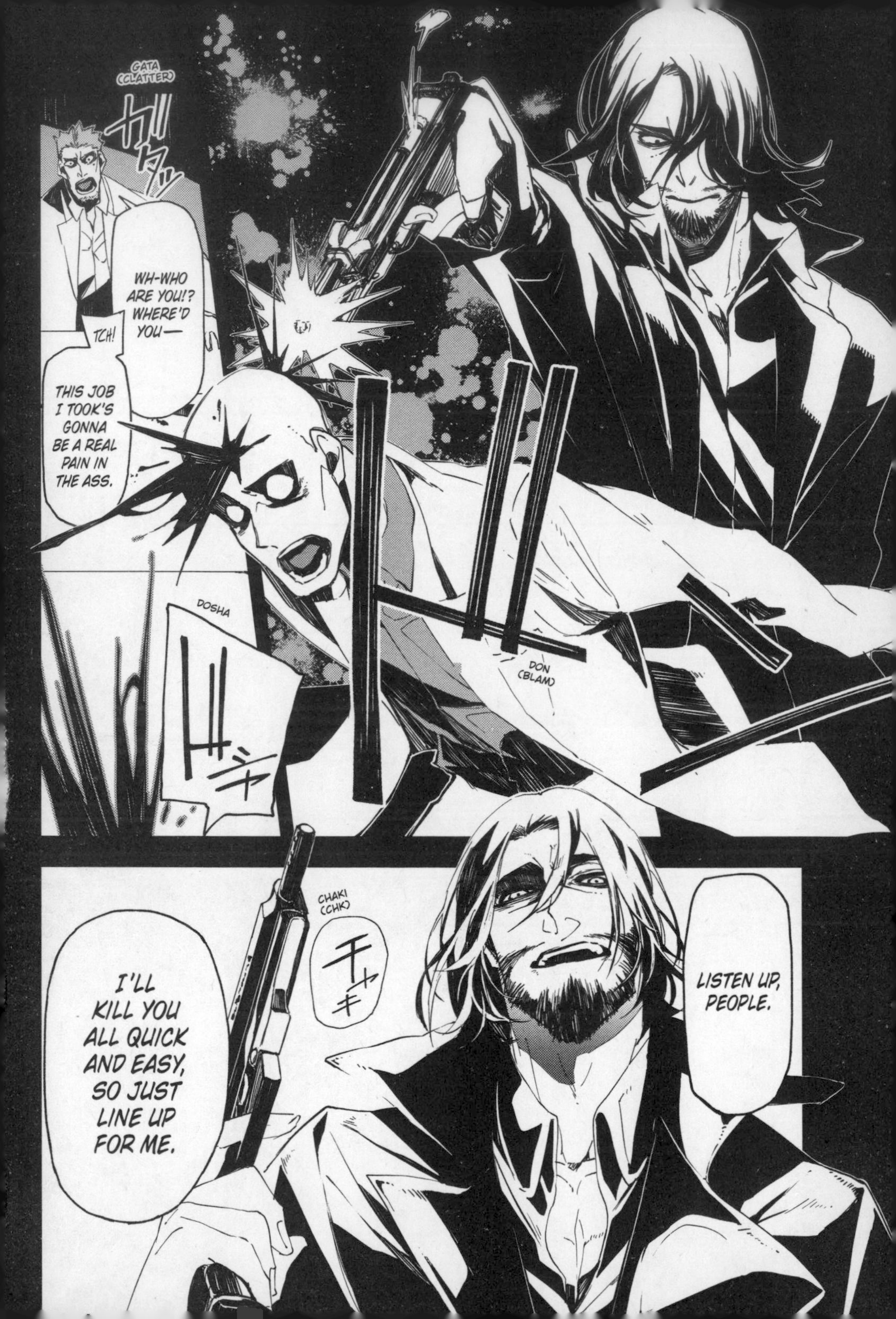
GATA (CLATTER)
WH-WHO ARE YOU!? WHERE'D YOU—
TCH!
THIS JOB I TOOK'S GONNA BE A REAL PAIN IN THE ASS.
DON (BLAM)
DOSHA
LISTEN UP, PEOPLE.
CHAKI (CHK)
I'LL KILL YOU ALL QUICK AND EASY, SO JUST LINE UP FOR ME.

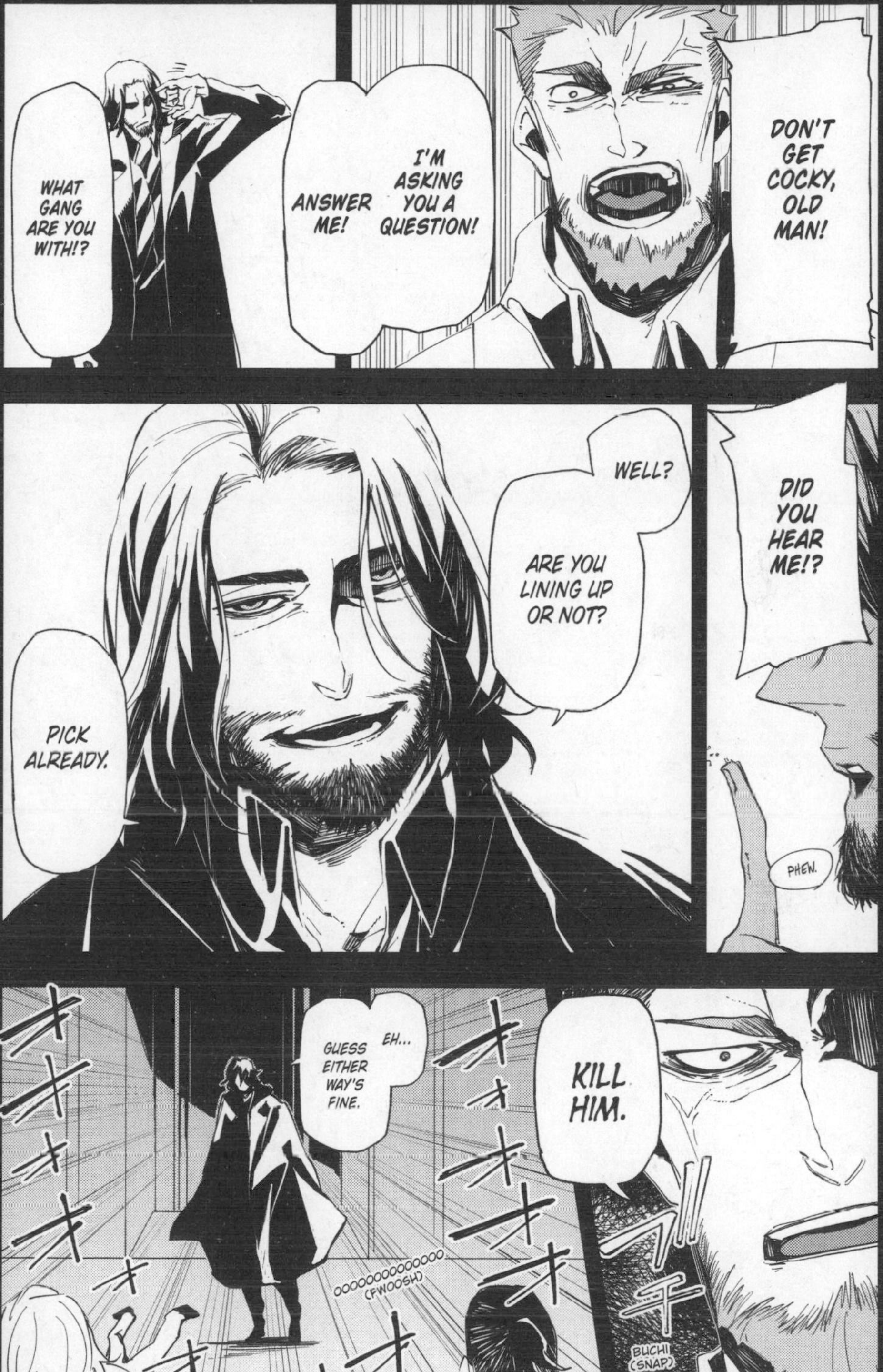
DON'T GET COCKY, OLD MAN!
I'M ASKING YOU A QUESTION!
ANSWER ME!
WHAT GANG ARE YOU WITH!?
DID YOU HEAR ME!?
PHEW.
WELL?
ARE YOU LINING UP OR NOT?
PICK ALREADY.
KILL HIM.
BUCHI (SNAP)
EH...
GUESS EITHER WAY'S FINE.
(FWOOSH)

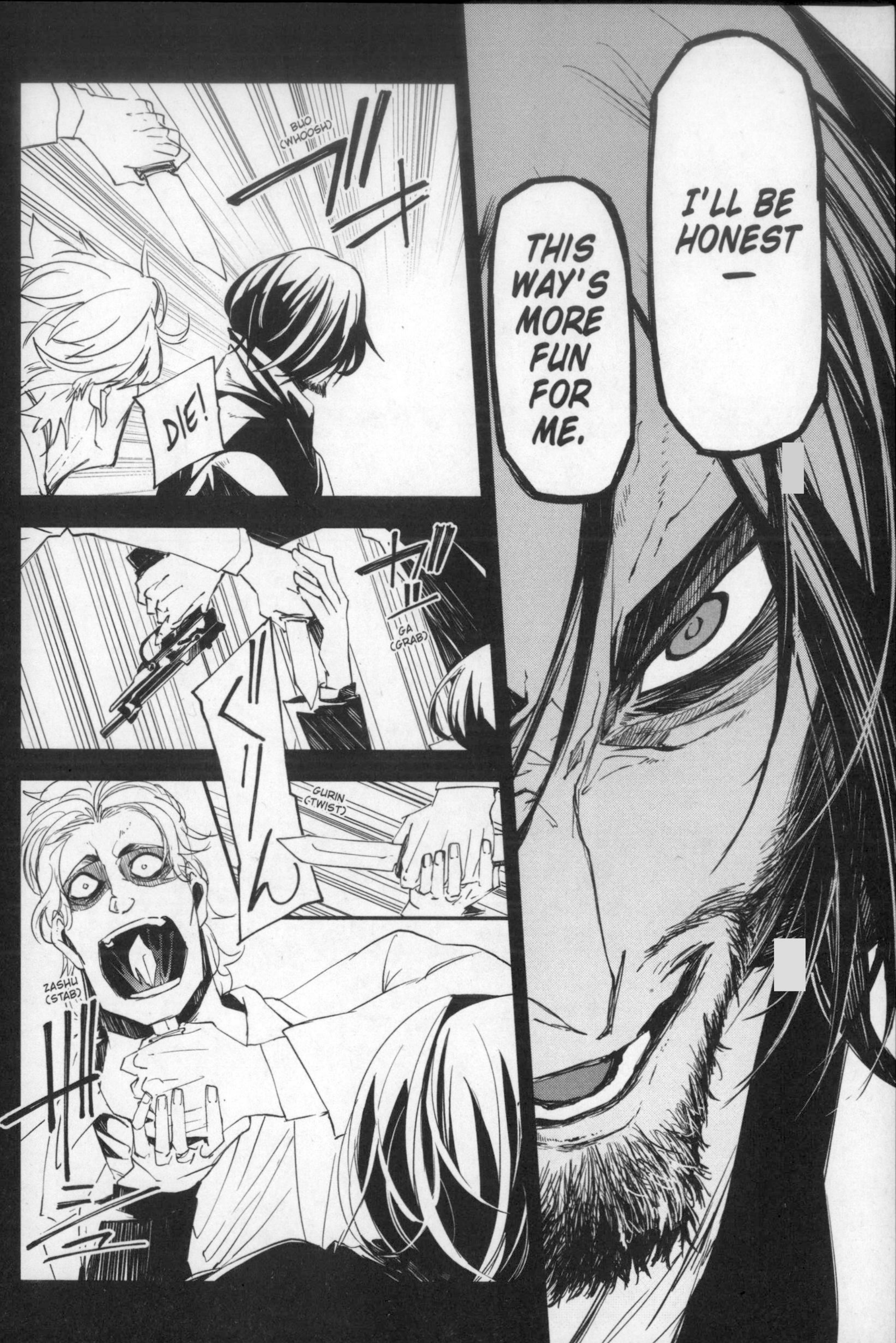
I'LL BE HONEST —
THIS WAY'S MORE FUN FOR ME.
BUO (WHOOSH)
DIE!
GA (GRAB)
GURIN (TWIST)
ZASHU (STAB)

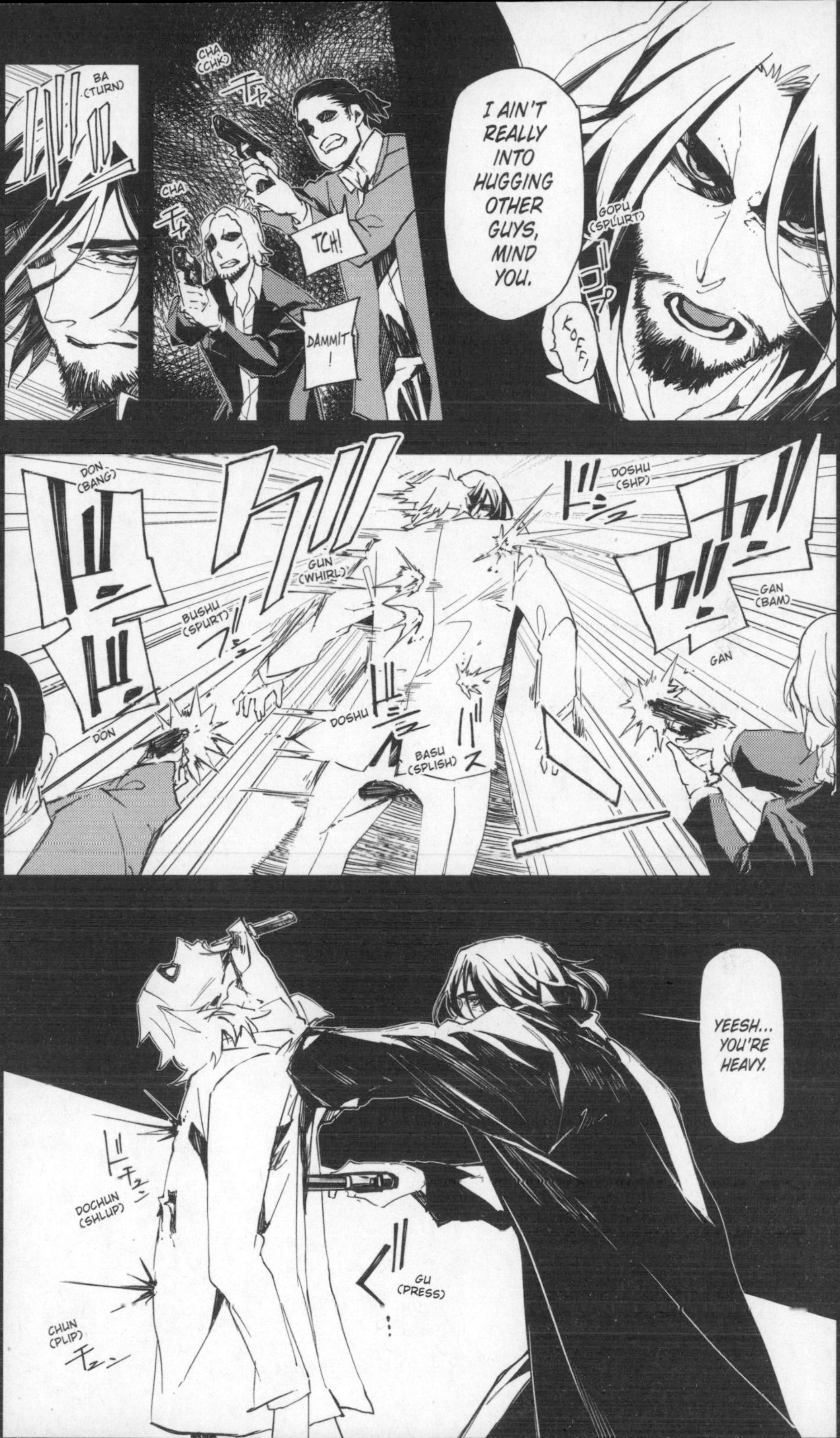
I AIN'T REALLY INTO HUGGING OTHER GUYS, MIND YOU.
GOPU (SPLURT)
KOFF!
CHA (CHK)
TCH!
CHA
DAMMIT!
BA (TURN)
DOSHU (SHP)
GAN (BAM)
GAN
GUN (WHIRL)
DON (BANG)
BUSHU (SPURT)
DOSHU
BASU (SPLISH)
DON
YEESH... YOU'RE HEAVY.
DOCHUN (SHLUP)
GU (PRESS)
CHUN (PLIP)

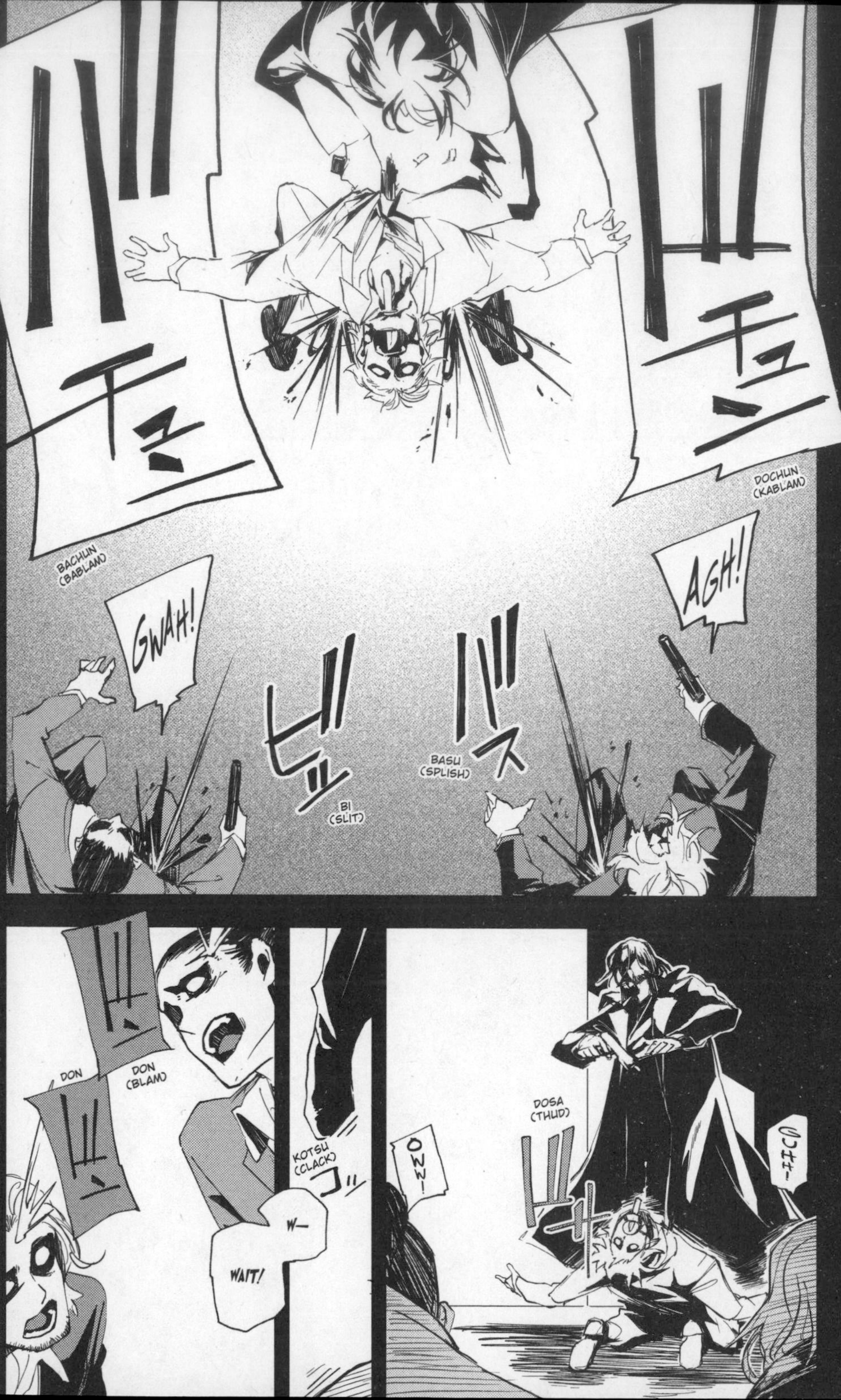
DOCHUN (KABLAM)
AGH!
BASU (SPLISH)
BI (SLIT)
BACHUN (BABLAM)
GWAH!
DOSA (THUD)
GUHH!
OWW!
KOTSU (CLACK)
DON (BLAM)
DON
W—
WAIT!

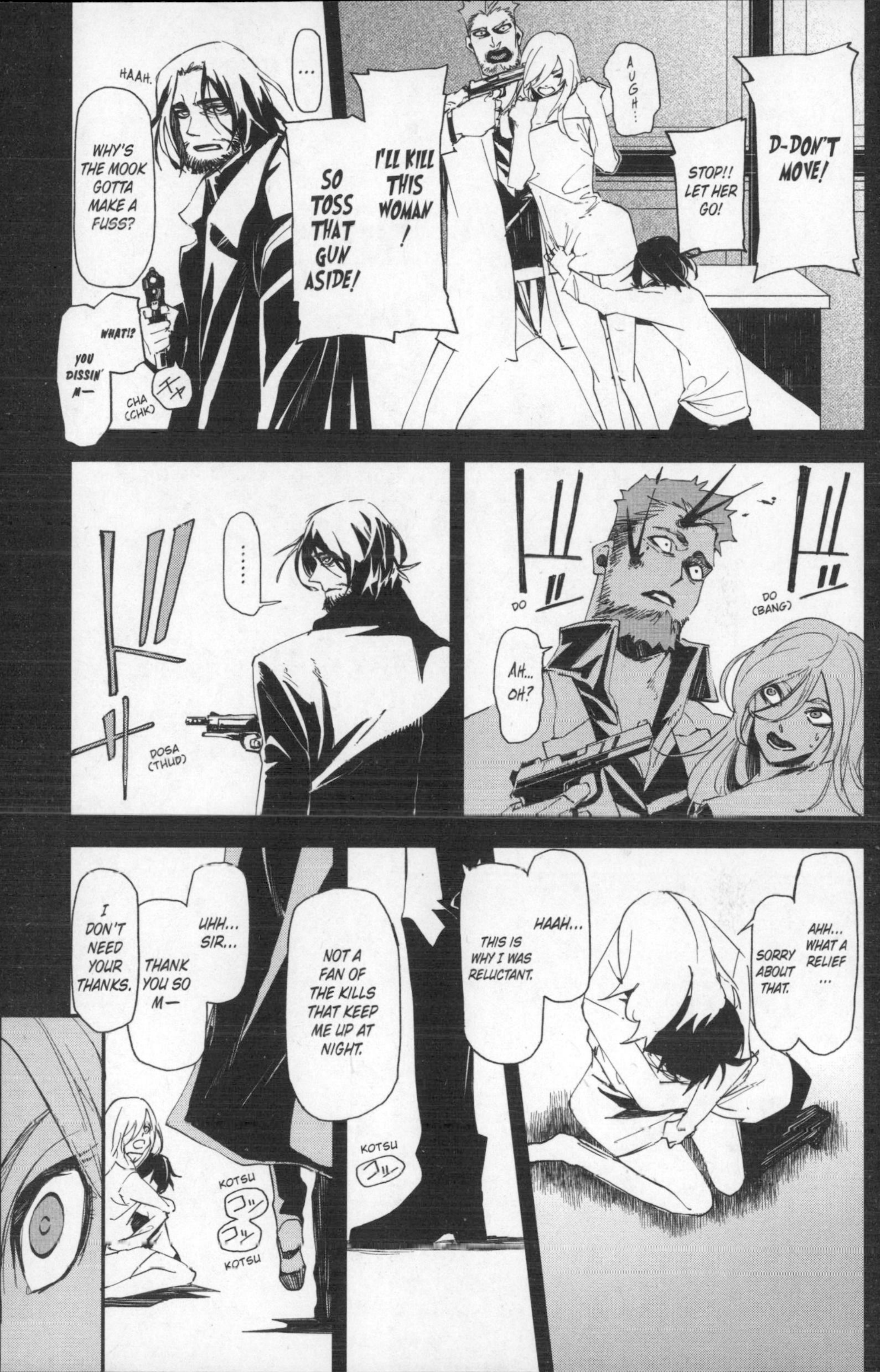
D-DON'T MOVE!
STOP!! LET HER GO!
AUGH...
I'LL KILL THIS WOMAN!
SO TOSS THAT GUN ASIDE!
...
HAAH.
WHY'S THE MOOK GOTTA MAKE A FUSS?
WHAT!? YOU DISSIN' M—
CHA (CHK)
DO (BANG)
DO
AH... OH?
......
DOSA (THUD)
AHH... WHAT A RELIEF...
SORRY ABOUT THAT.
HAAH...
THIS IS WHY I WAS RELUCTANT.
NOT A FAN OF THE KILLS THAT KEEP ME UP AT NIGHT.
KOTSU
UHH... SIR...
THANK YOU SO M—
I DON'T NEED YOUR THANKS.
KOTSU
KOTSU

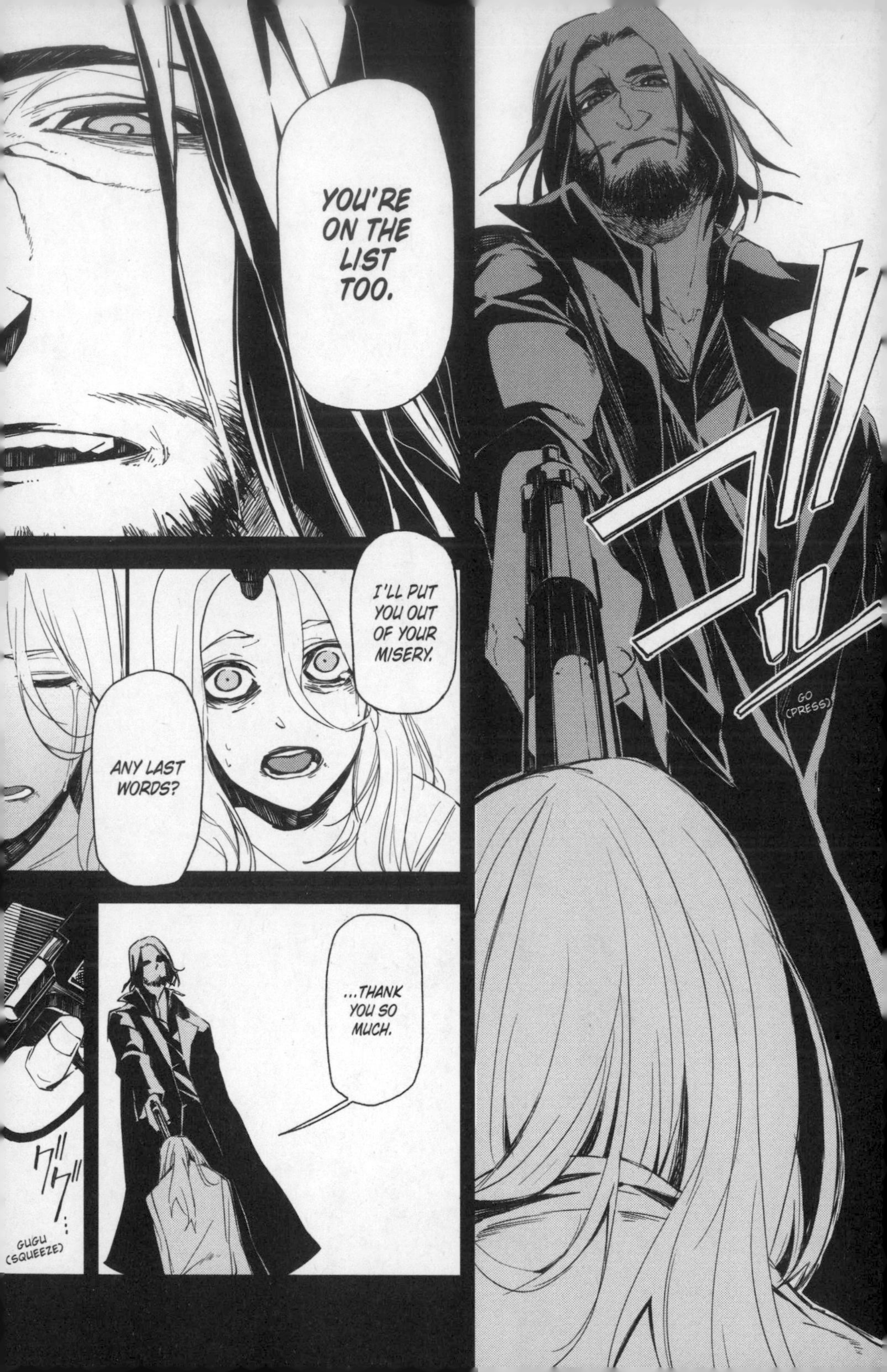
GO
(PRESS)
YOU'RE ON THE LIST TOO.
I'LL PUT YOU OUT OF YOUR MISERY.
ANY LAST WORDS?
...THANK YOU SO MUCH.
GUGU
(SQUEEZE)

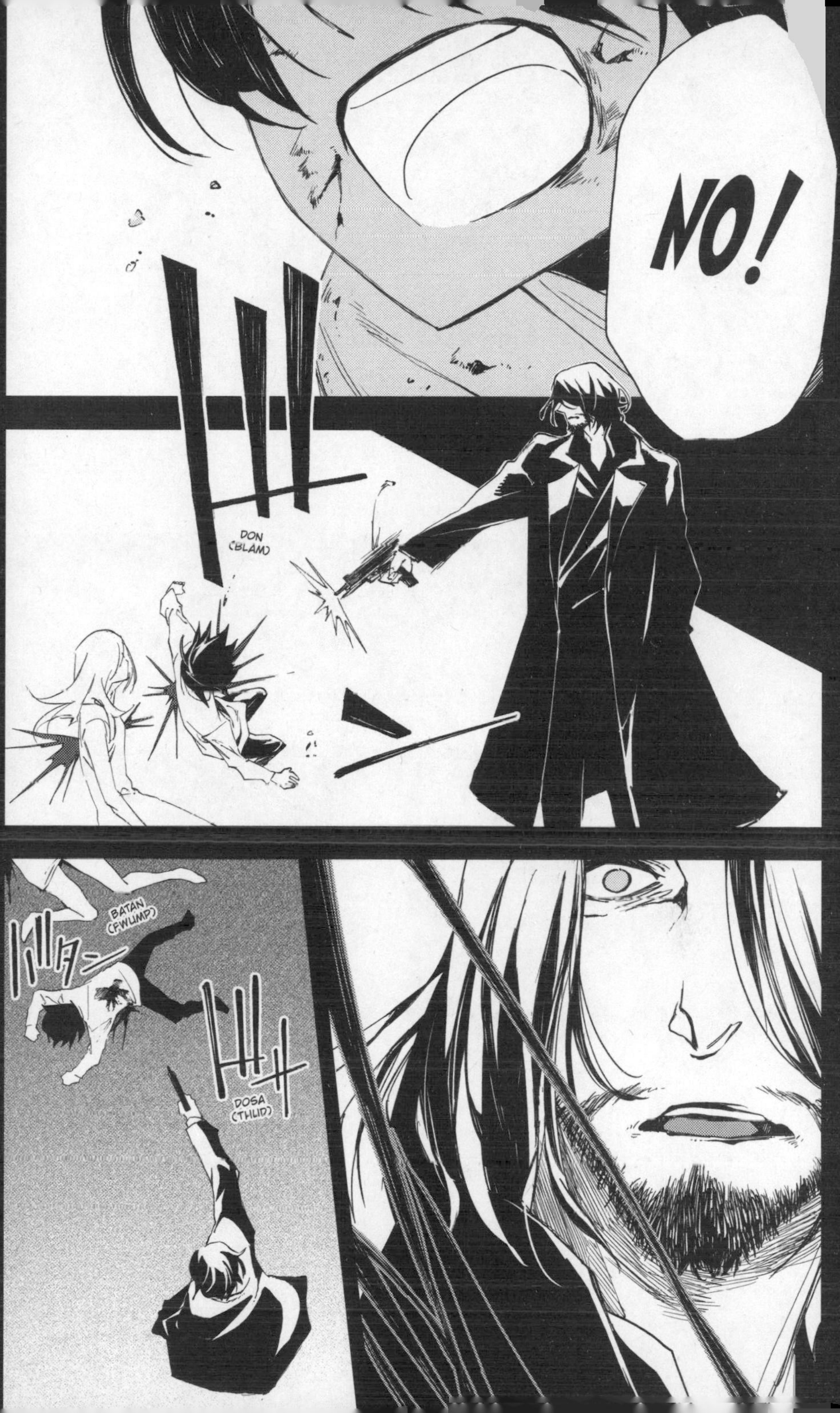
NO!
DON (BLAM)
BATAN (FWUMP)
DOSA (THUD)

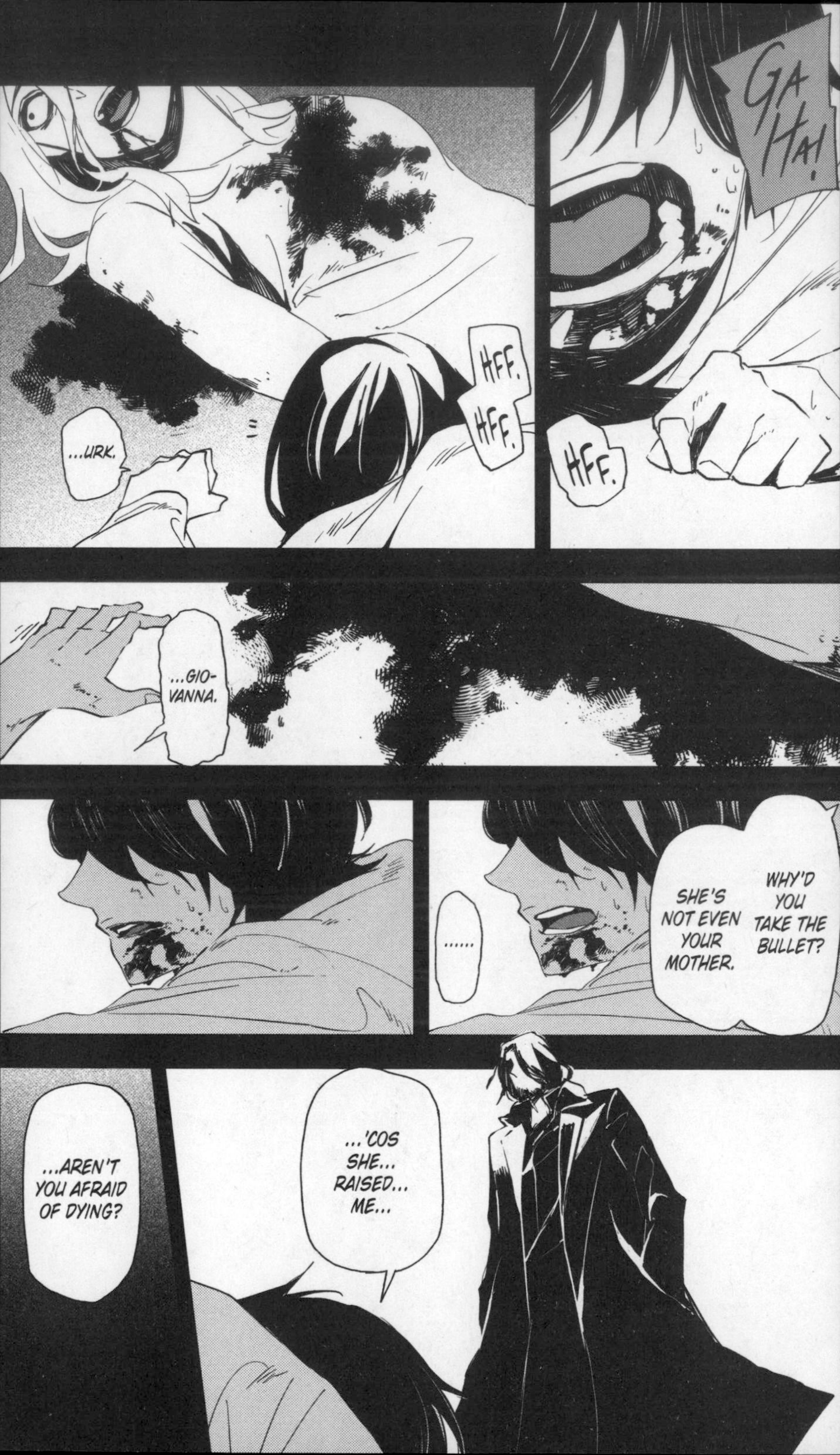
GA HA!
HFF.
HFF.
HFF.
...URK.
...GIO-VANNA.
WHY'D YOU TAKE THE BULLET?
SHE'S NOT EVEN YOUR MOTHER.
......
...'COS SHE... RAISED... ME...
...AREN'T YOU AFRAID OF DYING?

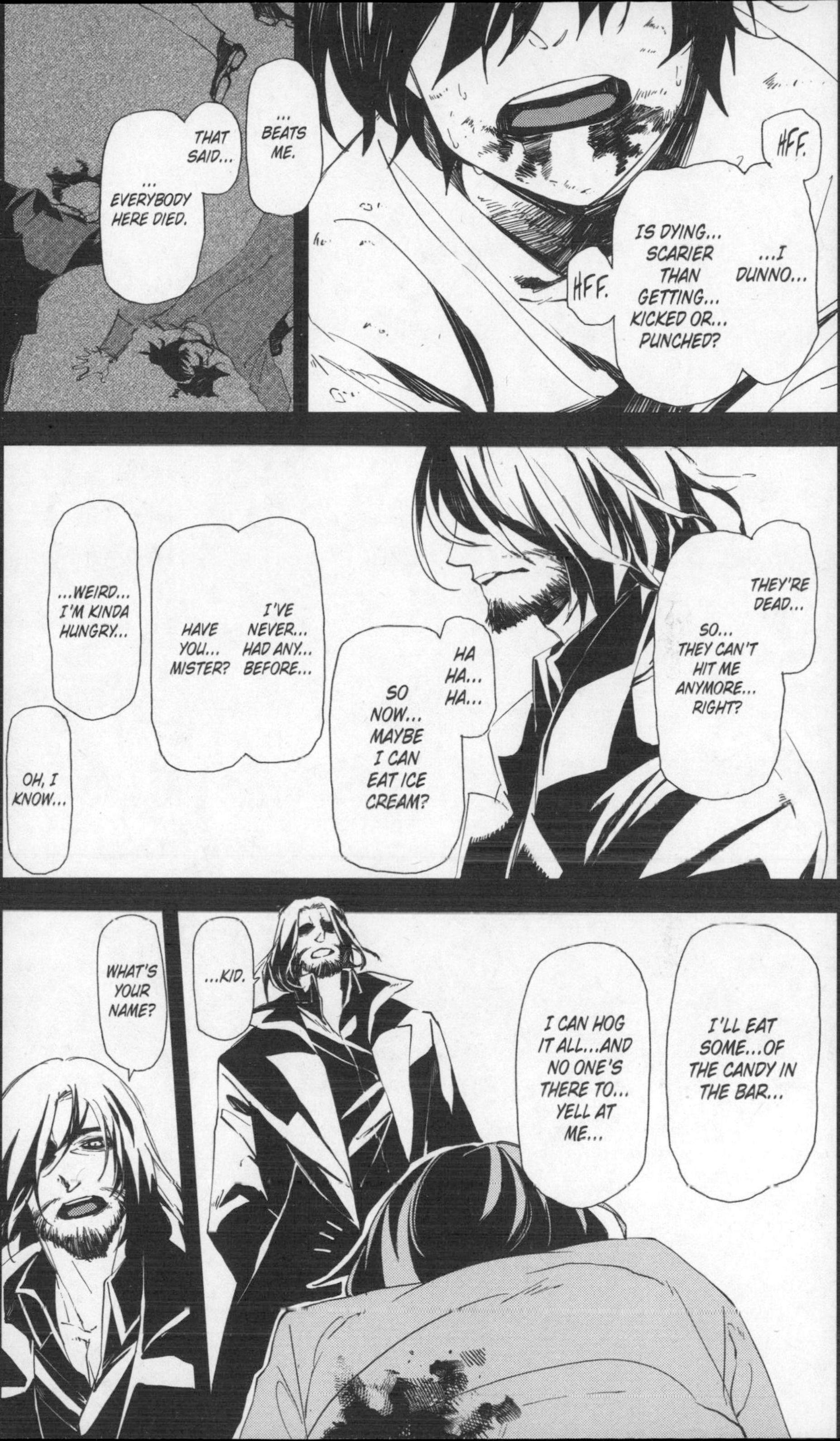
HFF.
...I DUNNO...
IS DYING... SCARIER THAN GETTING... KICKED OR... PUNCHED?
HFF.
... BEATS ME.
THAT SAID...
... EVERYBODY HERE DIED.
THEY'RE DEAD...
SO... THEY CAN'T HIT ME ANYMORE... RIGHT?
HA HA... HA...
SO NOW... MAYBE I CAN EAT ICE CREAM?
I'VE NEVER... HAD ANY... BEFORE...
HAVE YOU... MISTER?
...WEIRD... I'M KINDA HUNGRY...
OH, I KNOW...
I'LL EAT SOME...OF THE CANDY IN THE BAR...
I CAN HOG IT ALL...AND NO ONE'S THERE TO... YELL AT ME...
...KID.
WHAT'S YOUR NAME?

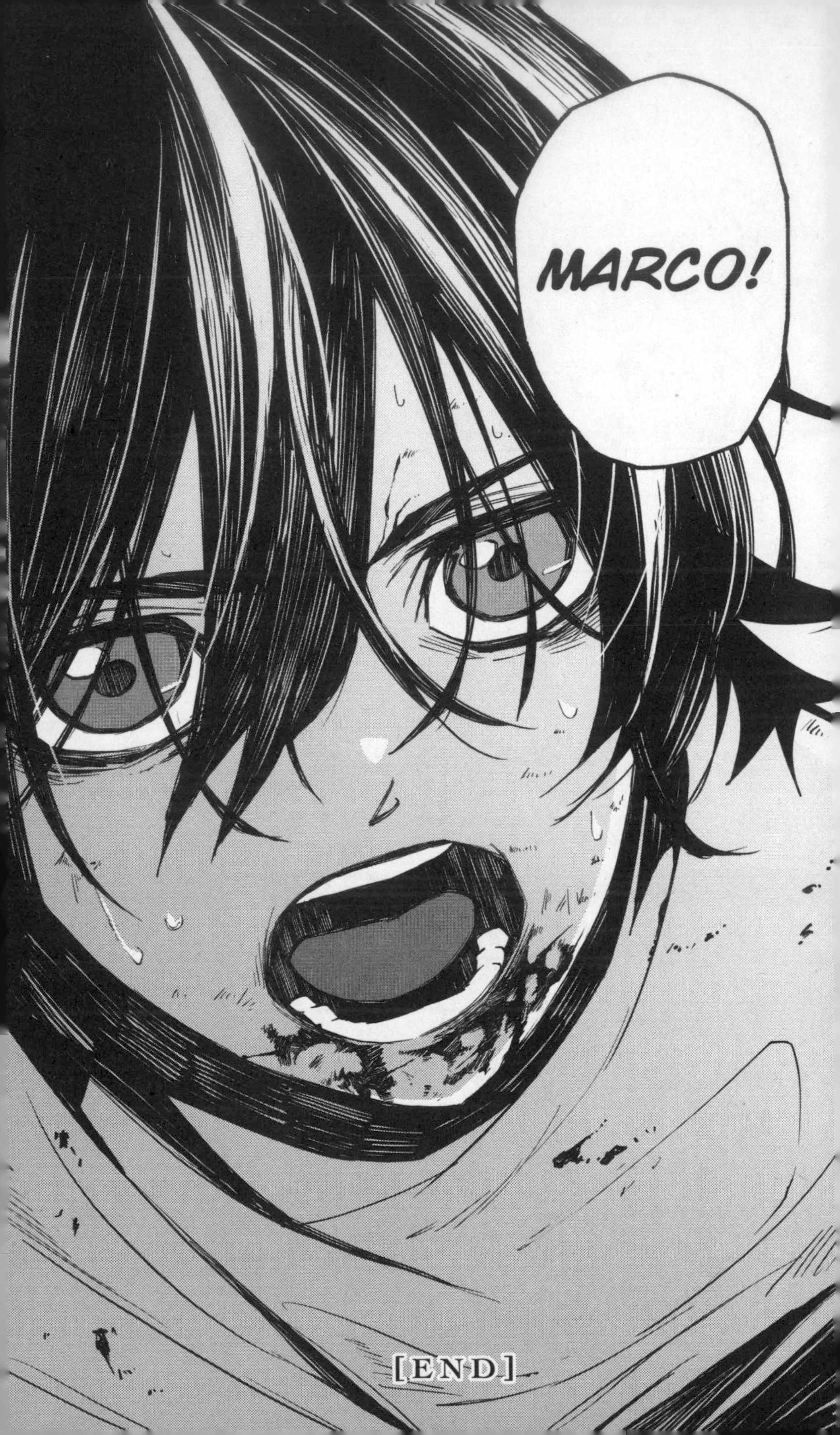
MARCO!
[END]

Translation Notes

COMMON HONORIFICS

no honorific: Indicates familiarity or closeness; if used without permission or reason, addressing someone in this manner would constitute an insult.

-*san*: The Japanese equivalent of Mr./Mrs./Miss. If a situation calls for politeness, this is the failsafe honorific.

-*kun*: Used most often when referring to boys, this indicates affection or familiarity. Occasionally used by older men among their peers, but it may also be used by anyone referring to a person of lower standing.

-*chan*: An affectionate honorific indicating familiarity, used mostly in reference to girls; also used in reference to cute persons or animals, regardless of gender.

-*sensei*: A respectful term for teachers, artists, or high-level professionals.

-*senpai*: An honorific used for upperclassmen and older, more knowledgeable colleagues.

Onii-chan: An affectionate term used for older brothers or brother figures.

PAGE 3

Comisu, or Comic Summit, is a reference to Comiket—short for Comic Market, a *doujinshi* convention where artists and authors from across the country gather to exhibit and sell their works. It's the largest such event in Japan.

Otaku, or as it's translated in the title of the series, "geek," is a Japanese term used to refer to hard-core fans of almost anything, but most commonly manga, anime, idols, and games.

Doujinshi are self-published books that are typically based on existing series, written and illustrated by passionate fans, as well as aspiring manga creators looking to get their start in the industry.

PAGE 9

This pushy cosplayer is referencing characters from several famous anime—Asuka from Neon Genesis Evangelion, and Lelouch from Code Geass.

PAGE 23

Fujoshi is a term meaning "rotten woman," and is used by female fans of the boys' love genre in a jokingly self-deprecating manner. It's a pun on the word *fujoshi* (meaning "woman") and the character *fu* (meaning "rotten").

PAGE 29

"-*taso*" is an intentional misspelling of "-*tan*." The "-*tan*" honorific is an even cuter way of saying "-*chan*," and in *katakana*, the Japanese syllabary used primarily for foreign words, "n" and "so" look extremely similar, so it can be easy to mix the two up. An English equivalent would be the intentional misspelling of "own" as "pwn" in the early days of online gaming.

PAGE 89

Yakuza is a term used to refer to organized crime syndicates that originated in Japan. Marco also adds "Giapponese" when referring to them, which is Italian for "Japanese."

PAGE 177

Hidakaya is a Chinese-style restaurant chain in Japan known for its *gyoza* dumplings and ramen.

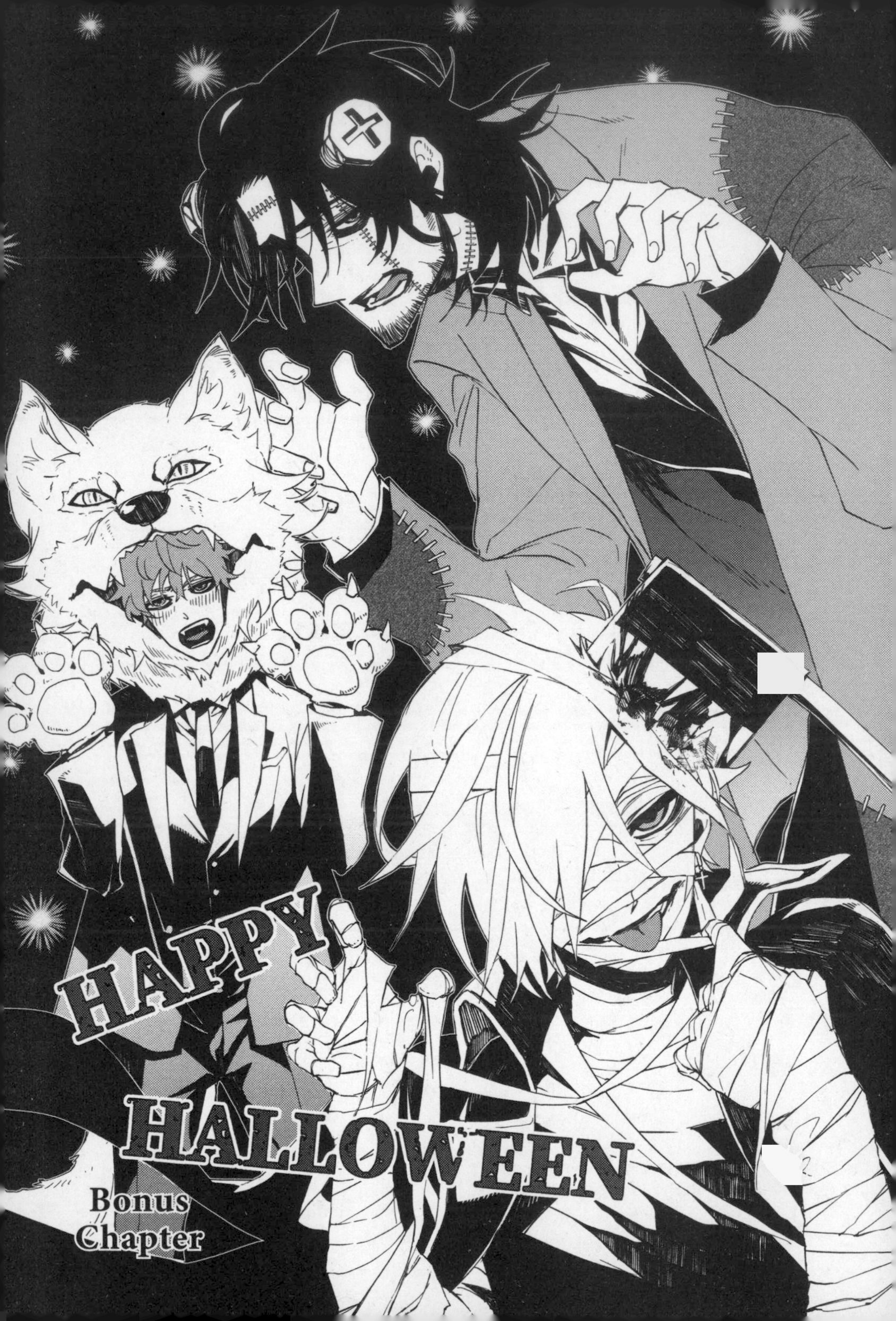
HAPPY HALLOWEEN
Bonus Chapter

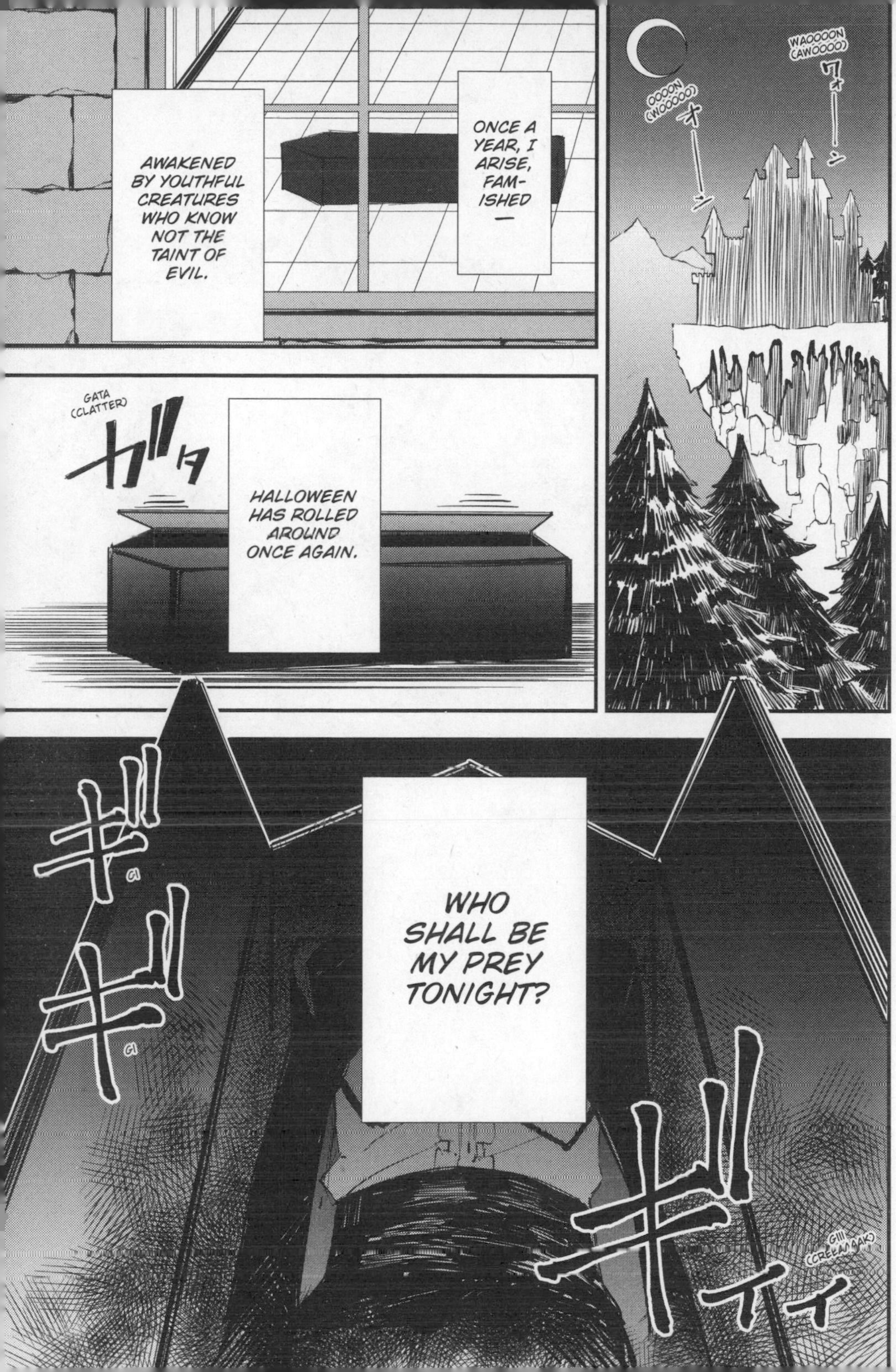

WAOOOON (AWOOOOO)
OOOON (WOOOOO)
ONCE A YEAR, I ARISE, FAMISHED —
AWAKENED BY YOUTHFUL CREATURES WHO KNOW NOT THE TAINT OF EVIL.
HALLOWEEN HAS ROLLED AROUND ONCE AGAIN.
GATA (CLATTER)
WHO SHALL BE MY PREY TONIGHT?
GIII (CREEAAAK)
GI
GI

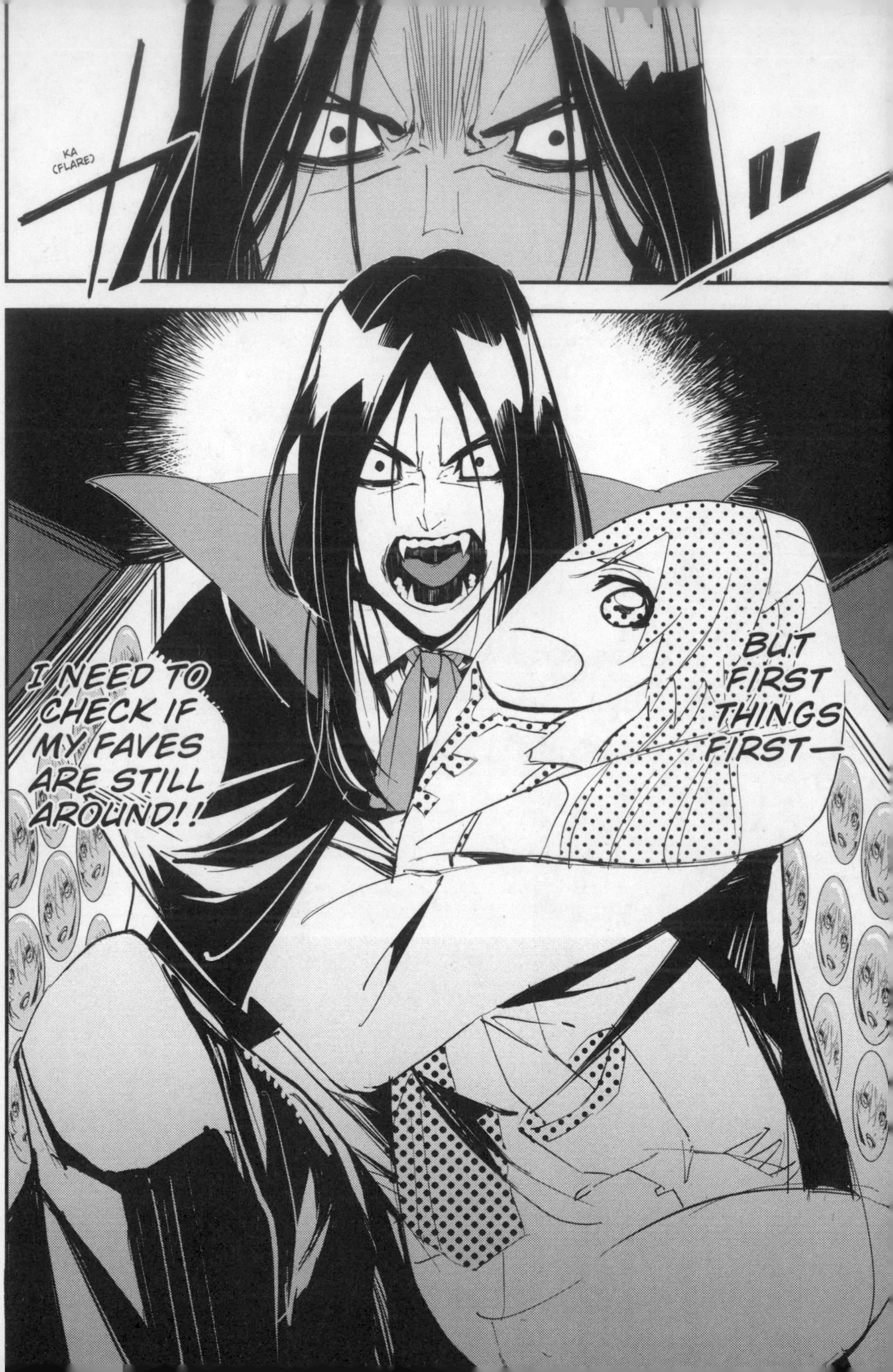
KA (FLARE)
BUT FIRST THINGS FIRST—
I NEED TO CHECK IF MY FAVES ARE STILL AROUND!!

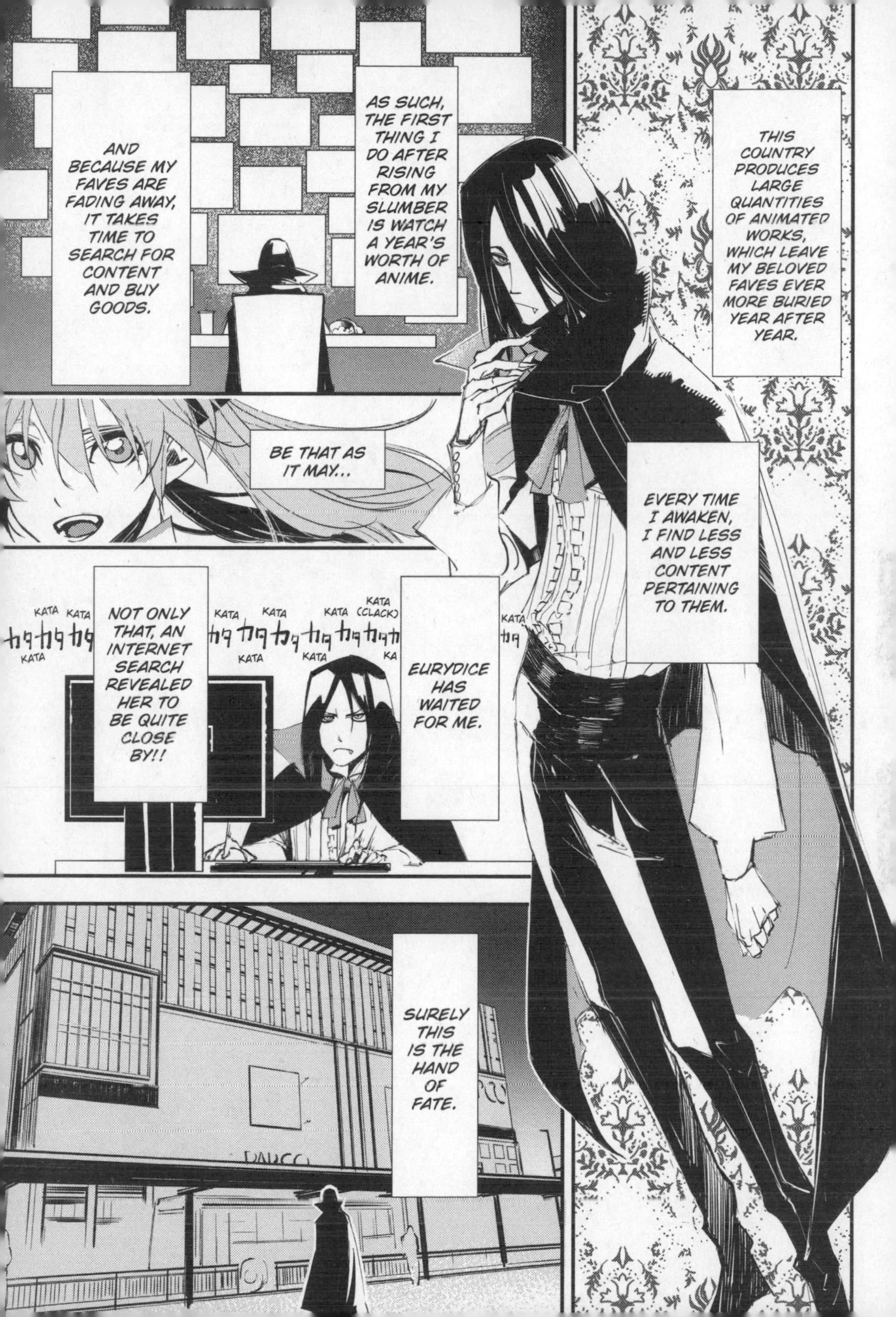
THIS COUNTRY PRODUCES LARGE QUANTITIES OF ANIMATED WORKS, WHICH LEAVE MY BELOVED FAVES EVER MORE BURIED YEAR AFTER YEAR.
EVERY TIME I AWAKEN, I FIND LESS AND LESS CONTENT PERTAINING TO THEM.
AS SUCH, THE FIRST THING I DO AFTER RISING FROM MY SLUMBER IS WATCH A YEAR'S WORTH OF ANIME.
AND BECAUSE MY FAVES ARE FADING AWAY, IT TAKES TIME TO SEARCH FOR CONTENT AND BUY GOODS.
BE THAT AS IT MAY...
EURYDICE HAS WAITED FOR ME.
NOT ONLY THAT, AN INTERNET SEARCH REVEALED HER TO BE QUITE CLOSE BY!!
KATA KATA KATA KATA KATA KATA KATA KATA (CLACK) KATA KATA KATA
SURELY THIS IS THE HAND OF FATE.

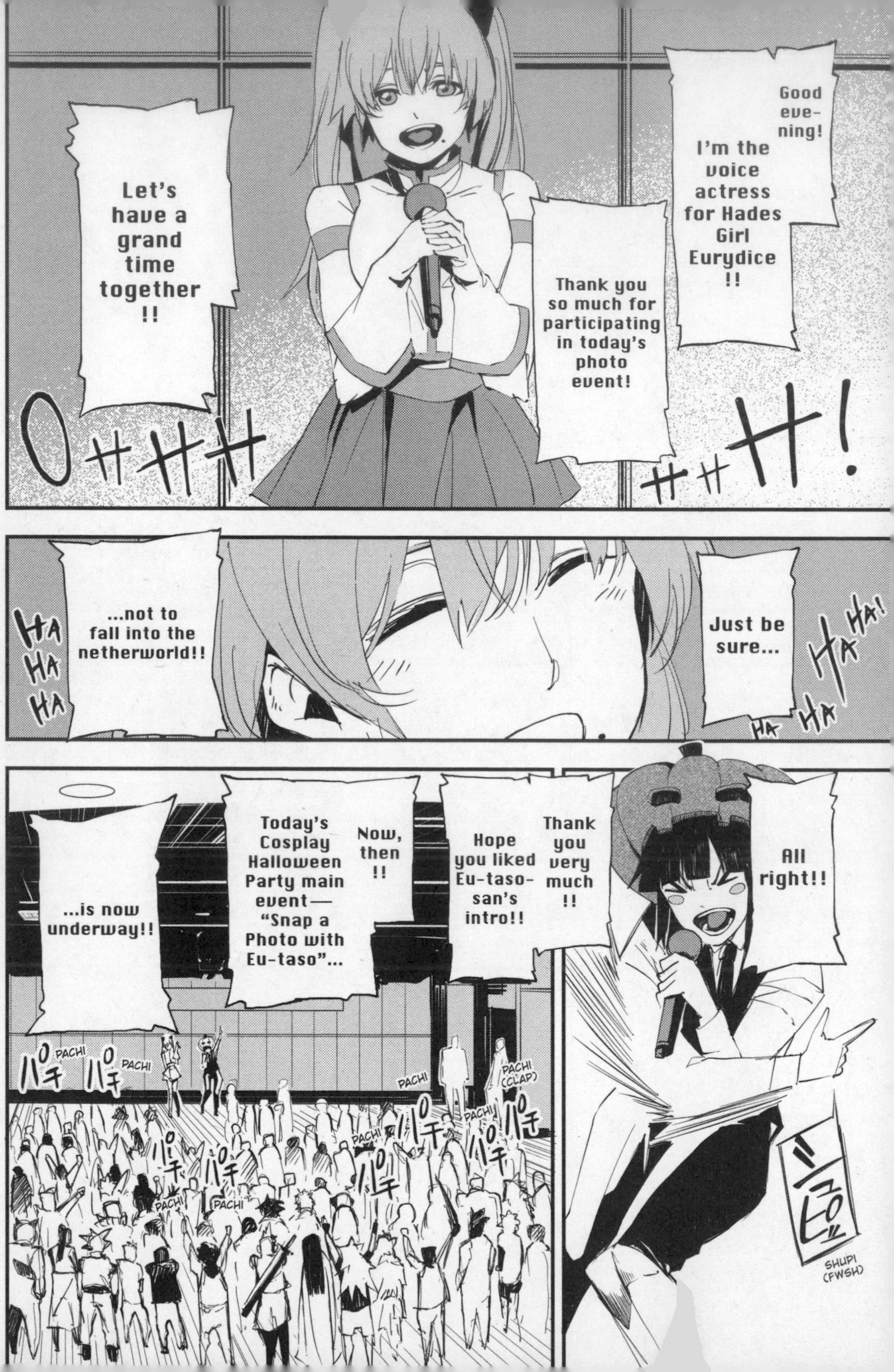
Good eve-ning! I'm the voice actress for Hades Girl Eurydice!!
Thank you so much for participating in today's photo event!
Let's have a grand time together!!
OHHHHHHH!
Just be sure...
...not to fall into the netherworld!!
HA HA HA HA HA
HA HA HA
All right!!
Thank you very much!!
Hope you liked Eu-taso-san's intro!!
SHUPI (FWSH)
Now, then!!
Today's Cosplay Halloween Party main event—"Snap a Photo with Eu-taso"...
...is now underway!!
PACHI PACHI PACHI PACHI (CLAP)
PACHI PACHI PACHI PACHI

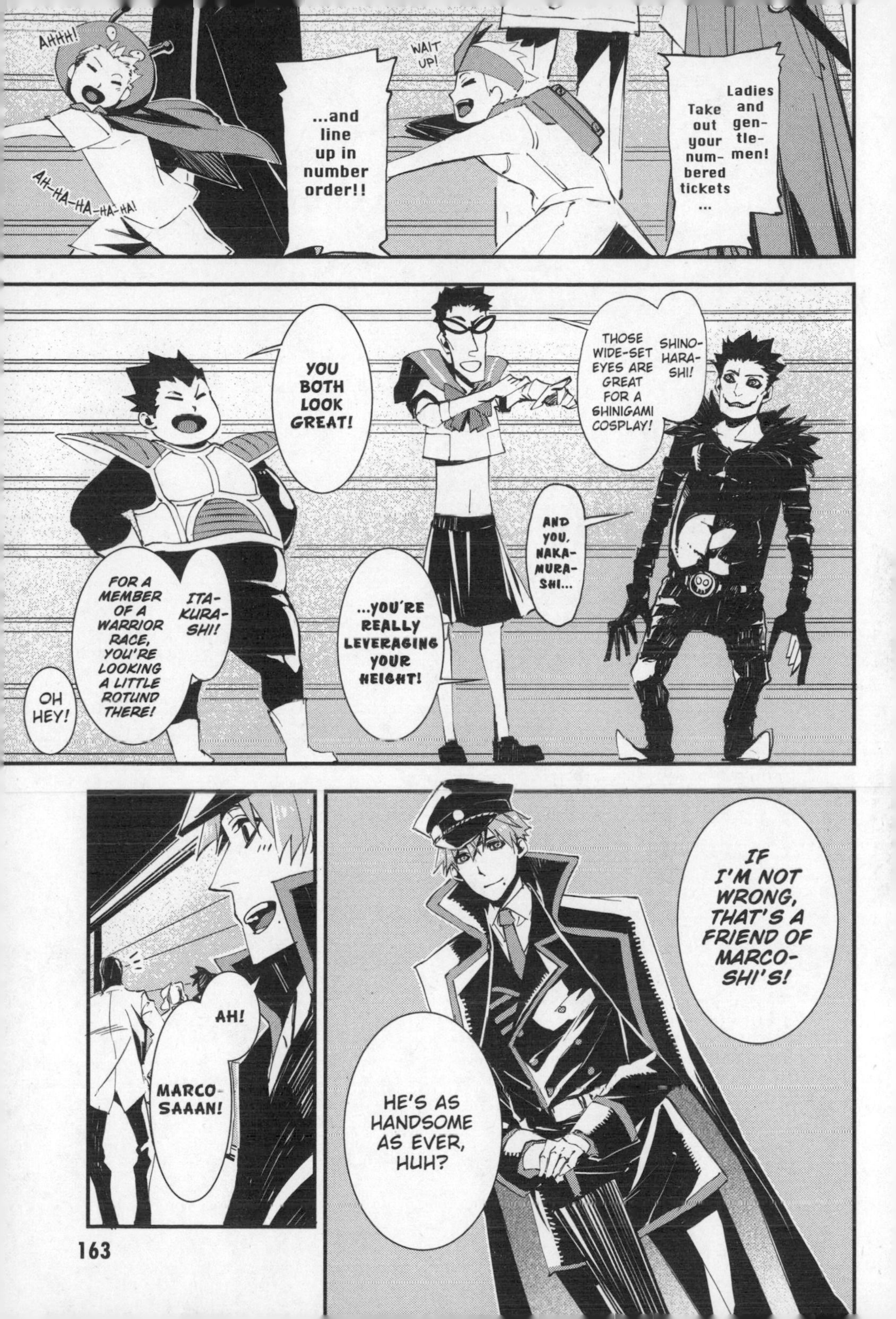
Ladies and gentlemen! Take out your numbered tickets...
...and line up in number order!!
WAIT UP!
AHHH!
AH-HA-HA-HA-HA!
SHINOHARA-SHI!
THOSE WIDE-SET EYES ARE GREAT FOR A SHINIGAMI COSPLAY!
YOU BOTH LOOK GREAT!
AND YOU, NAKAMURA-SHI...
...YOU'RE REALLY LEVERAGING YOUR HEIGHT!
ITAKURA-SHI!
FOR A MEMBER OF A WARRIOR RACE, YOU'RE LOOKING A LITTLE ROTUND THERE!
OH HEY!
IF I'M NOT WRONG, THAT'S A FRIEND OF MARCO-SHI'S!
HE'S AS HANDSOME AS EVER, HUH?
AH!
MARCO-SAAAN!

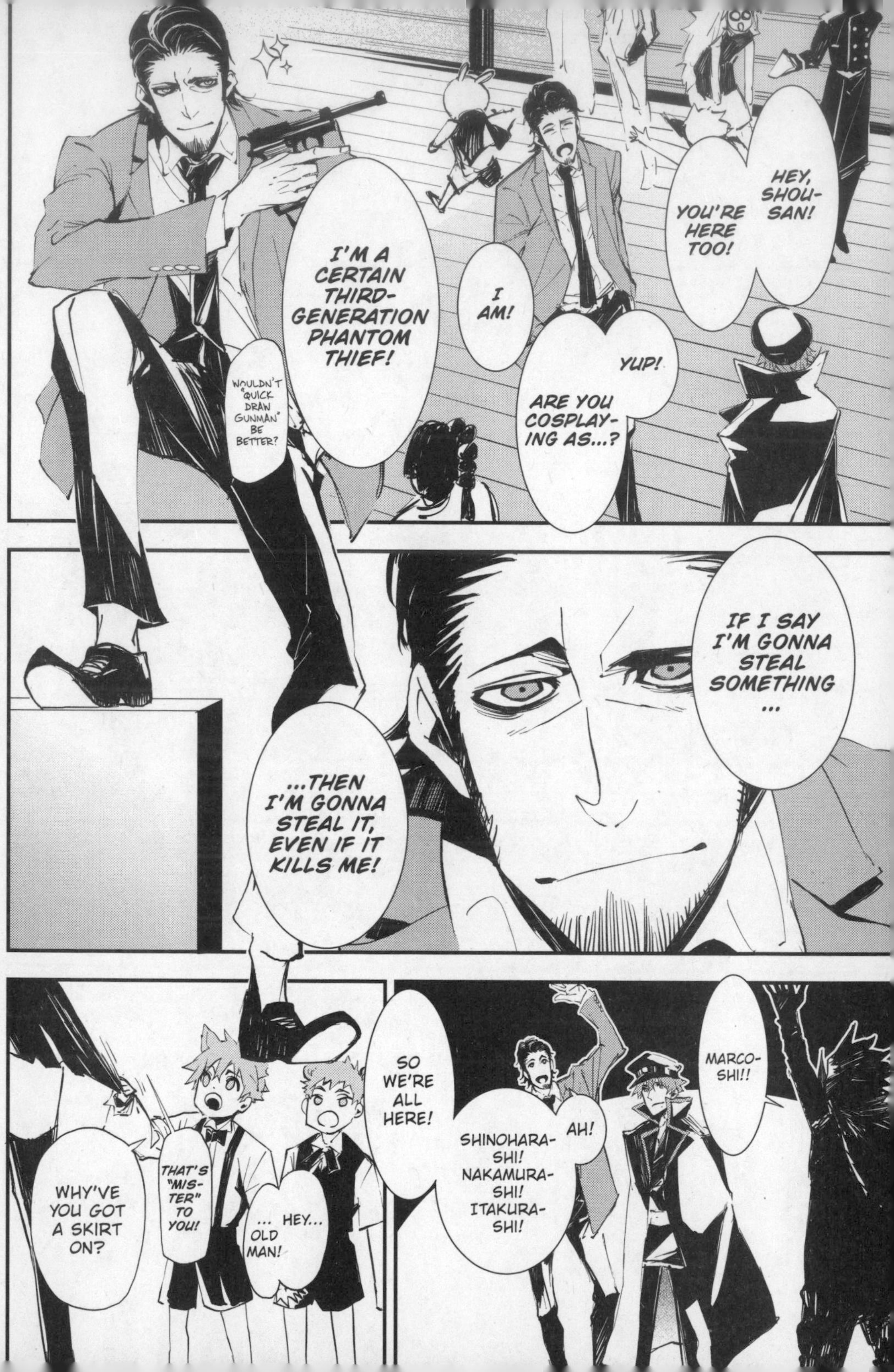
HEY, SHOU-SAN!
YOU'RE HERE TOO!
I AM!
YUP!
ARE YOU COSPLAYING AS...?
I'M A CERTAIN THIRD-GENERATION PHANTOM THIEF!
WOULDN'T "QUICK DRAW GUNMAN" BE BETTER?
IF I SAY I'M GONNA STEAL SOMETHING...
...THEN I'M GONNA STEAL IT, EVEN IF IT KILLS ME!
MARCO-SHI!!
AH!
SHINOHARA-SHI! NAKAMURA-SHI! ITAKURA-SHI!
SO WE'RE ALL HERE!
... HEY... OLD MAN!
THAT'S "MISTER" TO YOU!
WHY'VE YOU GOT A SKIRT ON?

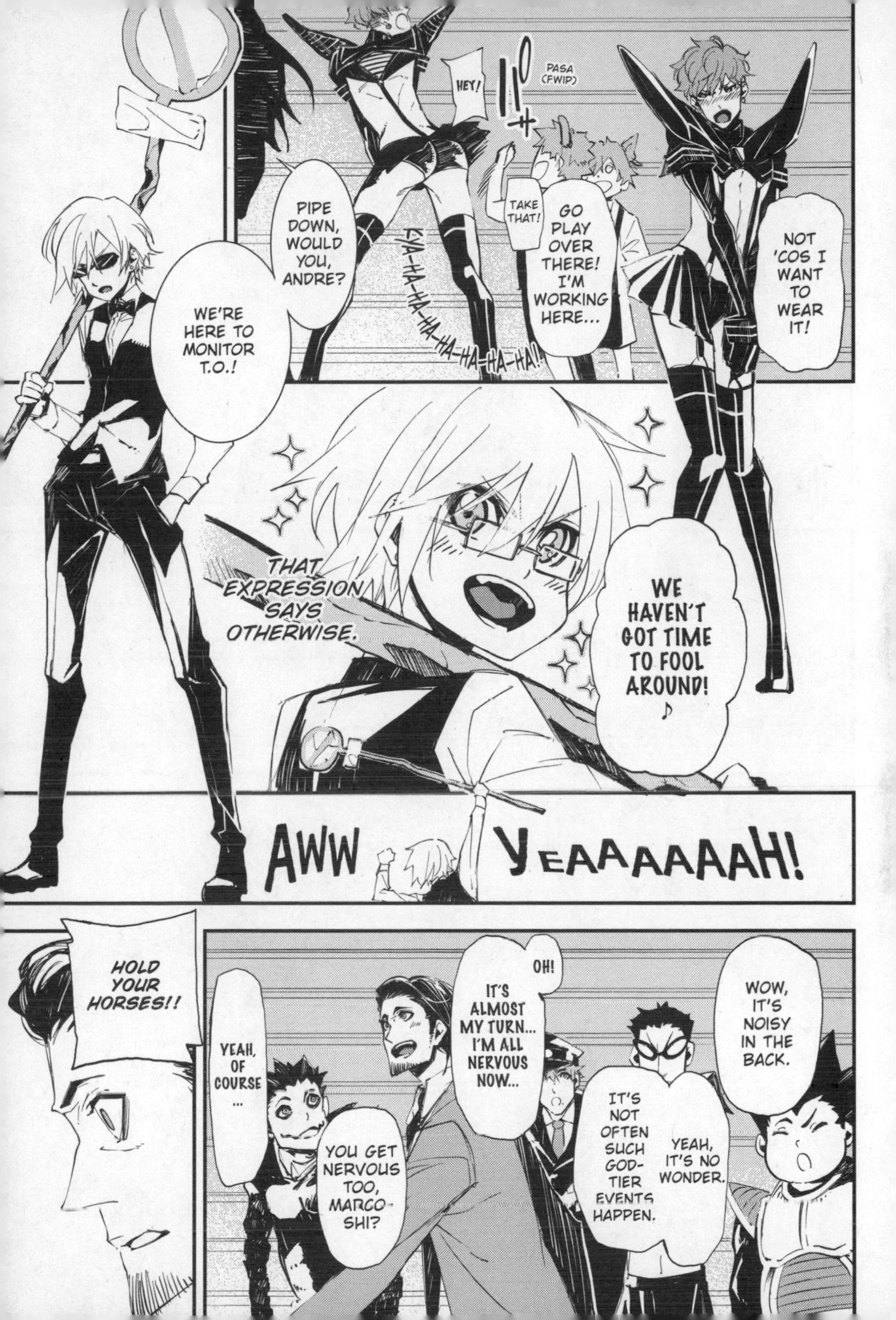
NOT 'COS I WANT TO WEAR IT!
HEY!
PASA (FWIP)
GO PLAY OVER THERE! I'M WORKING HERE...
TAKE THAT!
KYA-HA-HA-HA-HA-HA-HA-HA!
WE HAVEN'T GOT TIME TO FOOL AROUND! ♪
THAT EXPRESSION SAYS OTHERWISE.
AWW YEAAAAAAH!
PIPE DOWN, WOULD YOU, ANDRE?
WE'RE HERE TO MONITOR T.O.!
WOW, IT'S NOISY IN THE BACK.
YEAH, IT'S NO WONDER.
IT'S NOT OFTEN SUCH GOD-TIER EVENTS HAPPEN.
OH!
IT'S ALMOST MY TURN... I'M ALL NERVOUS NOW...
YOU GET NERVOUS TOO, MARCO-SHI?
YEAH, OF COURSE ...
HOLD YOUR HORSES!!

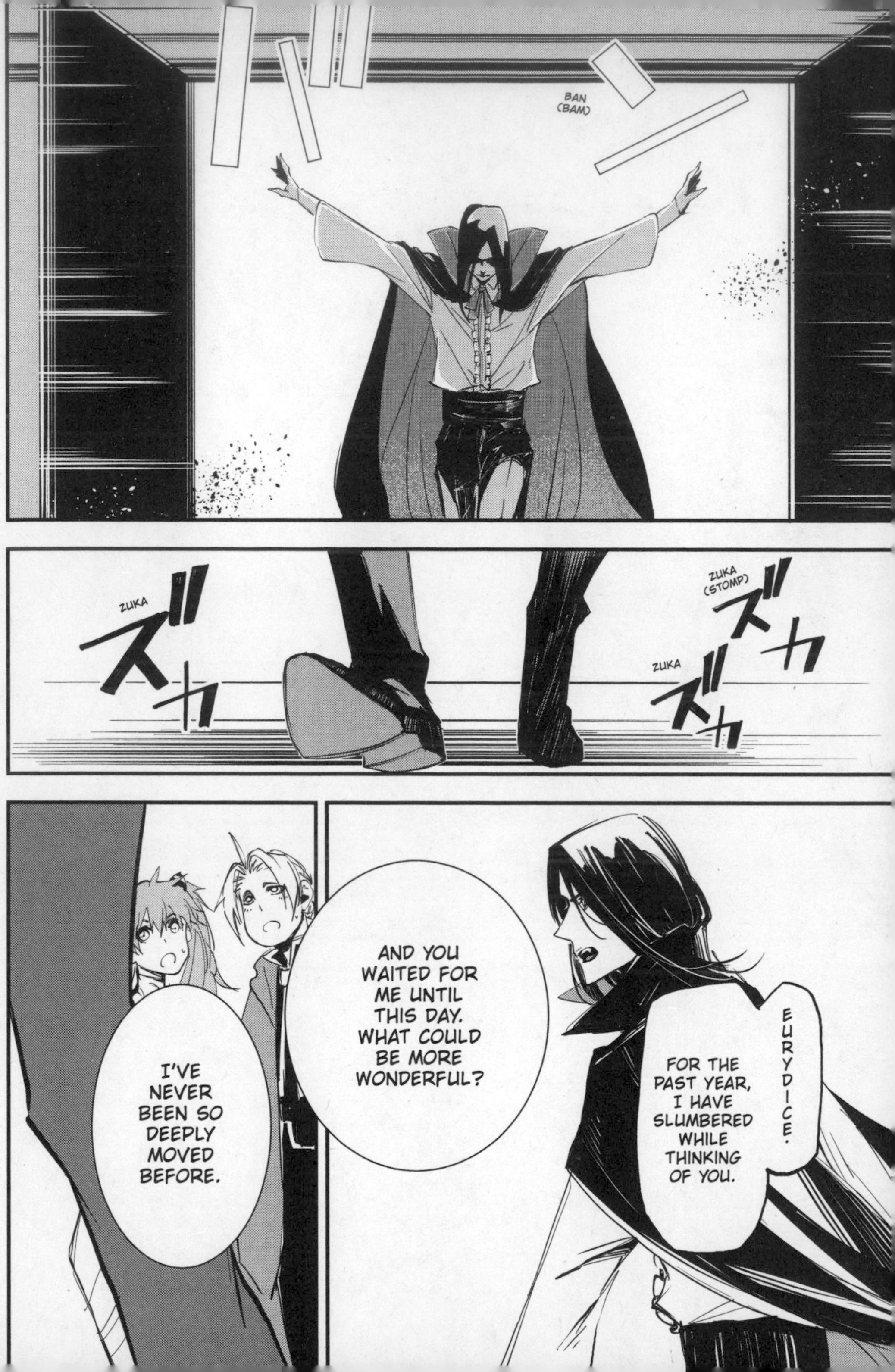
BAN (BAM)
ZUKA (STOMP)
ズカ
ZUKA
ズカ
ZUKA
ズカ
EURYDICE.
FOR THE PAST YEAR, I HAVE SLUMBERED WHILE THINKING OF YOU.
AND YOU WAITED FOR ME UNTIL THIS DAY. WHAT COULD BE MORE WONDERFUL?
I'VE NEVER BEEN SO DEEPLY MOVED BEFORE.

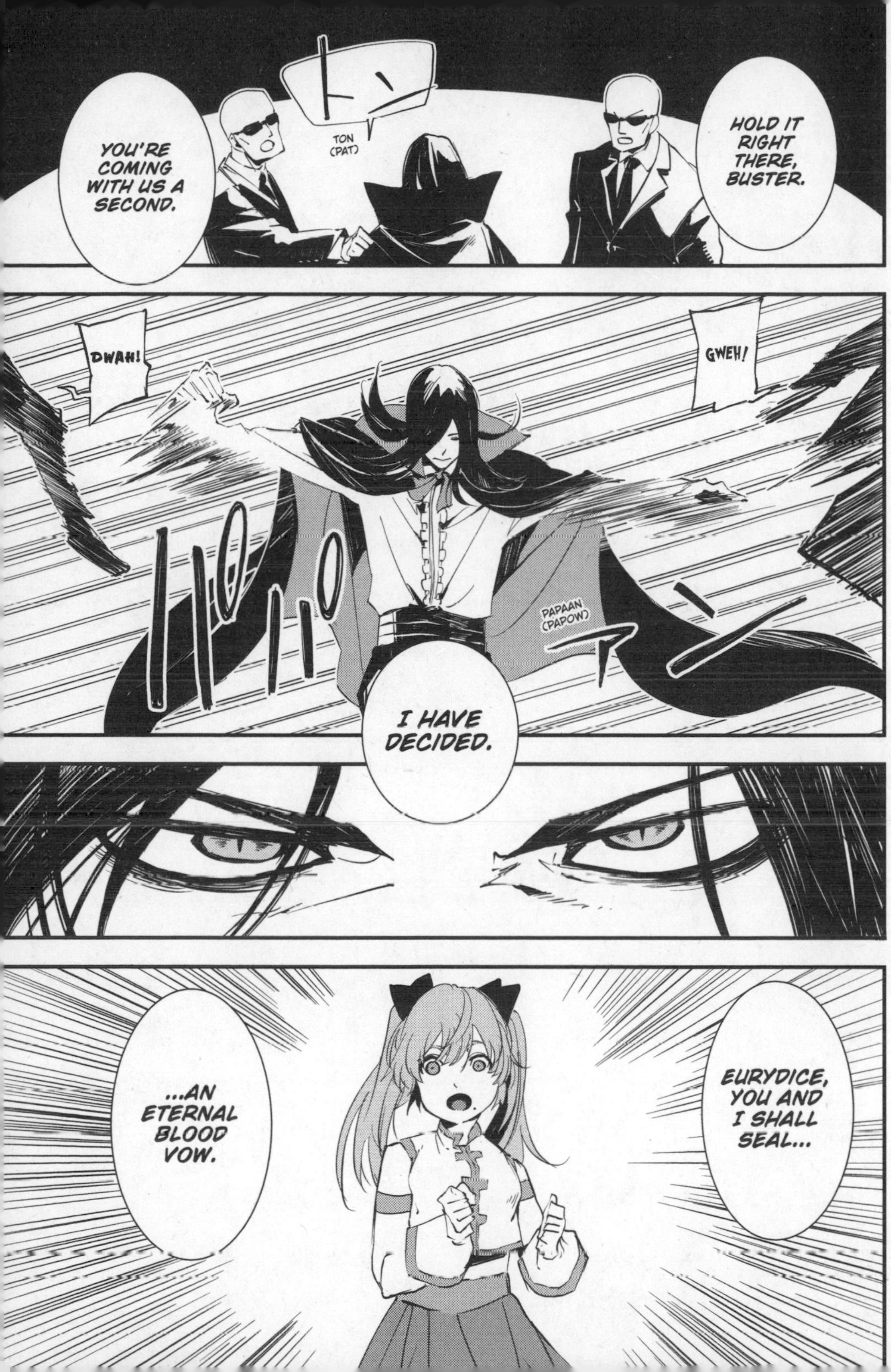
HOLD IT RIGHT THERE, BUSTER.
TON (PAT)
YOU'RE COMING WITH US A SECOND.
GWEH!
DWAH!
PAPAAN (PAPOW)
I HAVE DECIDED.
EURYDICE, YOU AND I SHALL SEAL...
...AN ETERNAL BLOOD VOW.

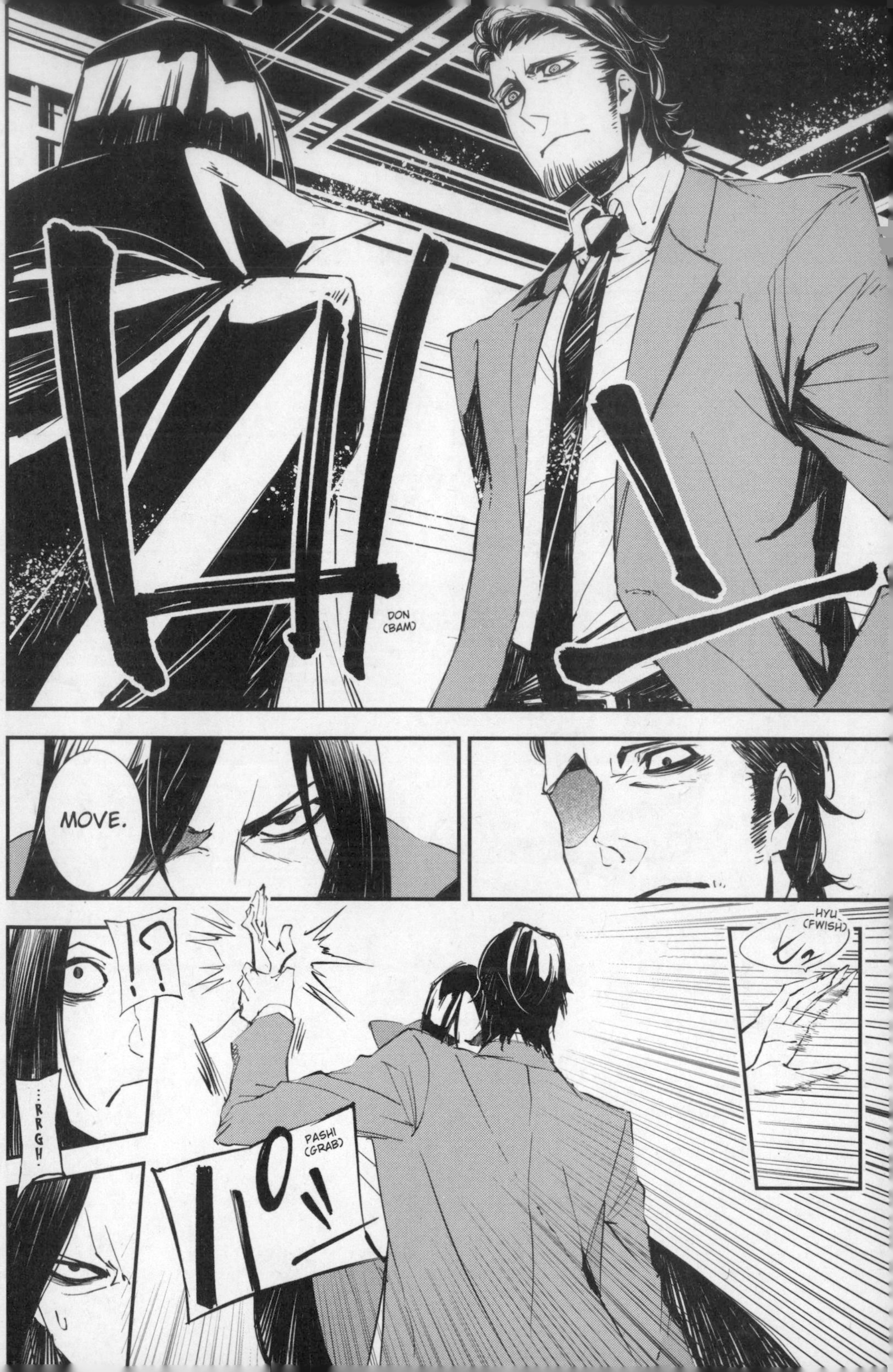
DON (BAM)
MOVE.
HYU (FWISH)
!?
PASHI (GRAB)
...RRGH!

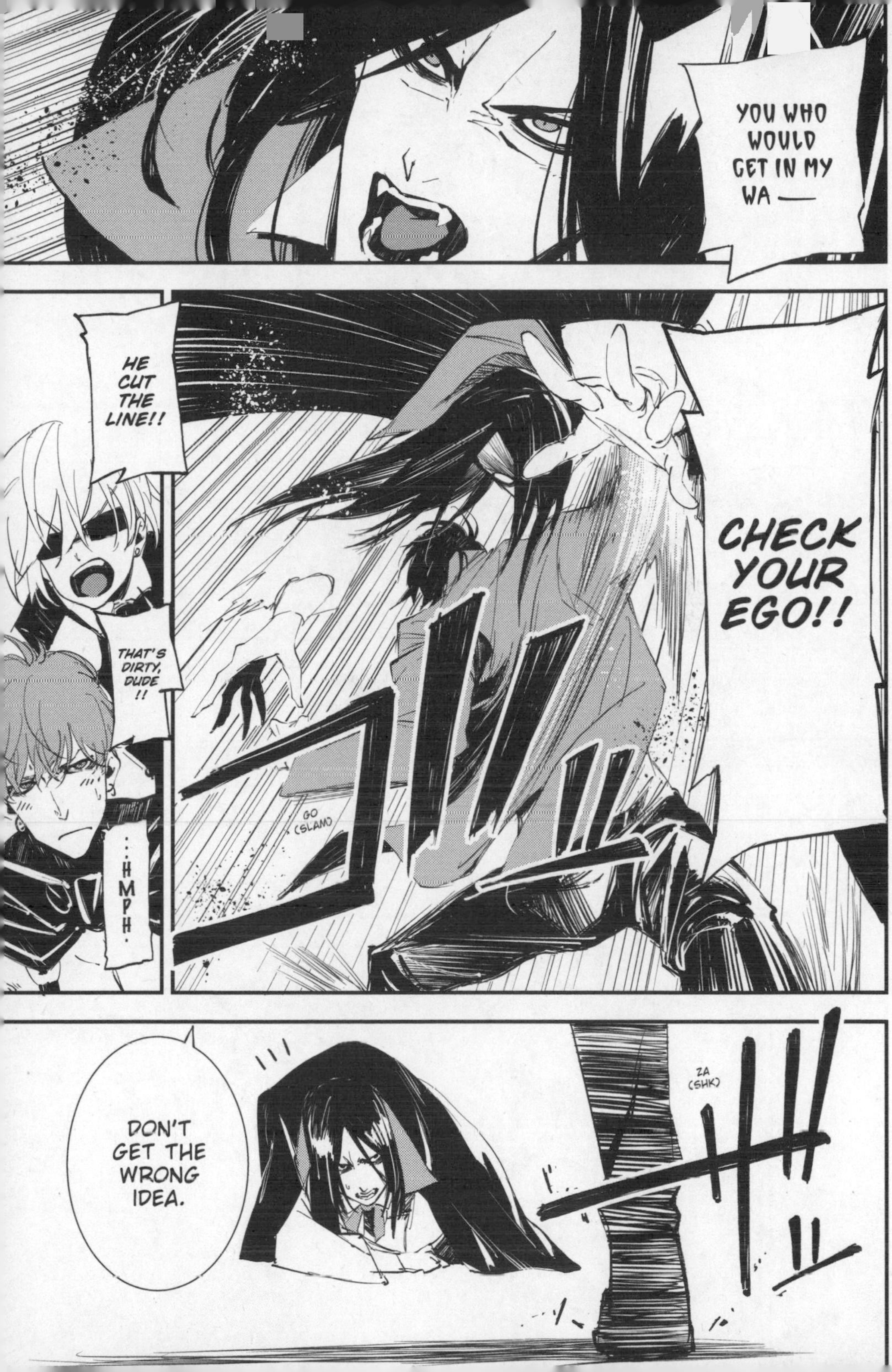
YOU WHO WOULD GET IN MY WA—
CHECK YOUR EGO!!
GO (SLAM)
HE CUT THE LINE!!
THAT'S DIRTY, DUDE!!
...HMPH.
ZA (SHK)
DON'T GET THE WRONG IDEA.

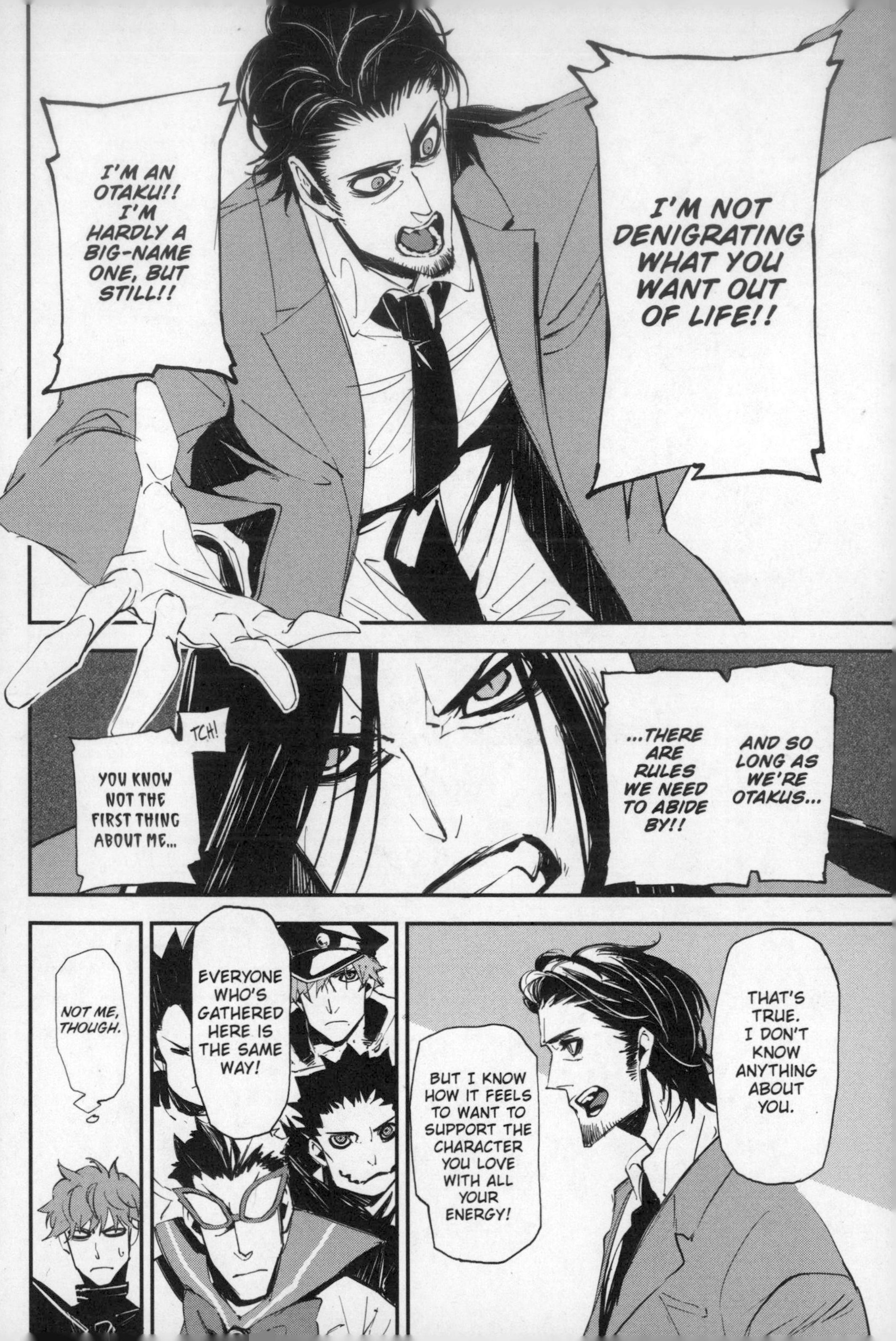
I'M NOT DENIGRATING WHAT YOU WANT OUT OF LIFE!!
I'M AN OTAKU!! I'M HARDLY A BIG-NAME ONE, BUT STILL!!
AND SO LONG AS WE'RE OTAKUS...
...THERE ARE RULES WE NEED TO ABIDE BY!!
TCH!
YOU KNOW NOT THE FIRST THING ABOUT ME...
THAT'S TRUE. I DON'T KNOW ANYTHING ABOUT YOU.
BUT I KNOW HOW IT FEELS TO WANT TO SUPPORT THE CHARACTER YOU LOVE WITH ALL YOUR ENERGY!
EVERYONE WHO'S GATHERED HERE IS THE SAME WAY!
NOT ME, THOUGH.

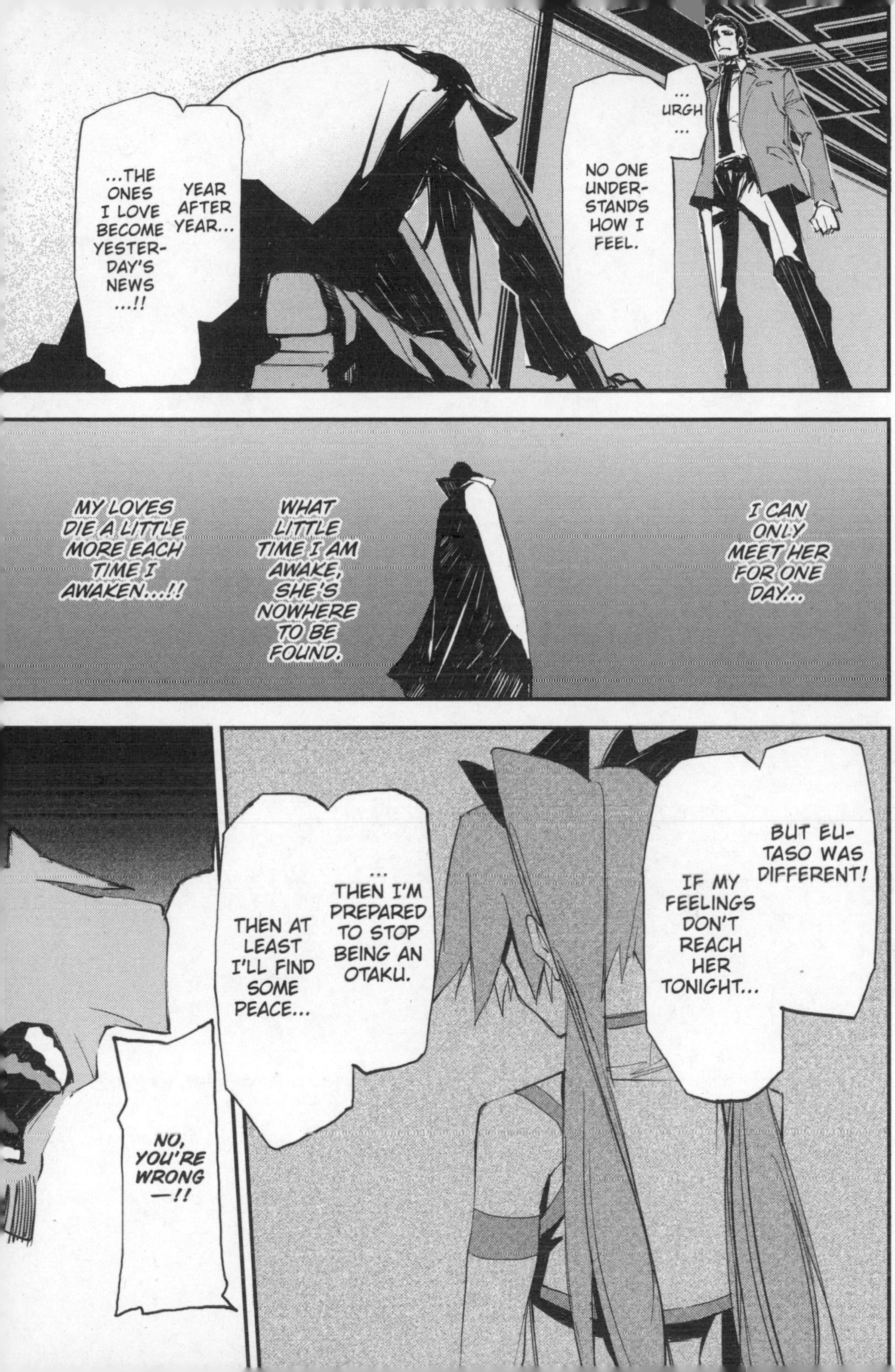
... URGH ...
NO ONE UNDERSTANDS HOW I FEEL.
YEAR AFTER YEAR...
...THE ONES I LOVE BECOME YESTERDAY'S NEWS ...!!
I CAN ONLY MEET HER FOR ONE DAY...
WHAT LITTLE TIME I AM AWAKE, SHE'S NOWHERE TO BE FOUND.
MY LOVES DIE A LITTLE MORE EACH TIME I AWAKEN...!!
BUT EU-TASO WAS DIFFERENT!
IF MY FEELINGS DON'T REACH HER TONIGHT...
... THEN I'M PREPARED TO STOP BEING AN OTAKU.
THEN AT LEAST I'LL FIND SOME PEACE...
NO, YOU'RE WRONG —!!

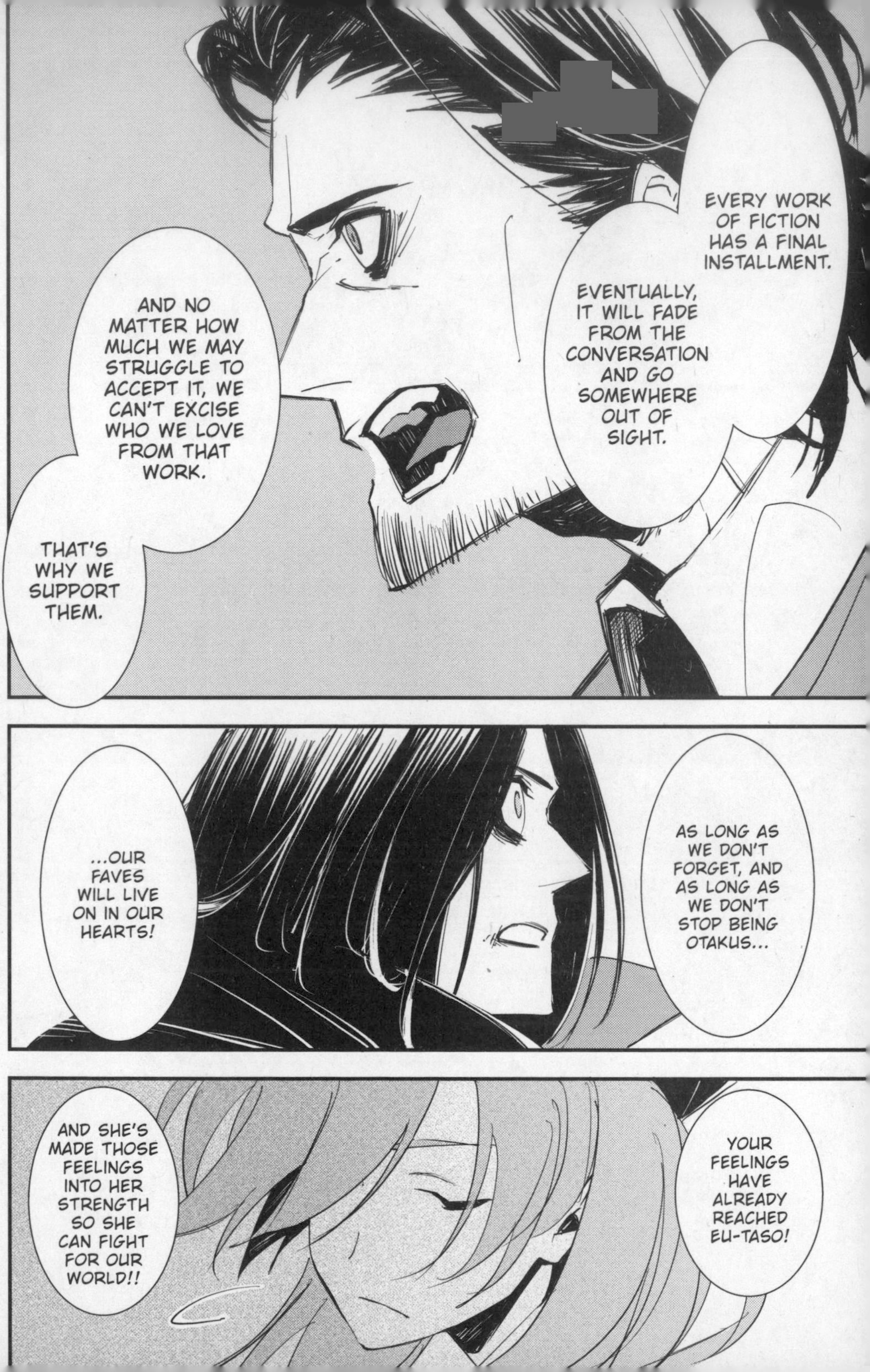
EVERY WORK OF FICTION HAS A FINAL INSTALLMENT.
EVENTUALLY, IT WILL FADE FROM THE CONVERSATION AND GO SOMEWHERE OUT OF SIGHT.
AND NO MATTER HOW MUCH WE MAY STRUGGLE TO ACCEPT IT, WE CAN'T EXCISE WHO WE LOVE FROM THAT WORK.
THAT'S WHY WE SUPPORT THEM.
AS LONG AS WE DON'T FORGET, AND AS LONG AS WE DON'T STOP BEING OTAKUS...
...OUR FAVES WILL LIVE ON IN OUR HEARTS!
YOUR FEELINGS HAVE ALREADY REACHED EU-TASO!
AND SHE'S MADE THOSE FEELINGS INTO HER STRENGTH SO SHE CAN FIGHT FOR OUR WORLD!!

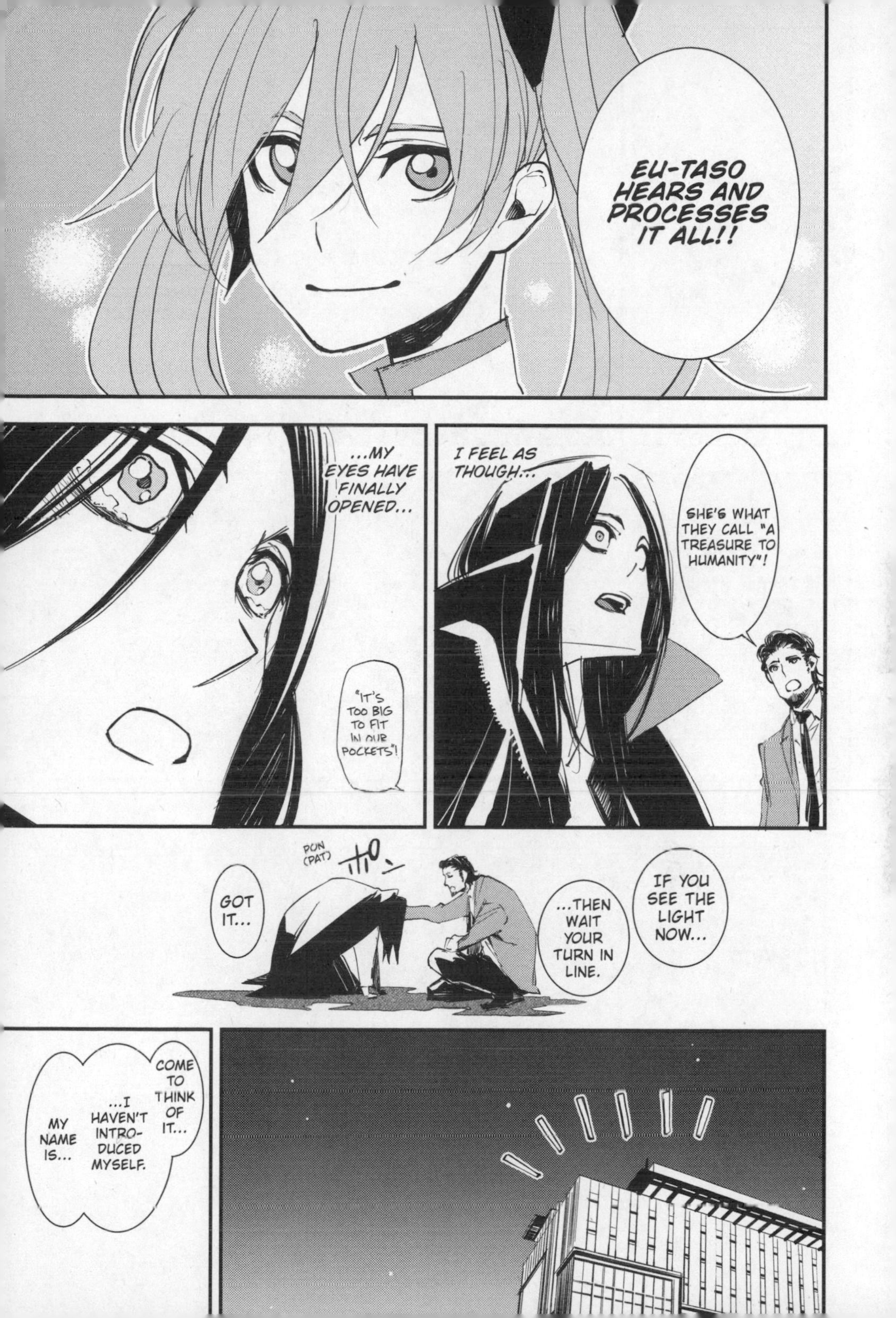
EU-TASO HEARS AND PROCESSES IT ALL!!
SHE'S WHAT THEY CALL "A TREASURE TO HUMANITY"!
I FEEL AS THOUGH...
...MY EYES HAVE FINALLY OPENED...
"IT'S TOO BIG TO FIT IN OUR POCKETS"!
IF YOU SEE THE LIGHT NOW...
...THEN WAIT YOUR TURN IN LINE.
PON (PAT)
GOT IT...
COME TO THINK OF IT...
...I HAVEN'T INTRO-DUCED MYSELF.
MY NAME IS...

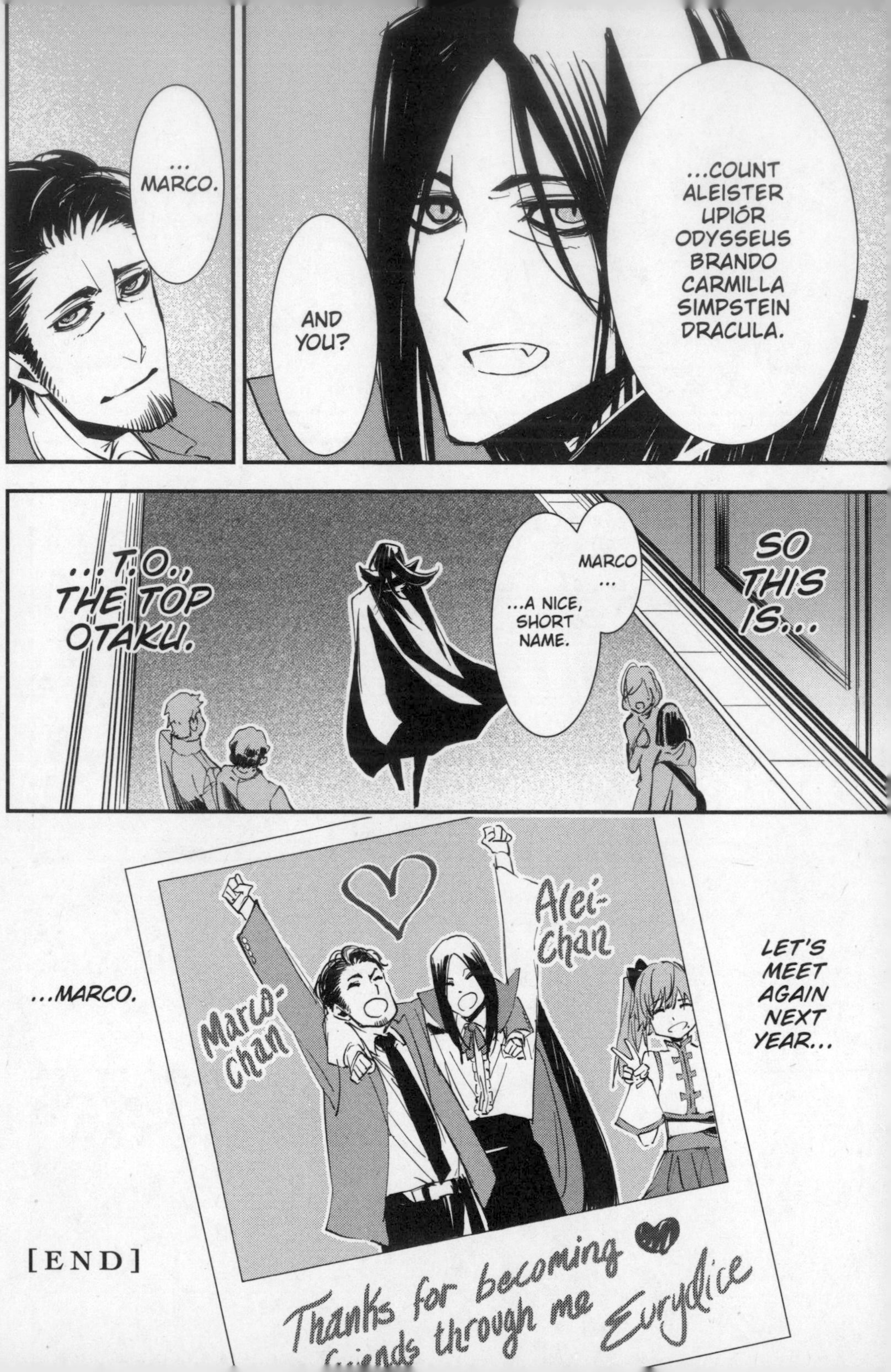
...COUNT ALEISTER UPIÓR ODYSSEUS BRANDO CARMILLA SIMPSTEIN DRACULA.
AND YOU?
... MARCO.
SO THIS IS...
MARCO ...
...A NICE, SHORT NAME.
...T.O., THE TOP OTAKU.
LET'S MEET AGAIN NEXT YEAR...
Alei-chan
Marco-chan
Thanks for becoming friends through me
Eurydice
...MARCO.
[END]

MARCO LETS HIS GUARD DOWN

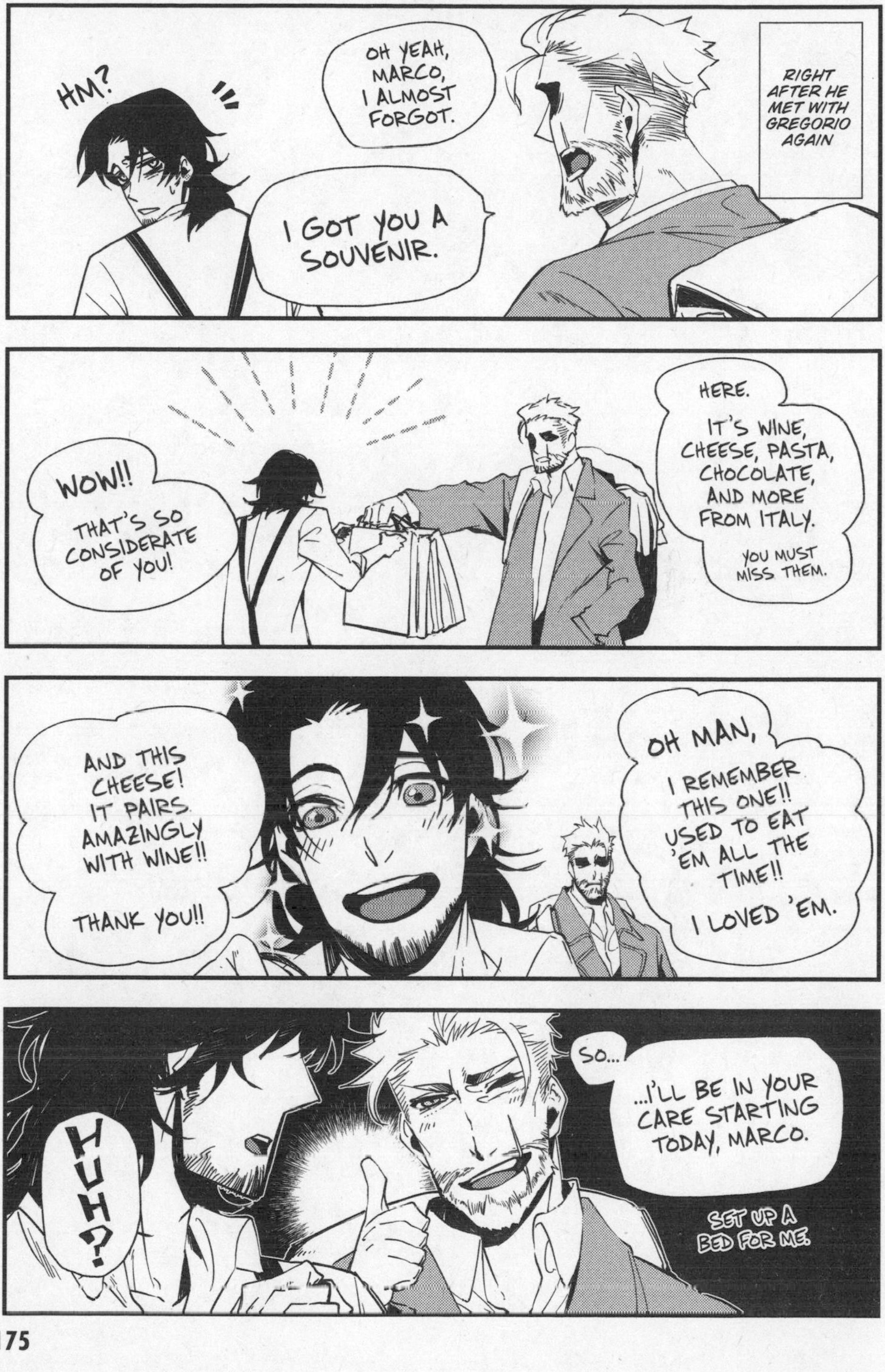
RIGHT AFTER HE MET WITH GREGORIO AGAIN
OH YEAH, MARCO, I ALMOST FORGOT.
HM?
I GOT YOU A SOUVENIR.
HERE.
IT'S WINE, CHEESE, PASTA, CHOCOLATE, AND MORE FROM ITALY.
YOU MUST MISS THEM.
WOW!!
THAT'S SO CONSIDERATE OF YOU!
OH MAN,
I REMEMBER THIS ONE!! USED TO EAT 'EM ALL THE TIME!!
I LOVED 'EM.
AND THIS CHEESE! IT PAIRS AMAZINGLY WITH WINE!!
THANK YOU!!
SO...
...I'LL BE IN YOUR CARE STARTING TODAY, MARCO.
SET UP A BED FOR ME.
HUH?

EXCERPTED FROM THE COMISU DOUJINSHI "THE BITTERSWEET SIGNAL!!"

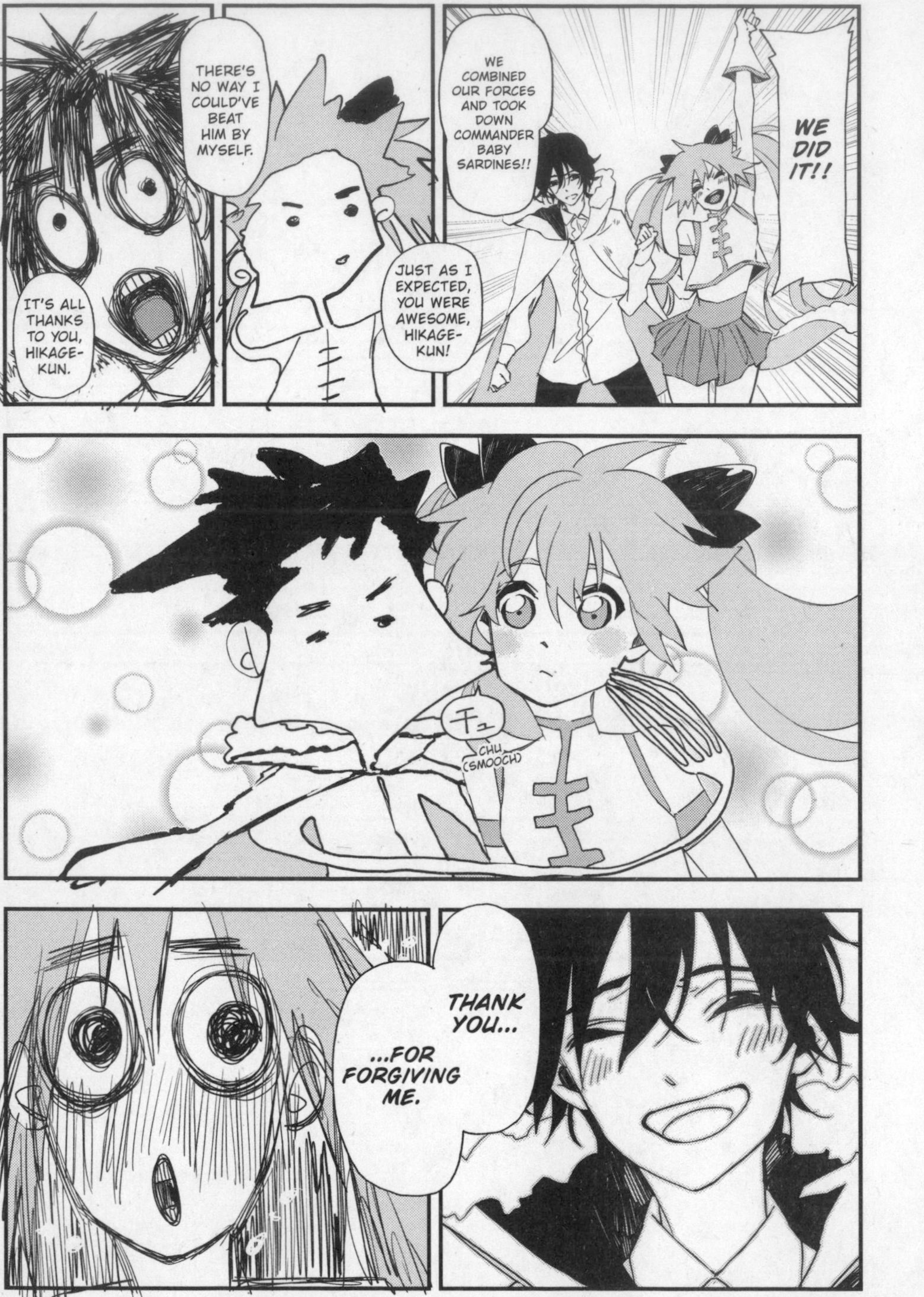
WE DID IT!!
WE COMBINED OUR FORCES AND TOOK DOWN COMMANDER BABY SARDINES!!
THERE'S NO WAY I COULD'VE BEAT HIM BY MYSELF.
JUST AS I EXPECTED, YOU WERE AWESOME, HIKAGE-KUN!
IT'S ALL THANKS TO YOU, HIKAGE-KUN.
チュ
CHU (SMOOCH)
THANK YOU...
...FOR FORGIVING ME.

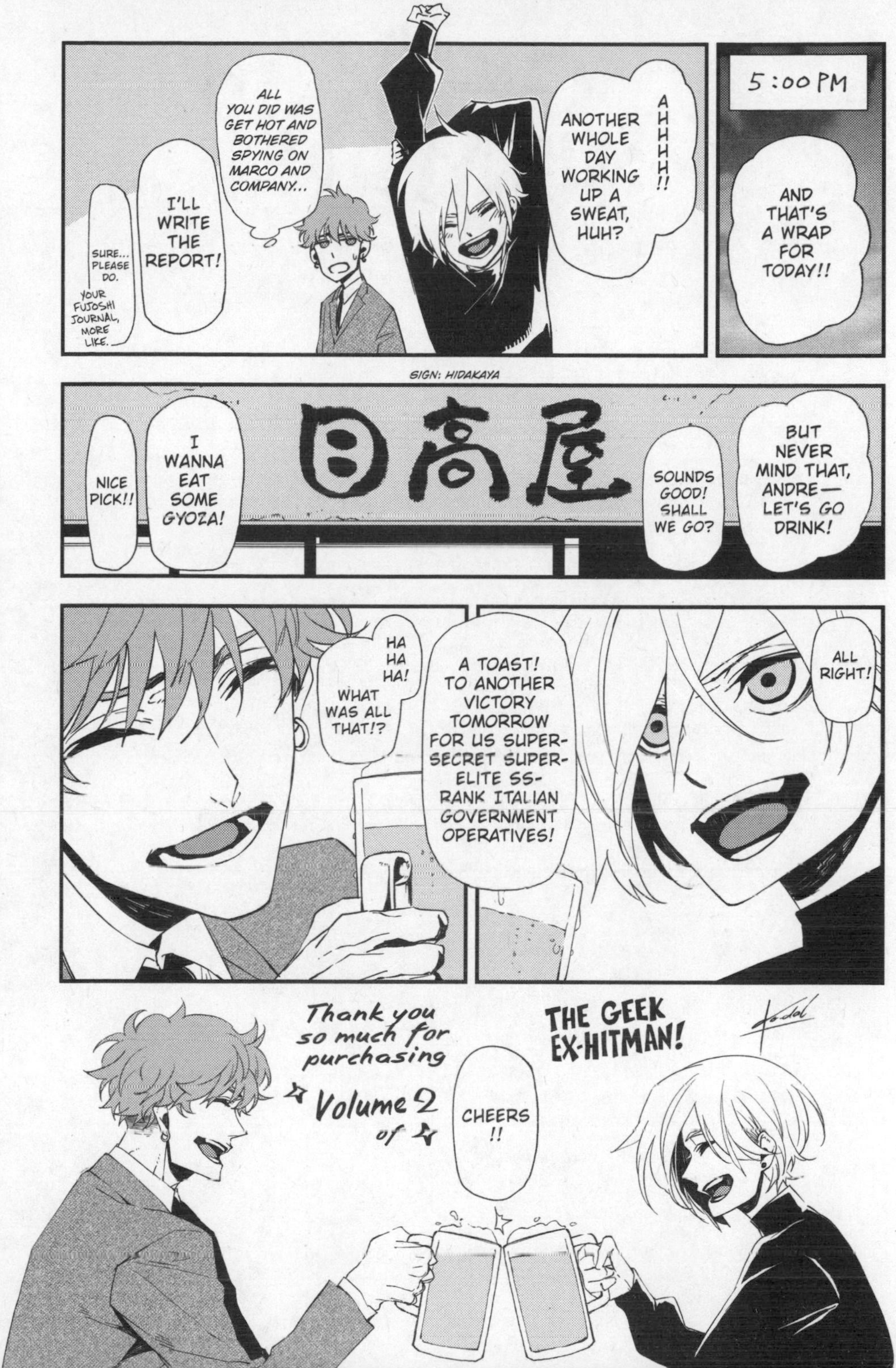
5:00 PM
AND THAT'S A WRAP FOR TODAY!!
AHHHH!!
ANOTHER WHOLE DAY WORKING UP A SWEAT, HUH?
ALL YOU DID WAS GET HOT AND BOTHERED SPYING ON MARCO AND COMPANY...
I'LL WRITE THE REPORT!
SURE... PLEASE DO.
YOUR FUJOSHI JOURNAL, MORE LIKE.
SIGN: HIDAKAYA
BUT NEVER MIND THAT, ANDRE— LET'S GO DRINK!
SOUNDS GOOD! SHALL WE GO?
日高屋
I WANNA EAT SOME GYOZA!
NICE PICK!!
ALL RIGHT!
A TOAST! TO ANOTHER VICTORY TOMORROW FOR US SUPER-SECRET SUPER-ELITE SS-RANK ITALIAN GOVERNMENT OPERATIVES!
HA HA HA! WHAT WAS ALL THAT!?
Thank you so much for purchasing Volume 2 of THE GEEK EX-HITMAN!
CHEERS!!

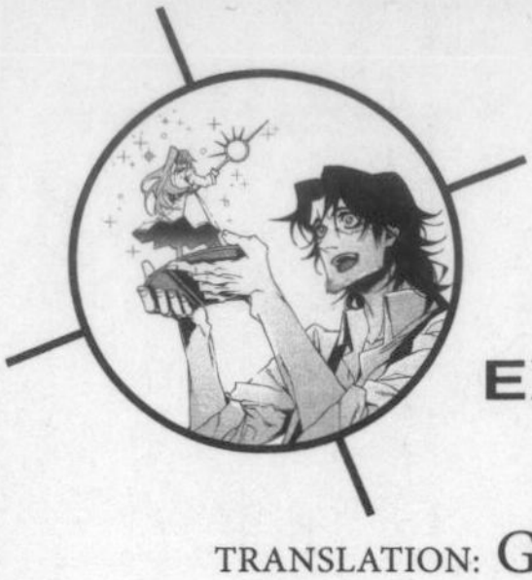

THE GEEK EX-HITMAN 2

Ko-dai

TRANSLATION: Giuseppe di Martino • LETTERING: Erin Hickman

This book is a work of fiction. Names, characters, places, and incidents are the product of the author's imagination or are used fictitiously. Any resemblance to actual events, locales, or persons, living or dead, is coincidental.

SONO OTAKU, MOTO KOROSHIYA. Vol. 2

First published in Japan in 2021 by KADOKAWA CORPORATION, Tokyo. English translation rights arranged with KADOKAWA CORPORATION, Tokyo, through Tuttle-Mori Agency, Inc., Tokyo.

Yen Press
150 West 30th Street, 19th Floor
New York, NY 10001

Visit us at yenpress.com
facebook.com/yenpress
twitter.com/yenpress
yenpress.tumblr.com
instagram.com/yenpress

First Yen Press Edition: October 2022
Edited by Yen Press Editorial: Mark Gallucci, Carl Li
Designed by Yen Press Design: Jane Sohn, Andy Swist

Yen Press is an imprint of Yen Press, LLC.
The Yen Press name and logo are trademarks of Yen Press, LLC.

Library of Congress Control Number: 2022935394

ISBNs: 978-1-9753-5075-8 (paperback)
978-1-9753-5076-5 (ebook)

1 3 5 7 9 10 8 6 4 2

WOR

Printed in the United States of America

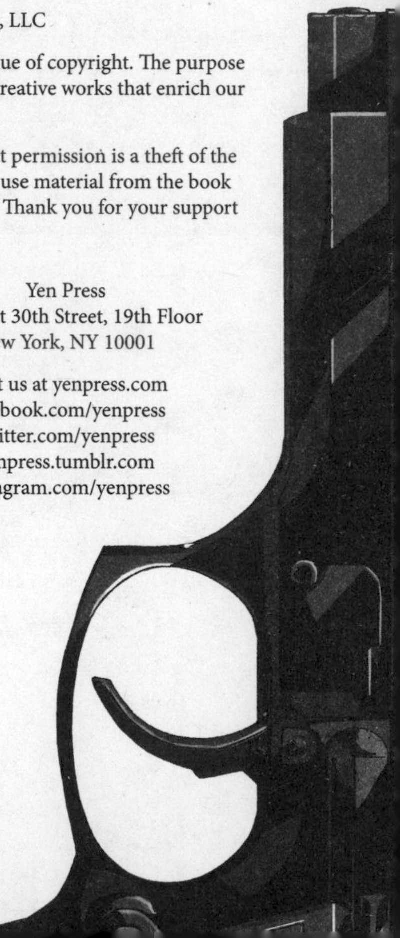